Managing Complexity in High Technology Organizations

Managing Complexity in High Technology Organizations

Edited by

MARY ANN VON GLINOW
SUSAN ALBERS MOHRMAN

New York   Oxford
OXFORD UNIVERSITY PRESS
1990

Oxford University Press

Oxford   New York   Toronto
Delhi   Bombay   Calcutta   Madras   Karachi
Petaling Jaya   Singapore   Hong Kong   Tokyo
Nairobi   Dar es Salaam   Cape Town
Melbourne   Auckland

and associated companies in
Berlin   Ibadan

Copyright © 1990 by Oxford University Press, Inc.

Published by Oxford University Press, Inc.,
200 Madison Avenue, New York, New York 10016

Oxford is a registered trademark of Oxford University Press

Library of Congress Cataloging-in-Publication Data
Managing complexity in high technology organizations / edited by Mary Ann Von Glinow
and Susan Albers Mohrman.
p.   cm.   Bibliography: p.   Includes index.
ISBN 0-19-505720-1
1. High technology industries—Management.   2. Organizational behavior.
I. Von Glinow, Mary Ann Young, 1949–   .   II. Mohrman, Susan Albers.
HD62.37.M355   1989   620'.0068—dc19   89-3030 CIP

Printing (last digit): 9 8 7 6 5 4 3 2 1

Printed in the United States of America
on acid-free paper

Preface

This book is about managing a growing segment of the global economy: high technology industries, systems, and people. It is also about the complexity associated with managing in high technology industries and organizations. The contributors to this volume are noted for their original and pioneering work in the field of high technology management. Collectively they have captured the high technology phenomenon, departing from traditional prescriptions and theoretical bases in an attempt to define the field's parameters. The majority of the selections are based on extensive empirical findings. This in itself is a departure from most treatments of high technology management. Moreover, for the first time a new framework is presented for dealing with the numerous complexities and challenges that managing in high technology industries and organizations poses.

The introductory chapter defines the scope of the book, presenting a case study of a high technology organization that at first glance seems in distress. However, careful examination reveals that the ceaseless threats and challenges illustrated in this setting, which would be debilitating to more traditional organizations, are the lifeblood of this firm. Some of the fundamental differences between high technology management and management within more traditional organizational forms are thus highlighted.

We quickly shift to global high technology management. Everett M. Rogers and Ying-Chung Annie Chen provide an in-depth analysis of domestic and foreign technopolii, the dense concentration of high tech firms and research labs that serve as energy centers for technology development and commercialization. This is followed by Jay Galbraith's chapter on global strategies and structures, which demand new organizational forms. Rounding out this section, Gerardo Ungson describes international competition in high technology industries, utilizing the United States, Japan, and EEC countries as examples.

The emphasis in the next four chapters shifts to organizational phenomena. Kathy Eisenhardt and Jay Bourgeois, who have studied top management teams in rapidly changing, "high-velocity," high tech environments, present some fundamental paradoxes for individuals forced to make decisions. Claudia B. Schoonhoven and Mariann Jelinek challenge the lessons of the past by proposing that altogether different forms of organizational structures exist in successful high technology firms coping with rapid technological changes. Thomas Kosnik offers insights into high tech marketing, which vary considerably from traditional marketing wisdom. Karlene Roberts and Gina Gargano take us into the realm of the high-reliability, high technology organization in order to examine the complexities and interdependencies associated with the successful functioning of a nuclear aircraft carrier.

The succeeding two chapters highlight specific problems in organizations that are technologically oriented. Dorothy Leonard-Barton discusses the implementation of new production processes and organizational learning strategies for handling the various problems that occur. Paul Adler challenges our thinking about traditional methods of organizing, explaining how the best results from implementation of CAD/CAM systems may be achieved. Both of these chapters highlight the importance of organizations as learning systems.

The final section deals with interpersonal problems within high tech firms. Allan M. Mohrman, Susan A. Mohrman, and Christopher Worley build upon the uncertain and interdependent nature of high technology work, presenting arguments and research that identify the team, rather than the individual, as the critical unit of analysis in high tech firms. Susan Resnick-West and Mary Ann Von Glinow challenge traditional methods of managing high tech workers, illustrating various shortcomings with poignant examples of culture clashes. Luis Gomez-Mejia and Theresa Welbourne examine compensation strategies in high technology firms and discuss recent innovations in this area that reflect a dramatic departure from traditional compensation schemes.

The final chapter synthesizes the various themes that have recurred throughout this book and offers a framework representing a first attempt at integrating diverse and complex areas associated with the high technology domain. This chapter tentatively provides answers to some central questions associated with high tech management. In so doing, it provides a framework for the key characteristics of high technology organizations, which is critical in formulating theory or offering concrete implications for practice. The challenges described in this book are enormous and the implications controversial. However, we all believe that it is time for a shift in our thinking about high technology management.

Many individuals were involved in the production of this volume. Our contributors have been a pleasure to work with because they are a dedicated, scholarly group, with boundless energy and enthusiasm concerning high technology. We owe special thanks to the entire staff of the Center for Effective Organization, which helped us with all aspects of production, often on very short notice. Thanks especially to Paul Huang, Marie Martin, and Annette Yakushi.

Thanks also to Edward E. Lawler III, whose good-natured encouragement and support for writing projects is a constant spur to action. We also appreciate the editorial assistance and general support we received from our editor, Herb Addison, and the staff at Oxford University Press.

We are grateful to our families for enduring kaleidoscopic turmoil at various times during the project.

Los Angeles   M.A.V.G.
January 1989   S.A.M.

Contents

Contributors

PAUL S. ADLER is Assistant Professor in the Department of Industrial Engineering and Engineering Management at Stanford University. His doctorate is from the University of Picardie, Amiens, France. He has conducted postdoctoral work at Harvard and has held faculty positions at Columbia University and the Brookings Institution. Dr. Adler has published widely on high technology industries and technologies in such journals as *California Management Review, IEEE Transactions,* and *Revue Economique.* His research has focused on managing the engineering–manufacturing interface, CAD/CAM implementation, technology strategy, machine tool computerization, and automation.

L. JAY BOUREGEOIS III is Associate Professor at the Colgate Darden Graduate Business School, University of Virginia. His research concerns strategic management in volatile environments, top management group processes, and strategy implementation. His publications have appeared in *Strategic Management Journal, Academy of Management Journal, Academy of Management Review, California Management Review,* and *Management Science.*

YING-CHUNG ANNIE CHEN is a doctoral candidate at the Annenberg School of Communications, University of Southern California at Los Angeles. Her research interests include the diffusion of cable TV systems in the United States, the study of "advanced wired cities" in Europe and in the United States, and public perceptions on the issues of "privacy" in a computerized society. She is also interested in issues of technology transfer, particularly the phenomenon of "technopolis."

KATHLEEN M. EISENHARDT is Assistant Professor in the Industrial Engineering and Engineering Management Department at Stanford University. Her research interests are in management in high-speed high technology environments. She is currently examining the strategic decision making of top management teams in the microcomputer industry and success factors of new ventures in the semiconductor industry. Her publications include articles in *Management Science, Organizational Dynamics,* and *California Management Review.*

JAY R. GALBRAITH is Professor of Management and Organization and a member of the Center for Effective Organizations at the University of Southern California at Los Angeles. Prior to joining the faculty at USC, he directed his own management consulting firm in Denver, Colorado, and devoted his time to consulting projects. He has also been Professor of Management at the Wharton School, University of Pennsylvania, and Professor at the Sloan School, Massachusetts Institute of Technology. While on leave from MIT from 1972 to 1974, Dr. Galbraith was affiliated with the European Institute for Advanced Studies in Management in Brussels, Belgium.

His principle area of specialization is organizational design, change, and development. More recently, Dr. Galbraith has concentrated on major strategy and structural changes in organizations.

Dr. Galbraith has had considerable consulting experience in the United States, Europe, and South America. He is frequently called in to consult on the design of corporate structures, international organization, project and product management systems, internal new ventures, and major organization changes. These projects have been with new companies, old and established companies, banks, telephone companies, high technology firms, and diversified corporations.

Dr. Galbraith has written numerous articles for professional journals, handbooks, and research collections. In addition, he has published three books: *Designing Complex Organizations* (1973), *Organizational Design* (1977), and *Strategy Implementation* (2nd edn., 1986).

GINA GARGANO is a doctoral student in Organizational Behavior and Industrial Relations at the University of California at Berkeley. Her research interests include organizational and environmental interdependence and complexity, alternative organizational forms, and employee rights in the workplace.

LUIS GOMEZ-MEJIA holds a Ph.D. degree in Industrial Relations from the University of Minnesota. He is a Research Professor in the Department of Management at Arizona State Unviersity. Dr. Gomez-Mejia has had more than eight years of field experience in compensation and personnel management at the Control Data Corporation, and the city of Minneapolis, and has been a consultant to various private and public sector organizations on compensation practices. Dr. Gomez-Mejia has had more than thirty publications on compensation and human resource management in such journals as *Personnel Journal, Academy of Management Journal,* and *Industrial Relations.* He is the editor of *Compensation and Benefits* and coauthor of *New Perspectives in Compensation.*

MARIANN JELINEK is Associate Professor of Management Policy at the Weatherhead School of Management, Case Western Reserve University. Previously, she held appointments at the State University of New York, Albany, McGill University, the Amos Tuck School at Dartmouth College, Worchester Polytechnic Institute, and Bentley College. She was educated at the University of California at Berkeley, where she received her Ph.D. degree; and at the Harvard Business School, where she earned her D.B.A.

Her teaching assignments include Policy and Advanced Manufacturing Technology and Corporate Strategy. Research and consultation interests center on effective management of innovation, strategic change, and manufacturing technology. Doctor Jelinek has published six books, including *Institutionalizing Innovation* (Praeger, 1979), and more than twenty articles, among them "Plan for Economies of Scope," an article with Joel Goldhar that appeared in the *Harvard Business Review.* A book on the management of high technology firms, *Patterns of Innovation* (with C.B. Scoonhoven), is forthcoming.

THOMAS J. KOSNIK holds a B.A. from Duke University, an M.B.A. from the Colgate Darden School, University of Virginia, and a Ph.D. in Business Administration from Stanford University. He is currently an Assistant Professor of Marketing at the Harvard Business School. His research focuses on marketing innovations, including new products, new markets, new marketing tactics, and new technologies to help marketing and sales professionals to achieve a closer relationship with customers as well as other functional areas in their firms. The industries in which Dr. Kosnik concentrates his research include computer hardware, computer software, systems integration, and public accounting.

DOROTHY LEONARD-BARTON is on the faculty at the Harvard Business School. She teaches, researches, and consults on the development and implementation of new technologies. During the past five years, she has focused particularly on the transfer of process technologies in high technology firms from research laboratories into operations.

In addition to teaching courses in manufacturing and the management of technology at M.I.T. Sloan and at Harvard, Dr. Leonard-Barton has taught in numerous corporate executive programs. Her writings have appeared in academic journals such as *Research Policy* and practitioner-oriented publications such as the *Harvard Business Review*. Her Ph.D. is from Stanford University.

ALLAN M. MOHRMAN, JR. is the Associate Director for Research and a Research Scientist in the Center for Effective Organizations, Graduate School of Business, University of Southern California. Before he achieved his present position, Dr. Mohrman was a faculty member in the College of Administrative Sciences at the Ohio State University. He earned his Ph.D. in Organizational Behavior in the Graduate School of Management at Northwestern University.

He has published in the areas of Performance Appraisal, Participation in Decision Making, Organization Change and Development, and Technological Impacts on Organizations. He is a coeditor of *Research for Theory and Practice* (Jossey-Bass, 1985). He is currently editing a volume on large-scale system change and is completing a manuscript on the design of performance appraisal systems.

SUSAN ALBERS MOHRMAN is a Senior Research Scientist at the Center for Effective Organizations in the Graduate School of Business at the University of Southern California. She has also been on the faculty of Organizational Behavior at the University of Southern California and has been a Visiting Lecturer at the Ohio State University in the School of Administrative Sciences. She received her A.B. in Psychology from Stanford University in 1967 and her Ph.D. in Organizational Behavior from Northwestern University in 1978.

She has published papers in professional journals and books on the topics of innovative approaches to the design of organizations, organization development and change, human resource practices, high technology management, high involvement management, union/management cooperative methodologies. She is editor of *Research for Theory and Practice* (Jossey-Bass, 1985), which explores innovative methodologies for the conduct of research which is designed to impact practice. *The Design of High Performing Organizations* will be published by Addison-Wesley in 1990.

SUSAN RESNICK-WEST is president of GRW Consultants, a firm specializing in change and performance management. She holds a Ph.D. from UCLA. Her research has focused on performance management systems, with special attention to the needs of high technology employees. Formerly Manager, Organizational Planning and Effectiveness, Xerox, Special Markets Group, Dr. Resnick-West was responsible for the design and development of entrepreneurial business in high tech environments. She is Adjunct Professor of Management and Organization at USC Business School and coauthor of the book *The Design of Performance Appraisal Systems,* published by Jossey-Bass.

KARLENE H. ROBERTS is Professor of Business Administration at the University of California, Berkeley. She is a Fellow in the Academy of Management and in the Division of Industrial and Organizational Psychology of the American Psychological Association. She serves on the editorial boards of the *Journal of Applied Psychology, Organizational Behavior and Human Performance,* and *California Management Review* and has served on the editorial boards of *Journal of Vocational Behavior* and *Academy of Management Journal.*

Professor Roberts received her bachelor's degree from Stanford University and her Ph.D. in Psychology from the University of California, Berkeley. She was a research associate in the Graduate School of Business at Stanford University and joined the faculty of the School of Business, University of California, as an instructor.

Professor Roberts publishes in the areas of organizational communication, research design in organizations, cross-national management, and the management of complex systems. Her research has been supported by the Office of Naval Research, National Science Foundation, IBM, and the Department of Labor. She has served in a consulting capacity to the U.S. Navy, National Institute of Education, National Institute of Health, SRI International, Bank of America, Public Broadcasting System, and Sears Roebuck and Company.

EVERETT M. ROGERS is Walter H. Annenberg Professor of Communication and Associate Dean for Doctoral Studies at the Annenberg School of Communications at the University of Southern California. For the past thirty-four years, he has been conducting research on the diffusion of innovations, and has authored a series of books on this topic, the most recent of which is *Diffusion of Innovations* (New York, Free Press, 1983). Rogers' interests also include the role of technology in high technology transfer. His work on this topic is included in *Silicon Valley Fever,* which he coauthored with Judith K. Larsen (New York, Basic Books, 1984). Rogers' latest book is *Communication Technology* (New York, Free Press, 1986).

CLAUDIA BIRD SCHOONHOVEN'S formal education includes a Ph.D. and two M.A.s, which were earned at Stanford University (1976, 1974, 1969). Her bachelor's degree is from the University of Illinois, Urbana. She also held a postdoctoral fellowship at Stanford University. She is currently a Professor of Organization and Management, San Jose State University, San Jose, California, and was a Visiting Scholar at the Stanford University Graduate School of Business and a Visiting Professor at the University of Santa Clara in 1986.

Her recent publications include "High Technology Firms: Where Strategy Really Pays Off," "Sociotechnical Considerations for the Development of the Space Station," and a book entitled *Patterns of Innovation: A Study of the Electronics Industry,* cowritten with M. Jelinek. Her paper, "A Time Series Analysis of Strategy and Performance in High Technology Firms" won the *Planning Forum Journal's* award as one of the three "Best Papers in 1986" in corporate and organizational planning. The paper was published in the journal in 1987.

Professor Schoonhoven is currently the principal investigator on grants from the U.S. Department of Commerce to investigate survival and performance of new ventures in the U.S. semiconductor industry. Her consulting, research, and publications are on organizational performance, innovation/technology management, organizational design, entrepreneurship, management of professionals, and space station design.

She was recently appointed Consulting Editor of the *Academy of Management Journal* (AMJ) and is an editorial board member of the *Administrative Science Quarterly*. She is a member of the Academy of Management, the Strategic Management Society, the Decision Sciences Institute, and the American Sociological Association.

GERARDO R. UNGSON is currently a Visiting Professor of Management at Nijenrode, the Netherlands School of Business, and an Associate Professor of Management at the Graduate School of Management, University of Oregon. He has also taught at the Amos Tuck School of Business Administration, Dartmouth College, the University of California-Berkeley, and the Pennsylvania State University. Professor Ungson has published more than twenty papers in refereed journals, and has coauthored two books: *Decision-Making: An Interdisciplinary Inquiry* (Boston: Kent Publishing Company, 1983), and *Managing Effective Organizations* (Boston: Kent Publishing Company, 1985). His forthcoming book, *Competitive Strategies in High Technology* (Lexington, MA: D.C. Heath, in preparation), is a result of a three-year study of eighteen firms in Silicon Valley. Professor Ungson has also given numerous presentations on the topics of corporate strategy, decision making, and industrial policy at academic conferences in the United States, Japan, Korea, and Europe. He is presently engaged in a collaborative project to study Korean companies. He has consulted for Rheems Industries, Motorola, Hilton Hotels, Weyerhauser, and Pierre Cardin and is presently on retainer for a multinational company in Kuwait. A former management consultant with the Economic Development Foundation (Philippines), he received his A.B. Mathematics, B.S. Management Engineering (with honors) at the Ateneo University (Philippines) in 1969, and an MBA (with high honors) and Ph.D. from the Pennsylvania State University in 1978.

MARY ANN VON GLINOW is an Associate Professor of Management and Organization at the University of Southern California. She received her Ph.D. from the Ohio State University. She has spent more than ten years researching the problems of attracting, motivating, and retaining high technology and professional workers and is author of *The New Professionals: Managing Today's High Technology Employees*. She has published her research widely and has worked with high tech firms, both domestic and international. Her recent work on technology transfer to China, as well as her work with the large Korean Chaebols, has strengthened her research findings on the complexity associated with managing high tech workers in a global economy.

Dr. Von Glinow has been active in the Academy of Management, where she served on the Board of Governors and as head of the R&D/Technology/Innovation Interest Group, and is currently the Program Chair for the O.B. Division. She serves on six editorial review boards, three of which directly involve high tech management. At USC, she is a dean's research scholar. She is also coauthor of *International Technology Transfer: The Case of U.S.-China*, to be published by Prentice-Hall in 1990.

THERESA WELBOURNE is a Ph.D. student in Human Resource Management at the University of Colorado at Boulder. She previously worked in industry, concentrating in Human Resource Management and Personnel at such companies as NBI, Inc., and Detroit Edison. Her current research centers around compensation and high technology management, and has appeared in such journals as *Compensation and Benefits Review* and *Human Resource Planning*.

CHRISTOPHER G. WORLEY is a doctoral candidate in the Graduate School of Business Administration at the University of Southern California. He is currently a research associate at the Center for Effective Organizations and an instructor in the undergraduate business program. He received his bachelor's degree in Environmental Psychology at Westminister College, a Master's degree in Environmental Psychology at Colorado State University, and a Master's degree in Organization Development at Pepperdine University.

Mr. Worley's research interests span both macro and micro organizational phenomena. His current work concerns strategic change and strategy implementation, organizational development, performance in high technology settings, and the implementation of large-scale change.

Managing Complexity in High Technology Organizations

1

High Technology Organizations: An Introduction

SUSAN ALBERS MOHRMAN AND
MARY ANN VON GLINOW

The high technology arena includes a critical portion of the economy of all developed and newly industrialized countries. The ultimate shape of the evolving global economy of the 1990s will most likely depend on how the various segments of high technology industries evolve. Who performs the research and development that create the knowledge underlying the rapid growth of high technology industries and seemingly unlimited potential for spawning new products and capabilities? Who harnesses that knowledge in new product designs? Where are these products manufactured? How are they distributed and to which markets? Who services the customers and ensures that they take advantage of the benefits offered by the latest generation of technology?

The answers to these questions depend, to a large extent, on the competencies that companies and societies develop to deal with the multifaceted and constantly evolving world of high technology business. This book deals with many aspects of high technology: the environment, management processes, structures, people, and systems that define the high technology arena. The contributors describe their experiences with high technology firms and venture to prescribe those procedures they have found to be successful.

This introductory chapter describes the terrain of the high technology arena and provides an overview of the contributions that follow. In providing a thumbnail sketch of various firms, we cannot do justice to the richness of the phenomena, our hope being simply to provide their flavor.

HIGH TECHNOLOGY FIRMS: A DIVERSE LOT

When we think of high technology firms, most of us intuitively know what they are. Four criteria are usually applied to determine whether firms are indeed "high tech":

1. These firms employ a large proportion of scientists, engineers, and technologists, compared with their non–high tech brethren.
2. High tech firms also have an unusually high percentage of research and development (R & D) expenditures. In fact, their ratio of R & D expenditures to sales is almost twice the average for all industries.
3. The emergence of new technology makes existing technology obsolete very quickly.
4. High technology industries have the potential for extremely rapid growth, since the applications of new technology make possible the emergence of a stream of new products and processes.

Other characteristics frequently mentioned include global markets, the existence of entrepreneurial firms that commercialize emergent technologies, complex products, and uncertainty in the marketplace.

As might be expected from this outline, the facets of high technology are numerous. They range from gene modification to robotics and artificial intelligence. Much of the public image of these firms and most of the academic knowledge come from the electronics industry—specifically from the world of cybernetic systems and communications. Equally representative is the pharmaceutical industry, in which biochemistry and biogenetic research provide knowledge underpinning the design of drugs and devices that interact in extremely complex ways with the intricate workings of the human body. Other high technology areas include the chemical, energy, aerospace, and instrumentation industries. Of course, others not perceived as high technology industries employ a large number of high tech workers and use high tech processes.

These firms exist in a diverse environment. Almost all face global competition from countries with extremely varied economies, cost structures, and social/governmental structures. Many are truly global competitors, operating within several countries with diverse cultures, regulations, ethics, and work forces. Those that compete worldwide in the global marketplace must deal with the changing requirements of doing business and the emerging shape of a transitional economy. Those that are "protected" from global competition, such as U.S. defense firms, often service the government as their major customer; they deal with rapidly changing and increasing sets of constraints, regulations, and restrictions.

High technology firms exist in a variety of technological environments. All are experiencing rapid development of product, process, administrative, and managerial technologies. They relate to a proliferating number of scientific disciplines and knowledge bases. Knowledge is advanced in a variety of settings, including universities, in-house research and development labs, and multifirm consortia such as Sematech. Most high technology companies today invest huge sums of money in basic and continuing education of their employees. It has been estimated that in 1988 four fifths of all money spent on education has come from large companies such as IBM, Hewlett Packard, and Xerox. These companies not only have in-house degree-granting programs, but expend considerable sums on their employees for alternative forms of education, facilitated by means of sabbaticals and leaves of absences.

Although we often think of high technology firms as existing in rapidly growing markets, many of the latter have reached maturity. Firms of varying size and age produce a wide variety of products, ranging from original products in new markets to established products in mature markets. In the electronics industry some firms compete in a commodities market, while others produce complex customized systems; some manufacture components while others manufacture products for retail distribution; still others assemble equipment manufactured by different companies. The economics and competitive requirements of these various environments are quite different.

The public impression of high technology has been formed largely by accounts in the press of glamorous start-ups (like Apple Computer), where employees wear jeans and drive Mazaratis to work, become millionaires in their early twenties, and take on the "big boys" with zest and (sometimes fleeting) success. Although it attracts less public attention, much high technology work is done in large, established corporations with all the trappings of a typical bureaucracy. Increasingly, the various elements of the high technology cycle, which extends from basic research to the sale and servicing of products, are performed by several companies in different countries that band together in innovative, strategic alliances.

We think of high technology workers as scientists and engineers who do knowledge work—the "gold collar" work force that sits at advanced work stations turning concepts into reality. The entrepreneurs belonging to this group have turned their concepts into companies. Others, who prefer the excitement of the research laboratory, wish to be protected from the exigencies of daily business. Less publicized portions of the work force include the manufacturing employees who perform repetitive jobs, monitor automated operations in fabs or on assembly lines, and perform test operations. A number of technical groups support manufacturing with process engineering and quality assurance activities. Sales, distribution, and field applications groups, as well as marketing and business development personnel, have one foot in the technical world of the engineer and another in the practical applications world of the customer. Finance and human resources employees perform the essentially "white-collar" tasks of keeping the books, assessing the financial viability of the business, and handling the myriad tasks associated with being an employer. The legal department deals with complexities of government regulations and patent protection. In some cases this means working with foreign governments to ensure smooth operations. All these groups include managers and individual contributors, and many also have planners and coordinators.

These various groups are necessary for the proper functioning of high technology firms. Their employees are, in a sense, high technology employees. As we move through the structure of this firm, talking, in turn, with employees from all these different disciplines, one has the impression of looking through a kaleidoscope. Each successive group represents one complete rotation of the kaleidoscope, so that the pieces that constitute the firm are viewed differently; those that were in the background now assume a front-and-center position, and vice-versa. Each has different values and aspirations. Each can expect to follow a different career path within the firm. Each measures firm effectiveness using different criteria.

FAST-PACED AND RAPIDLY CHANGING LIFE IN A HIGH TECHNOLOGY FIRM

We have spent many days observing what goes on in high technology firms, talking to various employees, and attending meetings. Our conclusion is that the essence of a high technology firm cannot be grasped by generalizing from other kinds of organizations. One way to get a sense of the richness of the high tech firm's fabric is to "walk through" a typical day, talking to various employees about their jobs, the challenges they face, and their concerns. One sees a very different world from that represented in the article in last week's *Business Week* or this month's best-seller. We cannot do justice to the numerous complexities in a short space; nevertheless, what follows is an attempt to sketch that "typical day in the life" of a high tech firm. We offer this thumbnail sketch to alert the reader to the type and kind of problems that run throughout this book—collectively forming what we call kaleidoscopic high tech management.

The following example is a composite of observations from two weeks spent in a small semiconductor company, a three-year-old start-up division of a larger electronics firm. We chose this case because the issues that arose and the events we observed are representative of those in a great number of other firms that we and all contributors to this volume have studied as well.

This company designed and manufactured two families of products using two different processes. Its products were largely sold to consumer electronics firms, primarily as commodities, although it also had a small but growing amount of business designing and manufacturing custom chips. At the time we visited the firm, it was three years old, had 350 employees, and was managed by its entrepreneur founder.

In the face of a down cycle in the industry, the company's sales were slowing and consequently the personnel growth rate was decelerating. Simultaneously, the company was making the transition from a small start-up with advanced products that showed large profit margins to a more mature firm with a catalog of products ranging from mature commodities with intense price competition to state-of-the-art new products. As part of this transition, the firm was systematizing its operations, or, as various employees put it, "getting discipline." This involved efforts to control manufacturing processes and costs and to shorten the new product development cycle.

We began our observations with the *executive staff,* since the strategy and direction emanating from this group subsequently ripples through the rest of the organization. This staff was wrestling with a number of thorny issues, each of which had major implications for the very nature of the firm.

First was the need, despite the market turndown, to make a major development commitment in each of its product families to remain state-of-the-art. This need was coupled with a desire to take advantage of opportunities for some large custom chips contracts that looked attractive in light of the widespread industry downturn. The success of the firm thus far had been based on several advanced products that had large profit margins. Now it was faced with the need for a strategy to achieve a more general presence in the market. The issue the team was grappling with was an insufficient resource base to adequately develop both families of products and simultaneously develop and produce custom chips. As they grappled with this issue, it was clear that at the table were the ultimate winners and losers—people whose jobs, skills, and interests lay in one or another of those three thrusts. Thus, there were strong pressures to pursue all three directions vigorously, from both within the team and the environment. The reality, however, was that the firm did not have the internal financial or technical resources to do all three well.

A related issue was the rapid price erosion in the industrywide profit margins on new state-of-the-art products by competition, which was occurring more rapidly than the firm could generate new products to take their place. The staff was dealing with the necessity of getting costs under control and reducing their new product development cycle substantially. Again, from their limited resource base, they were looking at tradeoffs: between investment in fabrication technology and investment in designers and design technology. These technologies were advancing so rapidly that the firm, once state of the art in both, was lagging behind. For this issue, too, there were potential winners and losers at the table. Some were going to be asked to do more with less; others would receive more to do more.

Finally, the staff was seriously considering establishing an offshore design facility. Its assembly and packaging operations were already located in Southeast Asia. The general manager saw long-term potential in moving part of its design work to an area that had excess design engineering capability and where design engineers were less expensive. In part, this move was being considered because the firm had recently experienced turnover among young design engineers who either went with other start-ups, where they were given a piece of the financial action (something not possible within the larger corporate context of this firm), or sought greater career opportunities in a larger, more established semiconductor firm.

The executive staff also dealt with a myriad of operational issues, some for information only, others involving decisions that had become necessary because they had not been resolved between groups at lower levels, because of developing trouble spots, or for some other reason. The review of specifications for joint Army-Navy (JAN) certification was proceeding slowly and involving a lot of overtime. Could they continue to press these people so hard? Some "hot lots" were tied up in the fab because of equipment problems. Was there a way to get those back on track? A key customer needed a visit from some "brass." Who was appropriate and available? The corporation was asking all divisions to have their executive staff go through a strategic planning workshop. What timing would work best?

We next moved to the *design engineering* area, where we began to see some of the operational manifestations of the issues being dealt with at the top. Two groups of design engineers worked to develop and provide redesign support to the two families of products. They had a backlog of new designs and an even bigger backlog of redesigns. Ambitious schedules for new product development and technology advances requiring frequent updates in current products were straining the capacity of this lean, young group. Uncertainty about strategic direction had contributed to some turnover of design engineers who feared that their expertise might become unneeded or, even worse, relegated to product update work instead of the more interesting new design work. In this high-pressure environment, important assignments were often given to new young engineers, who received little day-to-day guidance from managers who were "always in meetings." Valuable time was lost before it was discovered whether their designs were off the track.

This group was caught in its own technology change. It was midway in a move toward advanced CAD systems. About one third of the design engineers had a new generation of advanced work stations. Some were learning how to use them; others were anxious to receive aid from these technologies but were still using the old ("very obsolete," even though considered state-of-the-art six months earlier) equipment. Even more vexing, layout specialists were quitting, understanding that the new technology rendered them unnecessary. This left unhappy design engineers who did not have the new system and did not have adequate support.

At a meeting, the design engineers discussed the apparent demise of the "womb-to-tomb" product teams that had been a priority in the year's objectives. They died, ostensibly, because design engineers were unwilling to take responsibility for the ongoing redesign requirements of the produce life cycle. These engineers opted to spend their time on the more glamorous up-front design efforts. Confronted with the consequences for business of this behavior, the engineers faulted the unwillingness of the corporation to adequately finance development work (they wanted another, less sophisticated group to do the redesign), the inability of the fab to make "perfectly good designs" work, and the overeagerness of the sales representative in promising new product updates that could not be delivered. As one last self-justification, they lambasted the company for losing good engineers because it failed to understand that engineers need special treatment and cannot be governed by blue collar practices. Clearly this group was not eager to get into situations demanding interfunctional cooperation.

The *fabrication* area was dealing with its own challenges. In the midst of trying to bootstrap its way to the introduction of a new generation of process technology, it was also being called on by quality assurance to more fully document its process and develop a more rigorous in-process QA procedure. Design wanted it to speed the "hot lots" (lots under development). The business demanded that it adapt to many product lines and a proliferation of new products as well as a large number of variations of existing products. This group worked long hours, moving from "fire to fire," solving a plethora of technical problems. They felt this climate resulted from too many different kinds of products, many of which pushed the limits of the current process technology, from changing priorities, and from design engineers who did not want to hear about or correct problems in their designs. From the fab's perspective there were too many people in the company who did not understand that being a low-cost producer required more emphasis on producible designs and more resources for manufacturing equipment and process development.

The *test* area, where the final check was made before products were shipped overseas to be assembled, was similarly bothered by what it saw as the lack of discipline in the fab. Test employees felt they received too much "junk," with little indication that fab had a systematic means of correcting the problems. However, their biggest concern (and also their most interesting task) was to develop the next generation of test equipment and processes necessary for the new generation of chips that were now on the drawing board. They were especially concerned that, although they had to develop the ability to test the product at the same time the product was being designed, they were getting very little communication from the design engineers to inform their efforts. They were essentially flying blind, knowing they were moving in generally the right directions, and hoping they were not too far afield.

Visiting the groups with field contact—*marketing, sales,* and *field applications*—we became aware of a somewhat different perspective. These groups were concerned with customer need and practical applications. (Contrast this with the design engineering supervisor who claimed that "there has never been a breakthrough because an engineer understood applications.") These groups needed the relative chaos of the new product development cycle to be translated into firm new product introduction dates, clear and complete documentation, and highly reliable products. When they dealt with the customer, they did not want to have to echo empty promises; their credibility was key to success, and it depended on the credibility of the whole design-through-production cycle. These groups questioned the value of the grandiose strategic plans, which did not seem to acknowledge what they perceived to be limitations in the system. They were reluctant to sell a product until they were sure it was available; thus, in the eyes of the product line managers, they were failing to create a backlog of orders that would maximally benefit the company from the high margins of the early product introduction. As one sales manager said, "*They* [design engineers] deal with dreams; *we* deal with reality." Witness the meeting we attended, in which the sales managers were deciding what products they could safely push. Applications engineers were concerned that engineers were allowed to do whatever they pleased, and that certainly did not include developing adequate documentation for new products.

Viewed by the "techies" as irrelevant overhead, the *support groups* turned the kaleidoscope once more. The controller, for example, had his people working long hours not only to keep the book, but also to develop new management information capabilities that would enable product managers to make better decisions about product mix and other factors that impact on financial performance. Although he admitted that these reports often fell on deaf or even hostile ears, he felt this capability was a key element of the company's transition from a start-up venture to a mature business. While we were there, the managers in finance met to consider measures they would take to shield their workers from the antagonism they experienced from the troops—who considered finance responsible for what they perceived as inadequate investment in new equipment and adequate manpower and bureaucratic hassles such as detailed expense reporting.

The *human resources group* dealt with some of the largest issues relating to the capability of the firm: turnover and recruitment and management development. Open requisitions were a constant irritant to an already overburdened work force, and human resources was a handy scapegoat for this problem. We observed that the vast majority of this department's time was spent on the recruitment process. A second major issue was that the company had many young, relatively inexperienced managers who had moved up quickly and often during the start-up years of the company. The organization had changed many times in its three-year history, and people found themselves in brand new jobs managing newly constituted groups. We witnessed a meeting to discuss this issue. Exit interviews indicated that a key reason for departure was inadequate and neglectful supervision by managers who spent all their time solving technical problems and paid little attention to their employees. The human resources group was deciding how to convince line management that the problem could not be solved merely with the new "quick-fix" reward system that the executive staff had requested.

This snapshot view of some of the concurrent issues in one high technology company should not be interpreted as a picture of a company in distress. In actuality, this company was financially quite solid and viewed as a technological leader. Furthermore, these same themes are repeated in field notes from the visitation of many high technology companies, large and small, start-up and mature, healthy and struggling. Many stresses are built into the high technology arena, as a natural consequence of the kind of work they do and the nature of the high technology environment. The next section enumerates a few of the obvious elements in managing this environment.

HIGH TECHNOLOGY FIRMS:
COMPLEXITY, UNCERTAINTY, AND INTERDEPENDENCE

When spending time in a high technology organization, one cannot help but be impressed by the extent to which technology is the dominant theme. Technology and technological applications are both the products of the organization and the tools of its work. New product development and technology development are closely linked. Technological knowledge is sought and developed. Maintaining up-to-date technological expertise is a primary career concern for many individuals populating these organizations. The coordination and motivation of personnel with highly expert technical bases is an essential management challenge.

Technical expertise comes packaged in the form of highly trained specialists. Most high technology organizations require a large number of specialties to function, and these specialties tend to arrange themselves in a pecking order. They vary in their scarcity (market value), their criticality to the design to production cycle, their levels of education, and their level of creativity. Technical "gurus" emerge, who assume a disproportionate role in the solution of technical problems and often a role in the status hierarchy that belies their position in the organizational hierarchy. Managers are reluctant to give up their role in technical problem-solving, and thus technical tasks migrate upward.

The multiple specialties required for the functioning of high technology firms often speak different technical languages and have been trained in different disciplines with different worldviews and different technical algorithms. The tasks of these groups must be integrated and coordinated in a manner that is difficult to specify at the onset.

Much of the work in these firms is complex problem solving of elaborate and ill-defined problems. The solution to these problems often requires invention. Most projects have multiple puzzles to be solved, and their solutions all have to be compatible with one another—the test problem has to be solved in a manner compatible with the design problem, and the design problem and the fabrication problem have to be compatibly resolved, and so on. All related problems must eventually fit into a "system" that works.

This complex set of tasks and people exists within a larger environment that changes rapidly, creating a great deal of uncertainty. The technologies that are applied to the products of these organizations, and are used by organizational members in accomplishing their task, develop and change rapidly. New product development cycles are being drastically reduced as the competitive environment becomes more intense. The marketplace changes and develops rapidly; as some product lines reach a point of saturation, others emerge, and the globalization of the economy proceeds at a relentless pace.

The speed and amount of change place huge burdens on the members of these companies to solve their puzzles quickly and to work out their interdependencies efficiently. All those specialties that do not like or know how to talk to one another must cooperate to solve the puzzles first. Steps that were once handled sequentially (design, produce, test) must be performed simultaneously. Individuals trained to be individual problem solvers must learn to be part of a team.

Another result of the rapidly changing and uncertain environment is the establishment of an atmosphere of risk. People in high technology organizations are preoccupied with strategy. They want to know how their company is going to ride the seas of change and competition and emerge a winner. They look for leadership and become disillusioned when they do not see it. They relentlessly second guess, based on their own reading of the "tea leaves"—technical journals, technical networks, and the popular press. If they lose confidence in the future of the firm, they look for greener pastures.

To survive, high technology organizations must constantly learn and develop. Everyone we encountered was learning something: engineers were learning a new computer system, finance people learning the new government accounting regulations, fab operators learning a new etching process; new managers learning to think like managers, executive groups learning what it is to be a truly global company. This learning process is compressed: engineers must begin producing immediately on their new work stations; field application engineers must master new products as soon as the specifications are released; those who strategize must learn quickly the competencies and degree of threat from brand new competitors and emerging strategic alliances.

Built into the competitive arena of high technology firms is the basic tension between the forces that might result in chaos—the fast pace of change, a high degree of complexity, and the huge amount of interdependence and the need of the business for predictability and control. The employees in these organizations are part of an elaborate organizational system governed by considerations of schedule, cost, and performance. Whether within the confines of a contract, a customer order backlog, or a product strategy to achieve timely and competitive market presence, people feel they are operating in a highly uncertain technical world within rigidly defined and frequently unrealistic business constraints. There is ongoing tension between the rational world of planning and control and the dynamic and unpredictable world of technological invention; between the need to control resources and the desire to unleash resources to enable extraordinary accomplishments; between the worries of economic viability viewed through such variables as productivity and return on investment and the technologists' concerns with the technical breakthrough and ability to remain state of the art.

As we rotate the kaleidoscope, we experience different perspectives on the rich and complex world of high technology. Although it is impossible, in a single volume, to expose all its facets, the contributors to this book have provided a rich array of perspectives.

In the succeeding three chapters, we begin with a global approach to the

complexities of high technology industries and firms. In chapter 2 Everett
M. Rogers and Ying-Chung Annie Chen define the role of the technopolis in
the innovation process and provide observations of numerous technopolii
around the world. They discuss how different location decisions influence
the culture of the firm. Their contention is that different national cultures
impact on high tech firms differentially in terms of strategic advantage. In
chapter 3 Jay Galbraith takes this perspective one step further. He predicts
that since the R & D process of high tech firms seeking competitive advantage is becoming so expensive, the wave of the future rests with the truly
global enterprise and with cross-cultural strategic alliances. In addition, he
predicts that these new alliances will demand new organizational forms. In
chapter 4, Gerardo Ungson examines three sets of international competitors
in the high tech arena—firms from the United States, Japan, and the European Economic Community (EEC). He describes the industrial policies of
each country and predicts the factors that will influence the effectiveness of
high technology in the future.

Designing organizations that can effectively handle the rapid rate of
change, the need for ongoing innovation, and the extreme technological interdependence is a high technology challenge. The next three chapters focus
on key issues relating to the design of high technology firms. In chapter 5,
Kathleen M. Eisenhardt and L. Jay Bourgeois III deal with the strategic
decision making process. They offer insights from their study of top management teams operating in the "high velocity" environment of the high
technology firms. They challenge classic models of strategic decision making and give us a detailed excursion into the microcomputer industry. Chapter 6 represents Claudia Bird Schoonhoven and Mariann Jelinek's longitudinal analysis of several highly successful high technology firms, which
illustrates how these firms structure themselves to promote innovation. The
authors challenge the classic wisdom that "organic" structures are best
suited to the high technology arena. Rounding out this segment, in chapter
7 Karlene Roberts and Gina Gargano present an in-depth analysis of the
sources of and solutions to extreme interdependence, using their studies of
nuclear aircraft carriers as an empirical example. The theme of interdependence is one that permeates the book.

The next three chapters stress the need for high technology organizations
to become effective at organizational learning. In chapter 8 Tom Kosnik addresses patterns in high technology marketing. He notes that because of the
many complexities associated with the technology and the interdependencies and rapid rate of change, marketers must learn a new way of operating.
They must be prepared to become knowledgeable about many aspects of the
firm, work more closely with other disciplines, and develop ways to continually update their knowledge.

In chapter 9 Dorothy Leonard-Barton presents findings from a study of
two competing organizations' introduction of new technology. She finds that
different corporate-level and plant-level strategies for introducing new technology have a significant impact on the ability of the organization to learn

how to use it. Next, in chapter 10, Paul Adler presents learnings from an in-depth study of the utilization of CAD and CAM systems. He contends that American firms are not getting the intended benefits of these systems of reducing new product development time and costs. He attributes this to the traditional organizational design of most U.S. firms and makes the case that fundamentally new organizational patterns must be learned.

The last section focuses on critical issues in managing human resources. In chapter 11 Allan M. Mohrman, Susan A. Mohrman, and Christopher Worley assess performance management in high technology settings. They build on the interdependence theme, noting that in most high tech settings, the team is the critical unit of analysis, not the individual performer. Their research is conducted in three large, mature, high technology firms, and they note that traditional performance management approaches have very little do with organizational effectiveness. In chapter 12 contributors Susan Res-nick-West and Mary Ann Von Glinow note that fundamental clashes arise in managing a high tech work force. If not managed properly, these clashes can become overwhelming barriers to organizational effectiveness. Drawing from a decade's worth of data collection, the authors offer suggestions for management of culture clashes. Chapter 13 rounds out this segment, with a cogent analysis by Luis R. Gomez-Mejia and Theresa Welbourne of com-pensation strategies in high tech industries. Drawing from a large sample, they critically examine what works and what doesn't. They discuss the theme that all three chapters share— that today's high tech firms have de-veloped unique human resource strategies and practices that mesh well with the nature of this industry.

Lastly, chapter 14 presents a state-of-the-art analysis of the kaleidoscop-ic components discussed in the previous chapters. Offered here is a synopsis of the existing knowledge, and a framework that begins to focus the domain more clearly. Common themes are extracted, and contradictions are exam-ined. In virtually all the chapters contributors have challenged the tradi-tional wisdom of management theories. The final chapter represents an at-tempt to model similarities and dissimilarities within an integrative framework. We conclude this volume by offering management implications, noting that there are still murky areas worthy of additional empirical inves-tigation.

2

Technology Transfer and the Technopolis

EVERETT M. ROGERS AND
YING-CHUNG ANNIE CHEN

The objective of this chapter is to identify the main lessons learned about the role of technology transfer in the rise of high tech centers that are emerging at various places in the world. A *technopolis* is a geographically concentrated high tech complex often characterized by collaborative R & D efforts between high tech industry and a research university or government-sponsored R & D institute, and by the presence of venture capital and entrepreneurial spin-off firms. A technopolis often contains a research park as the core of the university–industry collaboration. A technopolis may or may not be planned by a government. Early U.S. technopolii such as northern California's Silicon Valley and Route 128 (near Boston) mainly evolved spontaneously, although in recent decades several technopolii in the United States, such as Research Triangle in North Carolina and Austin, Texas, represent a trend toward greater government involvement.

Although the technopolis phenomenon first appeared in the United States around 1960, the term itself was coined by the Japanese. In 1980 the Ministry of International Trade and Industry (MITI) published its "Technopolis Concept" in *Visions for the 1980s,* a plan to construct some twenty high tech centers patterned after Silicon Valley and Japan's Tsukuba Science City. The term has since come into vogue more widely, as evidenced by a recent conference on "Technopolis: Emerging Issues in Technology Commercialization and Economic Development," held in Austin, Texas, in 1987, and a book based on that conference (Smilor, Kozmetsky, and Gibson, 1988).

This chapter presents an analysis of ten technopolii: Silicon Valley in northern California, undoubtedly the most widely known technopolis; Austin, Texas, probably the most rapidly rising technopolis in the 1980s; Cambridge, England, and Route 128, which represent highly spontaneous high technology development; and Research Triangle in North Carolina, Sophia

An earlier version of this chapter was presented at the Pan-Pacific Conference IV, Taipei, Taiwan, May 17–20, 1987.

15

Antipolis in southern France, Tsukuba Science City in Japan, the Shenzhen technopolis (near Hong Kong), the Beijing technopolis in China, and the Hsin-Chu technopolis in Taiwan. The latter six technopolii were carefully planned and represent a high degree of governmental involvement.

Why is there currently such great interest by governments, private companies, and scholars in the technopolis? To governments a technopolis represents the creation of jobs and the production of income (and hence taxes). National governments desire their firms to remain competitive in the worldwide microelectronics industry that drives the information society. To a private high tech company, a technopolis is perceived as a business opportunity in which it can gain an advantage in technological innovation from the relatively facile technology transfer that occurs in a technopolis because of the propinquity of R & D to the users of technology. For many firms, a technopolis is also a place where new competitors are likely to spin off from existing firms. For social scientists, a technopolis represents an important type of contemporary social change, and thus a phenomenon that deserves careful study. The technopolis is the heart of the *information system,* in which a plurality of the nation's labor force is employed in information work. Information workers include all occupations whose main function is gathering, processing, or disseminating information and producing information technology. In the United States today about 60 percent of the work force consists of information workers. *Information* is patterned matter-energy that affects the probabilities available to an individual making a decision (Rogers, 1986, p. 10). Later in this chapter we argue that technology is essentially information.

HIGH TECHNOLOGY INDUSTRY AND TECHNOLOGY TRANSFER

A *high technology industry* is characterized by (1) highly skilled employees, many of whom are scientists and engineers; (2) a fast rate of growth; (3) a high ratio of research and development expenditures to sales (typically about 1:10); and (4) a worldwide market for its products. In a high technology industry, the technology is changing continuously at a rate faster than in other industries. So high tech is high not because its technology is complicated or sophisticated, but because the technology is changing rapidly. The main high tech industries today are electronics, aerospace, chemicals, pharmaceuticals, instrumentation, and biotechnology. Certain subindustries within electronics, such as semiconductors and microcomputers, possess a technology that is advancing particularly rapidly, so microelectronics is the highest of high tech.

Technology transfer is a process in which technological innovations are exchanged between individuals and organizations who are involved in R & D, on the one hand, and in putting technology into use, on the other (Rogers and Valente, 1988). Conventionally, technology transfer was thought to involve a physical or material product. In recent years, however, as research and development activities have increasingly incorporated software, processes, and other nonmaterial components into their products, we have realized that technology transfer is basically the communication of technical information. Eveland (1986) points out that "technology" is essentially information and "transfer" is essentially communication; thus, technology transfer is basically the communication of technical information. Usually technology transfer in the United States is from a research university to nearby private companies, but it may also flow in the opposite direction or be a two-way processes.

Technology is a design for instrumental action that reduces the uncertainty in the cause–effect relationships involved in achieving a desired outcome (Rogers, 1983). We usually think of technology as a tool for accomplishing some function. The tool may be a metal model or it may be a machine. For example, the authors wrote the present chapter on a microcomputer using WORDSTAR, a computer software product. A single item of technology is usually called an *innovation,* defined as an idea perceived as new (Rogers, 1986). Thus, a technology is essentially a closely bundled set of innovations (Rogers and Valente, 1988).

A *research university* is an institution of higher learning whose main function is to conduct research and to provide graduate student training in how to conduct research (Rogers, 1986, p. 15). The research university's role in an information society like the United States is analogous to that of the steel factory in the industrial society. It is the key institution around which growth occurs, and it determines the direction of that growth. Each of the technopolii in the United States (as will be illustrated) centers on a research university. However, in some other nations, the role of the research university is filled by a government-sponsored research institute. The general point here is that *a local source of technological innovations flowing from some kind of R & D organization is a prerequisite for a technopolis, particularly at its initiation.* Silicon Valley could not have begun in the 1960s without Stanford University, although today Stanford is not a particularly crucial element in Silicon Valley. Similarly, a technopolis was emerging slowly in Austin, Texas, until 1983, when the MCC (Microelectronics and Computer Technology Corporation) located there; the MCC decided on Austin because of a desire to neighbor with the University of Texas (Gibson and Rogers, 1988).

For the technological innovations resulting from R & D in a research university (or its counterpart) to benefit society, the technical information must be *transferred* from an R & D unit to private high-tech firms. These companies then transform (i.e., commercialize) a technological innovation into a new product that fills the needs of potential buyers. Thus technology transfer lies at the heart of the technopolis. It is the fundamental process. Increasingly, the nature of nation-to-nation and company-to-company competition (and collaboration) lies in the process of effective transfer of technological innovations from R & D organizations to high tech firms. One function of the technopolis is to serve as a system in which technology transfer is facilitated (Rogers and Valente, 1988).

Because information is such a highly valued commodity in the information society, those individuals who produce new information are superelites (Bell, 1973). Scientists, R & D workers, and engineers are high priests of the information society. These individuals gain their unique status through graduate-level training at a research university. Brainpower is thus the vital ingredient of the technopolis in the information society. The scientific–technological elites of the information society receive wealth and social status, earned through their advanced formal education and, in many cases, their entrepreneurial spirit. For instance, the approximately 250,000 high tech workers in Silicon Valley include 15,000 self-made millionaires and two billionaires (Rogers and Larsen, 1984). These superelites typically have several years of graduate-level education in a technical field like electrical engineering or computer science, and then were involved in launching a successful high tech microelectronics firm around a technological innovation.

COMPARISON OF TEN TECHNOPOLII

Table 2.1 briefly summarizes the background of each of the ten technopolii of our study, which we take up in approximately the order of their founding and their current size.

Silicon Valley

Silicon Valley has immense riches, a sunny, much-admired climate, and is the world's center for producing advanced communication technologies: Semiconductors, microcomputers, computer peripherals, and lasers. Silicon Valley is unique in demonstrating the role of entrepreneurial spirit in creating high tech spin-off companies in the microelectronics industry. Silicon Valley has been called "the world capital of the information society" (Rogers and Larsen, 1984). Silicon Valley is the oldest, largest, and most widely known technopolis in the world.

The rise of Silicon Valley was closely tied to Stanford University. Frederick Terman, an electrical engineering professor, was the "godfather of Silicon Valley" (Rogers and Larsen, 1984). Terman believed in close contact between the university and high technology firms. In 1938, Terman loaned $538 to two of his graduate students, William Hewlett and David Packard, to start the first high tech electronics company in Silicon Valley. Today, both Hewlett and Packard are billionaires, and their company is the biggest success story in Silicon Valley. In 1951, Terman conceived the idea of a university industrial park. Stanford Industrial Park is the first of its kind, and the most successful; it served as a model for scores of other high tech parks in the United States and abroad.

The other "godfather" of Silicon Valley is Dr. William Shockley, who launched the semiconductor industry. Shockley Transistor Laboratory, founded in 1955, gave birth to Fairchild Semiconductor, which in turn became the spawning ground for scores of spin-offs. The many entrepreneurial spin-offs from Fairchild Semiconductor marked the take-off of Silicon Valley in the 1960s.

Six key factors account for the rise of Silicon Valley: (1) technical expertise, (2) infrastructure, (3) venture capital, (4) job mobility, (5) information-exchange networks, and (6) learning entrepreneurial fever from local role models (Rogers and Larsen, 1987). Silicon Valley represents a special kind of information society heartland based on continuous technological innovation, vigorous competition, and the entrepreneurial spirit.

Today about 3,000 microelectronics manufacturing firms crowd this 10 × 20 mile technopolis, and all of the space has been gone since 1980. Housing has become so prohibitively expensive that it is difficult for Silicon Valley to attract workers (especially workers at lower pay levels) or even experienced engineers. During the 1980s, Silicon Valley typically served as the location for the company headquarters and the R & D function of a newly-founded microelectronics company, with the company's manufacturing facilities located elsewhere in the United States (for example, in Phoenix, Arizona; Portland, Oregon; Austin, Texas; or Colorado Springs, Colorado) or overseas (in Malaysia, the Philippines, or India, for example). By 1987 only one-third of the production capacity of semiconductor manufacturers remained in Silicon Valley. So the high degree of agglomeration of microelectronics firms in Silicon Valley from 1960 to 1980 was then followed by a disagglomeration of production facilities to a dozen other technopolii in the U.S. and overseas.

This recent disagglomeration led to speculation of a decline in Silicon Valley. Yet available statistics show that 60 percent of all semiconductor start-ups since 1987 are located in Silicon Valley, and the total number of Silicon Valley electronics employees has more than doubled since 1981. Silicon Valley displays a form of economic transition to a future information economy in which R & D, designing, marketing, and strategic planning are key information worker functions and constitute the primary economic activities.

Route 128

Route 128 owes its birth to MIT, particularly to MIT's president in the 1940s, Carl Taylor Compton. A firm believer in university–industry interaction, Compton encouraged MIT faculty to consult with local firms and founded the American Research Development Corporation (ARDC), a venture capital firm, to provide start-up funding to spin-off firms. Fred Terman's idea of a science park at Stanford University was an idea derived from MIT. Thus Route 128 was the genesis of technopolii in the United States and in the world.

Route 128 obtained its name because the high tech companies were first concentrated along Highway 128 around Boston. Since then it has expanded to other areas near Boston. The Route 128 high tech complex developed in the late 1950s, and grew to early success by 1971, thanks to defense and

Table 2.1 A Comparison of Ten Selected Technopolii

High Tech Complex	Location	Was the High Tech Complex Spontaneous or Planned?	Research University	Is Venture Capital Present?	Is Entrepreneurial Spirit Demonstrated by Spin-offs?	Current Number of Firms	Current High Tech Employment	Percentage of Foreign Firms or Joint Ventures	When Begun?	Climate and Quality of Life
1. Silicon Valley	Santa Clara County, Calif. (near San Francisco)	Mainly spontaneous	Stanford	Yes	Yes, but may be decreasing in the late 1980s	3,000	250,000	Perhaps 5%	First company in 1938, but really grew after 1960	Sunny climate; high quality of life
2. Route 128	Boston, Mass.	Mainly spontaneous	MIT	Yes	Yes	About 700	175,000	Very few	First companies in 1940s, but really grew after late 1950s	Good quality of life
3. Research Triangle	Near Chapel Hill, Raleigh, & Durham, N.C.	Planned	University of North Carolina, N.C. State, & Duke	No	No	50	23,000	Almost none	1958 (began to grow after 1966)	Good
4. Austin	Austin, Tex.	Originally unplanned	University of Texas at Austin	No	Few, except for 50 spin-offs of Tracor	800	60,000	Almost none	First company in 1955, but really grew after MCC founding in 1983	Good

Name	Location	Planning	University	Col5	Col6	Col7	Col8	Col9	Year	Quality
5. Cambridge	Cambridge, U.K.	Completely unplanned	Cambridge University	Yes	Yes	450	About 16,500	About 25%	1960s	Outstanding cultural life
6. Sophia Antipolis	French Riviera	Planned	University of Nice	Yes	Yes	150	6,000	About 80%	1969	Fabulous climate
7. Tsukuba Science City	Tsukuba, Japan (near Tokyo)	Planned	University of Tsukuba	Little	Few	200	About 15,000	Some	Construction begain in 1968, finished in 1980.	Considered a sterile environment
8. Hsin-Chu Industrial Park	Hsin-Chu, Republic of China (near Taipei)	Planned	National Chin-Hwa University	Yes	Few	About 80	(Unknown)	Many	1981	Good
9. Shenzhen Special Economic Zone	Shenzhen, Guangdong Province, People's Republic of China (near Hong Kong)	Planned	University of Shenzen	No	No	700	(Unknown)	About half	1979	Very good
10. Jongcuacun	Beijing, People's Republic of China	Originally spontaneous	Beijing University, Science Academy, others	Yes	Yes	170	About 10,000	None	1982	Good

aerospace contracts with the U.S. government. In the early 1970s, recession struck this area, and 12,000 engineers and technicians were laid off. However, the combination of a research university, a surplus of experienced engineers, and a group of venture capitalists created a renaissance along Route 128. In the late 1970s and early 1980s, Route 128 became a synonym for minicomputers, a technology that played a pivotal role in Route 128's comeback.

Today Route 128 draws its academic resources mainly from MIT, and much less from Harvard, Boston University, and the University of Massachusetts. Route 128's high tech products are not limited to microelectronics. Biotechnology, for example, has become an important industry supported by Harvard University's excellence in microbiology. Even in a state like Massachusetts, known for its high tech industry, high tech employees make up only 12 percent of total employment (Miller and Côté, 1985). High-technology industries are generally capital-intensive but not labor-intensive.

Research Triangle, North Carolina

Research Triangle is the largest *planned* high tech complex in the world. It began in 1958 when Governor Luther H. Hodges had the vision of turning the Raleigh–Durham–Chapel Hill metropolitan area into a technopolis. Three universities are the points of the triangle: North Carolina State University, Duke University, and the University of North Carolina. Before 1958, this triangle was largely an uninhabited swamplike tract. Research Triangle offers low taxes, freedom from unionized labor, and a nice climate.

In 1981 Research Triangle received a big boost when then Governor James B. Hunt established the Microelectronics Center of North Carolina (MCNC) in Research Triangle Park. MCNC is designed to improve the quality of microelectronics research and education in North Carolina. To date over $82 million of state government funds have gone into the MCNC. This center helped elevate the status of Research Triangle as a major high tech center in the United States. Although a showcase for planned research parks, Research Triangle has not yet generated entrepreneurial spin-offs. But it has raised the ranking of North Carolina's personal income from forty-fifth thirty years ago to thirty-seventh place today among fifty states.

Austin, Texas

Austin, the capital of Texas, is a growing city that had already attracted Intel, IBM, Texas Instruments, and other microelectronics manufacturing plants (with about 30,000 employees) before it made a sudden leap to high tech stardom in 1983. The dramatic change occurred when the Microelectronics and Computer Technology Corporation (MCC) chose Austin over fifty-seven other U.S. cities as its headquarters site.

The MCC is a research consortium of twenty major electronics firms in the United States, founded to compete with the heavily government-subsidized Japanese Fifth-Generation Computer Project (ICOT). William C. Norris, the former president of Control Data Corporation, initiated the idea of the MCC, and helped push it through to reality. When the MCC was founded in 1982, its legality in relation to antitrust regulations was unclear. The U.S. Department of Justice gave the MCC the "yellow light," indicating that it would not prosecute the MCC at that time. In 1984, thanks to lobbying by the MCC and its twenty shareholder companies, the National Cooperative Research Act was passed into law, thus freeing R & D consortia like the MCC from certain antitrust regulations. By 1989, more than 150 R & D consortia had been founded in the United States.

The MCC presently has 20 member companies, 454 researchers and staff members, and an annual operating budget of $75 million. Austin won the MCC by promising a $23.5 million building for the MCC at the University of Texas' Balcones Research Park, and $40 million from the University of Texas to expand their electrical engineering and computer science programs. Since 1983, the MCC attracted R & D units of several of its twenty-member companies to relocate in Austin (e.g., 3M, Motorola, and Lockheed). 3M transferred 3000 R & D workers to Austin in 1984 (Farley and Glickman, 1986). The agglomeration of R & D workers to Austin in 1984 is part of an important trend, because *entrepreneurial spin-offs are more likely from R & D employees than from production workers in microelectronics companies.*

The MCC caused a spectacular building boom in Austin from 1983 to 1985, characterized by escalating housing costs and the construction of surplus office space. In 1983, the average price of a home in Austin was $88,464. Two years later, this figure was $107,000, an increase of 21 percent. During the 1983–85 period, twelve large office buildings were constructed in Austin, more than doubling the square feet of office space and creating a vacancy rate of 40 percent, the highest in the nation. Austin's skyline was so altered by the office building construction that local wags claimed the building crane had become the new state bird.

The University of Texas has not only played a key role in attracting the MCC to Austin but has for some years played the seed role in agglomerating the Austin technopolis. The "Hewlett-Packard" of Austin is Tracor, founded in 1955 by Frank McBee, who earned his B.S. and M.S. degrees in engineering at the University of Texas. By 1987, Tracor had 2200 employees and had fathered sixteen direct spin-offs (including Continuum, with 700 employees, and Radian, with 973 employees and four of its own spin-offs). Counting both direct and indirect spin-offs, Tracor has spawned fifty new high tech ventures, indicating a high degree of entrepreneurial activity in Austin (Smilor et al., 1988).

By 1988 only two spin-offs from the MCC had occurred, but more are expected. Another indicator of the key role of the University of Texas in the rise of the Austin technopolis is shown by the results of a recent survey of

103 high tech firms in Austin: half of these companies had some type of direct connection with the university, such as hiring a UT professor as a consultant (Smilor et al., 1988).

In 1988 Sematech (Semiconductor Manufacturing and Technology Institute), an R & D consortium with fourteen member companies, located in Austin. Like MCC, Sematech represents a response to Japanese competition, but with even larger stakes. Sematech has a $250 million annual budget (including $100 million from the U.S. Department of Defense) and will provide 800 jobs. Competition for Sematech was even more severe than for the MCC, with 135 sites in thirty-four states submitting proposals. Although the state of Massachusetts made a $440 million bid for Sematech, Austin won by providing a $68 million package, including $50 million from the University of Texas to purchase a building for Sematech, plus plenty of political clout. U.S. Representative Jake Pickle of Austin led the lobbying to get Sematech's $100 million annual appropriation through the U.S. Congress. MCC officials tipped off Texas leaders that Sematech was coming soon after it was formed in May 1987, thus giving Austin a head start in their campaign. Since half of the Sematech member companies were the twenty shareholders of MCC, Austin was evidently considered a good site for Sematech.

Cambridge, United Kingdom

The high tech complex in Cambridge is usually referred to as the "Cambridge phenomenon" (Segal, 1984). This prestigious university town is the site of a burgeoning high tech industry created largely by incidental unplanned local initiatives developing around one of the oldest universities in the world.

Cambridge University allows its faculty members to work with local industries, which was not possible in other English universities. The organizational culture of Cambridge University calls for its academic staff "to devote themselves to advancement of their subject, to give instruction to students and to promote the interests of the University as a place of education and research" (Segal, Quince, Wicksteed, 1987, p. 31). Beyond this general expectation, a Cambridge professor is free to work with outside high tech firms, as a consultant, for example. Thus Cambridge University's policy concerning university–private company relationships amounts to a "benign, laid-back, supportive and non-interventionist policy" (Segal, Quince, Wicksteed, 1985, p. 33). Officially, Cambridge University was not an active promoter of the Cambridge phenomenon. Nor did the British government play any role in fostering the Cambridge phenomenon, although it is now trying to encourage other technopolii, each centered on a university. As the main analysts of this technopolis (Segal, Quince, Wicksteed, 1987) stated, "The Cambridge experience . . . has a multiplicity of causes . . . which in its totality has been unplanned" (p. 1).

One trigger in creating the Cambridge technopolis was a local branch of Barclays Bank. In the 1960s this bank not only started investing in high tech firms but provided an advisory manager to help these new entrepreneurial projects. Today 450 high tech firms are included in the Cambridge phenomenon.

Sophia Antipolis, France

For the past decade or so, the national government of France has pursued a public policy of assisting French firms to compete more effectively in the worldwide high technology market, especially in microelectronics. Examples of French projects that have been pursued in light of this national policy are (1) the "wired city" project in Biarritz, in which households and businesses are connected by two-way interactive cable television, and (2) the Minitel project, in which videotext terminals were provided free to 3 million French households (Williams et al., 1988). "France, Inc." is thus evolving into a European version of "Japan, Inc.," in which government and private high tech firms collaborate (1) to conduct R & D in order to create technological innovations and (2) to commercialize this technology into new products, which are marketed domestically and then sold on the world market. The French government's investment thus translates into an international competitive edge for French high tech firms.

Sophia Antipolis is another example of the France, Inc. policy. A large research park was established in 1969 with national and local government funding. The setting is exquisite, in the heart of the European sunbelt. Sophia Antipolis (named for the Greek god of knowledge, connoting "anti-city") is located on the French Riviera, near the beautiful city of Cannes on the Mediterranean. Here is a technopolis driven mainly by one factor: a high quality-of-life. The Sophia Antipolis research park contains many foreign firms, including those from the United States, like IBM, DEC, and Dow Chemical. About 150 companies are located in Sophia Antipolis, employing 6000 workers and providing 19,000 service jobs.

The initial inspiration for this technopolis came from Senator Pierre Laffitte, a local resident who had served in the national legislature in Paris and as director of the French School of Mines. He took the lead in envisioning Sophia Antipolis, and obtaining government funding for it. It is now well underway.

Tsukuba Science, Japan

Tsukuba Science City is a planned technopolis that lies in a 3-by-12-mile crescent shape about 35 miles north of Tokyo. Tsukuba City, launched in 1963, represents an investment of $5 billion in public funds (Bloom and Asand, 1981). Much of this funding was obtained from the sale of the land on which government research institutions had been located in Tokyo, before they moved to Tsukuba.

The original purposes of building Tsukuba Science City were (1) to ease the serious housing problems in Tokyo and (2) to build new, modern facilities for government research institutes outside of crowded Tokyo. Tsukuba was meant to be a science city, one that emulates places like Novosibirsk Science City in the U.S.S.R., which was set up to use the natural resources in Siberia (Tatsuno, 1986, p. 265). Planning for Tsukuba Science City began in 1960, but relocation of the forty-three national research institutes was not completed until 1980. Its goals are to facilitate high tech development and foster regional economic development. Tsukuba Science City is the model technopolis for these twenty future technopolii in Japan.

The development of the Tsukuba technopolis was inspired by Silicon Valley, although its structural arrangements more closely resemble those of Research Triangle in North Carolina. The Japanese government started with the high technology agglomeration process, seeding it with a core of government-funded research institutes. MITI is so concerned about technology transfer from government research institutes to private industry that it created a unit responsible for this process: the Agency of Industrial Science and Technology (AIST). AIST is headquartered in Tokyo, but most of its activities are in Tsukuba.

In addition to the forty-three government-funded R & D institutes, Tsukuba has two new research universities, one of which is Tsukuba University. Presently, Tsukuba City includes 6500 researchers in government institutes plus several thousand researchers in private companies. The public research institutes in Tsukuba City represent one third of all the national research personnel and 50 percent of the national R & D budget. Although spin-off high tech firms have not yet characterized Tsukuba Science City, a number of semiconductor and electronics companies have moved their R & D operations there. Many are situated in three science parks in Tsukuba.

A major drawback in creating a dynamic community characterized by close university, private business, and government communication has been the sterile nature of the city. Tsukuba City is not yet considered very livable by Japanese standards. The "Tsukuba syndrome" consists of skin rash, diarrhea, and other health problems that reflect individuals' maladjustment to the life-style of this new city. Tsukuba has an unusually high suicide rate. This technopolis, with a total population of 150,000, lacks an adequate number of bars, restaurants, and other services that the Japanese consider essential to urban life. Many residents of Tsukuba City still maintain a residence in Tokyo, spend the weekends there, or even commute every day.

Hsin-Chu Industrial Park, Taiwan

Hsin-Chu Industrial Park was launched in 1980 by the Taiwanese government to create a showcase for future high technology development. Like Singapore, South Korea, and Brazil, Taiwan has become a newly industrialized country. Cheap labor is no longer the foundation of its export-based economy or the main attraction for foreign investment. Taiwan's competitive edge in export was especially blunted in recent years by China, Malaysia, and other developing countries, which offer cheaper labor for manufacturing clothes, shoes, and furniture for export to industrialized countries. Taiwan is therefore now pursuing the high tech industry.

Hsin-Chu Industrial Park combines (1) the idea of the Stanford Industrial Park and (2) the experience of export processing zones (EPZs), tax-free enclaves established by a government to encourage foreign-owned firms to locate there and provide jobs. Hsin-Chu Industrial Park focuses on microelectronics and maintains a close link with nearby Ching-Hua University, a research university with academic strength in the natural sciences. Structurally reminiscent of the export processing zones in Kaoshung, Nantz, and Taichung, the Hsin-Chu Industrial Park has a distinct set of financial and operational incentives for investors, both foreign and domestic.

About eighty companies are located in the park, with annual sales exceeding $750 million and an annual growth rate of 66 percent (*Commonwealth*, 1987). Only new companies are allowed to locate here. Most of these are owned by native Taiwanese, but there are also a number of joint ventures with foreign investors. Many entrepreneurs are overseas Chinese who either immigrated to or worked in the United States after completing their graduate degrees there. Thus, one function of Hsin-Chu Industrial Park is to rectify the brain-drain problem.

Strategies employed by companies in Hsin-Chu Industrial Park differ substantially from those of companies in the old EPZs. First, companies are motivated to develop innovative technologies to fill a market niche in the worldwide high tech market. The goal is to attract joint ventures with industrialized countries (*Commonwealth*, 1987). Second, a number of firms have set up offices in the United States (especially in Silicon Valley) to handle marketing or even to conduct R & D. Companies in the park actively seek foreign partners for the purpose of technology transfer from foreign companies.

Shenzhen Special Economic Zone, China

The Shenzhen Special Economic Zone is the largest of the four special enterprise zones (SEZs) set up by the Chinese government along China's southeastern coast to implement a new economic strategy of attracting foreign capital and technology. The SEZs represent a new Chinese policy "toward integration into the capitalist world economy" and serve as the "key connecting points along the Western Pacific Rim" (X. Chen, 1988, p. 1).

From 1980 to 1986 these four doors accrued $1.28 billion in overseas capital, or one fifth of the total foreign investment in China. Shenzhen alone is responsible for 60 percent of total foreign investment and almost 80 percent of all new factories in the four SEZs since 1980. The city grew from 1.16 square miles in 1979 to 120.5 square miles in 1987. Population in Shenzhen increased from 23,000 to 350,000 in the same period. Once an agricultural area, Shenzhen has transformed itself, winning the title of "a city built in one night."

China SEZ strategy is to transfer both technology and management style from multinational companies. Foreign investment in processing and assembly work in Shenzhen decreased from 23.9 percent in 1979 to 3.4 percent of total investment capital in 1984, while joint ventures constituted more than 95 percent of the foreign investment in 1984. Independently owned foreign enterprises are limited.

The other side of technology transfer in Shenzhen involves the close relationship between a research university and private firms. The University of Shenzhen, a technical university launched with the assistance of the United States, in the long run will provide the type of technology transfer found in most other technopolii of study here. Shenzhen is under state control, and entrepreneurial spin-offs are rare.

The highly planned technopolis in Shenzhen has yielded both expected and unexpected results. On the one hand, Shenzhen is faced with a dilemma of being simultaneously an "overseas import zone" and a "domestic export zone" (X. Chen, 1988). Most of Shenzhen's products are sold in China's domestic market, which is lucrative for most foreign investors. Production is thus often geared for domestic consumption rather than for export. On the other hand, Shenzhen provides a sharp contrast with the rest of China, economically, ideologically, and culturally; it even has its own currency.

Jongcuacun, China

Jongcuacun is a street in Beijing on which some 170 computer-related companies have located since 1982. This minitechnopolis began spontaneously, unlike the Shenzhen technopolis in which the government of China is strongly involved. The Science Academy, Beijing University, and some fifty government-funded research institutes are located in the same section of Beijing as Jongcuacun. The Computer Institute and the Computer Software Institute are government-supported R & D institutes.

The most important firm in Jongcuacun is Stone Computer Company, sometimes called "China's IBM." It had 700 employees and annual sales of 137 million in 1987. Other companies are relatively small; they make microcomputers, printers, and computer software programs, publish computer books and magazines, and produce training videotapes about computers. Many of these firms have only their headquarters and R & D functions on Jongcuacun Street, with their manufacturing facilities located elsewhere in China. Typically, a firm in the Jongcuacun minitechnopolis is partly owned by the Chinese government and partly by private individuals.

Jongcuacun is thus the first real technopolis in China, one which evolved spontaneously like Silicon Valley, the Cambridge phenomenon, and Route

128. The Jongcuacun technopolis displays a great deal of entrepreneurial spirit in a socialist economy.

LESSONS LEARNED ABOUT TECHNOLOGY TRANSFER AND THE TECHNOPOLIS

Technology Transfer in the First World and Asia

Technology transfer in Euro-America seems to be somewhat different from that in Third World countries, especially in East Asian nations. Technology transfer in the United States results from the development of information as a valued commodity in an information society. It occurs through the close relationship between a research university and private companies. The information-producing capability of research universities is thus channeled to high tech firms. Research parks are one mechanism for this technology transfer strategy.

In Asian countries (but much less so in Japan) technology transfer generally has a foreign component. It involves transferring technical knowledge from a Western nation to a Third World country in Asia. The establishment of export processing zones is one embodiment of this type of international technology transfer. Many Third World countries like South Korea, Taiwan, Singapore, India, Mexico, and Brazil have pursued this strategy of imported technology transfer to create an export-based economy. As these nations emerge as information societies, a second wave of learning is needed. This second wave involves indigenous efforts to upgrade the technological expertise in a nation.

The new technopolii in Asia are basically built on the EPZ model, which offered tax incentives and other special benefits to attract foreign investors. But with the EPZ, a research park is transplanted from the First World in order to launch the infrastructure for an information society in Asia. The indigenous component of the second wave of technology transfer is illustrated by three aspects of the technopolii:

1. Joint ventures with foreign firms to facilitate technology transfer.
2. A close university–industry relationship to strengthen local R & D and also the R & D–marketing interface.
3. A number of domestic entrepreneurial firms, which allows high technology to trickle down to the rest of the nation.

The new type of technology transfer in Asia attempts to reverse the brain drain. For several decades, as these Asian nations acquired technologies from the West, they lost their best brainpower to the United States. Returned overseas citizens are helping to launch technopolii in Taiwan and India (Singhal and Rogers, 1989). The returning entrepreneur often brings considerable capital, as well as technological know-how.

We conclude that *a technopolis is an ideal mechanism to facilitate technology transfer both in Western nations and in East Asia.*

The Role of Government

Experiences in the United States and England show that government involvement was not essential in the birth of the older technopolii such as Silicon Valley, Route 128, and Cambridge. Presence of a research university was the main factor in the initiation of these three technopolii. In many of the early technopolii, a particular individual played the role of *champion:* Fred Terman, the electrical engineering professor, dean of engineering, and provost at Stanford University, in Silicon Valley; Karl Compton, the president of MIT, in Route 128; and North Carolina Governor Luther Hodges, in launching Research Triangle. All three of these technopolii began in the 1960s. In more recent times, an individual champion is less important in the rise of a technopolis. Instead, a national or local government facilitates the rise of a technopolis.

The most successful technopolii under study, however, were usually not under direct governmental supervision. Research Triangle had the strong, consistent support of the state of North Carolina for thirty years, but this technopolis began to take off only after the first eight years of strong promotion and heavy state government investment. Former Governor James B. Hunt devoted about 25 percent of his time for eight years (1976–84) to recruiting high tech companies to Research Triangle Park. From 1981 to 1987, the state government invested $82 million in the Microelectronics Center of North Carolina (as stated previously). Clearly, government promotion of a technopolis can be very expensive; a rapid response should not be expected.

Japan has successfully pursued a planned approach to creating the high tech complex at Tsukuba Science City, and it is now extending this approach to other technopolii in Japan. However, the Tsukuba technopolis took more than twenty years to reach maturity and still has not seen the outburst of entrepreneurial spin-offs witnessed in Silicon Valley.

In most East Asian nations, governmental planning and investment are necessary to bring a technopolis to life. The conditions contributing to the rise of Silicon Valley, Route 128, and Cambridge do not exist in most Asian nations today. An excellent research university, nearby private industry, and an ample amount of venture capital are not easily found in one place in these Asian Countries.

We conclude that *long-term government commitment is necessary to launch a technopolis today.*

IMPORTANCE OF THE RESEARCH UNIVERSITY AND THE SCIENCE PARK

Physical proximity greatly facilitates technology transfer. A technopolis must have its own source of cutting-edge technology, such as a research university or a government-funded research institute, because the results of R & D do not travel far. One reason for locating science parks on a university campus is the importance of geographical closeness in high tech technology transfer.

The pioneer technopolii in the United States, Silicon Valley, Route 128, and Research Triangle, started as a result of the marriage of a research university and a nearby industrial park. The Stanford Industrial Park was created very early in the rise of Silicon Valley, but in Cambridge the research park was founded *after* a community of high tech firms was in place. The arrival of a privately owned R & D consortium (the MCC) in Austin in 1983 was the main factor putting this new spot on the high tech map. So a research university plus its research park is only one combination that can generate a technopolis.

University–industry collaborative R & D centers in microelectronics, like the MCC and Sematech, represent a new and important force on the U.S. university campus, one that has generated a great deal of policy controversy. "Few subjects have received as much attention recently as the prospect of closer relations with American business" (Rosenzweig, 1982). Some academics worry that closer relationships with private industry may distort university research priorities, and overemphasize applied research at the expense of basic research. The following are three main points of potential conflict between the U.S. research university and private firms:

1. Restrictions on the communication of research results, resulting from company secrecy policies that may conflict with a scientific desire for free communication.
2. The relatively short-term orientation toward research of private firms versus the longer-term orientation of university scientists.
3. The priority agenda for university research may be affected by corporate sponsorship, which emphasizes scientific fields with direct potential for commercial payoff.

The research university is invaluable in the development of a technopolis, as is the establishment of a research park nearby. In East Asia today, where technical expertise and venture capital do not match the level in the First World nations of North America and Europe, government-funded research institutes seem to play a role in high technology transfer similar to that of the research university in the United States. Government-funded research institutes in the United States are relatively unimportant in technology transfer.

The main analysts of the Cambridge technopolis concluded that "There is no doubt that throughout Britain and much of the industrial world expectations of what a science park can realistically achieve by way of fostering new technology industry have been greatly inflated" (Segal, Quince, Wicksteed, 1985, p. 29). On the basis of our analysis of the ten technopolii in this study, we conclude that *a science park can help create a "critical mass" of high tech companies more quickly by (1) agglomerating them in one place (2) close to a research university.* But a science park is not necessary for a successful technopolis to develop, as the Cambridge phenomenon and Route 128 show. In Cambridge today, only 10 to 15 percent of the high technology firms are located in the science park (Segal, Quince, Wicksteed, 1987, p. 29).

Importance of Spin-offs

The ultimate bottom line for growing a technopolis is a high rate of high tech spin-offs. Individuals in a technopolis achieve millionaire status not by working for a salary, but by launching a new firm that grows rapidly and thus becomes highly valued on the stock market. Their net worth is a paper value that escalates when a new high tech firm "goes public." The 15,000 millionaires in Silicon Valley got rich by launching start-ups, or joining one soon after its founding, and being rewarded with stock option that later became very valuable.

A high rate of start-ups characterizes Silicon Valley, Route 128, and Cambridge. As mentioned previously, Austin has about fifty spin-offs from one firm, Tracor, that was founded in 1955. The six other technopolii of our study do not yet have many spin-offs. Until they do, these technopolii will not make a major impact on their national economy. Entrepreneurial companies play an important role in economic development because of the jobs they create. For example, Birch (1978) found that two thirds of all new jobs created in the United States from 1969 to 1976 occurred in companies with fewer than twenty employees. Birch and MacCracken (1984) found that for the period 1977–81, a somewhat smaller percentage of new jobs developed in small firms. About 50 percent of the high tech firms in the Cambridge technopolis have fewer than ten employees. About half of the 16,500 employees in Cambridge high tech firms work in the eight largest firms (Segal, Quince, Wicksteed, 1987, p. 20). As in Silicon Valley, the Cambridge technopolis consists of many small firms and a very few large firms. And in both technopolii, most new jobs are created in the smaller firms (Segal, Quince, Wicksteed, 1987. p. 21).

Most high tech spin-offs are triggered by a technological innovation. The usual entry ticket to the microelectronics industry is a new technological product. The promising potential of the new product helps to attract venture capital to start the new company. The new firm's growth is then fueled by sales of the new product, and thereafter by a strategy of continuous technological innovation. The new technology may come (1) from in-house R & D activities (hence the 10 percent of sales that are invested in R & D by high tech companies) or (2) from a nearby research university or government-funded research institute. "High-tech companies thrive on state-of-art, which they harvest and apply to market opportunities" (Miller and Côté, 1985).

To compete effectively, a new high tech company must outgrow other companies producing the same product. Such rapid expansion puts great strain on the new firm, as it seeks to navigate this "adolescent transition" from being a small, informal group into becoming a large bureaucracy (Rogers and Larsen, 1984). The number of employees may double annually for the first several years of a high tech firm's existence. Ultimately, the new firm must change from an entrepreneurial orientation to maintenance-type management as the firm becomes an established bureaucracy, and thus it may become a parent to a new family of high tech spin-offs, each led by an entrepreneur with a vision of a new product who felt stifled in the established corporation.

New spin-off firms are more likely to be launched by R & D workers than by manufacturing workers in high-technology companies. Austin had about 30,000 high tech employees before MCC arrived in 1983; most worked for companies headquartered in Silicon Valley, such as AMD, Intel, and Hewlett-Packard, which manufacture semiconductors and computers. The R & D work (and thus the spin-offs from the parent companies) were in California, with production engineers and assembly-line workers in Austin. After 1983 the arrival of the MCC changed this situation, and Austin began to rival Silicon Valley as a high tech microelectronics R & D site. We predict, therefore, that more spin-offs will occur in Austin in future years as the entrepreneurial spiral is fanned.

Even though a research university may be crucial to starting a technopolis, at least in the United States, most R & D scientists do not become entrepreneurs (Miller and Côté, 1985). Unlike a scientist, the entrepreneur is motivated by a desire to take risks and earn big money.

Technological entrepreneurs are expert in technological innovation but usually lack the business management skills needed to launch a new high tech company (Miller and Côté, 1985). This lack of business acumen on the part of entrepreneurs is why venture capitalists are important in a technopolis; they not only provide capital to a high tech start-up, but also supply business management advice, often on a daily basis, to the entrepreneur (Rogers and Larsen, 1984). Because of this need for constant contact between venture capitalist and entrepreneur, venture capital does not travel far, perhaps not more than fifty miles. Hence, each technopolis must have its own cadre of venture capitalists.

Quality of Life

The ten technopolii of the study are prototypes of information-creating centers in an information society. They are distinct from the traditional centers of manufacturing industries. U.S. technopolii are in the Sun Belt, Cambridge is located in a nice medieval town in England, and Sophia Antipolis is on the French Riviera. Besides a pleasant climate, these areas have little pollution and a beautiful environment. The new Japanese technopolii are all located in scenic spots, accompanied by detailed regional planning to provide the life-style conveniences that were originally lacking in Tsukuba Science City.

The quality of life in the Asian technopolii is generally above that in the rest of the country in terms of cleanliness, convenience, attractive housing, and climate. Life-styles in these technopolii are generally Westernized, which may cause cultural conflict and stress for individuals who live there. Tsukuba Science City has a higher suicide rate than the national average and people complain of the "Tsukuba syndrome." Shenzhen is so drastically different from the rest of China in life-styles and ideology that it is considered a "special zone."

Agglomeration in the Technopolis

Why are high-technology microelectronics firms concentrated in a technopolis in each of our countries of study rather than being scattered throughout the nation? *Agglomeration* is the spatial concentration of some quality in an area. High tech firms are even more agglomerated than other industries, some of which are also quite agglomerated (e.g., U.S. auto manufacturing in Detroit, the film industry in Hollywood and in Bombay).

Agglomeration of a technopolis occurs for several reasons:

1. A research university or an R & D institute is often the seed for a technopolis. The first new high tech firms spin-off from this seed institution, and, later on yet newer high tech firms spin-off from the earlier spin-offs. Proximity to the seed institution thus causes agglomeration.

2. Technological progress in high tech industry is so rapid and business competition so intense that information exchange must be direct and interpersonal. In Silicon Valley, much information exchange takes place through informal networks in bars or at parties (Rogers and Larsen, 1984).

3. A spin-off usually does not travel far from its parent company. An established technopolis provides an infrastructure for entrepreneurial business operations. Suppliers, buyers, financiers, markets, skilled personnel, and an information network exist in the special cocoon of the technopolis. The advantages of being able to tap this local infrastructure lead to agglomeration. Entrepreneurs do not want to move, remove their children from their school, or disrupt existing personal networks by moving the parent firm. With agglomeration, as one Silicon Valley entrepreneur remarked, "The only difference is that you turn into a different driveway when you go to work in the morning" (Rogers and Larsen, 1984). To leave this enriched milieu would be disadvantageous for a struggling new high tech firm.

Now we see more clearly the unique role of the research university (or its counterpart) in the technopolis. Typically, a technopolis begins to sprout around a research university. Hewlett-Packard, the first high-tech firm in Silicon Valley (founded in 1938), spun off directly from Stanford University. A critical mass did not begin to form until H-P and several other early firms moved onto the Stanford Industrial Park in the mid-1950s, attracted by the technological advantages of spatial proximity to Stanford University's growing prowess in microelectronics R & D (Rogers and Larsen, 1984). A science park can be a key factor in encouraging agglomeration, and thus a technopolis.

The Cambridge technopolis began in 1881 when Cambridge Instruments was formed. Segal et al. (1985) estimates that 55 percent of the 450 companies are direct spin-offs from Cambridge University, and most of the remaining 395 high tech firms are spin-offs of the fifty-five spin-offs. *Direct spin-offs from a research university spark the agglomeration process in the early stage of forming a technopolis.*

Agglomeration of high tech firms in a technopolis is important because it results in concentrating a "critical mass" of successful entrepreneurs, which then support and reinforce each other in the uncertain situation of launching a new company.

Collaboration in the Technopolis

One salient characteristic of a technopolis is a collaborative form of relationships, rather than pure competition. Rapid technological change and intense competition in a high tech industry encourage domestic and international collaboration. Companies that are competing with others in the same industry (e.g., computers or semiconductors) may collaborate to fund R & D microelectronic centers like the MCC or Sematech, where they work together in research on common problems. Such collaboration not only helps these companies compete with other companies in the United States; it also enables these companies to compete with the Japanese.

This major shift from strict competition to certain forms of collaboration characterizes "Japan, Inc." Ouchi (1984) advocates collaborative relationships, which he terms "M-form organization," as the most effective means for American firms to recapture a competitive edge in high tech from their Japanese counterparts. In an M-form arrangement, the system of operating units are partially interdependent, in that no organization can give orders to any other unit. So they cooperate to mutual advantage. "The M-Form Organization succeeds only if it maintains its balance" (Ouchi, 1984, p. 24).

We conclude that *the technopolis represents a certain degree of collaborative relationships despite competition in a high tech industry.*

EXPORTING SILICON VALLEY: DIFFUSION OF PLANNED TECHNOPOLII

Silicon Valley, in the parlance of Americans, Asians, and Europeans, is almost synonymous with high tech and technopolii. The United States originated the "high-tech complex" idea, and Japan, after learning from the example of the former, is radiating its experience to other Asian countries. Striking similarities are observed among the ten technopolii studied in the present chapter; however, some important differences—especially in terms of the overall growth pattern of the technopolis in each country—are evident.

When a new Silicon Valley is created in the United States today, considerable government support is required. These newer Silicon Valleys in the United States and Asia have not yet produced many entrepreneurial spin-offs, partly because of a lack of venture capital. The planned technopolii may not be expanding through entrepreneurial spin-offs, but they are certainly growing by attracting outside entrepreneurs to the local site.

Clearly, each technopolis is not invented independently of previously existing technopolii. *The idea of the technopolis has diffused from Silicon Valley throughout the United States and the world.*

TECHNOPOLII AND THE INFORMATION SOCIETY

Technopolii are undoubtedly key outposts of the information society. However, there is an inherent contradiction between the expected structure of an information society and the structural arrangements of the present technopolii. Scholarly literature on the information society (e.g., Bell, 1973) stresses a decentralized structure, where the infrastructure is a telecommunications network, information is the raw material and main commodity, and the physical need to cluster people, material, and capital on the nodes of transportation is eliminated. Contrary to such predictions, the present technopolii demonstrate a strong degree of clustering. Will the present phenomenon of agglomeration gradually give way to decentralization?

Change toward decentralization of mature technopolii may be on the horizon. Many Silicon Valley firms are branching out to other high tech locations, because of geographical limitations and skyrocketing real estate values in Silicon Valley. It is the manufacturing divisions of these companies that are scattering. The concentration today of company headquarters, venture capital, markets, and R & D activities in a technopolis seems likely to continue for some time. But in certain technopolii a decentralized separation of manufacturing and R & D-related activities eventually occurs. Decentralization may also take the form of multiple technopolii in a nation, as is occurring in the United States and in Japan.

3

Technology and Global Strategies and Organizations

JAY R. GALBRAITH

Technology, acting directly and indirectly, is the most powerful shaper of global strategies and organizations today. Gerald Hage identifies 1975 as the year of the beginning of the new competitive era (Hage, 1988). In that year R & D spending increased 6 percent in real dollars over previous years. Every year since then U.S. firms have increased real spending from 4.5 percent to 8 percent per year. Through the compounding effects of percentage increases, the United States in 1988 will spend twice as much in real dollars on R & D than it did in 1975. Abegglen reports that Japanese firms have increased real R & D spending 17 percent per year since 1978 (Abegglen and Stalk, 1985). The ramifications of the increase in resources devoted to technology are to drastically alter the nature of competition, the role of governments, the types of business strategies, and therefore the kind of social organization needed to conduct economic activity today and in the future.

This chapter traces the effects of the new technological competition on the business environment and its impact on new organization forms. The first section discusses the environment in terms of the direct and indirect effects of technology. The second section analyzes how businesses are adopting strategies to deal with the new environment. Finally, the organization forms, both old and new, used in this chapter are described. Figure 3.1 illustrates the factors that make up the environment, the strategies, and the organization forms. Overlays and network organizations are discussed in this chapter.

BUSINESS ENVIRONMENT

Technology has a direct effect on business strategies but also an indirect effect on other factors such as the role of governments. In this section, the factors in the environment that are shaping the new business strategies are

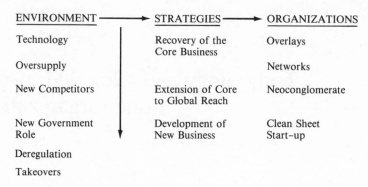

Figure 3.1   Framework for Analysis

Technology

The previously quoted statistics on rates of growth in investment in R & D, indicate that U.S. companies double their investments in R & D every ten to twelve years. Japanese companies are doubling theirs every five to six years. These investments greatly increase the fixed costs of doing business. To cover the increased costs of product and process development, companies need greater volume than their domestic home markets provide. This search for world-scale volumes has greatly increased the level of competition in most markets.

The increased investments are also shortening product life cycles. With fewer years over which to write off the product development costs, companies need more volume per year to reach break-even points. The result is a search for markets in more countries to replace fewer years of volume. The level of competition increases even more. Thus, the immediate effect of investing in new technologies is to escalate global competition by forcing companies to seek world scale outside their domestic markets.

Oversupply

The problem with more firms seeking worldwide volume is that worldwide demand is not growing fast enough to accommodate them. The United States is no longer a source of growth as it deals with its twin deficits. Europe has grown at less than 2 percent per year over the last ten years. The West Germans, ever fearful of inflation, are reluctant to stimulate their economy to act as a source of growth. The less developed countries have demand but not much foreign exchange to pay for anything. The Pacific Rim countries are growing but have not yet opened their markets to foreign goods. The result is more competition for less growth.

New Competitors

The new competitors are largely companies from Pacific Rim countries, which need not be described here (Kotler, Fahey, and Jatusripitiak, 1985). Suffice it say that they are all following the Japanese model and moving from labor cost advantages to world-scale plants to proprietary technologies for competitive advantage. The result is that the world has more and more effective suppliers of its products. These more effective competitors raise the level of competition another step.

New Role for Government

One reason the new competitors are quite formidable is that they are teamed with their governments. Government has always been active in international trade, but the nature of its interventions has changed. Initially, government regulated trade through tariffs and subsidies. Most trade was in raw materials and commodities. Now trade has expanded to include industrial and consumer products. These products are manufactured and distributed by multinational oligopolies. It is more efficient for countries to negotiate directly with IBM, Sony, and Siemans to get local value added. So governments have shifted from regulation of markets to direct negotiation with oligopolies.

The most recent change, however, is to the active actual participation of government in the competitive process. Technology is again a driver of this change. The new role is clearest in newly emerging industries and technologies. Governments shelter new industries like biotechnology. They also relax antitrust laws permitting cooperation among local competitors in developing new technologies at precompetitive development stages; that is, increasingly governments are forming and funding consortia and nonprofit corporations to create and disseminate new technologies before they are developed into commercial products. For example, the European Community has funded ESPIRIT to develop semiconductor and electronic products.

A scan of the *Business Week* issue for September 19, 1988, indicates this new role in the United States. First the Federal Communications Commission is setting standards for introducing high-definition television (HDTV). Among other features, the standards limit the Japanese and provide American companies, if any are interested, with a window of opportunity to catch up. Second, the National Research Council is concerned about progress in photonics and proposes a national effort. The National Photonics program is to fund companies, government laboratories, and universities in a cooperative program. Third, Japan refuses to open its research on superconductors at its universities. The United States has complained and is launching a bill through Congress for a five-year, $600 million program to support Superchip Corporation in work on superconducting chips, and Superconductivity Applications, Inc., on work on wire and electrical applications.

The effect of this most recent shift in government role is to shift the basis of competition to country versus country rather than company versus company. The intercompany competition remains in the markets. But trade blocs are more active in promoting technology for their local competitors.

Deregulation

Another feature of today's environment that increases competition is deregulation in financial, telecommunications, media, transportation, and other markets. These moves are often the direct result of technology and investment levels in new technology. Communications technologies, for example, instantaneously move money around the world in the form of bits. The biggest change is taking place in Europe. By 1992 all of the nontariff barriers to competition are to be eliminated. The actual dismantling of these barriers will take longer, but many changes are already occurring in anticipation of the 1992 deadline. Europe is becoming a much more competitive marketplace.

Takeovers

The increased level of competition requires strategies from management to deal with the new environment. The stock markets undervalue the stocks of companies that do not respond. In the less regulated financial markets investors, both friendly and unfriendly, bid to take over these undervalued stocks. If management needs an additional stimulus to respond to the new competitive environment, the takeovers are providing it.

Summary

The mid-1970s saw the start of the new global competition. It was then that investment in R & D and the rise of new competitors from the Pacific Rim created an excess of supply in most industries. In this new competitive arena governments are both deregulating some markets and actively participating in precompetitive phases of new industries. The more competitive markets and global, deregulated financial markets are imposing strict disciplines on managements. New strategies and new organizations are the result.

THE NEW STRATEGIES

The response of Western companies to the new competitive environment has been a sequence of three strategic steps. First, they act to recover the cost and quality competitiveness of their core businesses. Next they extend these businesses globally. Finally, the priority shifts to the development of new sources of revenue. The companies still work on cost competitiveness and global extensions, but growth and development assume a higher priority in resource allocation when the business generates an excess cash flow. Technology plays a different but key role in each of the three strategies.

Recovery

The new competition had its beginnings in the middle and late 1970s, but the first strategic response to it came in the early 1980s. Western companies faced deeply depressed earnings caused jointly by the recession of 1981–82 and the new competition. Companies from the United States experienced the highly inflated dollar as well. During this era the massive recovery efforts on the core businesses began. These efforts have progressed from cuts and layoffs to longer-term programs. Today firms are relying on responsive integration, consolidation, vertical disintegration, and employee involvement.

Initial efforts centered on cuts. These came in spending, layoffs, plant closures, concessions, smaller staffs, early retirement, and so on. Everyone downsized. These efforts dropped break-even points so that firms could survive a recession, but they did not restore competitiveness.

Today recovery efforts are centered on longer-term areas. Quality programs are being implemented throughout organizations, and vice presidents of total quality management report to the CEO. Chief financial officers conduct a worldwide search for capital as U.S. interest rates increase the cost of money.

Technology comes into play in several ways. In automation, technology is used to reduce labor cost. It is used in robotics and automation for quality and flexibility. Management and professional functions are now being automated by computer-aided design (CAD), engineering (CAE), manufacturing (CAM), software engineering (CASE), and so on. Currently, the establishment of computer-to-computer linkages is reducing intermediate information processing steps in sequential processes, with a reduction of clerical costs and an increase in quality. The computer's greatest impact on management processes is its facilitation of a more responsive and integrated organization.

The responsive-integration efforts of firms are a direct response to the new competition. Many companies are discovering that there are hidden costs in the interfaces between functions like engineering and manufacturing or sales and manufacturing. Engineers were previously unconcerned or unaware that trivial design changes could produce major savings in manufacturing costs. Development costs can be drastically reduced if new products are brought to market faster. The faster, more integrated development processes are called "simultaneous engineering" in Detroit or "concurrent design" at Hewlett-Packard. Responsive integration is now a basis of competition. Firms are designing quality and cost-effectiveness into their products and services from the beginning. As product life cycles decline, the product development cycles are declining. The customer is also demanding more customized products, faster delivery, and newer technologies. To stay competitive the firms have to provide responses that are customized, integrated, and faster.

A second strategic change is consolidation. A number of factors are causing firms to consolidate, pool, and centralize activities that require specialists, use expensive equipment, and require large expenditures on R & D. When companies want to minimize the number of people, they create a central pool and time share them. Various staff and specialist organizations are being consolidated. To stay state-of-the-art and be able to afford expensive equipment, research activities in an area are being consolidated in "centers of excellence" or other similar units.

Consolidations are also occurring across companies, through acquisitions and mergers. A number of mergers were attempted in the pharmaceutical industry. Achieving scale in R & D is always a factor in these acquisitions. Unisys, after merging Burroughs and Sperry is again looking for other acquisitions to get the scale to develop and deliver today's computer technologies. Similarly, mergers among Europe's national champions in the computer business are being discussed. Scale is needed in computers to combat IBM, DEC, Fujitsu, and Hitachi and to capitalize on 1992. Thus, the increased level of spending on R & D and on automated plants and processes is causing consolidation to achieve the scale needed to cover higher break-even points.

Technology is also a powerful factor in the next recovery technique—vertical disintegration. Previously, high-performance companies did everything themselves. To ensure high-quality supplies and guaranteed outlets for their products companies performed all activities in the value-added chain. This policy led to extensive vertical integration managed by monolithic hierarchies such as in General Motors and IBM. But in today's competitive environment companies can no longer afford to do everything and do it well. Companies are therefore doing only what they do well. At the limit, companies perform only those activities in which they hold a competitive advantage. Outside sources are sought to perform the remaining activities. In a competitive environment, a company cannot afford a second-rate performance in any activity. If its own performance is not competitive, then the firm must buy from someone who is.

However, the same forces for vertical integration still exist; that is, firms still need a guaranteed source of supply. But companies do not have to own all the suppliers to receive the guarantee. They create sourcing relationships, alliances (teaming), minority investments, and joint ventures and join the government-sponsored consortia referred to earlier.

Firms in the paper industry are an example. Not typically considered high technology, paper is becoming R & D intensive. Previously paper companies vertically integrated all the way from owning forests to making pulp and paper and converting paper into products such as packaging. Today the packaging revolution has increased R & D expenditures for new products. Process control computing has increased R & D in process innovation. Biotechnology is causing land and timber companies to invest in R & D to create supertrees, which grow to maturity in fewer years. Very few companies can afford all of this R & D investment; fewer still are good at all the different types of R & D. In response to more R & D spending, various supply and technological exchange arrangements are occurring in the industry. Some are simple vertical disintegration, in which a subsidiary that supplied the company is sold to a vendor who is consolidating. Long-term supply contracts and minority investments by the previous owners are used to guarantee a source of supply.

The newer arrangements are those that exist between competitors. For example, Toshiba and Motorola have formed an alliance to exchange technology; Motorola will provide microprocessor technology and Toshiba will provide dynamic RAM (random access memory) process technology. The firms will continue to compete in the marketplace. McDonnell Aircraft and General Dynamics are teaming together in a bid for the Advanced Tactical Aircraft (ATA). Neither can afford the risk of the investment nor to stay in all technologies. These are not the usual contracting/subcontracting relations. They involve greater sharing of data and cooperation between competitors who are both system integrators.

Finally, competitors are coalescing, with government encouragement and sponsorships, into consortia of various kinds. The government sanctions the collusion between competitors in precompetitive phases of technology development. Often the government provides funding and opens national laboratories. More recently, serious discussions in the United States are revolving around having the Department of Defense pick technological winners and fund their development as the Japanese ministries have done. At the moment it is not clear how successful these cooperative efforts are going to be. But they are all being caused by the new technological competition.

In summary, firms are acting in a number of ways to restore competitiveness in their core businesses. Initial efforts at downsizing through cuts give way to programs to consolidate activities, to increase integration and responsiveness, to automate all activities, and to disaggregate by buying more activities outside the company. The final phase in this process begins with the recognition that recovery is a never-ending process. At this point companies begin programs for employee involvement to launch a process of continuous improvement. Everyone in the company takes responsibility for improving cost and quality performance.

The overall effect of the recovery efforts is to create paradoxes for the organization. Companies must be both more competitive and more cooperative. They must now fight harder for market share and profits; yet they must cooperate, even with competitors, to share expensive technologies so that all benefit. Technology itself creates paradox. Workstations with the power of mainframes, microprocessors embedded in everything, and flexible manufacturing all reduce scale economies and enhance the competitiveness of small firms. On the other hand, the next central office switch will cost billions. Semiconductor plants cost hundreds of millions because of the sophisticated technologies in them. Costs such as these favor large firms. Responsive integration favors small fast acting units. Consolidation and pooling encourage large firms. The challenge for organizing is to design social systems which are viable in the face of the paradoxes.

Extending the Core Business to a Global Business

The next step companies are taking is to make their core businesses into global businesses. No longer can international business strategy be the sum of the country or regional strategies of subsidiaries. Business unit strategies must be more global from the outset. However, there are differences in the degree to which a business is a global business. Similarly, countries vary in their degree of participation in the economic process. As a result, subsidiaries vary in the degree to which they can be localized and business units in the degree to which they are global.

The degree to which a business is global depends on the structure of the industry in which the business is conducted (Prahalad and Doz, 1987). One of the determinants of industry structure is the percentage of sales invested in R & D. A consumer goods business investing 0.5 percent of sales in R & D is not a global business. In pharmaceuticals, electronics, and biotechnology, however, where 12 to 15 percent of sales go to R & D, world scale is needed to cover the fixed costs of product development. In industries requiring world scale, products need to be designed from the beginning to be capable of sales in more than one countries. Hewlett-Packard cannot afford to design a personal computer for the United States, one for Europe, and a third one for the Far East. Instead they design a common platform with capability for localization later. The same process occurs at Allen-Bradley for its factory automation products. The basic product is designed to be capable of modification to fit multiple markets.

Investment in state-of-the-art factories also increases fixed costs and necessitates a search for world-scale volume. Businesses such as semiconductors, auto components, and processing industries all have heavy investments in factories. As distribution and service businesses invest in computer hardware, software, and networks, their capital costs increase. Many businesses with increasing fixed costs are becoming more global in order to achieve world scale; to do this they need a product development process that integrates multimarket needs and coordinates multisite efforts.

Other factors also determine the degree to which the structure of a business is global. One factor is whether competitors and customers are also global in their businesses. Another is the degree to which markets are homogeneous across countries. Homogeneity allows more universal products and fewer tradeoffs in pooling international market requirements.

In summary, a number of factors determine whether or not a business is global. One of the key parameters is the percentage of sales that is invested in R & D. To get the volume to cover higher break-even points, the business must seek world scale and become global. For almost all high technology businesses, more increased investment in product development is requiring global product strategies and more universality in their product lines. No longer can products be designed for the U.S. market only. Worldwide marketing strategies are being implemented to determine worldwide needs.

Along with forces that are making for more globalization and integration across countries, there are forces that cause more fragmentation of activities and the need to tailor policies to individual countries. The international strategy area has its paradox also. As host governments become more active, especially in high technology industries, they are forcing businesses to become more locally attuned and to add value in their country. To get access to markets and attain world scale, companies must accommodate the countries' demands for technology transfer, value added in their country or a joint venture with a local partner. Companies must also compete in areas where the cutting-edge technology is first introduced. Increasingly, high technology products are being introduced simultaneously all over the world, but products like television sets are introduced in Japan first while software is introduced in the United States first. For competitive intelligence, companies must be in these markets. Other companies are doing their development in a variety of countries, capturing unique national competencies in the process. Organizations are locating design activities in northern Italy, manufacturing research in Japan, and R & D in Israel (one of the few countries without a shortage of electrical engineers), to name a few examples.

These last forces tend to fragment an organization and scatter activities around the world. They act in contradistinction to the forces for integration. Like the forces of recovery, globalization creates both strong and conflicting pressures for organizations. They must integrate global business strategies and yet fragment the actual performance of the work in a variety of countries. They must also demonstrate that they are good local citizens.

Telecommunications is a good example. The next central office switch will be a multi-billion-dollar effort. Only a few designs can generate enough sales to exceed break-even points. Switch designers need world scale and a fairly universal product base from which to adapt to local markets. However, switches are purchased by government-owned Post Office–Telegraph and Telephone Ministries, who insist on buying local. To get the business, AT&T, NEC, or Siemans must be local and global simultaneously. Organization design for strategy implementation under these conditions becomes a challenge.

DEVELOPMENT

Strategic priorities for technology firms are now shifting and will be different in the 1990s. Recovery pressures on costs and quality will continue, as well as pressures to think globally about the businesses. But development has already begun to assume a higher priority in resource allocation decisions. At some companies the new expression is: "What are you doing for the top line?" That is, companies realize they cannot remain competitive by simply closing plants and offering early retirement. They need new sources of revenue to grow and develop. Also the revived core businesses are generating more cash than can economically be reinvested in them. Leaders are now being challenged to search for new growth sources.

The new development strategies being adopted by Western organizations are targeting services, software, technology, and financial services as new growth sources. There are a number of reasons for their selection. First these industries are the growth areas for Western economies. In a growth market, the competition for market share is less fierce and profit margins are higher. Second, many organizations already perform the services, generate software, or create technology for their own internal needs and discover they are good at the activity. A business can be built from these internal seeds. Third, many industries in these areas are restructuring because of technological change and/or deregulation. The newcomer has an advantage in an industry undergoing restructuring. Current industry participants have invested in the old technology and are slower to adopt the new rules of competition. Financial services is the best example of an industry that is restructuring because of technology and deregulation. Many of the largest and most profitable financial service businesses are the former credit subsidiaries of General Electric and IBM.

The high technology businesses are targeted as new growth sources for several reasons in addition to those already mentioned. First, Western countries with trained and expensive work forces can best compete in the high-performance ends of the markets. This end of the market is driven by technology, performance, and design. The home markets of companies are early testing grounds for the products. Second, new technologies such as biotechnology, photonics, and superconductors generate tomorrow's industries. Early entry in a growth industry reduces battles over market share and serves as a future source of earnings. Third, these industries are most likely to be protected at home initially and subsidized by defense spending. Fourth, technology itself restructures industries and provides openings for a newcomer. Open systems architectures are changing the computer industry, application-specific semiconductors are changing the chip business, and so on. Thus, industries that are restructuring or emerging because of technological change present developmental opportunities to Western companies. These companies may or may not have been high technology companies before the new competitive era.

An example of an industry that is restructuring is the food industry. As in financial services, government is apparently going to play a less protectionist role by the late 1990s. Over time the subsidies are going to be reduced. The technology of farming favors the large farmer. The size of the average farm increases as professional businesses replace the family farm. The consumer is king in the food business as surpluses abound. The consumer in the United States wants nutrition and health as well as good taste. The new technologies of breeding and biotechnology allow us to "design"

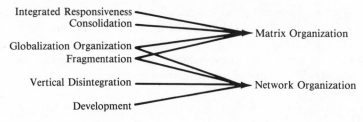

Figure 3.2   Strategy and Organization

new food products by creating animals with low cholesterol, desirable muscle texture, and taste. Companies such as British Petroleum and Volvo must respond to this new customer-driven business. Consequently, food industry strategy and organization will be driven by R & D and new product development. Brand recognition and a superior product created through biotechnology become the keys to competitive advantage.

In summary, companies are seeking new sources of growth by entering new businesses based on services, software, and technology. These services and technologies are usually ones that the organization has mastered in serving its core businesses. Technology businesses in particular lend themselves to new sources of revenue. They are future growth businesses or present opportunities for restructuring existing industries into new sources of revenue. As a result, firms like General Motors, British Petroleum, and Procter & Gamble are becoming high technology companies.

Throughout the 1980s and 1990s companies will follow this strategic sequence. Most companies went into a recovery mode in the early 1980s. They will be pursuing global and development strategies in the 1990s. Aerospace, on the other hand, developed in the 1980s, but the post-Reagan defense budget has placed it in a recovery mode in the late 1980s. For most companies, all of these strategic steps are in process at any one time. For a particular business unit, however, recovery, globalization, or development will take top priority.

Organizing for Competitiveness

Implementation of these three strategic steps in the new competitive environment is reviving some old organization forms and giving rise to some new ones. Those that are of particular significance for technology companies are today's Matrix Organization and Network Organizations. Figure 3.2 portrays the strategic forces that are creating the need for these social forms.

As was mentioned earlier, the strategic forces are causing paradoxes for companies. To be responsive and integrated, companies need small, fast-acting business units. But to get critical mass in a technology, companies need large functions. The solution for some companies is to use a functional organization with product, project, or program overlays. Previously, these overlays or functions were referred to as matrixlike organization. The forces for the network organization arise from all strategies. Vertical disintegration in recovery and market access in globalization lead to joint ventures and various alliances. These same alliances also lower the barriers to entry for a new business. They give a new business global access and let them build volume quickly. It is in these new business developments that the network is most likely to arise.

Today's Matrix

Today's matrix organizations are arising from the conflicting strategic actions described earlier. At the business unit level, pressure for consolidation arises in the recovery of cost competitiveness. As firms seek to reduce duplication, achieve scale in functions with expensive equipment, pool highly specialized talent, reduce the number of people, and consolidate purchasing power, they are forming functional organizations. Consolidations are occurring in businesses from General Electric's major appliance business to Hewlett-Packard's computer business. At the same time, market pressures are causing firms to respond to the customer faster and with more varied offerings. To be responsive to customers and deliver new products faster, firms try to create small, closely coupled interdisciplinary teams. These are best organized as small autonomous divisions like the old Hewlett-Packard model. But even here conflicts arise. The design and operation functions are best organized on a product basis to deliver products rapidly; sales and service functions are best organized on a customer basis to respond to unique market needs.

The result of conflicting pressures to consolidate and be responsive lead to different organizational bases for different functions. It is not difficult to find businesses in which purchasing is centralized and organized around vendor types. The component manufacturing is centralized and organized around manufacturing processes. R & D is centralized and organized by technology. Design, assembly, and test operations are decentralized and organized by product line. Sales and service are a single unit organized partly by geography and partly by customer type. These functional alignments are necessary to get superior competitive performance from each unit. However, functional organization creates barriers to integration around a customer or product for fast response.

The answer has been to create processes varying from informal relations to formal product teams to product managers that are overlayed on the functional organization. These overlays or teams are temporary product, market, or customer organizations for integration and represent a form of quasi-structure (see chapter 6 in this volume).

A similar situation prevails in the international sector. Conflicting strategic pressures to integrate global businesses across countries and to scatter value-added activities and respond to local governments must be dealt with simultaneously. Those organizations that were organized by country, such as IBM and DEC, are creating product business unit overlays with world-

	U.S.	Japan	Europe	Pacific/L.A.
High End	$	$	$	$
Mid Range	$	$	$	$
Low End	$	$	$	$
Peripheral	$	$	$	$

Figure 3.3 Planning and Budgeting Matrix

wide business teams and global product managers. Companies that were organized by worldwide line of business, such as Motorola, are creating country overlays with country teams, country site managers, and country managers. Each overlay is to create integration not achieved through the structure. Various forms of matrix organization occur because businesses vary in how global they are and host governments in how active they are. As a result business managers are strong in some cases and country managers in others. For both business unit organization and international organization, the matrix is back. It may be called product management or something else, but it is an overlay or matrix-type organization nonetheless.

Today's matrix is different in its successful applications. Successful companies manage the matrix shown in Figure 3.3, with a planning and budgeting process. functions could be substituted for countries or regions as columns with no loss of meaning. The figure shows product lines (high end, mid range, low end, peripheral equipment) in a matrix across countries and regions. The box at the intersection of product and region contains the planned revenues, costs, profits, and market shares for that product in that region. The first requirement for a successful matrix is an information system that reports costs and revenues for all the categories. Second, the company needs a planning process to agree on all the entries. The planning process is a negotiation process between product managers and geographic managers to determine revenue, profit, and market share by product and by country. The adopted plan then becomes the target for all managers. Performance becomes a task of meeting all the targets and the reward system is based on the agreed-upon plan.

Planning systems are also becoming more event driven and less calendar driven. Rather than being an annual exercise, plans are revised when events require revision. These frequent revisions require that the process be computerized.

All of these features are difficult to implement. This difficulty is why most organizations fail at matrix. The problem for managements facing the twin demands of consolidation and responsiveness is to learn to function with the kind of management process described previously. In short, matrix and overlays are not a structural problem but one of management process and management selection. The design of information systems, planning process, budgeting processes, performance measurements, performance assessment processes, and reward systems around matrix management issues are key. Selection of managers who can negotiate, influence without authority, become team players, and live with ambiguity is a companion design issue. Although the strategic steps to restore competitiveness are clear, companies are still grappling with the previous issues to learn how to implement those strategies.

THE NETWORK ORGANIZATION

Ray Miles has labeled a new form of organization emerging today as the Network (Miles and Snow, 1986). Instead of monolithic, vertically integrated hierarchies like those of IBM or Procter and Gamble today, companies of tomorrow will be loosely coupled, flexible arrangements between a number of firms. Each firm will perform only what it does best and link with others through sourcing arrangements, long-term contracts, alliances, minority investments, and joint ventures. These forms arise as companies disintegrate vertically, expand globally, or grow rapidly in new businesses.

The organization design issues for the network organization revolve around the firm that assumes the responsibility for design and maintenance of the network. This firm has the broker role in the network and is called the hub firm. The broker role can be played by the corporate headquarters of a company or by the headquarters of a business unit. This section focuses of the business units, which face network design issues of two types. One issue is the need to create a presence in all key markets worldwide. Key markets are those that give world-scale volume, those in which key competitors are present, and those in which state-of-the-art technology is introduced first. To achieve a presence in all key countries, the hub firm must form joint ventures or alliances with local firms. The hub firm must design its international network. A second issue for the hub firm is "What activities in the value-added chain for an industry will the firm own and perform?" This second issue is the focus here.

Current predictions are that firms are vertically disintegrating (Miles and Snow, 1986) or disaggregating. Indeed firms are buying more services and components rather than performing or making them themselves. However, the same pressures for vertical integration still exist. Firms still need guaranteed sources of supply and outlets for their products over the business cycle when supplies are short and channels full. Firms still want to collect profits from the upstream and downstream portions of the industry. The source of profits in an industry will change over the business cycle from upstream to downstream. When chips are in short supply, semiconductor firms make money; when chips are plentiful, systems manufacturers make money. The result is that companies are in transition from vertical integration to *vertical control*; that is, companies are finding ways to achieve the benefits of vertical integration without the costs of ownership. The price, however, is that management must learn to influence partners they do not control or own. Like matrix management, a premium is placed on managing relationships.

The design decisions to be made for the hub firm include: (1) What activities should be owned by the company and which should be acquired though arrangements with other firms? and (2) What kind of relationships should be negotiated and managed with these other firms to achieve adequate control?

The pattern of response is emerging in recent business start-ups, like Sun Microsystems, Nike, Reebok, Genentech, and businesses that are establishing themselves in restructuring industries. Established companies in established industries are not vertically disintegrating, although they may sell an activity when it can be easily separated. It is in the new developmental areas that network organization emerges in its extreme form. An example from the food industry illustrates the issue.

British Petroleum owns breeding and feed subsidiaries. The idea is to create a male/female pair of cattle, hogs, turkeys, and other species. They provide the breeding stock and feed for nutrition to producers (farmers) who raise the stock. They take minority investments in packers and processors to guarantee a market for farmers using their breeding stock. The packer also allows them to control distribution to retailers and other outlets. The control of distribution allows them to use brands for their products as Frank Perdue has done with chickens. Brand recognition and a superior product through biotechnology become the keys to competitive advantage. Companies like BP that usually vertically integrated the entire product flow now only perform the product design (breeding animals and seeds) and control the brand and marketing. This means they own only a breeder and control distribution with a food processor that manages the brand. Castle and Cooke does this with Dole brand pineapples. Currently, it is trying the same approach with other fruits and vegetables. In consumer businesses, vertical control is therefore exercised by owning technologies to create products, owning the brand, and performing the marketing. All other activities are necessary to deliver the product to the customer but are secondary and provide smaller margins. By performing the dominant functions in the value-added chain, a hub firm can thus exert vertical control without owning all the activities along with chain.

In commercial businesses like computers and biotechnology, the research function is a key basis of control. Sun Micro Systems attempts to control the value-added chain by continually introducing new technologies that everyone can use. Sun is pursuing open architectures that change the structure of the industry. The results can be seen in personal computers in which open architectures and an IBM standard have moved the dominant activity away from the computer manufacturer to the component provider. It is Intel and Microsoft that make money in PCs. Anyone can make the computer but everyone must use Intel's microprocessor and Microsoft's operating system. Hence, Sun created a chip called SPARC and engaged in a joint venture with AT&T for a standard UNIX operating system. It has formed 250 agreements with value-added resellers and original equipment manufacturers to distribute its technology. In addition to its own sales force, Sun has 250 other sales forces to sell and distribute its products. Critical mass is reached rapidly through networking.

The ability to use technology as a hub from which to control a network depends on laws that protect intellectual property and pricing schemes that allow inventors to reap downstream profits. For example, Castle and Cooke is fighting to prevent other distributors from using their proprietary seeds. They want only "their" farmers to use the seed and only their branded products to be grown from them. But at the heart of their lawsuit is the question, "What can be patented or copyrighted to protect intellectual property?" Indeed the success of the technology development strategy of Western firms depends on the protection of intellectual properties, especially in other countries. But even in Western countries the limits of protection are being established and challenged. The lawsuit brought by Apple against Hewlett-Packard for allegedly copying the "look and feel" of the Macintosh interface is a good example and a case to follow.

Pricing schemes for securing downstream profits from a technology without vertically integrating downstream are also arising. Cetus Corporation, a research boutique, has invented a biotechnology process with a potential to create some useful pharmaceuticals. They have formed a joint venture with Perkin-Elmer to create a machine that can be purchased by Ciba-Geigy, Upjohn, and others to create these pharmaceuticals. The joint venture has priced the machine low so that lots of laboratories such as university labs can buy it and create drugs. But the joint venture wants a royalty of some 10 percent from all pharmaceuticals created with their machine. This pricing scheme is one more variation on Gillette's original concept of giving away handles to sell blades. Another pricing concept has been introduced by an architect in Berkeley, California. He charges a usual fee for building designs but also wants 1 percent of the sale price every time the building is resold. All of these schemes are attempts to brand and profit from one's intellectual and artistic properties. The creator is attempting to profit without creating a vertically integrated organization to make, sell, and distribute the final product to the ultimate consumer. The schemes also place power with the creator of the intellectual property, so that the company performing creation can act as the broker or hub in the network organization.

Firms also use other approaches to achieve vertical control. One is simply size. Using purchasing and selling volume, a hub firm deals only with smaller suppliers and customers. Sears has controlled suppliers by buying from small manufacturers and being their dominant or only customer.

A second approach is to use financial services. The big companies entering the food business, which were mentioned earlier, are also using their financial services subsidiaries or going into joint ventures with other financial services companies to control the value-added chain. To farmers who use the company's breeding stock, they provide loans. For those farmers who use their breeding stock, and also buy their feed and sell to a packer, they provide loans with favorable interest rates. In addition, they can reduce the risk to the farmer and packer by guaranteeing price spreads. Through their financial services subsidiary, they use futures markets to hedge their own risk or trade as appropriate. Companies like IBM and AT&T are starting these activities as well. Their customers are buying large systems and networks, and much of the profit comes from financing the packages. Through these mechanisms, the large companies achieve the same results as vertical integration would achieve, but they avoid the capital investment of owning all the stages in the industry. Instead of being an owner of the farms and packers, or of subsystem manufacturers and software developers, they are the bankers. By controlling technology, controlling the brand, and being the banker, the companies achieve vertical control.

The fourth mechanism is information networks. Firms all along the value-added chain "plug into" the hub firm's network. They all need to adopt compatible systems and standardized accounting and information systems. All the firms in the network benefit by having upstream and downstream visibility. Such visibility reduces uncertainty, lowers inventories, and increases responsiveness to end users. On the other hand, it increases the hub firm's control. If you want to do business with General Motors, for example, you have to adopt MAP, their new computer language, and plug into their system.

In summary, network organizations require a hub firm or broker firm to create and maintain the network. Firms that perform this role achieve vertical control and avoid the costs of ownership required by vertical integration. Vertical control is achieved by performing the dominant function in the value-added chain, being the biggest firm in the network, being the banker to the network and designing and maintaining the information network for the network organization. A number of issues remain, however. These vertical control relationships are loaded with conflicts of interest and require constant negotiations.

The second design decision for the hub firm is what activities should it own and perform and which should it farm out to others in the network. From the preceding discussion it is evident that hub firms must own and control the dominant functions in the business such as product design and marketing the brand. Others, such as financial services and information systems design, are useful but not necessary. An examination of Benetton shows the design logic.

Benetton is not usually thought of as a high technology company. Indeed the fashion industry is probably not high technology. But Benetton performs only the high technology and design-intensive activities of the industry. By any criteria it is a high technology company. It designs the equipment, products, processes, information systems, and advertising. Any capital- or labor-intensive activity is subcontracted. In many traditional industries, high technology firms are restructuring the entire industry as Benetton has done in high fashion. Benetton has chosen to perform only a few of the activities along the value-added chain. They perform the marketing function, produce the product design (fashion clothing for young women), and control the brand. The manufacturing activities of weaving and sewing are performed by outside contractors. Some manufacturing functions are performed by Benetton. They buy wool and machinery for all members of the network. They design the equipment and the computer-aided design processes. They perform the dyeing, an activity in which they have a proprietary process to dye garments after they are made. They perform 1 percent of the manufacturing to gather the intelligence to negotiate with the rest of the network and get quick turnarounds on new product trials. Thus, Benetton is big when it is advantageous to be big (when buying) and small when it is good to be small (labor-intensive sewing). They do the difficult things (manufacturing technology) and the proprietary things (dyeing).

All of the sales take place through agents who deal with independent stores in a franchiselike arrangement. Benetton handles the distribution and designs the information system for rapid response to fashion trends. General Electric Information Systems runs their network. Their financial services subsidiary provides banking and leasing services to all members of the network. Benetton also has a venture capital subsidiary to finance new high technology fashion start-ups.

In summary, first are disaggregating and buying some portion of activities they used to perform. When vertical disintegration occurs, vertical control is still necessary. Control can be obtained by performing the dominant function, being big, being the banker, and running the information system. These functions allow a firm to play the broker role and be the hub of the network.

Network organizations are currently in fashion; it is an appropriate form for many applications. However, vertical integration is not dead. In the oil industry, the producing countries are attempting to reintegrate the industry by arranging for downstream assets. In semiconductors the vertically integrated Japanese firms can cut the price on semiconductors to gain market share versus U.S. manufacturers. The Japanese vertically integrated producers can profit from low-cost semiconductors by selling electronics products more profitably and subsidizing their semiconductor divisions, which their U.S. competitors cannot. Strategic analysis rather than management fashion should determine the design choice.

SUMMARY

This chapter has described how technology is changing the competitive environment in which business activity is taking place. Organizations are making their core businesses more competitive with emphasis on responsive integration, consolidation, and vertical disintegration. They next extend those businesses globally. When cash flow is generated above the core businesses' needs, development becomes the highest priority.

To implement these new strategies, firms are adopting matrixlike organizations, network organizations, neoconglomerates, and green field start-ups. In this chapter we described today's matrix organization and emphasized the network as the newest of the organization forms to be used in the 1990s, as development becomes the dominant strategy.

All of these organization forms reduce (but do not eliminate) the importance of formal structures and authority. They increase the need for skills at negotiating and influencing without authority. Those companies that were previously successful at matrix organization have an advantage over others who must learn both matrix and network skills.

The companies that were used as examples in this chapter are often not considered to be high technology. The author wanted to make the point that most manufacturing firms are now becoming high technology firms. General Motors, Procter and Gamble, food companies, paper companies, and fashion companies are all being driven by technology; that is, their strategies and organizations are the result of their use of technology to recover and develop in the new global competition. Those companies in the industries mentioned earlier that do not think of themselves as high technology firms will be at a disadvantage in the new competitive era.

4

International Competition in High Technology: The Case of the United States, Japan, and Europe

GERARDO R. UNGSON

Firms confront today's agenda for international competition amidst the throes of change. For nearly two decades, scholars have predicted the emergence of new industries based on the creation and processing of information that would usher in a postindustrial society. Consistent with such predictions, these high technology industries—computers, semiconductors, computer-aided design and manufacturing (CAM/CAD), telecommunications, and software—have provided much of the dynamism in the recent development of world economy. Competitiveness in these industries is particularly crucial for many industrialized countries such as the United States, Japan, and Germany, which have slowly been losing their grip on maturing, smokestack industries to newly industrializing countries such as Korea, Brazil, and Taiwan. A belief that is gaining wide recognition is that the future of industrialized countries in a postindustrial society may lie in their ability to sustain their competitiveness in high technology industries.

Viewing high technology in the context of international competition, some key trends have emerged: the United States still enjoys a strong strategic position, especially in advanced high technology products and services, but this position is wilting against escalating Trans-Pacific competition; Japan has emerged as a strong and formidable competitor who is widely regarded as dislodging the United States from its preeminent position in the future; and Europe, with few exceptions, is slowly declining in its competitiveness, and needs a massive "catch-up" strategy to survive. And survival for firms in these countries will depend on their abilities to muster their management skills, natural resources, and national institutions to compete in this area. While the trends discussed earlier conform to conventional wisdom, no clear consensus has emerged on which country will assume technological and economic preeminence in the future.

This chapter examines patterns of competition in high technology, with particular attention to international rivalries between Japan, the United States, and the European Economic Community (EEC). It compares high technology with traditional, capital-intensive industries; discusses the industrial policies of Japan, the United States, and the EEC in relation to competition in high technology; evaluates how institutional differences in these countries are transformed into competitive advantages and corporate strategy; and presents specific implications for managing high technology in terms of business, technological, and public policies that bear on the issue of enhancing the competitiveness of U.S. firms.

THE NATURE OF HIGH TECHNOLOGY

High technology industries differ from traditional capital-intensive industries in many fundamental ways. Competitive strategies in high technology industries are primarily determined by changes in technology (Porter, 1980; Riggs, 1983). Innovations in microelectronics, for example, have led to significant changes in designing computers and telecommunications. New advances in CAM/CAD technology have altered the manner in which semiconductors are designed and manufactured. And manufacturers of futuristic consumer products await developments in superconductivity that might make their products commercially viable.

High technology industries also exhibit distinguishing characteristics in terms of growth rates, technological diffuseness, and internal structure (Ungson, 1988a). High technology industries account for the ten fastest-growing sectors in the United States over the past thirteen years (*U.S. Industrial Outlook*, 1987). In semiconductors alone, the average annual growth rate from 1971 to 1985 was 33 percent; CAD/CAM and software sectors registered even higher gains, with growth rates ranging from a low of 46 percent to a high of 300 percent (*U.S. Industrial Outlook*, 1986, 1987). High technology industries also offer products and services that have relatively short product life cycles (e.g., 3 to 4 years) compared with traditional, capital-intensive industries (e.g., 15 to 20 years). Moreover, innovations in one high technology industry oftentimes create new markets in others. As an illustration, advances in miniaturization and semiconductor technology have accelerated the growth in telecommunication, CAM/CAD, analytical instrumentation, computers, robotics, software, consumer products, and defense applications. For this reason, semiconductors have been dubbed "the crude oil of the 1990s." (This phrase is attributed to William Sanders of Advanced Microelectronics Devices.) Finally, high technology firms are populated with scientific personnel, requiring more technical skills than conventional industries (Riggs, 1983).

Accordingly, competing in high technology creates new and different demands for managers. Since product life cycles are significantly shorter, there is more pressure to recoup initial investments over a shorter time period.

Because the pace of technological innovation can render previously accepted products and technologies virtually obsolete within a short period of time, firms constantly jockey for positions to make them competitive in world markets. De-skilling, re-skilling, and dislocations create social anxieties that spill across as disturbing features in the workplace. Collectively, the need for a rapid, timely, and appropriate response to competitor's actions affects all phases of management, whether this be financing for research and development, pricing newer products in the marketplace, investing in new plant capacity, or training and developing persons to adopt to a high technology movement.

INTERNATIONAL COMPETITION IN HIGH TECHNOLOGY

Historically, U.S., Japanese, and European high technology firms have competed in distinctive ways. Since the discovery of the transistor in 1949, the United States has enjoyed economic and scientific supremacy in high technology, with modest competition from Great Britain. The success of U.S. firms as innovators in the field was facilitated by early Pentagon funding in semiconductors. The climate for innovation was enhanced by the unique structure of a "Silicon Valley" that combined the benefits of venture capital funding, university research, and a cluster of budding entrepreneurs into one area (Reid, 1984). Moreover, the implosion of growth markets (computers, software, CAM/CAD) arising from innovations in microelectronics was easily accommodated by the large size of the U.S. domestic market, paving the way for even more innovations.

In the past, Japan had relied on both the United States and Europe for key innovations, which they secured through licensing and cross-licensing agreements. Through superior production techniques, ingenious "reverse engineering" capabilities, and institutional support from the Japanese government and ministries (Abegglen & Stalk, 1985; Johnson, 1985), Japanese firms have excelled in driving down the costs of these products for commercial consumption. Videocassette recorders (VCRs), first produced by Philips in 1971, are an example. Although Philips' VCRs contained many appealing features that had yet to be configured into Japanese VCRs, they were very expensive and limited in terms of recording capability (e.g., one hour maximum recording time). Japanese firms, notably Sony and JVC, took the lead in refining video recording to the point that recording capabilities were enhanced (e.g., two or more hours of video). The Sony Betamax and JVC VHS systems were quickly adopted by other Japanese manufacturers who poured enormous investments to produce them in heavily automated factories. In time, prices had dropped to affordable consumer levels, earning Japanese companies dominant market positions against Philips European VCR system and other foreign competitors (MacKintosh, 1986).

Playing a "catch-up" role, European firms are presently examining how to work within the constraints imposed by the EEC to become competitive in high technology. Although a number of European firms, notably Philips and A. G. Siemens, are not lacking in innovation, as represented by their success in the videorecorder and the compact disc, they have not been able to diffuse these products at a competitive level. The limited size of individual European markets, a preference to compete in the U.S. market instead of their own, and myopic managerial strategies developed over the years account for their failures (MacKintosh, 1986).

From a global standpoint, U.S., Japanese, and European firms have taken distinctively different approaches to building their strengths in high technology. For many U.S. high technology firms, the answer lies in the tenets of a free market system. That is, success accrues from a healthy climate of innovation, such as that fostered by Silicon Valley, as well as a belief in the unencumbered access to Japanese and European markets. For Japanese high technology firms, the answer lies in their ability to exploit advantages in their national institutions. Some analysts have argued that selective targeting of industries by Japanese bureaucracies and nationalistic procurement practices within their interfirm groupings (*keiretsu*) account for their favorable market position (Borrus, Millstein, & Zysman, 1983; Ungson, Bird, & Steers, 1988). And, for European high technology firms that have only recently awakened to the reality of being totally dominated by their competitors, the answer might be in finally creating a truly united common market, such as those called for in imperatives for complete unification in 1992 (Dekker, 1985; Mackintosh, 1986).

The emergence of the Japanese as a serious threat in high technology markets once dominated by U.S. firms accentuates the contrast between market approach favored by U.S. firms, and calls into question which approach might be more effective in future competition. Table 4.1 traces the performance of Japanese semiconductor firms from 1974 to 1987. Specifically, in 1974, Japanese firms held a mere 14 percent of the world market—a figure that catapulted to 45 percent in 1987. An inescapable conclusion is that Japanese gains were made at the expense of the United States and Europe: North America (primarily the United States) dropped from a 72 percent share in 1974 to 42 percent in 1987, while Europe also dropped from 11 percent in 1974 to 8 percent in 1987. And there is every indication that such a trend will continue into the 1990s. Semiconductors are used as an example, but we think the experiences of semiconductor firms are representative of other high technology sectors, and similar trends might occur with others in the future.

Although some U.S. high technology firms still believe in the tenets of the free market system, their devastating loss to the Japanese in the 64K and the 256K RAM battles have provoked questions whether the free market alone is sufficient to deter Japanese competition. By and large, their responses have been to lobby for import relief against Japanese products, based on claims of "unfair" competition and dumping charges against particular Japanese firms. Other strategic responses have been documented (Ungson, 1988a), but these to do not appear to have significantly warded off the Japanese onslaught.

Table 4.1 Worldwide Semiconductor Production (1974–1987, $M)

Segment	1974	1975	1976	1977	1978	1979	1980	1981	1982	1983	1984	1985	1986	1987
North America	1,900	1,570	2,170	2,590	3,420	4,670	6,360	6,050	6,205	7,850	12,250	9,300	9,800	12,220
Europe	290	250	275	400	455	600	710	790	835	1,040	1,545	1,460	1,940	2,375
Japan	375	350	595	695	1,220	1,555	2,290	2,815	2,990	4,420	7,800	7,050	10,540	13,755
Row	40	30	40	50	65	90	130	160	165	200	225	280	530	850
Total Merchant IC	2,605	2,200	3,080	3,735	4,980	6,915	9,490	9,815	10,195	13,510	21,820	18,090	22,810	29,200
Captive ICs	400	440	675	1,050	1,300	2,010	2,695	2,900	3,160	3,625	4,280	4,800	4,850	5,120
Total WW Discrete*	2,900	2,250	2,900	3,150	3,700	4,090	4,460	4,730	4,450	5,070	6,650	5,965	7,190	7,800
Total WW semiconductor	5,905	4,890	6,655	7,935	9,980	13,015	16,645	17,445	17,805	22,205	32,750	28,855	34,850	42,120

*Includes captive.

SOURCE: *Status 1986: A Report on the Integrated Circuit Industry* by William McClean (ed.). Copyright 1986 by Integrated Circuit Engineering Corporation. Reprinted with permission.

What disturbs corporate officials and public officials is that the same pattern of Japanese success in such industries as steel, automobiles, consumer electronics, and motorcycles is once again occurring in semiconductors—an industry that many consider to determine the pace and the extent of industrial growth and development (Borrus et al., 1983). There is hardly any question that loss of its position in semiconductors would have adverse consequences for the continued leadership of the United States in other high technology industries. Even so, the trade controversy and protectionistic flurries obscure a critical point, that is, the *basis* of the *endurance* of Japanese strategies in the long run. The prepotent question, initially raised by Borrus et al. (1983) and one with far-reaching implications for future U.S. competitiveness, remains: Will future success in high technology be determined by competitive advantages derived primarily from *national institutions* or from *technological/market forces?* While this question can be debated in the context of emerging industries like CAM/CAD, software, telecommunications, and biotechnology, historical events in semiconductors provide a more unequivocal answer that favors institutions. To substantiate this argument I now turn to the pattern of competition in the world semiconductor industry.

INTERNATIONAL RIVALRY IN SEMICONDUCTORS

Semiconductors, broadly defined as materials with properties of both a conductor and an insulator, are generally considered to be strategically important because they represent key intermediate inputs to other electronic industries such as computers, telecommunications, and consumer electronic products. Because semiconductors have been the fastest-growing industry in the last thirteen years (*U.S. Industrial Outlook,* 1987), they determine the extent and growth of other electronic industries. Since the complete picture of the Japanese assault on the dRAM market has been extensively reviewed in other published sources (Borrus et al., 1983; Okimoto, Sugano, & Weinstein, 1984; The Semiconductor Industry Association Report, 1983), I will simply present the fundamentals of the competition here.

Finan and LaMold (1985, p. 164) argue that before 1977 competitive success in semiconductors was based on four factors: consumer acceptance of product design, availability of second-source suppliers, aggressive pricing, and credible delivery acceptance. At the early stage of the product life cycle, competition focused on product development as several firms competed to have their product design become the industry standard. Mostek's design of the 16k dRAM is one example of a clear favorite. Once a favorite was selected, other firms typically entered the race as second-source producers, competing on the basis of price, marketing and distribution, quality, and reliability (Finan & LaMold, 1985). Since funds obtained from a mature product were typically invested in a new product, it was important for firms to maintain the cycle of investment and reinvestment (McKenna, Cohen, & Borrus, 1984).

The Japanese entry into the 64k dRAM market in the late 1970s to early 1980s changed the competitive rules in the industry. Japanese firms used their strengths as low-cost manufacturers of the product to aggressively attack the U.S. market and exploit the financial constraints experienced by U.S. firms during recessionary periods. In 1981–82, for example, Japanese firms began to introduce enormous quantities of the 64k RAM at sharply reduced prices. When the prevailing price for the device was $25 to $30, Fujitsu offered $15. By the end of 1981, prices had dropped to $7.75, with several Japanese merchants quoting prices as low as $5. These strategies enabled the Japanese to garner more than 90 percent of the 64k RAM market share, and a disproportionate share of the 256k RAM market (The Semiconductor Industry Association Report, 1983; McLean, 1986).

The Japanese entry strategy was based on a buildup of memory production capacity, which was ensured, in no large part, by government measures aimed at protecting the domestic market. Moreover, since Japanese firms tend to carry large fixed costs as a result of high interest rates and fixed wages, they often price at a level to cover their high fixed costs even if this is lower than world market prices (Ungson, Bird, & Steers, 1988).

The success of the Japanese ushered in new competitive parameters—an emphasis on prices and timely delivery. Instead of the conventional emphasis on research and development, competition had shifted to becoming a low-cost producer, a strategy that was enhanced by the Japanese strengths in manufacturing and process refinement. As part of the Japanese emphasis on better handling equipment, air purifying techniques, comprehensive clean room measures, and well-trained personnel, Japanese products were regarded not only as lower priced but with reliable high quality as well (Okimoto et al., 1984).

In changing the competitive rules of the game, Japanese firms have adversely affected U.S. semiconductor firms in a number of ways. Generally, they have minimized the traditional strengths of U.S. firms in product development in favor of process development in which they excel. Such actions have prompted several U.S firms to retreat to smaller niches in the market, which they think are impervious to Japanese entry strategies, if not to leave the market entirely (Borrus et al., 1983).

Taken together, these events signify much more than a loss of profits and market share for U.S. firms. Moreover, although one can point to numerous shortcomings in U.S. corporate strategies, these shortcomings do not fully explain the Japanese rise to dominance. That Japanese success extends across a number of different industries, and not any particular industry, highlights the critical role of institutions in *creating* competitive advantages for Japanese firms. The pattern of Japanese success raises fundamental questions of whether macroeconomic policies alone—a route favored and pursued by U.S. policymakers—are sufficient to guarantee success in high technology. The contrarian view is that national institutions (e.g., industrial policy, educational policy, management systems) may be the important factor, if not one of the prepotent variables, that may determine the future winners in high technology competition.

U.S., JAPANESE, AND EUROPEAN FIRMS—A REAPPRAISAL

If the success of high technology firms ultimately rests on enduring institutions that support them, then how might we assess policies enacted by the United States, Japan, and the EEC? This section reviews the patterns of institutional support as congealed in formal industrial policies (Ungson and Van Dijk, 1987).

Assessing U.S. Industrial Policies

For decades the United States has used generic policies, such as varying the interest rate and selective tax policies, to support particular industries or firms. When interventionist policies are made, such as the bailing out of Lockheed or Chrysler, or when the U.S. government invests in particular sectors (semiconductors), there is no real consistency in these policies. Accordingly, some writers have described these policies as uncoordinated, fragmented, noncohesive, and even chaotic (Magaziner & Reich, 1983).

Even so, it is no secret that many U.S. high technology firms have, in fact, benefited from their proximity to various government contracts. Until 1970, government-supported R & D and Pentagon expenditures in semiconductors were considered important stimuli in developing the industry. At present, the VHSIC program, sponsored by the Defense Department, provides more funding for semiconductor research than similar programs in Japan and has considerably enlarged the U.S. domestic industry. Other factors favor the technological leadership of U.S. high technology firms. The pouring of venture capital, into Silicon Valley and other sites continues to accelerate. And high technology industries can only benefit from policies to develop similar "Silicon Valleys" (e.g., Austin, North Carolina Triangle, Boston, Minnesota), if not new initiatives to develop precompetitive, collaborative consortia (e.g., Sematech).

Even so, questions remain regarding the adequacy and direction of R & D expenditures. Although Pentagon funding continues, it is doubtful that these efforts will translate quickly into commercial applications. In fact, the attention placed on defense-related projects may steer efforts away from commercially oriented applications (Okimoto et al., 1984). And the excitement surrounding the creation of precompetitive collaborative consortia in semiconductors is tempered by U.S. practices that impede their competitiveness. U.S. antitrust regulation, for example, limits the formation of mergers and alliances necessary to match the size and financial resources of Japanese firms and EEC-sponsored research projects. Because many U.S. firms are evaluated in the short term—a situation dictated primarily by quarterly stock market reports—they are discouraged from building up the long-term capital investments and R & D that are needed to match Japanese expenditures.

Assessing Japanese Industrial Policies

In contrast with the United States, Japan views its industrial base in terms of a portfolio, in which particular industries are "targeted" for development, restructured, or scaled down. A major thrust of Japan's effort to contribute to semiconductors was the well-publicized program for industry–government cooperation in VLSI research. Associated companies included NEC, Toshiba, Hitachi, Fujitsu, and Mitsubishi. Research and cooperative laboratories were staffed by engineers from these five companies. As a result of this project, more than 1000 patents were issued, and about 460 technical papers were published—a remarkable organizational success (Okimoto et al, 1984).

Compared with the United States, the Japanese have a strategic emphasis on semiconductors, which has led to a more coherent strategy for promoting exports and protecting their domestic market. Unlike U.S. trade policymakers who construe the world market as subject to policies that promote efficiency in resource allocation, Japanese lawmakers regard their market in terms of a "development state," and have restricted the entry of foreign competitors accordingly.

However, Japan's success may result in its own undoing. Japanese semiconductor firms now dominate the standard memory market and are gearing up to compete with U.S. firms in more advanced circuit chips, telecommunications, and supercomputers. Japan's key problem is slower economic growth, which has occurred at a time when it had become dependent on export trade to fuel its growth and when other countries, notably Europe and the United States, are starting to erect protectionist measures to save their industries. Slower growth also places heavy institutional pressure on the government to invest in Japan's social infrastructure, instead of its historical preference for rapid growth and economic development. Compared with other industrial countries, Japan lags behind in social security and welfare spending (Lincoln, 1988).

There are also other indications that some elements that have contributed to Japan's remarkable growth in the last three decades are starting to weaken (Lincoln, 1988). Younger Japanese have critically questioned the slow and conservative career paths in the hierarchical structure of Japanese firms. Unlike their parents and grandparents, younger Japanese prefer rapid movement in an organization that eclipses traditional seniority considerations. Finally, as Japan grows into a full world power, the demands on it to assume a greater role in civil defense and the world debt problem are bound to intensify.

Assessing European Industrial Policies

In general, the decline of traditional industries has forced many European governments to support these industries to keep people in the work force. However, there is a growing awareness that this "employment" policy is not tenable. Within the EEC, there is a need for new industrial initiatives that go beyond the traditional policy covering agricultural products (viz., the Common Agricultural Policy).

There are a number of joint efforts between European firms supported by EEC. Though still in the embryonic, precompetitive stage, a collaborative project call ESPRIT (European Strategic Programme in Informational Technology) aims at "the achievement of technological parity with, if not superiority over, world competitors within 10 years" (*ESPRIT Report,* 1986). Within this broad mission, ESPRIT intends to strengthen the European technology base, develop a European telecommunication policy, create a common market for European Community Information Technology, and use rules and instruments of the Treaty of Rome to create a favorable climate for European high technology. It declares, "There will be no Europe without a European new technology policy; there will be no new technology in Europe without collective European action."

Simply stated, Europe needs help to catch up and remain competitive with the United States and Japan. Many analysts believe the key to success lies in greater collaboration among countries in the EEC. A united Europe can lead to a massive market of 271 million consumers (319 million with Spain and Portugal), compared to 230 million in the United States and 119 million in Japan (MacKintosh, 1986). The community could represent the world's biggest market and its biggest trading power! A future event that is capturing the imagination and interest of a lot of people is the Single Act, which proposes a genuine European economic area without internal frontiers by 1992. If implemented, these would mean the elimination of 300 technical barriers—the first step leading to a truly unified Europe. If it is successful, European high technology firms should be able to innovate products and reap the benefits of being a first mover and achieve a scale of economics across a large market—an objective that has eluded them in the past.

Unfortunately, the elegance and intellectual appeal of this proposal do not break down the political obstacles that prevent its realization. European integration, or a truly united market, means the elimination of regional protection and other impediments to a free market. For many years, Europeans, notably Philips, have advocated such a policy. Standardization of the requirements for electronic components, the abolishment of short-term protection of (state-owned) "national champions," and closer R & D collaboration are part and parcel of Philips' proposal (Dekker, 1985). However, if history is a guide, integration does not bode well for the European community; the lack of government commitment made unification policies the victims of short-range political expediencies. Finally, even with the impetus behind community-sponsored programs such as ESPRIT, the MEGA-Project of Siemens and Philips, and various others (RACE, EUREKA), the question remains whether their funding is adequate to match the scale of U.S. and Japanese investments.

IMPLICATIONS FOR MANAGEMENT

Imagine two contrasting scenarios:

Scenario 1. By the year 2000, the sale of electronics products will reach $1.3 trillion on a worldwide basis, propelled mainly by the invention and diffusion of faster and smaller semiconductors. Capitalizing on the benefits afforded by Sematech and other consortia as well as their traditional strengths in small-scale entrepreneurship, U.S. high technology firms lead in the development of advanced microelectronic products. End-users of semiconductors strengthen their market positions by quickly incorporating innovations into their products. Japanese firms still remain the principal rival to the United States, although their weakness in software technology limits their advances in telecommunications and computers. European firms still anchor their hopes on community projects such as ESPRIT, but they have simply been outspent by their U.S. and Japanese rivals. Given their interdependencies, U.S., European, and Asiatic firms begin to form collaborative alliances. Meanwhile, U.S. and Japanese firms brace themselves for the next battle that will determine technological leadership in 2015: mastery of superconductivity.

Scenario 2. Buoyed by their success in successively dominating sectors of the high technology market, Japanese firms finally overrun the United States in the 1990s. This touches off a domino effect in the United States as advanced semiconductors, computer products, peripherals, biotechnology, electronic consumer products, and even telecommunications fall into the hands of the Japanese and other foreign competitors. The reduction of the United States to a second-rate power creates feverish protectionist sentiments, resulting in numerous punitive trade measures and government procurement policies passed by the U.S. Congress. Meanwhile, consumers and industrial buyers in the United States begin to feel the pinch of higher prices. Alarmed by what has happened the European Common Market legislates even higher tariff protection, creating what is then called "Fortress Europe." The prices of high technology products begin to soar, leading to serious geopolitical imbalances. Country-bashing becomes commonplace as the embattled firms prepare for the next round of protectionism.

Although there is nothing more intriguing than engaging in some sort of crystal ball gazing, the preceding scenarios are not intended to be forecasting exercises. Because high technology industries are extremely volatile and fraught with uncertainties, it is very difficult to predict the future. In fact, a number of high technology firms have eschewed formal forecasting methods in favor of highly flexible organizational structures (Ungson, 1988a). *There-*

fore, instead of attempting to predict outcomes, the key task for managers in high technology industries might lie in understanding how particular trends lead to particular outcomes. By monitoring such trends, managers can adequately plan for change. Earlier I discussed how market and institutional factors determined changing patterns of international competition in the semiconductor industry. Based on this discussion, I will now show how particular trends might determine whether future competition will result in greater collaboration or in an unavoidable collision, and how collaboration or collision might, in turn, affect the competitiveness of the parties involved (Ungson & Van Dijk, 1987).

Fragmentation Versus Consolidation

An important trend that warrants the attention of high technology managers is the pace at which multidomestic firms evolve into global industries. Converging market and technological forces lead to large, concentrated, and global industries. This is evident in the semiconductor memory segment, where the growing preference of buyers for standardized products sold worldwide at lower prices established its global status. The global nature of semiconductor memory products can be contrasted with higher-state microprocessors for which demand still extends across different specialized buyers and market segments.

The fragmentation of new markets that arise from product differentiation favors the loosely coupled network of several entrepreneurial firms such as those in Silicon Valley. For as long as markets remain fragmented, smaller firms, which typically sell to specific niches, should be able to avoid direct confrontation with larger and better financed firms, which prefer to sell their products across a wider spectrum of buyers. Without being wedged in by larger competitors, smaller U.S. firms should be able to continue developing new products, processes, and services.

Consolidation of the market, however, as is evidenced in the trend toward greater globalization of high technology products, changes the parameters of competition. As markets converge, it becomes economical to configure activities within the firm to capitalize on the scale-economies and other synergies afforded by interproduct linkages. As such competition shifts from product/service differentiation to cost leadership (Porter, 1980), the ensuing battleground is likely to pit larger, vertically integrated firms in Japan, such as NEC, Fujitsu, against the megaprojects in Europe (e.g., Philips-Siemens joint venture, ESPRIT). In such a scenario, it is questionable whether smaller U.S. firms—which have historically been the source of many innovations but are not lacking in capital and production experience—can successfully compete against their larger and better-financed rivals (Borrus et al., 1983). If smaller U.S. firms do fade or merge with larger ones, it is uncertain whether the resulting large-scale alliances and consortia such as Sematech and SRC could provide the appropriate structure for continued new product innovations. For even with successful firms like Sematech, U.S. firms still need to adapt the new technology to low-cost manufacturing in their own plants, which in itself constitutes a large investment (Borrus, 1988).

"Active" versus "Passive" Trade Policy

Competitive policies are fueled by protectionist sentiments that are congealed in proactive ("active") or reactive ("passive") trade policies. The success of the Japanese high technology firms is reflected, perhaps unfairly, in huge deficits with the United States, prompting imperatives for a more "active" trade policy ranging from trade barriers to reciprocal market access. An active trade policy is also reflected in numerous charges filed against the Japanese for unfair trade practices such as predatory pricing and favored government procurement policies. While Japan has continued to unveil packages containing market access initiatives that appear to address U.S. concerns, the countervailing view is that both market and capital liberalization are a bit too slow and cumbersome. Some fear that deteriorating relations resulting from unfulfilled expectations between Japanese and U.S. policymakers jeopardize what remains of the General Agreement on Tariffs and Trade (GATT) system that sustained the postwar prosperity for years (Bergsten & Cline, 1987).

The evils of protectionist measures and "closed markets" are well-articulated in many economics textbooks; however, the repercussions of these measures in high technology can have far-reaching, devastating effects. Since semiconductors provide the key intermediate input to a host of other industries (e.g., computers, telecommunications, instruments), increasing their costs through tariffs (or indirectly through import quotas) could lead to significant cost increases in other industries as well. An example is computer firms in Europe, which face the twin disadvantages of not having a truly competitive semiconductor industry at home to finance them and needing to deal with 17 percent tariff on all incoming semiconductors from abroad. Moreover, there is mounting evidence that the success of U.S. semiconductor firms in limiting the production of Japanese semiconductor chips has led to shortages and higher chip prices for U.S. computer firms.

Additionally, initial measures by both U.S and European firms to curb the flow of Japanese memory semiconductors into their markets have only prompted the Japanese to move into more complex chips, a strategy that places them on a straight collision course with the United States. As one management consultant from Silicon Valley said, "The dumping issue of NC and Fujitsu may just hasten the Japanese entry into the custom and semi-custom market. Already, they have stepped up both their investment and efforts into gallium arsenide and C-MOS chips. The government, in this latest ruling, may have inadvertently accelerated the Japanese timetable by five to seven years." All in all, trade policy can spell the difference between more collaborative or more collisive competition in the future.

The Myth and the Reality of Joint Ventures and Strategic Alliances

Joint ventures, alliances, and triadic associations ("triads") have become fashionable topics in high technology, primarily because these are seen as collaborative structures that benefit all parties (Ohmae, 1985). In a world replete with trade tensions, there is nothing more soothing or reassuring than an image of Europeans, Japanese, and Americans working together in developing new technologies. The need for alliances and triads occurs from the accelerating tempo of technological change that has reduced product life cycles and lead times for developing products. There are no benefits for entrepreneurs since there is hardly any time-lag for competitors to match or improve the product. As a result, present innovators need to penetrate the global market at once, in sharp contrast with their predecessors who could reap the economic benefits of their new products at home before taking them abroad. In this context, the only viable structure that would accommodate the needs of these competitors is the triadic association, in which two or three firms can use their differences to build one strong team rather than competing and destroying each other (Ohmae, 1985). Since firms that are not members of the "triad" are likely to face considerable strategic disadvantages in competing against firms entrenched in alliances, the pressure for triadic associations will only increase (Ohmae, 1985).

Yet alliances or triadic associations have to be evaluated in terms of the motives of the participating firms and their perceptions of the rewards of such alliances. Ohmae correctly assumes that each party stands to benefit from the exchange when the alliance is initially conceived, but he does not expound on what incentives might sustain their participation over time. Clearly, parties form partnerships to overcome vulnerabilities in projects that they cannot accomplish on their own. For example, Japanese firms engage in joint ventures to obtain technological skills that cannot be as easily transferred or secured through licenses (LSI Logic-Toshiba). It also has been suggested that Japanese pursue partnerships when they are threatened by significant protectionist measures (Toyota-GM). Similarly, U.S. firms pursue these avenues to gain access to Japanese markets.

Over time, however, asymmetries develop between the partners. This results when one partner is able to acquire more skills than the other. Hamel and Prahalad (1988) have suggested that learning from others depends on the strategic intent of each party (i.e., the desire for internalizing a partner's skills), the extent to which each partner is open (i.e., the relative access to proprietary capabilities of the other), and the receptivity of each partner (i.e., how hard each partner works to learn from the other). For example, the Japanese are able to learn much faster about their partners' territory and practices than their partners can about them. At the conclusion of the partnership, it is the Japanese who emerge as winners in the exchange, and what initially appeared to be short-term advantages have now become long-term liabilities. For this particular reason, some, if not many, U.S. high technology firms have been critical of their collaborative ventures with the Japanese in the past (Reich & Mankin, 1986). If such a trend continues, competition between triad members can become more divisive rather than collaborative as was initially envisioned.

Success or Failure in Utilizing Institutional Strengths

There is no shortage of recommendations for improving the competitiveness of the U.S. high technology firms in relation to foreign competitors. Consider the following proposals: emulate its industrial policymaking (*Business Week*, July 4, 1983; Magaziner & Reich, 1983); adopt Japanese-style management techniques (Ouchi, 1981; Pascale & Athos, 1981); mandate punitive trade measures; reformulate antitrust legislation (Yamamura, 1986); promote consumer savings and capital formation (Palmer, 1983); provide incentives for scientific training (Botkin, Dimancescu, & Stata, 1984); and shift away from short-term incentives, to long-term stock appreciations, for example (Ungson et al., 1988).

Central to these recommendations is the need to use underlying institutions (e.g., tax rates, antitrust legislation, educational systems). Unfortunately, because these recommendations are long-term and go beyond the "quick-fix" mentality, there is the danger that they will be bypassed in favor of short-term, political thinking. Accordingly, the issue may not primarily concern the intent and context of these proposals, but the collective will to make some of them a reality. To the extent that U.S. firms are able to capitalize on their institutional strengths and leverage them into competitive advantages, a more benign competitive atmosphere should ensue. On the other hand, should U.S. firms fail in this effort, competition is bound to be fierce in context and protectionist in sentiment.

Among the most prominent institutional changes in the competitive landscape is the appearance of various forms of interfirm collaboration, some of which were discussed earlier: strategic alliances, triads, joint ventures, interlocking networks, cross-licensing agreements, and consortia. Despite the ubiquitousness of these forms and the excitement they have generated, these still have to be linked to competitive advantages and strategies (Ohmae, 1985; Gerlach, 1988). For us, these new forms signal new competitive rules for competing high technology industries. Interestingly, we see a juxtapositioning of roles for U.S. and Japanese firms. For U.S. firms that have been successfully innovative in small entrepreneurial settings, the shift to large-scale megaprojects such as Sematech and SRC creates pressures for them to innovate in larger, collaborative environments. And for Japanese firms that have historically relied on large R & D consortia, the challenge is to develop their innovative capabilities at a level that matches their strengths in manufacturing and diffusion. This is partly addressed by Japan's technopolis strategy (see chapter 2 in this volume). The extent to which U.S., Japanese, and European firms are able to capitalize on their institutional strengths may determine their competitiveness in the future.

IMPLICATIONS FOR FORMULATING TECHNOLOGICAL POLICY

Technological policy must give priority to the goals of developing, sustaining, and enhancing U.S. competitiveness in both product and process technologies in strategic high technology sectors. A good industrial policy can harness collective resources beyond the firm level to achieve economies of scale and scope that can translate into competitive advantages for individual firms. Thus, technological policy should not be cast as a substitute for a firm's corporate strategy, but as a complement to it. While the contents of technological policy have yet to be precisely defined, a number of key elements are needed.

First, the U.S. advantage in product development must be sustained. Historically, U.S. firms have had the edge in innovating streams of new products, while Japanese firms excelled in incorporating innovations into new products and delivering them quickly to the marketplace. While this might have worked well in the past, when U.S. firms had focused on computer applications and the Japanese on consumer electronic-products, such is no longer the case. As the markets for U.S. and Japanese firms have started to converge, the Japanese have stepped up their efforts at product development and have made impressive gains in several sectors including advanced semiconductor circuitry. For many U.S. firms, innovating to keep ahead of competitors may be the crucial strategy to avoid being drawn into costly price wars as had happened with many standard commodity products. Therefore, it is critical that U.S. firms sustain this edge in product innovation.

Second, every effort must be made to restore the present U.S. competitive disadvantage in production. Cohen and Zysman (1987) have debunked the belief that manufacturing has become obsolete in the transition from an industrial manufacturing to a postindustrial service economy. To the contrary, since high technology services are inextricably related to manufacturing, weaknesses in production are bound to lead to competitive disadvantages in services. Similar linkages are already apparent in the semiconductor industry. The lack of participation by U.S. firms in standard commodity semiconductors may restrict their competitiveness in more complex circuitry. And because semiconductors provide strategic inputs to a host of other high technology sectors, the loss of relative competitiveness in semiconductors may limit the long-term effectiveness of these end-users.

Third, there is the need to strengthen R & D management, particularly in smaller firms. Technically, innovation can occur in any part of the organization, but it is within the R & D function that they are expected. One of the more frustrating problems plaguing U.S. industries is the transfer of product or process from the R & D laboratory to the production shop floor. Conventional prescriptions for improving the transfer process stress the role of "product champions," the education and training of the R & D staff, and closer integration between the R & D function and corporate strategy. Although we expect R & D management to reside principally within the technical function, and not as a peripheral staff function, it should accentuate the link between product/process innovativeness and corporate competitiveness.

Fourth, there is need to explore possible synergies derived from university–government–industry collaboration. One such evolving structure is the consortium, defined generally as partnerships between universities and nonprofit organizations with the objective of funding and developing research. Two prominent examples are the Semiconductor Research Corporation (SRC) and the Microelectronics and Computer Technology Corporation (MCC). Sematech, a collaborative effort of the semiconductor industry with the participation of the U.S. chip tooling and materials suppliers, also fits this mold. These consortia have targeted research programs designed to enhance the competitiveness of U.S. high technology firms. Sematech, which conducts research and development from the laboratory to actual production, is particularly important if U.S. firms are to regain their manufacturing competence.

Although the technological goals of consortia are impressive, it is too early to determine what their actual benefits to U.S. firms might be. Despite the fact that research in these types of endeavors remain generic, proprietary interests are high, and there is already growing criticism that the "best" personnel are not sent by member companies to participate in consortia activities. And there is the fundamental issue whether U.S. firms, historically accustomed to innovating on a smaller scale, can effectively do so on a larger scale. Nonetheless, consortiums and other mid-scale research activities represent a creative infrastructure that meets the competitive challenge of the 1990's.

Finally, technology policy has to be integrated with longer term, less focused policies such as technical education and antitrust legislation. An alarming trend for U.S. high technology, well documented by Botkin, Dimancescu, and Stata (1984), is the growing scarcity of technically trained personnel. For the sake of comparison, Japan has been producing more engineers than the United States though it has only about a half the population of the United States. Because knowledge-intensive industries are closely linked with technically trained personnel, the growing gap between Japanese and U.S. engineers does not bode well for future U.S. competitiveness.

Antitrust legislation, specifically those laws directed at joint R & D research, is another area that might make the difference between the two competing countries in the future. Yamamura (1986) has argued that the U.S. antitrust structure effectively restricts joint research activities among large firms, while the Japanese structure promotes it. Both systems have benefited their firms in specific contexts, but we believe the rising costs of R & D—which have become almost prohibitive—will work more to the advantage of Japanese than U.S. high technology firms. The success of large-scale projects, such as Sematech, SRC, and MCC, will depend on further interpretations of U.S. antitrust laws and how much Americans are willing to support policies that appear to promote the interests of particular sectors. Unfortunately, both educational and antitrust policies are broadly focused and may not be as tightly linked to success in high technology. Should these policies be neglected, U.S. high technology firms might find themselves in the unenviable position of having their destiny controlled by foreign competitors that have more favorable social, political, and economic environments.

Charting Strategic Decisions in the Microcomputer Industry: Profile of an Industry Star

KATHLEEN M. EISENHARDT AND
L. J. BOURGEOIS III

How do executives make strategic decisions in industries with rapid and discontinuous change in demand and technology? How do these executives cope with the continual entry and exit of competitors? How do they choose among a variety of technical and market options? In short, how do top management teams make decisions when the pace of change creates a "high-velocity" environment?

This chapter is based on an inductive study of the strategic decision-making processes of firms operating in the high-velocity microcomputer industry (Bourgeois & Eisenhardt, 1987, 1988; Eisenhardt & Bourgeois, 1988; Eisenhardt, 1989). By high velocity, we mean those environments in which rapid and discontinuous change occurs in demand, competition, technology, or regulation in such a way that information is often inaccurate, unavailable, or obsolete. High-velocity environments involve continuous instability overlaid by sharp spikes of discontinuous change (Sutton, Eisenhardt, & Jucker, 1986). According to this definition, biotechnology, banking, and microcomputers are high-velocity industries. In contrast, although they score high on a dynamism index (Dess & Beard, 1984), cyclical industries such as machine tools are not.

The microcomputer industry is a prototypical high-velocity environment. The industry began in the mid-1970s as entrepreneurs took advantage of the new microprocessor technology. As will be described more fully later, the industry had a very high rate of technological change. It was also characterized by rapid changes in competition and demand. For example, the leading firms in 1983 were Texas Instruments, Commodore, Sinclair/Times, Atari, and Apple. By 1984, only Apple and IBM remained as major competitors. In some market segments, growth rates topped 100 percent per year.

Our initial research phase concentrated on the strategic decision-making processes of four microcomputer firms, two of which were successful and two that were not. We then expanded the study to include eight and then twelve firms, and more than seventy executives. The intent was to investigate the strategic decision-making process in a high-velocity environment. Previous research had emphasized large corporations such as DuPont, Xerox, and Chrysler (Chandler, 1962; Quinn, 1980), nonprofit organizations such as universities and government (March & Olsen, 1976; Janis, 1982), and laboratory simulations (Vroom & Yetton, 1973; Schweiger, Sandberg, & Ragan, 1986). In our view, such studies cannot capture the information vacuum and precarious nature of firms in fast-paced industries.

The design of the study is what Yin (1984) termed "multiple case." This design relies on a replication logic (Yin, 1984)—that is, the logic of treating a series of cases as a series of experiments—each case serving to confirm or disconfirm the inferences drawn from previous ones. Although a multiple-case design is more demanding than a single case, it permits induction of more reliable and richer models.

We interviewed every member of the top management team of each firm, including the chief executive officer (CEO) and other corporate officers. The teams typically included the heads of sales, finance, manufacturing, and engineering as well as the CEO. The interviews began with general questions regarding the firm's competitive strategy. Each executive was then asked to describe functional strategy, decision climate, and interpersonal interactions among the executive team. In the second portion of the interview, we traced the "story" of a strategic decision recently made within the firm. We used interview questions that concentrated on facts and events, not respondents' interpretations of their own actions or those of others.

We also gathered secondary source data, including financial results, press releases, journal articles, product data, and business plans, and we observed several executive meetings. We then carefully combed these data for patterns to develop our propositions.

The data indicated that the top executives in successful firms engaged in a fundamentally different strategic decision-making process than did the executives in the less successful firms. Specifically, our findings are a set of hypotheses in the form of three paradoxes:

The *first paradox* is that top management teams of successful firms use highly rational and analytic decision-making processes, but they execute those processes in a short time period. Rapid decisions would seem to make sense in high-velocity environments. But rational, deliberate analysis would appear to require time, particularly in an information-scarce industry. Hence the paradox: quick yet rational deliberation. By contrast, the poor performers were often reactive in their strategic decision processes—they responded to outside events, rather than acting proactively—and they conducted few analyses and considered few alternatives. Often, they mulled over their choices for a long time, frequently for more than a year.

The *second paradox* is that successful firms are led by decisive, powerful CEOs, but their top management teams are equally empowered. Powerful, decisive entrepreneurs are the norm for start-up industries, but teams in which each functional vice president is more powerful in his own arena than the CEO, are not. The paradox: CEO power greater than the team's, and individual team member's power greater than the CEO's. Only among the low-performing firms did the CEO exercise the greatest influence in each decision area.

The *third paradox* is that the top management teams of more successful firms make bold, risky decisions that often challenged established industry norms, yet preserve safety by postponing decision implementation as long as possible through the use of carefully planned execution triggers. As a result, these firms might pioneer a leapfrog in technology or distribution, but they would plan to execute incrementally. The paradox: successful firms implement risky decisions safely.

We found that the top management teams in successful firms were able to resolve these paradoxes in their strategic decision-making processes. By contrast, we found that the top management teams of less successful firms lacked most, or even all, of these characteristics.

In this chapter we illustrate the strategic decision-making challenges of high velocity environments that give to these paradoxes. We also describe how these paradoxes were played out in one firm. From the study, we selected a high-performing firm, which we refer to as Zap Computers. At the time of the study (1984–85), Zap was emerging as one of the premier firms in the microcomputer industry. Zap has since continued its rise to the top of the industry. The firm's success in dealing with the three paradoxes make it a particularly rich case for illustrating the results of our study.

We begin this chapter with a sketch of the microcomputer industry. We then highlight the strategic decision-making challenges posed by the microcomputer industry, and illustrate their resolution at Zap by tracing the story of an actual strategic decision process. We conclude with several managerial lessons for strategic decision making in high-velocity environments.

THE MICROCOMPUTER INDUSTRY, 1976–87

The microcomputer industry began quietly in the mid-1970s as electronics hobbyists started tinkering with the newly developed microprocessor. From this modest beginning, the industry has become one of the most rapidly growing and dynamic industries within the U.S. economy. By 1987 the annual shipment of personal computers alone exceeded $20 billion and represented about 30 percent of the worldwide computer dollar shipments by U.S.-based vendors. This compares with only 7 percent in 1980 and close to 0 percent in 1976 (Sharma & Bourgeois, 1988). Equally impressive are the achievements of some of the firms within the industry. For example, Apple Computer was the first U.S. company to reach the Fortune 500 within five years of founding, and Compaq was the first to reach $100 million in sales in its first year of operation.

The original PC, a crude machine capable of communicating with the user in machine language only, was developed in 1975 by Ed Roberts of MITS, an Albuquerque-based company, and sold as a "to-assemble" kit to computer hobbyists (Sharma & Bourgeois, 1988). The unexpectedly favorable market acceptance of this machine stimulated the entrepreneurial spirit of engineers and businesspeople, and soon a number of companies jumped into the fray. In 1976 Commodore became the first large, established company with extensive channels of distribution to enter the market, introducing the Commodore Pet in October. In 1977, the most notable new entrants were two Californians, Steve Jobs and Steve Wozniak, the hobbyist/founders of Apple Computer.

In the early days the microcomputer industry was characterized by a missionary zeal in promulgating the new technology, and a counterculture style of managing. Jeans and open-collared shirts, sported by bearded computer mavericks, were the norm for office attire. Fun often ranked with profitability among key corporate goals. The chief users as well as the designers and company presidents were hobbyists at heart and regularly exchanged technical information with each other at forums such as the Homebrew Computer Club and the Presidents Only poker game. One flamboyant entrepreneur even funded his employees to found firms to compete with his own. The atmosphere in the companies was casual, and the MBA was an infrequently spotted species.

The 1970s were a formative period—a time of experimentation with new technology. However, that all changed in the early 1980s as start-up fever swept the industry. Demand exploded and products proliferated. Apple proved to be an appealing example to many would-be entrepreneurs. Almost everyone wanted to achieve the "entrepreneurial dream," exemplified by Apple, of building a successful company and garnering personal wealth. The number of microcomputer start-ups surpassed earlier waves of venture activity in mainframes and in minicomputers. Lured by venture capital and the opportunity of microprocessor technology, the number of start-ups soared to unprecedented numbers. *Business Week* (1982) estimated that 140 new companies were founded between 1977 and 1982. The industry rocked and surged upward. Motorola introduced the 68000, a 16-bit microprocessor with an 8 MHz clock, which served as the hardware platform for many new microcomputer products. AT & T licensed its proprietary UNIX operating system to all comers, and the 64K RAM memory chip roared onto the scene. The market and technical opportunities seemed unlimited.

What triggered the frenzy of the early 1980s? Entrepreneurs and their venture capital backers at last began to understand the fundamental importance of very large scale integrated circuit (VLSI) technology in general, and the microprocessor innovation in particular. The impact of the VLSI revolution was immense. For example, the raw computing speed of the Motorola family of microprocessors increased by a factor of 50 between 1975 and 1984 (Bell, 1984). Semiconductor firms introduced further enhancements such as math coprocessors, which "turbo-charged" the microprocessor. These semiconductor innovations, coupled with enhancements in software and computer architecture, in turn triggered substantial improvements in the price/performance ratios of computers. For example, the $4 million IBM 3081 mainframe computer delivered 0.6 floating point operations per second (FLOPS) per dollar while the IBM PC delivered 6.7 FLOPS per dollar—increasing price/performance by a factor of 7 (Bell, 1984)! On average, the microcomputer delivered approximately ten times the price/performance ratio of its big brother in a machine the size of a breadbox.

The low cost, small size, and ease of programming meant that hundreds more products could be built from microcomputer technology than were feasible from the older minicomputer technology. Not surprisingly, then, microcomputer products ranged from the portable or laptop computer, costing little more than $1000, to superminis based on micro technology, costing $250,000. The price/performance improvement and the miniaturization of components opened the way for interconnection among computers, and thus provided a much larger and more flexible array of computing alternatives (Bell, 1984).

The start-up fever of the early 1980s was also fueled by the explosion of venture capital. Changes in the tax treatment of capital gains and investor fascination with high-technology ventures combined to produce an abundance of capital for new microcomputer firms. However, venture capitalists brought more than money to the industry. As venture capitalists heightened their involvement in the microcomputer industry, organization structures became more traditional, entrepreneurs began writing business plans, and firms endeavored to present an acceptable front to large businesses who were becoming the principal customers (Sharma & Bourgeois, 1988). Many of the new entrepreneurs traded in their sandals and jeans for Bally shoes and business suits. They hired MBAs. They transformed their offices into "showcase" surroundings, designed to impress would-be Fortune 1000 customers.

Before the 1980s the battle for leadership was fought in the home computer market. However, the new generation of start-ups such as Altos, Convergent Technologies, and Fortune Systems, targeted the business segment. They began marketing high-performance, sophisticated systems based on the new generation of more powerful microprocessors. These microprocessors served as the "brain" for products ranging from single workstations to systems for two to eight users (*Business Week*, 1982). Customers could obtain the performance of a low-end minicomputer at a much lower price. By 1981 these machines were making substantial inroads into the low end of the traditional minicomputer market (*Business Week*, 1982).

Another group of start-ups—Apollo, Stratus, and Synapse—packaged microprocessors in systems priced at more than $30,000 and ranging up to $250,000. These systems included sophisticated software and innovative architecture to solve computing problems that challenged the higher-end products of the older minicomputer technology, especially in the engineering workstation and transaction-processing segments of the industry.

The biggest event of 1981, however, was the entrance of IBM into the industry. In August of that year, IBM announced its first-generation microcomputer, then called the "Personal Computer." The entrance of IBM was critical to the industry for several reasons (Sharma & Bourgeois, 1988):

1. IBM owned 70 percent of the mainframe market sold to the Fortune 1000. Because of this dominant position, "IBM" were the three best known letters in the computer industry. The firm's entry legitimized the microcomputer industry.
2. The firm adopted an "open architecture" for its microcomputers. This was an invitation to third parties to develop hardware and software for the machine. This third party involvement led to faster product innovation and price cutting, which in turn expanded the market.
3. The industry participants finally knew what IBM was doing—at last, Big Blue's cards were "on the table." This allowed the competitors to plan strategic responses.

The entry of IBM accelerated the tempo of the industry. According to Bell (1984), 1982 brought the introduction of the Winchester disk drive. In 1983, Pyramid introduced its revolutionary RISC architecture computer, the 90X, while Synapse unveiled its symmetric, high-availability multiprocessor. In 1984, Motorola fueled its microprocessor war with Intel by introducing the 68020 chip with floating point arithmetic, instruction cache, and 16 MHz clock. The year also brought the introduction of the Macintosh by Apple. And 1985 marked the release of the 256K RAM memory chip.

The industry spawned many kinds of competitors. Major firms such as Digital, Data General, Texas Instruments, and Hewlett-Packard exhibited the deliberate style of established firms, while a gambling approach characterized many of the start-up firms. However, even among the newer firms, there were highly diverse approaches to managing. For example, the *Wall Street Journal* (Bulkeley, 1987) description of two combatants, Apollo and Sun, captured the diversity of styles among microcomputer firms. Apollo was described as building an image of solid, long-term reliability. It was a company moving to a more buttoned-down, traditional corporation. In contrast, Sun was characterized as ebullient and even "loony." The firm was well known for its April Fool's pranks, frequent beer bashes, and uproarious celebration of Halloween. Its corporate style typified "protocol-free" California.

The turmoil of the 1980s was accompanied by rapid changes in demand and competition. Although shipments of multiuser microcomputers doubled between 1981 and 1984, and personal computer shipments topped 7 million per year in the same time period (*Business Week*, 1986), the number of competitors also grew rapidly. Moreover, constant technological jolts shook and even shocked the industry. There was no dominant design and very little standardization of individual technical choices. For example, the pioneering operating system, CP/M, was challenged first by proprietary operating systems such as that of Apple. It was then challenged by the UNIX operating system, which AT&T licensed to all comers. IBM then hooked up with Microsoft to produce the DOS operating system option. Choices among these options were difficult for microcomputer executives. No one knew which, if any, operating system would become the industry standard—and for how long. Yet industry executives had to choose among the options in order to design products, and once chosen, operating systems were difficult to change because the design of an entire product hinged on this choice.

Microprocessor technology was equally volatile. In fact, the jump from the 8-bit to the 16-bit and then the 32-bit microprocessor created the need for changes in operating systems in the first place. In addition, Intel, Motorola, and later National Semiconductor carried on microprocessor "wars." Each jump in microprocessor technology made microcomputers based on the older technology obsolete almost immediately. Microcomputer executives were forced to guess when these spikes in technology would occur. Staying with older microprocessor technology risked product obsolescence, while jumping into newer technology risked leaping into unproven technology.

Industry executives also faced volatility regarding distribution channels and computer architecture. The industry began with use of mail-order and retail distribution channels. Should a firm sell through these traditional outlets or switch to others such as a direct sales force, manufacturer's reps, or resellers who repackaged the equipment under their own label? IBM surprised the industry with its open computer architecture in the personal computer. Before the IBM move, most producers used proprietary, closed architectures. Should a firm move to the open architecture strategy? Pyramid and Ridge inaugurated RISC-based machines, which then very successfully competed against full instruction set computers. Should a firm adopt the RISC-based computer architecture as a long-term strategy?

The market and technological turmoil of the 1980s brought success to firms such as Sun and Apollo, but it humbled others. For example, Gavilan and Osborne developed excellent products, but made mistakes in the timing of product introductions and manufacturing planning. They are now out of business. Other firms such as Durango and Synapse were too late with their product; both ran out of money as their venture capitalists tired of waiting for the dream to happen. Even mighty Digital Equipment stumbled. The firm produced a "me, too" machine that was obsolete before it hit the market. Texas Instruments entered the market and subsequently withdrew. Early winners such as Convergent, Corvus, and Televideo struggled to repeat initial successes. By 1984, the industry had encountered its first slowdown in demand. This further squeezed the marginal competitors out of the industry. Many of the entrants, including Morrow, Northstar, Eagle, Victor, Durango, Molecular, and Osborne, are now gone. Although the downturn in demand ended as industry sales ramped up in 1986, many executives still find that success is elusive in the microcomputer industry. And the pace of change continues.

STRATEGIC DECISION MAKING IN HIGH-VELOCITY ENVIRONMENTS

Many approaches to developing strategy rely on extensive processing of industry information (Hofer & Schendel, 1978; Porter, 1980). However, the rapid change and discontinuous jolts of high-velocity environments such as the microcomputer industry create a situation in which information is often inaccurate, incomplete, and obsolete. Thus, executives are faced with strategic choices for which they have poor and often no data. In the microcomputer industry, such choices as distribution channels, financing, microprocessor, and operating system are little more than "shots in the dark."

For example, consider the choice of microprocessor, a crucial strategic decision given its centrality in the design of a microcomputer. A top management team could choose to design its new product around a new microprocessor, which is not yet functional, or it could stay with existing technology. The information needed to make this choice is often faulty. Semiconductor firms are notoriously optimistic about the promised features of new microprocessors, compatibility with existing software, and delivery schedules. Information is often incomplete as well. For example, it is not always known which microprocessor will become the new industry standard. There are often rumors afoot, but rarely does an executive team actually know what will happen. Information may be obsolete. For example, has another microprocessor vendor already designed a chip that will make the one under study by the executives obsolete? Have competitors already incorporated the new design features, or is a new computer architecture being developed that makes the chip under study irrelevant?

Executives could conduct extensive analyses of technology and competition, but both are likely to change before the study is complete. This suggests that the usual strategic decision models, which involve gathering data, formulating alternatives, and then making a choice, are too information-dependent and time-consuming in a high velocity environment.

Decision-Making Strategy

Given that information in such fast-paced environments is at best questionable, what is an appropriate decision strategy? One possible strategy is the *imitation* or *me, too* approach. For example, a number of microcomputer firms followed one another into the small business microcomputer market. Although such an imitation strategy may seem attractive, it leads to overcrowded niches, such as occurred in this segment of the industry as well as in the disk-drive industry. In the case of the small business segment, some of the early entrants such as Televideo and Convergent were initially quite successful, but ultimately they and most other competitors could not successfully differentiate their products. Competition became fierce, overcapacity ensued, and profit margins plummeted.

Another strategy is simple to *wait and see* how the industry will shake out and then follow the strategies of the survivors. For example, a top management team could delay its choice of distribution channel until the successful choice becomes apparent. However, this decision strategy is an option only for the truly dominant competitor such as IBM. For most other competitors, the windows of opportunity are lost to those who wait. For example, Altos entered the multiuser microcomputer market early, captured the premier distribution outlets, and honed its manufacturing process on early volume. Later entrants such as Molecular and Durango were forced to use secondary distributors and were saddled with higher costs. Neither firm is now in business.

If both the "imitation" and the "wait and see" strategies are flawed because they are too slow, perhaps a *gambling* decision strategy is appropriate. That is, executives could simply make their bets and hope for the best. Certainly executives sometimes beat the odds and guess correctly, as did Osborne executives with the introduction of the world's first portable computer. However, as Osborne's managers learned, the odds of guessing correctly more than once are very small. When they gambled again with the early announcement of a new product, they miscalculated several key demand and production factors. The firm is no longer in business. The gambling decision strategy neglects the need, especially for resource-constrained young firms, to avoid mistakes. Although the strategy solves the delay problems of "imitation" and "wait and see," it heightens the probability of making fatal errors.

The problem with each of these decision-making approaches is that they fail to confront the key issue of strategic decision making in high-velocity environments: quick maneuvering without making mistakes. Several of our successful executives offered analogies to describe how they achieved both of these dimensions. One executive likened the process to race car driving: reflex is critical, but it helps to know the course. Equally colorfully, another executive compared strategic decision making in the microcomputer industry to playing video games—a far different image from the calculating chess player. Using these simple analogies as starting points, we probed our case data for patterns that distinguished successful firms from the less successful. We defined success in terms of CEO self-report and economic performance. The "best" firm grew at rates of 25 to 50 percent per quarter and is now a billion-dollar corporation. The three worst went bankrupt within a year of the study. Our efforts produced three paradoxes of strategic decision making that the successful microcomputer firms resolved and unsuccessful firms did not:

1. A quick, yet rational, strategic decision process.
2. A decisive, powerful CEO, yet an equally empowered top management team.
3. Bold, yet safe decisions.

In the following sections, we illustrate how the very successful top management team at Zap resolved these paradoxes in their strategic decision process.

ZAP: A SUPERSTAR IN THE MICROCOMPUTER INDUSTRY

Zap (a pseudonym to ensure the confidentiality of those executives observed for this study) is a manufacturer of microcomputers for professionals. The firm sells to a small number of OEMs and universities and is noted for its innovative technology and aggressive style. The firm is widely considered to be one of the premier success stories in the microcomputer industry. The firm's financial performance has been spectacular, with growth fluctuating between 25 and 100 percent per quarter. Most observers agree that Zap is an industry superstar.

The president of Zap is bright, energetic, and young. He holds an MBA from a prestige program. He is not a technologist himself, but others on the team are. He is regarded as a people-oriented, consensus-style manager. The top management team has a blend of experienced industry pros and young innovative comers who seem unaware of what cannot be done. Several of the senior vice presidents provide fatherly counsel to the president on an informal basis, and the president uses these executives as sounding boards and as a proxy for experience.

Zap executives are performance-driven. The executive suite exudes a feeling of breathlessness that is characterized by bursts of energy, rapid communications, and short sentences. Zap executives place a premium on acting rapidly, and they appear to spend little time engaged in casual conversation with one another. There is a "no-time-for-BS" orientation among Zap executives.

The strategic decision studied at Zap was "should the firm form a strategic alliance or go public to raise additional funds?" Zap executives had always planned to one day "cash in" by going public. However, Zap executives did not focus on this decision until one June when they observed potential problems with cash flow in the coming months. These problems surfaced in the budgeting process. The cash flow projections that triggered this decision were part of the very analytic orientation taken by Zap executives. As one executive told us, "We over-MBA it."

In light of these apparent cash flow problems, Zap executives sought outside confirmation. The vice president of finance described the team's first move as follows: "We were suspicious of the in-house model, so the banks and the investment bankers wrote new models. They all came up with the same answer (that is, cash flow problems on the horizon)."

With this background in finance, the president took charge of the decision. Initially, the team considered the alternatives of bank loans and additional venture capital—their past avenues to obtain additional financing. However, by July the option of going public had come to the fore. The pres-

ident described to us several key issues surrounding whether the firm should
go public:

> What drives what we do in this case is IBM. It impacts timing and (stock) val-
> uation. We're expecting them to have a product announcement in January. There
> are two points of view on this. One, is that we should go public now—prior to
> the product introduction—so that it won't have a depressing effect on our stock
> price. The other is that we should wait until IBM shows its machine, and once
> the public (customers) sees how lousy it is, then we should go public. So the first
> factor is IBM.
>
> The second factor is liquidity—liquidating peoples' holdings in the firm. Liquid-
> ity is good for each individual's net worth. But it's also bad. There is a question
> of whether people will sell their stock, get rich and just leave.
>
> The third item is the "war chest syndrome." We need a deep war chest to weather
> a variety of things: IBM's moves in the marketplace, losing people, losing cash.
> When you've got a big war chest, it's easy to go out and borrow more money.
> It's when you don't have any money that it's hard to come up with more, or to
> go public.

However, the president was not the only Zap executive to have a perspective on whether the firm should go public. Several were concerned by
the constraints and scrutiny associated with being a public firm. They noted
that revenues and earnings would have to be smoothed for quarterly reporting purposes because Wall Street punishes volatility. This smoothing would
constrain the operations of the firm. For example, the vice president of
R & D said, "To go public we need to keep our lines [growth rates] more
even." The VP of engineering added that going public "also means a lack of
flexibility. Companies are judged on a short-term basis, so there is a lot more
scrutiny." The VP of finance claimed that "there is quarter to quarter pressure on earnings—(we would have to avoid) hiccups."

Another concern was that a public offering would reduce the attractiveness of the firm to "star" R & D recruits. The VP of finance outlined this
issue for us. Every employee is a stockholder. Going public diminishes the
attractiveness of the firm to new key employees since it would mean that
"ground floor" equity positions would no longer be available. The VP of
engineering echoed the view that being a public company would mean the
loss of a major recruiting tool.

Overall, although most top executives at Zap stood to gain substantial
financial rewards from a public offering, there were mixed feelings about its
timing. One VP, an Osborne veteran, wanted to go public immediately; several others preferred to wait.

While Zap executives analyzed their various options, the strategic alliance alternative surfaced. This option first emerged on an airplane flight in
midsummer. As the president recalled, "I developed it with Jim [VP of en-
gineering] on an airplane. We were just sitting there for a few hours and just
started talking." During the course of the conversation, the option took
shape. The president described the strategic alliance option as follows:

The idea is to talk to 10 or 12 corporate investors who make strategic sense. . . . My motivation for this is that the structure of the industry is going to change dramatically. If we can be seen to be in partnership with some very strong play-ers—and this partnership is not just financial, of course, we also have some tech-nological reasons to be in partnership with them—then we will float to the top of the shake out [in the industry]."

Subsequently the president talked with board members over breakfast at a local pub. The president also sought the counsel of the VP of sales, one of the veteran executives on the team, and again sought the advice of the VP of engineering. During this time period, the president used staff meetings to keep the others informed. As he described it, "Everybody gives advice in-formally. They are my devil's advocates." The officers used the staff meet-ings to question the president on the status of the decision and to voice their opinions on the various options. There was substantial conflict among the executives. However, most were content simply to express their opinions.

The president ultimately favored the strategic alliance option. While con-tinuing to keep the VPs informed and involved, the president laid out a cal-endar and convinced the Board of the merits of his plan. However, simul-taneously, the president directed the team to make plans for an initial public offering. Every functional executive was instructed to formulate plans to go public as it related to their area of the firm. Thus, by August the decision to seek a strategic alliance was made, with going public poised as a backup option.

Events continued to move at a quick pace. The president summarized the events of the fall for us: "By August we were interviewing a few inves-tors. By September we had agreed with one. We signed [the alliance agree-ment] in October and the money was in November. If it hadn't worked, we would have gone public in December."

Thus Zap executives pursued the strategic alliance option, but simulta-neously programmed the initial public offering to occur, given some key con-tingencies and specific triggers. If the triggers were encountered, the VPs had developed action plans for their functional area within the firm. With these plans in hand, Zap was poised to move very quickly if the strategic alliance option had failed or the timing of an initial public offering became favorable.

THE FIRST PARADOX: A QUICK YET RATIONAL STRATEGIC DECISION PROCESS

The Zap case illustrates resolution of the first paradox: quick, yet rational, strategic decision process. Consistent with the paradox, the Zap strategic decision process was highly analytical. It was triggered by the formal bud-geting system. Consistent with rational analysis, Zap executives also ana-lyzed a relatively wide range of options for Zap's projected cash flow prob-lems, including additional venture capital, bank loans, a public offering, and a strategic alliance. Zap executives also considered a variety of factors in making their choice, including quantitative ones such as the likely amount of cash to be raised in each option and less tangible ones such as the effects on recruiting R & D stars. Moreover, this use of rational analysis and quantitative data was typical of strategic decision making at Zap. For example, Zap's president volunteered the exact quantitative targets for revenue, and administrative, selling, and R & D expenses. We also found that Zap executives reviewed a much wider array of quantitative measures on a regular basis than did most top management teams. These measures included revenue/employee, margins, backlog, scrap, cash, and inventory. Finally, Zap executives relied on weekly financial modeling simulations to run their business.

However, at the same time, Zap executives moved quickly: the alliance decision was made in less than four months and executed shortly thereafter. Zap executives belied the old saw, "analysis paralysis." Rather, the firm's budgeting system enabled Zap executives to diagnose impending cash flow problems quickly—before they were out of control. Zap executives also maintained the speed of the process by using what we have termed "qualified consensus" (Eisenhardt & Bourgeois, 1988) to resolve conflict. The Zap president attempted to gain consensus from his entire top management team, but when it was not forthcoming, he made the choice himself. Finally, Zap's president made particular use of the expertise and industry wisdom of his more senior executives. While he kept all informed, he focused his conversations on the most knowledgeable members of the team. This too cut decision-making time.

In contrast, the less successful teams were unable to combine rational analysis with decision speed. In most cases the strategic decision was triggered by external events. For example, at one less successful firm, the decision to develop a new product arose at the insistence of board members. At another such firm, the decision arose from a lawsuit directed at the firm. Also, in these less successful cases, the executive teams analyzed few alternatives, often only one. There was also much less use of quantitative data. For example, we asked one CEO to describe his quantitative targets. He replied that he had none; rather, integrity was key for him. Overall, at the less successful firms, the decision process was incremental, rather than rational and analytic as was the case at Zap.

Regarding the speed of the decision process, many of the less successful teams took more than a year to make their decisions. Among these firms, we observed several patterns (Eisenhardt, 1989). In some cases, CEOs delayed in the hopes that the team would reach consensus, but this consensus never happened. In other cases, we observed that the CEO analyzed and made the decision alone, without consultation. However, this often proved too time-consuming in light of the CEO's other duties. Overall, the teams at less successful firms seemed to become paralyzed by the turmoil and ambiguity of the industry. As an executive at one such firm told us, "Yes, you don't know any more even though you wait. Maybe we saw too much mystery, maybe we needed more gut."

THE SECOND PARADOX: A DECISIVE CEO, YET AN EQUALLY EMPOWERED TOP MANAGEMENT TEAM

The Zap case also illustrates the resolution of the second paradox: decisive CEO, yet an equally empowered top management team. Zap's president made a decisive move that was not popular with many of his executives. However, he kept each of them informed, especially in staff meetings, and the executives all conveyed their views to the president. Although his decision was at odds with the preferences of some of the VPs, the executives told us that their views were heard and thoughtfully considered. The president also maintained an empowered team by delegating the major tasks of the initial public offering to each VP for his or her own area. More generally, the president was described as "decisive" yet also as having a "consensus style" and being "people-oriented." We verified this qualitative data with quantitative results from questionnaires. We computed a power map at Zap, which indicated the power of every executive in each of five functional areas (marketing, R & D, operations, finance, organization) as rated by the entire team. At Zap the president was a very powerful individual, but the functional executives (except the VP of finance) retained the greatest power in their own areas.

In contrast, in less successful firms, there was no balance of power between the CEO and the rest of the top management team. In several cases CEOs had almost absolute control of power. They were described by phrases such as "THE decision maker," and "he runs the whole show." Power maps for these top management teams indicated that the CEO dominated decision making in every functional area. The result of this highly autocratic power structure was often extensive politicking and a stymied strategic decision process. In other cases, the CEOs appeared relatively powerless. Bickering among top management blocked decision making. Although many views were heard, very little new information was conveyed. As time dragged on, these firms missed strategic windows, and performance faltered.

THIRD PARADOX: A BOLD DECISION, YET A SAFE, INCREMENTAL EXECUTION

Finally, the Zap case illustrates the resolution of the third paradox: bold, risky decision, yet safe, incremental execution. The choice of a strategic alliance was, at the time of the study, an innovative one. Most firms sought additional venture capital or took their chances in the initial public offering market. However, this bold move was not an isolated occurrence. Zap executives were known throughout the industry as innovative and aggressive competitors.

Although making an innovative move, Zap executives mitigated the risk of their choice by negotiating with several alliance partners simultaneously, expanding their bank credit lines, and carefully planning the timing and actions associated with the going public alternative. Regarding the public offering, Zap executives identified decision triggers and all functional VPs had coordinated plans for execution during a public offering. With regard to the alliance option, Zap's president proceeded with negotiations with several potential allies. Thus, if the strategic alliance proved unworkable or if stock market or other conditions changed suddenly, the firm was poised to shift quickly either to another alliance partner or to a public offering.

In contrast, our less successful firms could not resolve this paradox. Several of the top management teams in these less successful firms simply chose to remain with the status quo or to pursue a familiar alternative. The financial performance of these firms was often stagnant. Other, less successful, teams did make bold strategic choices. However, in several such cases, the choice was never actually executed. In other cases, the teams made bold choices, but also pursued a risky path of execution. For example, one team made a risky technology leap to an operating system that was still being programmed by one of the major software firms. However, these executives did not couple that move with a safe execution strategy. When the operating system was delayed, these executives had to delay their product because they had no fallback position. The firm ran out of money and was not recapitalized by its investors.

In summary, Zap executives were able to confront the critical constraints of speed, decisiveness, innovation, analysis, and caution in a way that other executives in less successful firms were not. These latter executives often seemed unable to deal with the extreme ambiguity of a high-velocity environment. They became either paralyzed by the uncertainty or impetuous and even rash—neither of which is successful in an environment that places a premium on rapid, high-quality decision making.

IMPLICATIONS FOR STRATEGIC DECISION MAKING IN HIGH-VELOCITY ENVIRONMENTS

Many scholars of strategic decision making have focused their efforts on large corporations (Chandler, 1962; Quinn, 1980; Mintzberg & Waters, 1982) or nonprofit organizations (Pfeffer & Salancik, 1974; March & Olsen, 1976). In these situations, perhaps a trade-off between quality and speed in the strategic decision process is viable (Vroom & Yetton, 1973; Janis, 1982). But the constraints faced by firms in high-velocity environments are much different. Managers cannot simply imitate the strategies of others or wait and see what will be successful. They cannot take too many gambles because even one mistake can be fatal. Rather, the velocity of the microcomputer industry and industries like it does not allow managers the luxury of trade-offs between decision quality and speed.

What are the implications of our studies for managers in fast-moving environments? We suggest the following:

1. Be alert to signals that suggest the possible need for strategic change. If possible, build those signals into real-time information systems that give

the decision makers a "jump" on diagnosing the need for strategic shift. In Zap, the formal budgeting system provided forecasts of monthly cash flow— a critical variable for fast-growing start-ups.

2. Continuously consider alternative options to the present course. If change comes quickly to the industry, there may be little time to adjust. Known alternatives can be analyzed and implemented quickly.

3. When pressure mounts to address strategic change, do not wait. Analyze many options, but do so quickly by focusing on key facets of the alternatives. This yields high-quality analysis in a short period of time.

4. Do not wait for consensus—it may never come. Rather, take counsel, especially from the experienced executives who have the most to contribute to the decision. Then act decisively. Busy executives do want a voice, especially in their own area of the firm, but they also want leadership. As we saw in Zap, the decision was not universally popular, but the managers were kept fully informed. Decisiveness at the top allowed them to "get on with business" at their normally furious pace.

5. Take bold actions because imitation and follower strategies are too slow. But, guard against error by maintaining an array of options for as long as possible. This allows the firm to switch to alternative options if and when discontinuities in the environment render the original inclinations obsolete.

In summary, there has been increasing interest in the linkage between superior performance and the resolution or paradox (Van de Ven, 1983; Cameron & Quinn, 1988). The story of the microcomputer industry and the strategic decision-making process of one of its most successful firms indicate that resolution of paradox is possible and even essential in the strategic decision processes of firms in high-velocity environments.

6

Dynamic Tension in Innovative, High Technology Firms: Managing Rapid Technological Change Through Organizational Structure

CLAUDIA BIRD SCHOONHOVEN AND MARIANN JELINEK

People look at organizational change as, "Somebody did something wrong." That's nuts, because there's absolutely no reason why an organization that you created two years ago has any relevance to the organization that you need two years from now. The beauty of this business is that the technology will always change (and thus) the organization, the interfaces, the customer interfaces, and the vendor interfaces are always going to change, because of the technology.

Les Vadasz, senior vice president, Intel

Eternal innovation seems the price of survival in contemporary economic competition, and this is especially true for high technology firms. Survival depends on maintaining a steady stream of innovative microelectronic products manufactured in high volume by frequently changing state-of-the-art technologies. In this chapter we ask how organizations that must continuously innovate over time can manage the dominant competitive issue of innovation. Our focus is not merely on the creation of a single high technology innovation; rather we are concerned with how companies create a *stream of innovations* that are commercially successful. Innovations that have repeated marketplace success are our concern.

We examine how companies organize for innovation, drawing from a longitudinal study of five highly innovative U.S. electronic firms that manufacture and compete in the semiconductor components, systems, and computer marketplaces. We interviewed more than 100 high technology managers and engineers and discovered that they do not view the organizing process in dichotomous, simplistic, either/or terms. Instead we found complex organizational processes in these companies, which did not conform to the simple organizing models that pervade contemporary management textbooks. Today's textbooks still describe organizations as either organic, and thus appropriately structured for innovation and change, or mechanistic, and thus appropriately structured for steady-state technologies and environmental stability. One best-selling yet typical management text notes that "a particular organization . . . should be structured depending upon whether it must be (1) relatively efficient and productive or (2) adaptive and flexible" (Donnelly, Gibson, and Ivancevich, 1984, p. 196). The dominant prescription, therefore, is that organizations should be structured for either efficiency or flexibility. However, what if conditions require both *flexibility and efficiency*? Neither of these simplistic recipes for organizing comes close to adequately describing the subtleties and nuances required to organize for a continuous stream of state-of-the-art innovations that also enjoy success in the marketplace.

It is clear from our research that commercial success is a function of an organization's innovative ability as well as its ability to efficiently produce what it has created. The old flexible-versus-efficient formula will not work because these companies must do four things successfully and simultaneously, not merely one. First, they must innovate high technology products. Second, they must innovate their manufacturing processes, because success depends heavily on more and more sophisticated manufacturing techniques. Third, they must efficiently manufacture in high volume a continuously changing set of products and manufacturing techniques—neither remains stable for long—so steady-state manufacturing is not possible, and yet manufacturing efficiency is incredibly important here, just as it is in other non–high technology industries. And, fourth, their innovative products must have high market cachet: it is the market test that ultimately determines success for these companies. This imposes a dynamic tension on the organizations to be simultaneously clearly structured for efficiency while adapting to organizational modifications required by changes in their technical and market conditions. The companies we have studied pass this test, time after time, product after product. The old organizing formulas do not work because they underestimate the complex set of activities with which high technology companies must simultaneously contend to be successful, and thus for which they must be organized simultaneously.

The old formulas will not work for a second reason. Microelectronic and contemporary electronic firms compete in environments that require both innovation and efficiency. Thus, external as well as internal conditions impose the dynamic tension. We agree with Lawrence and Dyer's assumption that a key environmental characteristic for these companies is high rates of technological change (1983). Where they and other contemporary theorists err, however, is in their failure to analyze the nature of the technological change. Both product and manufacturing process innovations characterize the semiconductor, systems, and computer industries. Whenever process change is required, new efficiencies must be gained quickly despite uncertainties associated with applying the new manufacturing methods. The "end game" of manufacturing, even in the highly dynamic semiconductor industry, nonetheless dictates a strong need for efficiency. Manufacturing costs must be as low as possible to compete in these industries. Similarly, if these companies are to efficiently develop new products, clearly an organic, amorphous structure will not allow them to create new product designs in the least wasteful manner possible. Efficiency is defined as performing or functioning in the least wasteful manner possible—an essential characteristic of contemporary electronic competition.

The companies included in our research are Intel, National Semiconductor, Texas Instruments, Hewlett-Packard, and Motorola Semiconductor—all highly successful in creating rapid innovations over time. We used a longitudinal research design and tracked the companies from 1981 to 1988, to record changes and shifts in the companies' products, markets, technologies, and organizations. We interviewed over 100 innovation-knowledgeable people in these firms, starting with their founders and chief executive officers, down through vice presidents, division general managers, and R & D managers, to design and manufacturing engineers. We sought the perspectives of those involved in innovation and its management from the top to the bottom of these companies. The reader will recognize some of the leaders of innovation we interviewed—Charlie Sporck, David Packard, John Young, Gordon Moore, Les Vadasz, and Jerry Junkins. Others equally crucial to our research have been less publicly visible: Ted Hoff, the inventor of the microprocessor, Ed Boleky, a fabrication manager, and Steve Pease, an applications engineer. It is through their words that we illustrate our major findings on how contemporary high technology firms organize for a stream of commercially successful innovations over time.

OLD RECIPES AND NEW REALITIES

How does Hewlett-Packard coordinate and effectively direct the work of 84,000 employees to produce a constant stream of new, complex products? How does National Semiconductor keep track of the roughly 3500 different types of complex microelectronic products it offers at any given time—products that account for less than half of its overall revenues? How do any of these companies manage the innumerable and shifting activities of thousands of people, products, and technologies that are their world? For a company to continuously produce commercially successful innovations, year after year, suggests that an explicit management of the innovation process takes place. It also suggests that a mechanism exists to capture the attention of employees in a systematic way.

The companies we have studied are large, by any standard, and very complex organizationally. Their employees create, develop, and manufacture complicated microelectronic devices that govern satellites, robots, and computers of all sizes. How do these companies manage to pull off such an incredibly complicated set of simultaneous activities whose results form the heart of the information technology essential to the success and well-being of every industrial nation in the years ahead?

It has been clear to us from the beginning of this research that no single innovative idea is enough. Any single idea, be it for a new product or a new technology, is overwhelmingly insufficient. Good, even great ideas must be marshaled, financially supported, in tune with the marketplace, and efficiently manufactured. At virtually every step of the way, these processes involve complex activities requiring a host of contributors whose participation must be effectively timed, coordinated, monitored, and redirected as the need arises. In short, these activities must be organized and managed effectively. Ad hoc chance events will not do as an organizing philosophy. Explicit organization is the key to capturing the attention of thousands of employees who routinely create complicated end products. The pace of technical development is so fast that entire existing product lines can be obsolete within two years. As Intel's chairman, Gordon Moore, observed, "Every two years almost our entire product line turns over. We can almost go out of business in two years if we don't do it right."

To cope with the torrid pace of technology development, we found four key aspects of structure in these companies that interact to coordinate the many complex activities required in constant innovation: (1) a dynamic tension between (2) formal structures and reporting relationships, (3) quasiformal structures, and (4) informal structures of the organization. We will deal with each in turn; however, throughout this chapter the underlying emphasis remains on innovation, technical excellence, manufacturing efficiency, and marketplace success, and thus predictability amid near-constant change. This seemingly contradictory reality is central to success in the high technology markets of today and, we believe, will be increasingly important in many industries in the future.

We first reviewed the existing literature as a guide for our research. Although there are literally hundreds of studies relevant to the organization and management of innovation,[1] most advice to managers is derived from a groundbreaking study by British researchers Tom Burns and G. M. Stalker (1961). Basically, the best advice from the past was that innovation is best served by organizing according to principles of "organic management." Organic management is thought to enable firms to deal successfully with unpredictable technical and market contingencies, and these abound in the companies studied. In the original study of the British electronics industry, the companies that were high performers and innovative were organically managed to deal with the changing technical and environmental conditions they faced. Since high rates of technological innovation and environmental change have been well documented in the semiconductor, systems, and computer industries (Webbink, 1977; Jelinek, 1979; Schoonhoven, 1985), organic systems appeared to be the structure of choice for the companies we were about to study.

What specifically are these "organic structures" and management systems? The authors described organic systems as "adapted to unstable conditions, when . . . requirements for action arise which cannot be broken down and distributed among specialists . . . within a clearly defined hierarchy. Jobs lose much formal definition [and] . . . have to be redefined continually. Interaction runs laterally as much as vertically. Communication between people of different ranks tends to resemble lateral consultation rather than vertical command" (Burns and Stalker, 1961, pp. 5–6).

This definition makes intuitive sense, and yet a closer look reveals that it is unsatisfactory. When their ideas are analyzed more carefully, four separate dimensions of organic structure are implied: (1) ambiguous reporting relationships, with an unclear hierarchy; (2) unclear job responsibilities; (3) decision making is consultative and based on task expertise rather than being centralized in the management hierarchy; and (4) communication patterns are lateral as well as vertical (Schoonhoven and Eisenhardt, 1985). Burns and Stalker illustrated ambiguous reporting relationships with unclear hierarchy by their experience with the president of an electronics firm. When he began drawing the management hierarchy, his sketch "petered out in unresolved dilemmas. . . . There was, therefore, a deliberate avoidance of clearly defined functions and of lines of responsibility at the top level of management which . . . carried down through the rest of the management structure" (1961, pp. 83–85).

The second element of organic structure described by Burns and Stalker is that job responsibilities are indeterminant or unspecified. Managers and engineers in the electronic firms studied were unable to clearly state their job responsibilities. The authors reported that a product engineer said "nobody is very clear about his title or status or even his function." A foreman said, "Of course, nobody knows what his job is in here" (1961, p. 93).

Because these findings have remained unchallenged, we were led to expect ambiguous organizational structures, unclear reporting relationships, and indeterminant job responsibilities, given the competitive conditions facing semiconductor and computer firms. In short, we should have expected to find what contemporary writers have called unstructured, loosely coupled, amorphous adhocracies (Toffler, 1970; Weick, 1976; Mintzberg, 1979).

THE CONTEMPORARY STRUCTURE OF INNOVATION

Clear Organizations and Jobs

Our microelectronic firms certainly faced unpredictable, unstable conditions with complex problems. However, the problem is that the first two dimensions of an organic structure are worse than useless for providing the precise and definitive coordination, tight controls, high efficiency, and tough decision making needed in the fiercely competitive global marketplace. In contrast, contemporary semiconductor and computer firms, imbedded as they are in highly turbulent and changeful technical environments, display well-articulated structures, definite reporting relationships, and clear job responsibilities.

These firms are far from unstructured adhocracies. Quite the contrary, we found universally explicit reporting structures and clear hierarchies in which executives, managers, and engineers know who their bosses are, who their bosses' bosses are, who their reporting subordinates are, and who their organizational peers are at equivalent hierarchical levels in their organizations. There was simply no evidence of amorphous reporting, unclear hierarchy, or not knowing who is supposed to do what, as Burns and Stalker reported finding. All of the semiconductor and computer firms we studied had explicit organizational charts, readily available, and formalized from the top to the bottom of their companies.

In a few of our 100-plus interviews, managers were cautious in sharing these data with us, because organization charts are regarded as serious competitive information that reveal how the company organizes its work. Organization charts also typically reveal valued key employees whom some companies prefer to remain anonymous, obscured from their competitors' knowledge. In these cases, when a manager was not comfortable showing the explicit chart to us, he instead sketched one in our presence. None "petered out into unresolved dilemmas." None had unclear reporting relationships. The difference between our findings and those of Burns and Stalkers is striking.

In addition to having clear structures, the innovative and successful companies we have studied also have clear job responsibilities. This, too, contrasts with the earlier organic management research as well as with contemporary theories about adhocracies. We found that employees' titles and jobs are clear; they easily stated their titles and readily described their responsibilities. These are also printed on their business cards and listed on the organization charts, which were shared with us, providing more evidence of clarity. Thus independent of title, there is high predictability of who has responsibility for what throughout these companies. There was no evidence in any of our interviews of Burns and Stalker's famous quote, "nobody knows what his job is around here." In contrast, we found that these are high predictability organizations with clear job responsibilities and reporting relationships.

To illustrate how clearly structured these organizations are, Edward Boleky, a fourth-level manager at Intel, described his title, job responsibilities, and place in the organization, while sketching his organization on a chalkboard during the interview.

> I'm the California Site Fabrication Manager, responsible for three of Intel's wafer fabrication areas located in California. I'm one of four people reporting to Gerry Parker [corporate vice president for technology development]. My organization right now is relatively simple [writing on the board] . . . so I have three fab managers reporting directly to me, and I have a fellow who is running a task force . . . that involves a 32-bit microcomputer, the 8386. The fellow that's heading that reports to me, also.

Boleky continued by describing the remaining levels of reporting relationships in his organization, for which he was directly responsible. He drew out the positions that reported to the four positions that reported to him. One might predict clear structuring in a manufacturing subunit like Boleky's, but what about the structure of technology development, the heart of the innovative activity at Intel? Surely uncertain research activities would be more ambiguous and less clearly organized.

To understand how companies like Intel achieve a smooth and expeditious transfer of responsibility from development into high-volume production, we interviewed several managers and engineers in technology development. One of these was Kim Kokkonen, project manager in Static Random Access Memory (SRAM) Development. Kokkonen supervised a relatively small group of engineers who were developing an advanced semiconductor process technology, complementary metal oxide semiconductor (CMOS) process, and the first two SRAM products to be produced using the new CMOS technology. The semiconductor process and the new products would be transferred into manufacturing—actually into Boleky's fabs, described earlier.

When Kokkonen was asked to explain the transfer process, he immediately picked up paper and pencil and began to sketch an organization chart and a time line to express relationships over time. The organization Kokkonen drew started with the chief operating officer, Andrew Grove, followed by a direct report, Gene Flath, followed by Gerry Parker, the vice president and director of technology development, down to the groups that reported to Gerry Parker, including Kokkonen's in Static RAM Development. This was the exact same set of relationships Gerry Parker had drawn for us in a prior interview. There was high agreement on what the development organization was, who reported to whom, and what the separate positions and departments were. In Kokkonen's own department, SRAM Technology Development, there were thirty-five engineers and six program managers. Having drawn the entire organization, Kokkonen used the sketch to describe responsibilities of the various functions:

> Okay, this is me down here [pointing to the organization chart], and this [other] group is working on an advanced CMOS process. There's another group that's very similar to mine that's working on a different definition of a product that attacks different market segments. There is yet another group doing something similar. There's a group which does nothing but circuit designs, which take advantage of technologies which have already been developed and designs new circuits using those technologies. Finally, there's a basic module development group that develops some of the basic capabilities that we need to have: equipment development—things that aren't product or market related at all. An example would be lithography.

After describing his own organization, Kokkonen continued to explain how new developments are transferred into manufacturing, again going to paper and pencil. Here he drew a three-year timeline which he used to describe technology development at Intel and all of the various groups that come into play along the development cycle. In doing so, he described a clear set of relationships between eight separate development and manufacturing groups, each of which was bounded by time horizons and milestones along the path of development. In addition to his own SRAM development project group, the eight groups with which he and his engineers interfaced were new technology engineering (NTE), fab sustaining engineering, process reliability engineering, product reliability engineering, assembly engineering, product engineering, technology development test engineering, and technology exploitation group (TXG).

What is remarkable about these eight separate organizations is that Kokkonen, the project manager of six engineers, had crystal clear recall of these "interfaces," to use his term. Kokkonen was clear on what each of these groups was called, when each came into play along the development path, what each group was responsible for—in short, the entire picture. There was no fuzziness here, nor any failure to understand who is responsible for what or ambiguity regarding who these groups are. Kokkonen succinctly described their responsibilities, the key interfaces, and the transition points:

> My technology in general has about the most complex set of relationships to other subunits because we have a lot of internal ties. We also tie into all of the manufacturing arms of the company, in trying to transfer things. So the . . . things that we tie into: first the fab environment. There's a particular group set up in fab called "New Technology Engineering" (NTE) whose *defined job* is to spend the last year of development with us and the year after transfer of a [new manufacturing] process in cleaning up bugs and in just getting it ready for a full manufacturing environment.

As it developed, NTE was only the beginning of this complicated set of relationships. As Kokkonen continued, the entire diagram he had drawn came to life, with a heavy emphasis on reliability for the process as well as for the new products. As Kokkonen moved through the complete description of the life cycle of innovation at Intel, the extensive size of the Intel development and manufacturing activities became apparent, as did the complexities of dealing with the multiple groups. The project manager had fluently described the large number of people and groups with which he and his engineers had relationships, and the logic of the interfaces was perfectly clear to the listener. As to how he had developed this clear overview, Kokkonen remarked, "I think it's forced on you. The first time I didn't know all of this, but to get to this transfer point [into manufacturing], you have to deal with all of these people. . . . You just learn."

Similarly, in each of the other interviews at our five companies, no executive, project manager, or engineer was unable to clearly describe his title, job responsibilities, or the organization's structure of reporting relationships and the myriad of subunits within the structure.

The clear structure of these firms is deliberate, not a bureaucratic mistake. John Young, president and chief executive officer of Hewlett-Packard, provided some insight into this unexpected finding. He succinctly explained why there are clear reporting relationships at Hewlett-Packard: "I just think it helps 84,000 people, particularly when you're having a lot of changes, to see what you've done, what we're trying to accomplish, to make it as clear as you can what are the central thrusts of the organization."

We believe this is an important finding regarding the contemporary, innovating organization. As both a product of prior successes and a requisite for future success, these companies are highly complex organizations. They all produce thousands of products in multiple divisions, using state-of-the-art equipment and processes. The pace of technology development required to remain among the most successful innovators is murderous and will continue to be so. As a consequence, employees must have high predictability within their internal organizational environments. Clear structures and job responsibilities provide this predictability.

The lesson we derive from these data is the importance of a managed structure. With explicit reporting relationships, there is little of the predicted ambiguity of organic systems, and none of the wasteful uncertainty about to whom to turn. Structure is actively used to guide employees in the firms, for delimiting responsibilities, identifying connections between positions and people, and insuring that attention is actively allocated to appropriate tasks. In the midst of frequent product and manufacturing process changes and external competitive uncertainty, structure within these companies is clear. It provides high predictability for the behavior for organizations and subunits and rapid identification of needed resources and decision-making authority.

How, then, do these companies organize for repeated innovation? Very explicitly. These firms are characterized by highly effective, very explicit organizations, with well-understood and clearly articulated relationships. In retrospect, it could scarcely be otherwise. The activities undertaken by these firms are complicated, and cannot be undertaken except by large, sophisticated arrays of multidisciplined talent, marshaling substantial resources of equipment, dollars, and information. Wafer fabrication lines frequently cost millions of dollars, and very large-scale integrated circuit fabrication processes have hundreds of complicated steps. Without meticulous coordination and control, these processes simply will not be successful. Ad hoc organizations or loose, organic structures often recommended for innovation simply *will not do,* for the long run. Even if ad hoc arrangements might once have worked, their repeated success would be impossible, given the complexity of relationships, technologies, and product changes. Innovation in these firms is too important to leave to chance, and too complex to handle without explicit coordination. These companies need reliable, repeatable methods to bring good ideas from concept to product to market.

There is a puzzlement, however. How can we account for the high clarity of formal structure when Burns and Stalker and others have argued that a fluid, ambiguous, ad hoc structure is adapted to high rates of external change? If they do not have fluid, ambiguous structures, how do these highly innovation organizations adapt?

FREQUENT REORGANIZATION AND DYNAMIC TENSION

Two major differences are found when our data are compared with the earlier work of Burns and Stalker and more contemporary theorists. First, these innovating organizations *reorganize frequently,* and as a consequence, responsibilities and reporting relationships change to meet modified external and technical circumstances. This finding illustrates that one way in which high technology organizations adapt to technological and environmental change is by reorganizing, changing the formal components of the organization, rather than by so-called organic structures in which position responsibilities and reporting relationships are continuously ambiguous. This finding is also consistent with earlier research on reorganization in high technology industries (Schoonhoven, 1980). Thus, although clarity of formal reporting relationships and of position responsibilities is a consistent pattern in the successfully innovative companies we have studied, these companies are far from structurally inert. We have discovered that these organizations adapt to change by reorganizing their formal structures.

The second difference in our findings from that of others is that a *dynamic tension* is inherent in semiconductor and computer firms faced with changing markets, technologies, and manufacturing processes. On the one hand, continuity, control, and integration between functions and departments are required for the orderly process of new technology development and reliable, high-quality manufacturing. On the other hand, changing environments and technologies require organizational adaptability and flexibility. We refer to this as maintaining dynamic tension: the ability to be flexible through reorganizations as well as sufficiently systematic to be efficient producers. Organic structures do not include this dynamic tension, we have found—tension between clear structures and frequent reorganizations—but instead focus only on constant, free-form flexibility through amorphous organizational forms. Organic structures ignore the continuity and predictability of action which a clear structure provides for the organization and for its external constituencies.

It is important to recognize that these companies do not move from one adhocracy to the next, as some futurists have envisioned or as some have suggested innovative, high technology firms do (Toffler, 1970; Mintzberg, 1979). Adhocracies have been described as the "structure du jour"—the structure of whatever works for today's problems. However, if managers in an adhocracy perceived their problems as changed tomorrow, the structure du jour would be changed. Adhocracies also carry a highly temporal, spurious connotation, in which "you had to be there to appreciate it." Others in a large organization may not know how your subunit is structured if they have not checked recently. Lack of shared understandings and predictability of behavior is theorized to characterize adhocracies in a fast-changing, turbulent environment.

Rather than being organic adhocracies, the highly innovative companies we studied changed their structures when the problems for which the current structure was designed had changed; they shifted from one existing, clear structure designed for specific problems to another clear structure, maintaining a dynamic tension among organizational elements.

MANAGING STRUCTURAL CHANGE

We found that changes in formal structure are one of the principal tools by which the organization's executives can continue to keep their companies innovative but attuned to the current and anticipated future problems to face the company. Reorganizing the company signals an adaptation to a changed environment and technical circumstances for which the current organization is no longer appropriate, rather than a mistake in the original organizational structure as outsiders who do not understand the dynamic nature of the business often assume. Les Vadasz of Intel Corporation remarked, "People look at organizational changes as, 'Somebody did something wrong.' And that's nuts, because there's absolutely no reason why an organization that you created two years ago has any relevance to the organization that you need two years from now."

Vadasz has the distinction of wearing Intel Badge #3, signifying that he was Intel employee number three, after its two founders, Gordon Moore and Robert Noyce. Currently an executive vice president and a member of the Intel board of directors, Vadasz has witnessed how Intel's environment and technology have indeed been modified over the years: "And things *have* changed. The beauty of this business is that the technology will always change, the organizations, the organizational interfaces, the customer interfaces, the vendor interfaces. That's always going to change, because of the technology. To assume that your organization makes sense today, just because it made sense five years ago is really incorrect."

The prevalence and frequency of reorganization was indeed interesting to observe in these companies. We first began our interviews in the summer of 1981, and we completed the most recent interviews in 1988. Over this eight-year period, all of the companies made relatively a large number of changes to their formal organizations, both at the corporate level and at the division level. Obviously higher-level changes are more visible from the outside and may represent more significant reorganizations. Many more changes at operating levels occur with fewer external signs, and these modify the structure in very important ways. The experience of just one of our study companies, Hewlett-Packard, will suffice to illustrate the frequency and pervasiveness of structural change in these firms.

Hewlett-Packard

An explicit example of frequency of reorganization can be seen by tracing the organizational changes at Hewlett-Packard over the period of our work. In 1982, within six months of the beginning of our research, Hewlett-Packard began to make some externally visible organizational changes. John Young, H-P's chief executive, explained to us that these were the first of a set of organizational modifications designed to address the changing technical and market conditions in their computer business.

In 1982 H-P had "a really big problem, which, in 1985, we are still in the final throes of executing," said Young. The problem was to change their entire computer line around to a new architecture and to create a new family of computers. The long-term technical issues were still very much in the development stage, but H-P nonetheless had innovative computer products to offer its customers. As a consequence, in December 1982 H-P reorganized the computer group itself into more of a centralized marketing activity as well as a product division. Young explained his thinking on the reorganization in 1982:

> I really didn't want to disturb the product side of things until we had that really bolted down [technically]. Now [in 1985] that we have made more [technical] progress, I've made another change in the organization, and I think we feel we're in a position to deal with that. Again, that's a difference in that particular product, and now we've engineered things. We have one whole group that's doing nothing but engineering this one computer system: 800 professionals in it. This is quite a different [organizational] arrangement than we've ever had before.

In July 1984 H-P again reorganized as its markets continued to converge. For example, their traditional industrial computer users who needed test instruments, also needed to link the instruments to personal computers. H-P's structure, composed of relatively autonomous divisions, had made it difficult to take advantage of the converging markets. One sales force sold instruments and a separate sales force sold computers, even to the same customers. The result, according to one observer, was that "You had within H-P an instrument company and a computer company treating each other at arm's length while trying to do battle with IBM" (*Business Week,* 1984).

In 1984, within eighteen months of the creation of the personal computer group, H-P introduced three new products: a lap-sized computer named the Portable and two new printers called ThinkJet and LaserJet. In October 1984 John Young remarked that "creating the personal computer group was an extremely good way of getting a focus on marketing. It was a way of communicating to everyone that this marketing was okay; that it's okay to eat quiche" (Saporito, 1984). It was also a way of signaling to H-P insiders as well as to outsiders that the organization was formally addressing a hitherto untapped activity.

In mid-1984, the new position of "chief operating officer" was created to centralize authority and relationships among the divisions somewhat. Dean Morton was appointed, and a corporate marketing division was also created at that time, merging the computer and instrument sales forces to sell what is now referred to as an "integrated solution," not merely separate machines. At this time, while the management and organization of the overall computer division was modified, the personal computer group's organization was not changed.

The creation of a corporate marketing division was a major departure from Hewlett-Packard's usual methods of organizing. But the products and the markets were changing, and so was its structure. Long renowned for its engineering elegance and as a seller to an appreciative, technically trained customer base, H-P's employees had worked hard during the following two years to develop an equally elegant marketing capacity. Its vice president of the personal computer group was quoted as saying, "I keep telling my engineers that they now have five minutes to make a sale, not five hours like we used to. We have to focus on apparent user benefits." Dick Alberding, in 1984 the newly appointed corporate marketing head, spoke explicitly of the Hewlett-Parkard shift from simply great technical products to market share. "The personal computer industry is a market-share business. If you own 10 percent of the business, it's important to know what the incremental costs are to get more." Responding to implicit criticisms of H-P's marketing expertise at the time, John Young publicly stated, "I don't think HP is bad at marketing. It's just that we needed to accelerate the marketing to complement the engineering."

In 1985 Young described the causes of changes in organization structure made in the late summer of that year. His comments are worth lengthy quotation, because they lay out so clearly the connection between marketplace changes, technical shifts, and how restructuring helped deal with these. Both formal structures and what we call "quasi-structure" are apparent in Young's thinking.

> We see a lot of changes in the marketplace, over a period of years, I guess, both on the product as well as the customer side. The customer for our kinds of products used to be technically sophisticated people, buying things for them to work on, on their own. As we both changed the kinds of business to more information systems content, and even the technical side of that, customers have been growing less and less willing to do it themselves.
>
> Let's say the customer has been looking for more complete answers to their business or technical problems. This is what put pressure on the factory side, to conceive and deliver and support and document solutions that were very sophisticated in nature. Of course, all of this means more teamwork, more things that have to work together, more interaction between pieces of the organization, and less and less departmentalization, such is possible in traditional, division organizations.
>
> So, we still believe in small work groups, and we call those divisions at Hewlett-Packard, but we simply have to find ways of getting them to work more cooperatively, and to make sure that the system disciplines that are so essential are put in place.
>
> So, basically what we did on the factory side, is we organized things more on market centers, as opposed to product centers. On the field side, we dissolved those product linkages and turned them around into more of a customer team organization. That's been going along for a year now, with a lot of work in reestablishing those informal communications back and forth.

Explicit in Young's comments is a focus on structure as a management tool and on the importance of the interaction between formal organization and the quasi-formal activities of teams. Equally visible, however, is a shift from the prior focus on technical elegance as the selling point to *solving customers' problems*. The problems have changed, and thus the structure was reorganized.

Expecting Structural Change

Employees come to regard structural change as a part of life in companies like H-P, National, and Texas Instruments. They expect future changes, as well. Some of these anticipated changes are finer tunings of structure at lower levels. For example, Douglas Spreng, the division general manager of H-P's computer systems division, shared a recent formal organizational chart with us. This chart reflected the changes in structure that John Young describes in the preceding paragraphs. Spring offered the chart with a telling observation about structural change at H-P: "Do you want a copy of the corporate organization chart? In fact I've got a couple of slides I can give you that show the relationships too. They're probably in transition; six to nine months from now, they will probably be changed."

Spreng's comment was a straightforward observation on anticipated future modifications in H-P's structure, offered neither flippantly nor cynically. Instead, he was simply reflecting on likely consequences of changes in the relevant technologies that affected current businesses—and important marketplace realities. For example, Spreng speculated on what the near future changes in the structure might be, relevant to the businesses he was most familiar with:

> My guess is what we'll finally end up seeing is three businesses separately managed. But we're still sorting that out, because the last year has been rather complex, and it's not as clearly definable as the other two sets of changes in the organization (which have been made). We're taking a little longer time, because we do not want to take false steps. It's really important I think for us, if we make a step, that we make it firmly, and we go from there. [We won't] . . . do any herky-jerky . . . as some of the things in the past [have been].

This thoughtful division general manager was among that set of participants whose formerly highly autonomous operations were seeing their autonomy somewhat curtailed by the reorganization. Nonetheless he felt the changes were positive and in the needed directions. Spreng commented on these events:

> We're reorganizing the structure of the company, I think, in a much more solid way. The company is changing tremendously from the old days of what our vice president calls the futile-abilities of the instrument divisions to a vastly integrated, highly leveraged company. At the same time we are growing at a very good clip, which is quite a challenge, but it is absolutely necessary for us to achieve that.

We don't want to become a centralized company like IBM—we're not going to become that. But we're moving toward a more coordinated, strategically oriented kind of a management balance between the entrepreneurship of the divisional units and the strategic overview, the guiding hands if you will. This computer business, which has basically overtaken the company, has dramatically changed the company at the same time.

Managing the Process of Structural Change

The process by which these companies reorganize is substantially partici-pative. After clarifying changes in strategic directions that the company will take, the members of the top management team (the management committee in H-P's case) sketch out the major skeletal changes in the structure. How-ever, it is at the group and division levels that middle- and lower-tier exec-utives determine structural changes in their own organizations.

Details of the reorganized structure *must* be worked out by lower-level managers closer to the impacted groups. Unless the company's top execu-tives want to take forever to design the optimal structure, some interim ap-proximations must be made. It is generally not possible for the top manage-ment team to be omniscient when reorganization occurs. As a consequence, they place their best bets on what they believe the structure should be, im-plement it, and then observe the results. Frequently there are some elements of the new structure whose changes could not be anticipated in advance. For example, Doug Spreng remarked on the consequences of some changes that took place at Hewlett-Packard in 1985:

> You change things around . . . and then complexity of the interactions becomes awesome. You think that you've got this situation bounded, territories under-stood and so forth, and then you find out: "No, these three other organizations over there are intimately affected by what you just did here. You had no idea." Yet, you know unless you want to take forever in reorganizing you're going to have to make some of these decisions on the front end and hope that you haven't screwed something else up. Or hope that you can fix it.

The necessity for fine-tuning the reorganized structure is anticipated. These necessary structural adjustments provide an important opportunity for lower-level managers to impact the structure in ways more finely tuned to the actual problems at lower levels of the organization.

When the reorganization results in problems, the lower-level managers participate to refine the structure for better working relationships. Some of these structural changes hint at the important relationship between the for-mal structure and informal interaction. For example, Doug Spreng described why he and a related division general manager were going to have lunch to discuss which of their divisions two laboratories should join in the newly reorganized company:

> There's a lot of concessions going on . . . when you get down to some of the details. Like the guy across the mall, here [another division general manager]. I

believe that at least one and maybe two of his lab groups ought to be within an organization that I've got. . . . I've already approached the subject and asked him not to make any changes in his organization until we get it resolved, because I believe that we've got it wrong right now, and I don't want to keep it wrong. It's easy for us to do that because we both trust each other, and we know we're not trying to build an empire. We're just trying to do the right thing for the company and get these people to where they can make their best contributions. . . . We're going to get together over lunch and talk about it some more. We're creating a document that shows what the recommendations are and why. I think the best thing about H-P is that we can work these things out.

Self-Designing Organizations

The preceding narrative about changes in H-P's formal structure over the four-year period from 1982 to 1986 amply illustrates the kinds of changes we saw taking place at each of the companies we studied. For each firm, the changes in structure were customized to meet the modifications managers perceived in their company's environmental and technological situations. As a consequence, the timing of when each company reorganized varied. The aspect of structure modified by any given reorganization also varied by company. It is important, nonetheless, that the changes in structure were customized to deal with each of the company's localized task environments, its markets, and its technologies.

Companies whose managers engage in this kind of behavior are said to produce "self-designing organizations" (Weick, 1977). These companies can be self-designing because of two factors. First, the people working within these organizations are highly self-critical regarding how they are operating and whether the current structure is facilitating goal accomplishment fast enough. The managers and executives we interviewed provide strong evidence that it is a norm—a shared agreement regarding appropriate and desirable behavior—to evaluate the quality and utility of the organizational status quo. The need for constructive self-criticism is an important shared belief. If an element of the organization is not functioning adequately, alternatives are considered. The current organization is revised if necessary, or major elements of the current structure are changed if more modest organizational changes are deemed inadequate. The key is that these executives and managers openly evaluate the utility of the status quo of the structure. There is strong agreement among the managers and engineers we interviewed that organizational self-criticism is appropriate.

Our research suggests that for organizations to be self-designing over time, widely shared agreements regarding this activity are essential. In our firms, such agreements are part of the organizations' cultures and visible in the managers' operating behaviors. It is expected and widely found from top to bottom, down to the level of engineers. Founders and top-level leaders are very important in helping to shape expectations and norms, of course. We found that members of the top management teams of these companies expressed a willingness to reorganize if it seemed appropriate. More important, this expressed readiness was acted on: real changes in structure took place with some frequency; the changes were well publicized throughout the companies. All of this produced a high tolerance for change among the people at lower levels in the organization with whom we spoke.

The second reason these companies managed structural change so effectively was their awareness of market, scientific, and technology conditions outside their organizations. The external environment was given scrupulous attention. Effective organizational change must target and adapt to major environmental and technological shifts. Structure is a deliberate artifact intended to suit an explicit purpose, not mere random change. Random structural changes will have unpredictable effects on organizational performance—an extremely dangerous situation in the intensely competitive environment these firms face. Consequently, awareness of the context to be adapted to must be blended with a willingness to change in addition to skill at structural arrangements.

Managers in these companies systematically try to understand their businesses even better. They do so by measuring nearly everything internally, monitoring their competition, tracking technology and product shifts, and seeking to understand impending competitive changes. These are quite deliberately self-conscious organizations, with information shared and used in the process of structural modification.

For example, it is simply routine that the companies rigorously measure manufacturing "yields," the percent of usable components ("chips") produced on a single wafer of silicon. It is pro forma that manufacturing cycle times are continuously recorded and analyzed and that changes in manufacturing equipment, organizations, and people are instituted to drive the yields up and cycle times further and further down. The equipment changes frequently; new manufacturing processes are introduced frequently; existing technologies are improved through process development; and new products are introduced on new and continuously improving technologies. It is not sufficient to be right once; it is a continuous battle under difficult technical circumstances.

Such extraordinary attention is driven by broad awareness of competitive hazards. "We've got to beat the Japanese through speed of development and consistently high quality" was one phrase we encountered frequently in our interviewing. The awareness of the external market extends deeply within the internal levels of these companies. For example, the chief executive of National Semiconductor, Charlie Sporck, spoke of a newly graduated engineer, a circuit designer, who had joined National just the year before. "His views of what the [semiconductor] business is all about are far from perfect. But he knows where his product stands relative to everybody else's. Very clearly. He knows it better than I do."

The changes in organizational structure previously described also illustrate the *dynamic tension* principle of organizing in each of these companies. Each time a reorganization took place, clear new reporting relationships were worked out, clear responsibilities were assigned to individuals and groups, and these responsibilities were refined to clarify any problems or ambiguities. These companies can move rapidly to introduce new products or technologies in pursuit of corporate goals because people in the companies know what other people are doing and how they can count on others to facilitate their own local subgoals.

If these companies need to reorganize or modify their structures, their managers are fairly clear as to why. Something is not working optimally. The managers of these companies are highly self-critical and analytic about organizational arrangements. As conditions change, the highly innovative commercially successful companies we have studied reorganize to adapt to the new and anticipated future conditions.

QUASI-FORMAL STRUCTURE

Teams, Task Forces, and Dotted-Line Organizations

Clarity of and changes in the formal structure are important ways in which these companies have organized for innovation; however, formal elements of structure are only a part of the story. Organization theory seems to recognize only two dimensions of organizational structure: formal structure captured in the organization chart as subunits, positions, and reporting relationships; and informal structure, the unsanctioned patterns of interaction devised around social and task requirements the formal organization has failed to take into account. We believe it is time to recognize a third, intermediate level of structure that prevails in the companies we studied.

The intermediate level of structure we have observed is labeled "quasi-formal structure." This intermediate level of structure is not formally characterized on the organization charts. Nor is it "informal," in the usually covert, unsanctioned, purely social, and even adversarial sense of this term (Blau, 1955; Connor, 1980; Gouldner, 1954; Leavitt, 1973; Roethlisberger and Dickson, 1939; Selznick, 1949). The term generally means "used in combination with"; something is "quasi" because it "resembles but is not the thing in question."

In these organizations, quasi-formal structure consists of an extensive use of committees, task forces, teams, and dotted-line relationships. The quasi-formal structures we have observed in these companies resemble formal structure because they are formally sanctioned by the organization and explicitly recognized as legitimate. They are typically not designated in form, specified in a formally defined charter, or delimited rigidly in terms of membership. Nor do they take the place of formal authority and the usual responsibilities. Instead, quasi-formal structure is used *in conjunction with* the formal structure but does not replace it.

Quasi-formal structure should not be confused with the "informal structure" of the organization because it is *not unsanctioned,* illegitimate, covert, or in any way outlawed or disapproved of. On the contrary, it is explicitly recognized, condoned, and encouraged by management at all levels. Because managers themselves participate in creating this level of the companies' structures, this is almost a formalized element of these organizations; quasi-structure is the accepted mode for the entire range of employee problem-solving groups, from engineers and technicians to high-level executives.

One way in which quasi-formal elements are different from formal structure is that they change with an even greater frequency than the formal structure, as problems are resolved or new problems appear. Another difference is that these groups are relevance-based and problem-focused and typically transcend whatever formal structural boundaries that might otherwise impede problem solving. Thus, quasi-structure serves as an important organizational facilitator, enabling explicit formal structures to work, amid the urgent need to solve frequently changing technical and competitive problems. Quasi-structure augments the formal structure and bridges the gap between the skeleton of the organization and the informal mechanisms for doing things.

Quasi-structure also saves companies from simply becoming adhocracies, paradoxically because it makes change and adaptation to problems much easier. The organization need not move to a "structure du jour," and continuous, formal reorganization need not be a constant problem, with structure losing its clarity or people constantly working in a high readjustment mode as a consequence of continuous change. Quasi-structure augments the formal structure: it demonstrates the utility of forming problem-focused groups across internal boundaries and thus helps create a norm of helpful interaction and relationships across boundaries, which makes the formal boundaries and their limitations less constraining.

In each of the companies studied we observed an extensive use of committees, teams, task forces, and dotted-line relationships that augmented their clear formal structures. These were used for one-time or continuously problematic circumstances that required off-line, additional technical and managerial time. The genesis of these units of quasi-structure varies. Sometimes they arise spontaneously, forming around common problems with people in other functions. Sometimes "management" at some level explicitly requests that a task force or committee be convened to deal with a specific problem. A concrete example will illustrate the speed with which elements of quasi-structure are created.

Richard Walleigh, a manufacturing engineering manager in the computer systems division at H-P, described an example of a spontaneously formed task force around the concept of total quality control (TQC). First, someone has to perceive the need for a joint focus on a problem and take the initiative. In this case Walleigh himself was the initiator, with the following observation:

> "Here's a great idea, we ought to do this." Then once you have the light bulb turned on, the next thing you do in H-P is get a group of people together and you start talking about it. It always requires a group of people to do practically any-

thing. There's so few things that you can do in your own department without influencing other departments, that it seems everything we do is in groups.

So . . . you get them charged up about it, get them working on it in their departments through an informal mechanism. You just put together a team of the relevant players and say this is a great idea, talk about it, and we then say, how can we implement it here? Then everyone starts working on [implementation]. The team sort of meets, works on the project until the project's done, and it gets developed. . . . It's our style here and its almost necessary. We do lots of things in teams, some formal and some informal.

Walleigh is not alone at H-P in his enthusiasm for teams. His CEO, John Young, fully understands and approves of the kind of teamwork Walleigh's narrative describes. Young corroborated Rick's account with his own examples:

We have a million task forces around, particularly a lot of them on technical and marketing kinds of things, that really are very complex subsets of the organization—things that never show on this chart. It also happens in our administrative things: all the way from the compensation task force, to you name it, to . . . just finding knowledgeable and respected people who want the chance to participate in this problem is probably the most frequent pattern we use for the kind of coordination and cooperative activity.

Not Matrix Management

It is important to define quasi-structure in terms of what it is not, as well as what it actually is. Quasi-structure is not "matrix management." In the 1960s an organizational form called the matrix structure evolved within U.S. aerospace firms, often under contract to the U.S. Department of Defense and other federal agencies. In matrix management, the corporation or its subunits are reconfigured so that employees within functional departments have two bosses: a functional boss and a second project boss. This is called a dual-authority structure because both bosses have the traditional rights of supervisors to assign tasks, evaluate work, and influence the rewards and promotions their matrix subordinates receive.

Matrix structures were regarded as a genuine structural innovation, since they were well adapted to the vicissitudes of congressional funding, long-term projects with overlapping time lines, and shifting organizational and personnel needs of the aerospace industry. Matrix forms were a clear departure from rigidly hierarchical, vertical organizations typically seen in most large organizations until that time. They are configured on paper as a grid with dotted-line relationships, in which an engineer, for example, would "report out" of his or her functional engineering group to a project organization as well. Thus, "dotted-line" relationships have become a shorthand for one's matrix boss in addition to one's functional boss.

Occasionally the managers and executives we interviewed spoke of matrix relationships. Invariably further investigation revealed that neither the entire corporation nor its divisions were structured as a pure matrix form. Rather project groups were created for technology or product development, which typically drew engineers from several organizations. Other relationships initially described as matrix were later revealed to be of the dotted-line form, rather than a pure matrix form of subordinates with multiple bosses in a dual-authority structure.

More often than not, a dotted line relationship in these companies designated a "for information only" relationship, in which it was considered important for two positions on different levels, existing diagonally across organizational lines, to communicate with regularity. In such a case, a dotted line was used to characterize the relationship. In another case a project supervisor explained that he was "matrixed" to several other groups and divisions; this, too, was revealed to be an information-sharing relationship characterized by committees or meetings to report on and solve problems with other disciplines and departments. A structure of dual-reporting relationships was clearly not the meaning when the term "matrix" was encountered in our research; rather, a number of organizational units were involved in sharing information, in the typical case.

More to the point, quasi-structures are both more formal in their recognized status as problem-solving groups and less formal in their authority relationships. These are colleague-based, problem-focused entities that exist for the duration of the problem. They are also far more pervasive, more deliberate, and more explicitly used than "informal" relationships or "cultural" linkages.

The matrix concept, pure or otherwise, was familiar enough that many of the managers were rather clear that they did not have a matrix structure. Indeed, some believed that a formal matrix structure reduces the organization's clarity and reduces its effectiveness. Peter Rosenbladt, an R & D manager of about 120 people at H-P observed the following:

> Matrix management, wherever it's been tried [at H-P], it's been very distasteful, because it is always resulting in undue complexity, unclear objectives, so we like to do it informally wherever we can. We have never successfully implemented a matrix of management that really does work, because it immediately means that everyone has at least two bosses, and that doesn't go well with things like who determines how well you did, what the priorities are, and those kinds of things.

Managing Quasi-Structure: Costs as Well as Benefits

Though pervasive, quasi-structure is not without its costs. At Intel, for example, it is used extensively. Les Vadasz described the prevalence of both task forces and dotted-line relationships: "We have a lot of multiple reporting relationships, dotted-line reporting relationships and shifts in organizations, especially if you look at project organizations, as the project reaches different stages. People from multiple organizations participate. . . ."

The use of multiple reporting relationships on Intel's technical projects efficiently allocates scarce human talent to needed technical projects.

However, some complications are associated with dotted-line relationships, according to Vadasz. Consistent with other research, dotted-line and team-based relationships in technical projects and other organizational applications produce what he described as "some interim ambiguity." As Vadasz explained, "There is a difference between knowing that you have ambiguity and knowing that "Hey, I want to work out of it." If you just ignore it, then you get chaos. What you have to struggle for is clear organization lines, knowing fully well intellectually that you will not be able to accomplish it perfectly, because you want to do what's right for getting the project done. But if you always struggle to get the cleanest possible line [of organization], you have less chaos." In short, in a rapidly changing technical environment, constant vigilance is the price of organizational clarity for a firm striving to prosper and survive, even though it may have a clear formal structure.

Another cost of maintaining innovation in a large corporation is that considerable time must be spent integrating across organizational boundaries. This is another aspect of quasi-structure: it simply takes time, even if that time is invisible at first glance. While Hewlett-Packard executives consciously strive to keep its organizational units small with divisions of approximately 1000 participants, it is nonetheless clear that coordination across some 50 such divisions is not a trivial task. Task forces, dotted-line relationships, and teams are omnipresent within H-P, as indeed they are in all the firms we studied. These quasi-formal elements of structure are an absolutely essential mechanism of organizing for innovation. Task forces and dotted-line relationships are part of the solution.

At each company people were cognizant of the essential part that committees and task forces played in problem-solving and coordination, and yet they were simultaneously critical of the time required for effective task force participation. At each company, managers were aware of the need to eliminate any elements of organization no longer essential. However, elimination was not always easily accomplished. Les Vadasz at Intel felt that quasi-structure had to be tended, just as any aspect of one's garden might be. Less useful elements must be cut back and pruned. "Do we have too many dotted-line relationships? I would say 'Yes, we do, because it is not easy to kill something.' People get used to the fact that they are there, they have a committee of some sort. . . . Although the committee has done its job and the problem is resolved, some committees nonetheless evolve into standing committees. . . . And we have to be able to prune them."

Vadasz indicated that Intel was cognizant of the need to eliminate unessential functions, committees that survive beyond their functional utility, and meetings that simply take up time. A key observation, however, is that when quasi-structural elements become ineffective, thinking gets "stale."

We are trying more consciously these days [to address the longevity of teams and committees]. For example, we have a very extensive council system. About a year ago, one of the best council systems we've had from the beginning was our die production work. Because of so many factories all around the world, we have to make sure the better processes are common enough in all the factories so that we have the flexibility to move things around. Well, those committees over the years got a little bit stale. So we made a major change and pruned it dramatically. There were more people who felt that it was a breath of fresh air and so it wasn't a big issue . . . to prune it.

The latent value of task forces, committees, and councils is that they present opportunities for lower-level engineers and managers to begin developing their leadership and group skills—both essential components for future managerial success in an innovative company. This value is not without its costs, however. Vadasz continued, "But I think the biggest problem [with task forces] is that somebody has to do the supervising. Someone has to guide them. You don't just create something and let them go. If you were to hire a manager and let the manager go without supervision, you generally end up with undesirable results."

We have concluded that the quasi-formal parts of structure—the committees, the task forces, the project groups—require as much guidance and monitoring as any other part of the organization. Managing quasi-structure is, for all its necessary openness and participation, a demanding responsibility. Despite the fact that lower-level managers "chair" such committees, the burden on management for guidance is nonetheless heavy. They are "absolutely not a freebie" according to Intel's Vadasz, because they require the participants' time as well as some additional managerial time. Time is scarce in the big innovation technology marathon these companies are running. In balance, however, the value of councils, task forces, and committees is an essential component if these companies are to accomplish the required interaction that must take place across disciplines, departments, and divisions to achieve the remarkable multidisciplinary technologies and products these companies produce year after year. Councils, task forces, and committees are an effective tool in the management of innovation. Though not without costs, these organizational arrangements deliver tremendous benefits in the management of innovation if they are monitored and attended, just like any other aspect of the organization that you expect to bear fruit.

COLLEGIAL INTERACTIONS IN A TEAM ENVIRONMENT

One element of classical "organic management" for which we did find substantial evidence was collegial interaction. In place of strongly hierarchy-based patterns of interaction found in more traditional organizations, our firms embody very strong norms and practices of nonhierarchical, problem-, expertise-, and interest-based interaction. The extensive use of committees and teams that cross organizational boundaries and are composed of multilevel people clearly facilitates a nonhierarchically based pattern of interaction. Norms that support collegial interaction patterns and expertise-based authority clearly facilitate a nonhierarchically based pattern of interaction.

Fundamentally in innovative high technology companies, multitudes of novel problems exist for which no established solutions are readily apparent. The sensible approach is to rely on each and every resource available. Thoughtful reflection on the problem and substantive contributions, rather than hierarchy or status, are more relevant in the highly competitive environment these companies face. Fast decision making is essential to effective competition, so standing on form and position merely impedes problem solving.

John Young at Hewlett-Packard described this phenomenon and the part it plays in maintaining an innovative organization rather well: "To make the structure as clear as you can is a long way from saying there are no ambiguities. There is a very big need for a collegial environment . . . to make it work . . . I think it's far more the style and the freedom of activity and association and communication back and forth that makes an innovative environment."

Consider that these companies deliberately hire the very best people they can. People who have the most recent technical training are highly valued: recent graduates from engineering and business schools, as well as experienced engineers, executives, managers, in addition to those they can hire or develop internally for support functions. Even production workers and equipment engineers need to be of very high quality. In an industry of class 1 clean rooms, which counts contaminants to integrated circuit production in parts per million or less, the users and maintainers of highly sophisticated electronic production equipment must be very knowledgeable. All of these employees are the highest quality that can be found.

Now, the cynical reader will remark, "Well, surely there are some laggards, lower quality, just plain zeros in each of these companies." Undoubtedly there are. What distinguishes these companies, however, is the widely shared belief that we must use whatever human resources we have to bear on a given problem. The norm that permeates these companies is that anyone with what seems to have good ideas or who is reflective will be relied on if their experience, expertise, or intellectual abilities appear to be relevant to the problem at hand.

Selection from among the thousands of people available in each of these companies is facilitated by the companies' structures. There are smaller work groups whenever possible, and the overall structure of each of the companies is clear. One can determine without great difficulty where additional help might be found, if the people in your current organization do not have the requisite knowledge or help resolve the problems. People become known to those around them, and there are continuous opportunities to solve problems.

There is a pervasive norm that people in these companies call a "team mentality." The team mentality involves the shared perception that "we are in this together, and it will likely take more than just myself to solve a given problem." Indeed, if the team mentality were stated as a norm to guide the behavior of new recruits to these companies, it would resemble this statement: "Given the complex technical solutions that we are seeking in addition to the complicated and uncertain market conditions we face, it is likely that more than just a single individual will be required to solve a given problem."

We asked a division general manager at Hewlett-Packard if the highly competitive computer market their company was facing might change the willingness of managers to cooperate with one another internally. Was the pressure on H-P as a company going to make it tougher for individual division general managers to survive and for their careers to prosper, and thus increase internal competition among such managers for future promotions—and perhaps reduce their willingness to collaborate? In contrast to what might be expected, the manager responded as follows:

> Oh, no, you have to be *more teamwork-oriented*. Teamwork is the only way we can preserve our thrust into the markets as a company. The divisional structure will [continue to] exist, but yet [the reorganization] allows us to work at a much higher plane of cooperation as an organizational entity. So teamwork is . . . our secret. We're finding measurement of teamwork coming up more and more in evaluations and in ranking sessions of managers. You just don't go off and do your own thing in this company anymore.

Informal, collegial interaction was widely practiced at the technical levels of the organizations we studied, as well as among the managerial ranks. At National Semiconductor, for example.

> Sometimes [innovation] happens in the men's room. One guy's talking to another guy, and another guy's standing, eavesdropping on the conversation, scribbling on a napkin. If you dropped down right now to the cafeteria, you would see it going on. Most of [the innovation motivation] comes out of, let's say, frustration or irritation with the way something currently works. And a guy says, 'You know, I really wish I had a fill-in-the-blank. What I had didn't do fill-in-the-blank.'' And the other guy says, "Well, you know, a few years ago I had a problem like that and what I did was x, y, and z." And then the chemistry starts, and the result is a product that solves the problem.

In the restrooms, in the cafeterias, and in the hallways—informal colleague-based interaction patterns permeate these companies.

CORPORATE SIZE: HOW BIG IS TOO BIG?

We cannot leave a discussion of structure without turning to the issue of organizational size. Large numbers of people pose significant problems for coordination in a fast-changing marketplace and with fast-changing technology. So, too, do broadly scattered operations, broad product lines, and global competition. Each of the study companies operates worldwide, in an increasingly global market and technical environment. All have revenues of over $1 billion, and their number of employees range from just under 20,000 at Intel to Hewlett-Packard's 82,000 and Motorola's more than 90,000 employees worldwide. These are large corporations by any measure. However, they have not always been large. Indeed, many of the founders and top executives remember when the companies were smaller and more manageable, as recently as ten years ago. Although Texas Instruments, Motorola, and Hewlett-Packard were founded more than thirty years ago, they experienced their most explosive growth in the 1970s, just as the younger companies, Intel and National, were also experiencing rapid growth.

The founders and their early executives unanimously recalled how much simpler it was to communicate in a small company. It was relatively easy to retain a close coupling between the various organizational functions. David Packard described how he and Bill Hewlett operated in the early days at H-P, after World War II: "When the company was small, [a close coupling] was almost automatic, because we were all involved in everything. In fact, when we were small, I'd spend a lot of time in the laboratory, and I'd spend a lot of time in the factory, and I spent a lot of time in the field. And so you did all these things yourself." Packard's experiences nearly duplicate the description Pat Haggerty gave of his early days at Texas Instruments: "It was here that the setting of objectives and being small and tightly coupled . . . was so important. We put good people at the thing, and they were very tightly coupled."

During World War II, the war boom gave Packard and his partner, Bill Hewlett, the opportunity to see the impact of boom–bust economies on organizations through their observations of the aerospace industry. Neither wanted to hire people only to lay them off. They preferred to build loyalty through a long-term commitment to the people who were hired—even at the near-certain risk of slower growth and a smaller organization. Packard remarked, "I'd been seeing a lot of activity in the aerospace industry where companies would go out and get a big contract and hire all the engineers. When that contract was over, they'd have to fire them, and they'd go and work somewhere else. So, I decided that we would try to build our business on a long-term basis and not go out and get a lot of contracts. We had a maximum of about 200 people during the war, so we were a very small business at that time."

These observations on the negative impact of growth through short-term contracts laid the foundation for Hewlett-Packard's renowned human resource policies—to build loyalty through a long-term commitment to the people who are hired. Thus, although H-P stayed small during the war, its postwar success in building high- and low-frequency measuring devices eventually necessitated hiring more people. With growth, Packard realized that "the first hurdle to get over is to recognize that you can't do all these things yourself. Then the name of the game is to try and get people to do things the way you'd do them, if you were doing it. So you try and develop people who would have the same ideas, the same approach, and the same philosophy, and so we developed a very close relationship."

As H-P grew, the two founders and their close associates developed some clear ideas on how they would prefer to continue to manage the business. Mr. Packard continued:

> As we got bigger we decided that the way to manage this business was to break it down in small enough units so that people could have expertise in a particular field. So the first thing we did, we built our engineering laboratories into two sections: one on low-frequency instruments and one on high-frequency instruments. That meant then that these people not only kept up with all of technology, but they knew what the market needed and it was their business to stay ahead of the game in their fields.

Thus, from the time when H-P began to grow, the governing principle for organizing was to break the company down into small enough units so that people could specialize on a more finite piece of the business and thus develop a high level of expertise in it. This appears to be a fundamentally important organizing principle: in some form, all of the study companies seek to maintain a "small feel," although they differ substantially on how this is done. We conclude that, in complex businesses such as these, despite the increased time and attention required, it just makes good sense to "keep it small," within the cognitive limits of the human mind to grasp and manipulate effectively.

Packard's successor, John Young, was among many we interviewed who paid deliberate attention to organizational size. He described the importance of explicitly organizing people, of explicitly keeping the organizational units within smaller, more manageable units, and of building the requisite linkages between divisions and groups in a large, innovative organization.

> We are a six billion dollar company. That's one business [and not a conglomerate]. We have 52 operating divisions, not because it's easy to have 52 operating divisions, but because we believe in those small work groups. That means about a thousand people per work group. It's more on the model of a small business, . . . because of the interaction.
>
> I think it is extremely important for people to see who you need to cooperate with and why cooperating is a growing, valued characteristic. . . . The only excuse for having a big organization, it seems to me, is one where you generally have those linkages, that can build on each other. But linkage is a big problem. And it takes a lot of time. So, we have had to articulate [why it's worth time coordinating], and the organization form is one way to help do that.

Because they have learned how to manage large size by grouping people into smaller units, the founders and executives of these companies do not appear to be overly concerned with becoming "too big" as corporations. We asked Gordon Moore, chairman of the board and a founder of Intel, if he saw any upper size limit, an optimal number of people beyond which Intel was not likely to grow as a corporation? With a broad smile, Dr. Moore observed, "We're in a business where you grow or you die. We'll grow as long as we can. We may start to worry when we get as big as IBM. . . ."

Size, then, is not the issue. Instead, it is coordination, cooperation, information sharing, maintaining a problem-solving focus, regrouping people into smaller work units, and maintaining collegial relationships through the quasi-structure of multiple teams and task forces.

CONCLUSIONS

In our judgment the key to the continued innovation success rates these companies enjoy is to be found in their careful management of structure. This includes much thoughtful reexamination of existing formal structures, in light of changing technology and market needs. Sustained enthusiasm for constant improvement in the organization's structure through reorganization, as necessary, provides a consistent signal to employees that change is neither undesirable nor to be resisted. Instead, structure is to be managed and adapted to changed conditions.

This, in turn, requires a willingness to invest valuable time in structure per se. Quasi-structural elements like crossdisciplinary, multilevel committees, task forces, and teams require fostering, attention, and support. Thus, quasi-formal relationships to coordinate and exchange information are legitimated in these firms by widespread investment of sanctioned time. This includes senior management time, given to participating in these as needed and supporting quasi-structure on behalf of the organization at large. Senior management commitment to the essential importance of quasi-structure is clearly not lip service. The interpersonal skills essential for working within organizations with extensive quasi-structural elements, like teamwork and cooperative ability, are increasingly used to assess managers' behavior. That Hewlett-Packard now includes cooperation and team skills as variables by which its managers are evaluated is among the most fundamental indicators of how important these issues are to the survival of the companies we have studied.

These firms show a consistent pattern of structure—formal, quasi-formal, and informal—that actively facilitates both innovative ideas and task-relevant cooperation. While they have thousands of employees, these companies clearly organize for innovation, they reorganize for innovation, and they retain the small company flavor by carefully fostering patterns of interaction usually associated with small companies. These behaviors are clearly encouraged by structure, but they are also an expected part of the cultures of these companies. Informal interaction and coordination were found everywhere: in the hallways, cafeterias, and even in the men's and women's rooms. The dynamic tension among all these elements is an important component of the management of innovation.

Above all, it appears that effective, explicit, and deliberate management of the innovation processes is the key to success in high technology companies, a point increasingly recognized by managers themselves, if not as widely as might be hoped in the organization theory literature. Contemporary innovation, particularly in research-intensive companies, is a very elaborate process, drawing on a wide array of technical specialties. Yet technology itself is by no means enough; adept organizing for innovation is essential to continued success over time. Clear organizational structures, frequent reorganizations, and an extensive use of quasi-structure contribute significantly to the long-term innovative abilities of the high technology companies we have studied.

NOTE

1. See, for example, three extensive reviews of the literature:

Tornatzky, Louis, et al. (1983). *The Process of Technological Innovation: Reviewing the Literature.* National Science Foundation, May 1983.

Van de Ven, Andrew H. (1986). "Central problems in the management of innovation." *Management Science* (May 1986).

Van de Ven, Andrew H. (1988) "Processes of innovation and organizational change." Technical Report of the Strategic Management Research Center, University of Minnesota, February 1988.

In addition to these review articles, a sample of other works illustrates the extensive literature on the management of innovation.

Hatch, M. J. (1987). "Physical barriers, task characteristics, and interaction activity in research and development firms," *Administrative Science Quarterly,* 32 no. (1987): 387–399.

Jennings, D. F., and D. H. Sexton (1985). "Managing innovation in established firms: Issues, problems and the impact on economic growth and employment." *Proceedings,* 1985, Conference on Industrial Science and Technological Innovation. Sponsored by National Science Foundation. The Center for Research and Development. State University of New York at Albany.

Lundstedt, S. B., and E. W. Colglazier, Jr. (1982). *Managing Innovation.* New York: Pergamon Press.

Mintzberg, Henry, and A. McHugh (1985). "Strategy formulation in an Adhocracy," *Administrative Science Quarterly,* 30 (1985): 160–197.

Tushman, M. L., and W. L. Moore (1982). *Readings in the Management of Innovation.* Boston: Pitman.

Tushman, M. L., and P. Anderson (1986). "Technological discontinuities and organizational environments." *Administrative Science Quarterly,* 31 (1986): 439–465.

7

Perennial Renaissance: The Marketing Challenge in High Tech Settings

THOMAS J. KOSNIK

In the last decade, interest in high tech marketing has skyrocketed. Books by Regis McKenna (1985), a prominent Silicon Valley consultant, and William Davidow (1986), an Intel Executive turned venture capitalist, have met a receptive audience among business practitioners who believe that marketing in high technology settings is fundamentally different from traditional marketing. A textbook by Shanklin and Ryans (1984) has been used in university courses by students searching for the elusive formula for success in high tech marketing. The business press has made folk heroes out of high tech entrepreneurs like Steve Jobs, founder of Apple Computer and Next, Inc.; Bill Gates, founder of Microsoft; and Ken Olsen, founder of Digital Equipment Corporation. High tech has become synonymous with high excitement.

But, along with the excitement, high technology is fraught with complexity, making it a difficult and risky business for the people making marketing decisions. John Sculley, a seasoned marketing executive at Pepsico who became the president of Apple Computer in 1983, provides a compelling account of the dangers of applying marketing tactics that were successful in the cola wars of the 1970s to the new battleground of microcomputers in the 1980s. Sculley (1987) asserts that the basic assumptions he carried from Pepsi about investments in advertising and R & D and the management of product inventory were inappropriate in a high tech setting. In the microcomputer business, the pace of technological innovation could rapidly transform technology leaders into followers and render inventory obsolete. Along with other factors, several of Sculley's marketing decisions contributed to stagnant sales and reduced earnings. In the midst of Apple's problems in performance, stormy disagreements erupted between Sculley and Apple

Special thanks to associate professor Rowland T. Moriarty of the Harvard Business School. His coaching and collaboration on earlier research provided a substantial contribution to the evolution of ideas in this chapter.

founder Steve Jobs, who left the company in 1985. In the face of increasingly sophisticated consumers, skeptical Wall Street analysts, and aggressive competitors from around the world, Sculley and his management team struggled to revitalize Apple. Their response to the crisis included retrenchment, rededication to technological innovation, and a commitment to nonstop renovation in marketing. Sculley's ability to adapt to the complexities of marketing in the fast lane was rewarded by a rebound in performance. After a flat year from 1985 to 1986, Apple Computer's revenues increased from $1.9 billion in 1986 to $3.8 billion in 1988, a compound annual growth rate of 43 percent. Earnings in the same period increased at an annual rate of 56 percent, from $154 million to $375 million (Alex Brown & Sons, 1988).

Although the business press is full of marketing war stories like the Apple turnaround described here, there is very little in the way of systematic, rigorous research on high tech marketing. This chapter reviews the best of existing conceptual and empirical research on the topic, in an effort to provide the reader with (1) a framework for analyzing the sources of complexity in high tech marketing and (2) the implications for marketers—and their managers—in high tech settings.

WHAT IS HIGH TECH MARKETING?

Before leaping into a discussion of the things that make high tech marketing more difficult than non–high tech marketing, it is important to define what each is.

Burgelman, Kosnik, and Van den Poel (1987) have defined technology as "the practical knowledge, know-how, skills, and artifacts that can be used to develop a new product or service and/or a new production/delivery system. Technology can be embodied in people, materials, cognitive and physical processes, plant, equipment, and tools." This definition includes both product technology (which is embedded in the product itself) and process technology (which is part of the production/delivery system). It also encompasses what Capon and Glazer (1987) call "management technology"—the knowledge of how to market the product and run the business.

Even if the preceding definition for technology seems reasonable, considerable ambiguity and definitional imprecision cloud most definitions of high technology, as we have seen throughout the chapters in this book. Consider these three definitions from the marketing literature:

- The U.S. Bureau of Labor Statistics labels any industry with twice the number of technical employees and double the R & D outlays of the U.S. average as high tech (Shanklin and Ryans, 1984).
- Regis McKenna (1985) asserts that high tech industries are characterized by complex products, large numbers of entrepreneurial competitors, customer confusion, and rapid change.
- Shanklin and Ryans (1985) apply the high tech label to "any company that participates in a business with high-tech characteristics: the busi-

ness requires a strong scientific/technical basis; new technology can obsolete old technology rapidly; and as new technologies come on stream their applications create or revolutionize demand."

On the surface these three definitions illustrate a divergence of opinion about what constitutes "high tech." However, Kosnik and Moriarty (1988) suggest two underlying dimensions that link previous definitions and distinguish high tech from low tech marketing situations.

The first dimension is *market uncertainty*—ambiguity about the type and extent of the needs of customers that technology can satisfy. Levitt (1975) argued powerfully that the difference between selling and marketing is that "selling concerns itself with the tricks and techniques of getting people to exchange cash for your product. . . . Marketing . . . view[s] the entire business process as consisting of a tightly integrated effort to discover, create, arouse, and satisfy customer needs" (p. 10).

Unfortunately, using customer needs as the foundation for marketing in high tech settings is problematic, because customers cannot articulate what they need (Kosnik, 1985; McKenna, 1985; Shanklin and Ryans, 1984). Kosnik and Moriarty (1988) present several reasons that the needs of customers in a high tech setting are likely to be more uncertain than the needs in a low tech situation. Their argument is elaborated later in this chapter. McKenna's (1985) definition (complex products, customer confusion, rapid change) and Shanklin and Ryan's (1985) definition (new applications create or revolutionize demand) of high tech marketing both include elements of market uncertainty.

Kosnik and Moriarty's (1988) second dimension is *technological uncertainty*. Market uncertainty is not knowing what the customers want from the new technology. A few unanswered questions of high tech customers include the following: "How will we use it?"; "What will it do for us?"; "Why should we buy it?"; and "How much is it worth?" Technological uncertainty is not knowing whether the technology, or the company providing it, can deliver on the promise to meet a set of wants or needs, once they have been articulated. This form of uncertainty is higher in situations in which the technology is new or rapidly changing. All three of the earlier definitions allude to this form of uncertainty.

High technology marketing involves high levels of both market and technological uncertainty. Figure 7.1 contrasts what I have defined as high tech marketing with three other types of marketing.

The first is *low tech marketing,* the application of known technology to meet well-established needs. Examples include a variety of mature, frequently purchased products ranging from milk and coffee to toothpaste and toilet paper. The second is *better mousetrap marketing,* in which new technology is introduced to solve an age-old problem. An example of this situation is a new drug, administered in familiar tablet form, that cures cancer or helps the buyer lose weight. The needs to be satisfied are clear. Whether the new mousetrap will do a better job is uncertain in the early stages. The third

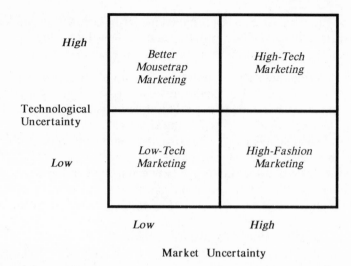

Figure 7.1 A Taxonomy of Marketing Situations Based on Technological and Market Uncertainty

situation is *high-fashion marketing,* in which the technology changes relatively slowly, but consumer tastes are difficult to predict. Examples include designer jeans, running shoes, and motion pictures.

The remainder of the chapter is devoted to the sources of complexity in high tech marketing. Some of the conclusions, as well as the practical implications, may be applicable to high-fashion or better mousetrap marketing problems as well.

SEVEN SOURCES OF COMPLEXITY IN HIGH TECH MARKETING

The central premise in this section is the assertion that marketing in a high technology environment is a complex task—more complex than the practice of marketing in other settings. This is not to suggest that low tech, high-fashion, or better mousetrap marketing problems are simple. In fact, marketing in any industry is a more complicated, demanding profession in the late 1980s and 1990s than it was a decade or two ago. Nor will the chapter demonstrate a statistically significant difference between high tech marketing and its counterparts in other settings. In fact, Moriarty and Kosnik (1987) point out that one glaring weakness of the existing empirical research is that few attempts have been made to verify the assumption that high tech marketing is unique. Despite the scarcity of objective data, most practitioners and academic observers believe that marketing semiconductor test equipment or monoclonal antibodies is more complex than selling soap, sleeping pills, or stylish clothing.

The evidence I have collected over a decade of working as a marketing practitioner and an academic researcher in the information technology industry, coupled with a review of the existing literature on high tech marketing, provides some support for the argument that high tech results in high complexity. During the period 1978 through 1988 I was involved as a participant–observer in eighty high technology marketing transactions. In thirty-six cases I observed organizations that were making a major purchase of information technology products or services. These products and services included computer hardware (mainframe, minicomputers, and microcomputers), computer software, high tech education and training, office automation consulting, and systems development services (the design and implementation of a "custom-built" computer system). In forty-four cases I was involved with companies that were trying to sell the preceding information technology products and services to a variety of market segments, including banks, educational institutions, federal government agencies, insurance companies, law firms, manufacturing firms, real estate developers, and computer software companies. There were more similarities than differences across the sample of eighty cases, regardless of the product or service, the year, or whether the view was from the buying or selling side of the transaction. By themselves, however, they do not address the issue of whether high tech marketing problems are different from their low tech cousins, or how high tech marketers should adapt traditional marketing practice to their particular environment.

To provide a point of contrast, I assembled a sample of fifty cases that have been written about real marketing problems in non–high tech situations, which I have analyzed and taught over the last four years as part of the introductory marketing course at the Harvard Business School. The cases were selected by two course heads (not the author) to present a broad and representative array of the marketing problems facing practitioners in the 1980s. In my sample, I included all cases taught in the first-year marketing course between 1985 and 1988 that were not "high tech." The fifty cases included 40 percent products for individuals or household consumption, including food, consumer durables, clothing, and health and beauty aids; 28 percent products targeted to organizational customers, including industrial consumables, equipment, and chemicals; and 32 percent products targeted to both home and institutional markets, including financial services, food, travel services, and ideas such as joining the priesthood, using birth control, and saying "no" to illegal drugs. There were some striking differences between the fifty "non–high tech" cases and the sample of eighty high tech marketing situations that will be discussed in detail later in the chapter.

In addition to the "qualitative" observation from eighty trips to the field and the marketing cases, I have designed experiments that simulate a complex buying decision involving new information technology. The results, which are also reported later in this chapter, corroborate the findings from the field research. After synthesizing the data from my own work and the research of others, I have isolated seven sources of complexity in high tech marketing:

- *Market uncertainty is high.* Customers are unable to articulate the latent needs that the technology might satisfy, assess the relative importance of newfound needs, or predict how their needs might evolve in the future. Thus, high tech marketers face the difficult task of shooting at an invisible, moving target.
- *Technological uncertainty is high.* The rocket scientists, engineers, and entrepreneurs who discover and exploit new technology are often unable to deliver on their enthusiastic predictions about what the technology will do, how reliably it will function, how soon it will be available, and how long it will last before it is rendered obsolete by another approach. Thus, the marketer must often sell promises rather than tangible products.
- *An ever-expanding set of new skills is required.* High tech marketers must build enough expertise in the key technologies to understand their market potential and to establish credibility with their counterparts in engineering and R & D. They must also learn enough about their customers' industries and functions to spot potential applications that the market has not discovered or articulated. The minimum acceptable depth of knowledge of the technology and the application is greater than in low tech settings. Hence, the marketing job is more complex.
- *Shorter product and technology life cycles result in fewer sustainable marketing advantages.* The paradoxical implication for marketers is that, although they have to know more about technologies and applications, the useful life of their knowledge and experience is growing shorter, making it extremely difficult to develop a sustainable marketing advantage over competitors.
- *Interfunctional and interfirm alliances are more frequent.* A marketing professional in technology-intensive businesses must often span functional boundaries to coordinate with key players in sales, field service, R & D, and manufacturing in their own organization. An increase in alliances between suppliers and customers and between competitors has required that marketers develop skills of diplomacy for sensitive and confidential negotiations between organizations as well.
- *International markets are increasingly important.* Several recent studies (Ambrosino, Green, Kein, and Lyons, 1988; Bank of Boston, 1988) suggest that (1) high technology companies of all sizes are experiencing more rapid growth in international than in domestic markets and (2) small, entrepreneurial companies in high tech industries are more likely to be involved in international markets than their low tech counterparts are. Each new country in which a company operates adds a layer of complexity to its marketing problems.
- *High tech often implies hypergrowth.* The growth rate of high tech companies, large and small, is often higher than that of companies in low

Figure 7.2 Sources of Market Uncertainty

tech industries. Although it is not necessarily harder to *sell* a fast-growing product than a mature one, the challenges of *building a marketing organization* in the midst of hypergrowth are both complex and critical to continued success.

The evidence related to each of the seven sources of complexity is discussed next.

Determining What Customers Want: Market Uncertainty

Why are the needs in the marketplace likely to be more uncertain in a high tech situation? Five questions that frequently raise market uncertainty are shown in Figure 7.2.

First, confronted with a radically new technology, customers may not understand what needs the technology could satisfy. A common example of this problem is the first-time purchase of a microcomputer. Many managers have had the experience of being forced to choose between desktops and laptops, hard disks and floppies, PCs and Macintoshes, without fully understanding how they would help in various management tasks.

Second, their needs, once known, may be subject to rapid and unpredictable changes as their environment evolves. Computer software to support income tax preparation in the face of changing federal tax code, and drugs to diagnose and treat a new disease whose causes are uncertain are both examples of products facing a "moving target."

Third, there may be questions about whether the market will eventually establish technical standards with which the products must be compatible if the buyer hopes to use them with other products, or to use it in conjunction with other people or organizations. The debate over VHS and Betamax format in the early years of video cassette recorders (VCRs), and the conflict over data communications standards in the Local Area Network (LAN) marketplace are examples of this type of market uncertainty.

Fourth, it is difficult to predict how fast a high tech innovation will spread. An example of this situation is the difficulty market researchers have had in predicting the future unit sales of innovations ranging from VCRs to office automation systems.

Finally, all of the preceding questions render it difficult to determine the size of the potential market. For example, in 1959, IBM turned down an offer from a start-up called Haloid Corporation to invest in a new xerographic technology because a consulting study predicted that the total market for the Xerox 914 was a mere 5000 units. A decade later, Haloid (which became Xerox Corporation) had sold 200,000 of the 914s and had become a billion dollar company (Jacobsen and Hillkirk, 1986).

Rigorous empirical research on market uncertainty is limited. Kosnik (1985, 1986) adapted a concept from March's (1978) work on ambiguity of preference that addresses several of the dimensions of market uncertainty. Kosnik defined a buyer's ambiguity of preference as a lack of clarity about the needs or goals a purchase should satisfy. Ambiguity may arise from ignorance about the needs, uncertainty about how they might evolve, or questions about how the rest of the market will behave.

Kosnik (1985) further developed an experiment to show how ambiguous preferences affect the buying process. The purchase decision was the selection of a computer system to enhance loan officer productivity in one of two banks—one with clear buying goals and one facing high ambiguity. There were two samples of subjects: fifty-four experienced computer systems consultants and sixty MBA students with at least two years of work experience, but limited experience evaluating computer systems alternatives.

Several significant differences in the buying process emerged. First, both the consultants and the MBAs in the bank with ambiguous preferences selected alternatives that preserved their client's flexibility by promising compatibility with other products and the ability to modify (customize) the product. The "flexibility index" of the set of products considered under high ambiguity was higher for both groups than under low ambiguity (a statistically significant difference at $p < .001$). (See Kosnik [1985] for details.) Second, those facing higher ambiguity of preference predicted that it would take more time and effort to reach a final decision on which product to buy ($p < .02$). Third, both samples that faced high ambiguity of preference were significantly more likely ($p < .01$) to hold discussions within the bank to clarify needs and to ask for consulting help from outside the bank.

These findings are the first attempt in the marketing literature to distinguish a variant of market uncertainty, ambiguity of preference, from technological uncertainty. They also suggest that "shopping" under high market uncertainty is a more complex buying task, leading to the expenditure of more time, an increase in internal discussions, and a greater tendency to call in experts to resolve the problem.

Other sources implicitly support the argument that ambiguity on the buyer side contributes to market uncertainty for the seller and thus to the complexity of the marketing task. McKenna (1985) describes the challenge facing high tech marketers as overcoming their potential customers' fear, uncertainty, and doubt (FUD). As mentioned earlier, McKenna (1985) defines high tech industries as having complex products. Shanklin and Ryans (1984) describe high tech executives as supply-side marketers. "With sketchy and quite likely discouraging hard information about the present market demand or about present consumer needs and preferences, supply side marketers develop and introduce products based upon intuition and judgment about future demand. . . . Many of them fail—that is to be expected—but a few also succeed" (p. 7).

Finally, Table 7.1 provides evidence that the elements of market uncertainty in high tech situations are significantly higher than in non–high tech marketing problems. To generate the percentages in the table, I first recorded whether or not each of the sources of market uncertainty was a significant factor for each of thirty-six high tech buying cases, forty-four high tech selling cases, and fifty non–high tech marketing cases (all of which were written from the selling company's perspective). A simple yes–no coding was used, in which "yes" meant that the source of uncertainty was significant in a particular case. The "yes" scores were then added and divided by the total number of cases in each sample to determine the percentage for which each element of market uncertainty was high. The table shows that all five sources of market uncertainty occurred much more frequently in high tech than in non–high tech situations. The similarity in percentages between the high tech buying cases and high tech selling cases in the table also suggests that market uncertainty is high from both the buyer's and the seller's perspective. The implication of the findings shown in Table 7.1 is that marketers of high tech products and services need to develop approaches to cope with high levels of market uncertainty.

Delivering on the Promise: Technological Uncertainty

Figure 7.3 shows five potential sources of technological uncertainty. The first is a lack of information about a product's *functional performance*—whether it will do what the seller promises. For example, when computer time-sharing systems were being adopted in the 1970s, both buyers and sellers of computers often encountered this type of uncertainty when trying to establish the response time (how fast the computer responded to a user at a terminal) of different machines under different usage conditions. Vendors made glowing promises about response time that were difficult to compare across suppliers without expensive benchmark testing, which few customers had the time to conduct.

Second, the company supplying the technology may not have an established track record for *delivery*. Uncertainty over delivery may arise in sev-

Table 7.1 A Comparison of Technological and Market Uncertainty in High Tech and Non–High Tech Marketing Situations

	Percent of Sample in Which Elements of Technological and Market Uncertainty Were High		
	Sample 1: High Tech Marketing Cases From Buying Organization's Perspective ($n = 36$ cases)	Sample 2: High Tech Marketing Cases From Selling Organization's Perspective ($n = 44$ cases)	Sample 3: Non–high Tech Marketing Cases From Selling Organization's Perspective ($n = 50$ cases)
Sources of Technological Uncertainty			
Will the new product function as promised?	81%	86%	16%
Will the delivery timetable be met?	81	100	16
Will the vendor give high-quality service when needed?	89	86	28
Will there be side effects of product or service?	86	82	14
Will new technology make ours obsolete?	82	80	8
Sources of Market Uncertainty			
What needs might be met by the technology?	83	100	18
How will needs change in the future?	100	100	36
Will the market adopt industry standards?	86	86	4
How large is the potential market?	69	64	16
How fast will the technological innovation spread?	89	86	22

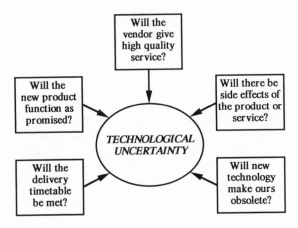

Figure 7.3   Sources of Technological Uncertainty

eral situations. The first shipment of a new product may be later than promised. The tendency of computer hardware and software manufacturers to miss promised delivery dates for new products is the rule rather than the exception. Such practices have led to a new phrase, vaporware, which refers to products that have been promised to the marketplace but may never be completed or delivered. Long after the first shipment of new products, shortfalls in the quantity available may occur as a result of manufacturing capacity constraints, often because of a bad guess about the potential market demand for a high tech product. For example, in 1988 a shortage of dynamic random access memory chips (DRAMs) led to shortages of products from many hardware vendors that relied on the chips for their desktop computers. Finally, uncertainty about delivery may arise from doubts about whether the supplier is financially healthy enough to stay in business. McKenna (1985) asserts that financial stability has a major impact on a company's ability to market its products. Buyers are reluctant to purchase from a firm in financial trouble because of the uncertainty that red ink raises about the future supply of additional products, parts, and service. Although the threat of bankruptcy is by no means limited to high tech firms, there are generally more entrepreneurial suppliers in high tech industries, and the long-term financial viability of a start-up is more uncertain that that of an older, larger company with an established record of financial performance.

Third, there is uncertainty about whether the supplier of a high tech product will be able to provide prompt, effective *service* to resolve problems that may arise if the new technology breaks down. Moriarty and Kosnik (1987) make it clear that high-quality service is critical across a variety of high tech and low tech settings. However, one factor that raises uncertainty about service in high tech marketing is the limited data on how the new technology will behave in the field. More mature technologies, such as those found in washing machines, televisions, and automobiles, have decades-long histories of problems and solutions that reduce the uncertainty about what might go wrong and the best steps to take to resolve each problems. Newer technologies have no track record, so even if the service technician arrives quickly, it is uncertain whether or when the breakdown can be repaired.

Fourth, there is a risk of *unanticipated side effects from the technology*. One example of such uncertainty occurred in the 1980s as the increased use of microcomputers and computer networks was accompanied by an increase in unauthorized access to business and government computer systems. Numerous press reports have discussed the resulting threats to businesses (e.g., embezzlement and computer fraud) by individual consumers, including violations of privacy and confidentiality and threats to the national defense (e.g., penetration of top-secret computer systems to learn about new weapons systems).

Finally, technological uncertainty may arise as a result of questions about *technological obsolescence*—whether and when the market will turn to another technology to replace what is offered by the current generation of products. The risk of obsolescence may occur long after a technology has found a stable market, only to be challenged by a new way to meet the market's needs. It can also occur when a new technology is introduced, if customers cling to their old approach just long enough to leapfrog the new technology to select an even more advanced approach introduced somewhat later. The marketer's risk in moving too quickly is that leapfrogging by competitors' products may send the new technology to an early grave. One example of this uncertainty is the introduction of compact disk (CD) audio systems in the 1980s. The sales of the CD players were just beginning to take off when digital tape players were introduced that promised the same quality of sound at a much lower cost. Uncertainty about whether digital tape would render CD technology obsolete even before it had achieved widespread acceptance led many potential CD buyers to "wait and see."

Table 7.1 shows that the five sources of technological uncertainty were an important factor in the vast majority of high tech buying and selling cases. They were rarely present in the sample of non–high tech cases.

The five sources of technological uncertainty raise concerns of buyers about the risks—to their companies and their individual careers—of adopting a high tech innovation. Kosnik (1985, 1986) found that experienced systems consultants were more likely than the less experienced MBAs to exclude any product from consideration that were not "tried and true" by other organizations. These findings are consistent with apocryphal stories about computer purchases in which alternatives to the market share leader, IBM, were avoided because "nobody ever got fired for recommending IBM." It appear that when technological uncertainty is high, experienced buyers favor alternatives that promise *security*. Security can be attained either through the size, stability, or overall reputation of the product provider or through the familiarity and trust that result from established relationships with people in the supplier organization.

So Much to Learn: The Expanding Skill Set Required for High Tech Marketing

Even in the simplest of situations, a marketer needs to learn about his or her product and target market segment. In high tech situations, however, the underlying product technology and the specific functions that might be supported are often much more technical and detailed than in low tech scenarios.

For example, in the computer software and services industry, marketers must have a working knowledge of the display screen technology, hard disk storage, operating systems, communications, data base and various print technologies, which provide the *technical environment* in which their software products operate. They must also learn about their customers' *industries* (such as banking or local government) and *business functions* (such as letter of credit processing or funds accounting). As a result, most computer software and services companies form project teams that bring functional, industry, and technological experts together to design and to sell the complex systems that are their products. Product managers in these firms often have a combination of an MBA with a computer science or engineering undergraduate degree. Many have previous functional experience in the industries their products serve.

In another example from the scientific instruments industry, the leading vendors of high-performance liquid chromatography (HPLC), a technique for separating chemical compounds, hire PhDs in chemistry for the sales force to ensure that they understand the technology and can use it to help solve customers' HPLC-related problems. The combination of highly educated sales and marketing professionals and the need for teams to provide expertise that one individual cannot offer is evidence of the complexity of the marketing and sales role in high tech industries.

So Little Time: Shorter Product and Technology Life Cycles Result in Fewer Advantages

Considerable evidence suggests that the average life cycle for high tech products in the late 1980s is shorter than it was a few years ago. At the same time, a number of world-class technology companies have substantially reduced the time required to move from concept to finished product in the new product development process. This ability to churn out more new products faster can be a source of marketing advantage (Clark and Fujimoto, 1986; Hayes, Wheelwright, and Clark, 1988; Takeuchi and Nonaka, 1986). Faster product development is one factor contributing to the shorter life cycle of products once they reach the market, because it takes less time to develop a new and better approach.

The shorter time to obsolescence for products and their underlying technologies suggests that the knowledge base of high tech marketers can rapidly become obsolete as well. Many technology companies invest in massive training programs to help their sales professional stay abreast of new developments in their product technologies, as well as those of competitors. A few firms have also developed programs to build expertise in target industries or applications.

The Marketer as Diplomat: Interfunctional and Interfirm Alliances

Interfunctional Boundary Spanning

Shanklin and Ryans (1985) provide a compelling argument for the importance of organizing in high tech situations to provide intensive linkages between organizations responsible for marketing and R & D. Their premise is that improved communication will stimulate ideas for new products and ensure improvement of existing products based on feedback from the marketplace. This recommendation provides a coping mechanism in situations that involve high uncertainty over both technology and the marketplace. Interaction allows marketing, which has the best information about the customers needs, and R & D, which has the best idea of the limits of the technology, to pool information and thereby reduce or manage the two forms of uncertainty.

The basic idea that uncertainty increases the need for cross-functional coordination has strong roots in earlier research. For example, Lorsch and Lawrence (1965) pointed out the importance of coordinating R & D and marketing (sales), on the one hand, and R & D and manufacturing, on the other. The issue of how to manage functional boundaries continues to be important for high tech organizations in the late 1980s. Schoonhoven and Jelinek, in another chapter in this volume, provide findings from their research that relate to this topic.

Cross-functional communication is likely to be higher in organizations making high tech purchases as well. Spekman and Stern (1979) studied the "buying center," the group in a buying organization responsible for making a purchase. They found that when uncertainty about the environment was high, communication increased between members of the buying center such as engineering and purchasing, which are the counterparts of R & D and marketing in the selling organization. As was mentioned earlier, Kosnik (1985) found that consultants and MBAs facing ambiguous preferences in the buying organization planned to spend significantly more time in internal discussions to help clarify the needs. The increased interfunctional involvement in high tech buying decisions has implications for marketing and sales professionals, who must cross functional boundaries not only in their own organization but in customer organizations as well, to ensure an effective selling campaign.

There is growing evidence of the need for coordination in low tech settings as well. For example, Procter & Gamble (P & G) has recently changed its product management organization, creating "business teams" of people from marketing, sales, production, and R & D to make decisions that in the past were made by brand managers. P&G's brands include many in mature product categories such as laundry detergent, toilet paper, and toothpaste. Even in these situations, marketers can ill afford to work in isolation from their counterparts in other functions. Although some integration may be useful almost anywhere, the arguments are most compelling for high tech settings, because of the complexity and uncertainty of information about both the technology and the marketplace.

The task of interfunctional coordination is often complicated by the relatively low status of the marketer in many high tech organizations. In most low tech consumer products companies, the product manager is a powerful and credible "hub of the wheel" for the brokering of influence and information. However, many high tech marketers must communicate and coordinate with scientists and engineers who are disdainful of their lack of technical credentials and with salespeople who question marketing's "value added" in an environment where, if you can't design it, make it, or sell it, you are an "overhead" item that consumes scarce resources better allocated to those who can. The exercise of influence in such situations is a more subtle art than in cases in which marketing enjoys greater power and prestige.

Interfirm Alliances
The 1980s have been marked by an increasing number of marketing alliances, either between suppliers and customers or manufacturers and distribution channels or among suppliers of complementary products (e.g., computer hardware and software) or competitors. Harrigan (1985) has discovered that, in contrast with other types of industries, high tech companies were less inclined to enter formal joint ventures with long-term legal covenants. Instead, they tended to favor looser, less formal agreements, which could be adapted or abandoned as the technology changed. Harrigan also describes several highly visible examples of high tech joint ventures, such as the Microelectronics & Computer Technology Corp. (MCC), which was founded in 1983 by fifteen companies to share the expense of advanced R & D for semiconductor, computer hardware, and software technologies. The point is not that high tech joint ventures never occur, but rather that flexible, disposable alliances may be more practical, and occur more frequently, than formal, long-term contracts when market and technological uncertainty are high.

There are numerous examples of these alliances in high tech settings. In 1985 Digital Equipment Corporation (DEC) established a Manufacturing Corporate Accounts Management (MCAM) program, whereby manufacturing executives who are familiar with how to use cutting-edge technology in DEC's operations met with their counterparts in DEC's leading customer organizations to exchange ideas on how to use new technology. The MCAMs also worked with DEC's manufacturing, marketing, sales, and product development organizations to provide a cross-fertilization of ideas in different functions.

In the 1985–88 time frame, there was a marked increase in alliances between computer hardware and software vendors who constituted one "channel" to the customer. For example, Tandem Corporation, a manufacturer of NonStop computers, built a group of 100 specialists in late 1985 with the responsibility of developing relationships with third-party software manufacturers. In the following year, it tripled the number of alliances with software suppliers to a total of 225 companies. In another example, Microsoft Corporation in 1987 had relationships with more than 300 hardware manufacturers to supply the operating systems for their microcomputers. *Systems Integration Age* (1988) has reported a marked increase in the number of relationships between computer software companies and consulting firms who specialize in customizing the software, installing it, and training users in the customer organization.

Relationships with various marketing partners are important as a way of building trust in the marketing exchange. The relationships can facilitate the flow of information from customers and channels that will reduce market uncertainty. It may also encourage customers or consultants to serve as "beta test sites" to run a new product through its paces, providing evidence of its performance limits and potential problems before it is introduced—thereby reducing technological uncertainty.

Von Hippel (1978) and Urban and von Hippel (1988) point out another benefit of strong supplier–customer relationships: lead customers are a major source of new product ideas. In a study of more than 160 major and minor product innovations in the fields of scientific instruments and semiconductor manufacturing equipment, von Hippel (1978) discovered that leading customers, not the marketers of the high tech systems, were the originators of ideas that led to commercially successful new products. Urban and von Hippel (1988) reported the successful use of a new methodology to elicit the new product ideas of lead users and demonstrated that the product concepts thus generated are attractive to customers who follow at a slower pace.

The Global Marketer: The Growing Importance of World Markets
High tech companies are increasingly turning to international markets for their products and learning that the decision to globalize has implications for all of marketing's "four Ps"—pricing, product policy, promotion (marketing communications), and place (distribution). One aspect of complexity is related to the fact that the marketer must become familiar with a new combination of language, laws, customs, culture, and distribution channels to get the product to the ultimate consumer. In addition, many high tech products must be made compatible with the technical standards in different countries, thereby complicating the design of the product to give it the flexibility to adapt to conditions around the world. In the computer industry, for example, the fact that different countries use different language symbols and characters, time and date formats, measures (i.e., meters and miles, pounds and grams), currencies, data communications protocols, electric power stan-

Table 7.2 Percentage of Sample Serving
International Markets

	Low Tech	High Tech
Manufacturing	29	69
Service	12	25

dards, and even paper sizes must all be taken into account in designing hardware and software products.

Although the issue of competing in global markets is not exclusive to high-tech industries, it appears that it may be more complicated for technology-intensive products than for simpler, more mature products. In a recent survey of 172 entrepreneurial companies in Massachusetts, Ambrosino, Green, Kein, and Lyons asked respondents to rate the importance of eleven problems that were "holding their businesses back." The respondents were classified as high tech and low tech manufacturing and service organizations. High tech manufacturing firms identified "limited access to international markets" as a much more important problem than did any of the other three segments of respondents. The problem was not a result of the fact that the other segments were already well established in international trade; in fact, the survey suggests the opposite pattern. The percentage of firms in each category that were serving international markets is shown in Table 7.2.

These results are corroborated by a study by Bank of Boston (1988), which sampled more than 400 high technology firms in thirty-eight states and five industries: biotechnology, advanced materials, photonics and optics, automation equipment, and test and measurement equipment. The study found that high tech companies in all five industries tended to enter international markets at an early stage in their development. Younger firms, founded after 1980, that exported enjoyed an increase in sales of 50 percent in the most recent fiscal year. Their counterparts who did not export increased sales by 44 percent. More mature exporting firms, founded before 1980, grew by 17 percent and nonexporters grew by 14 percent in the same period.

The Bank of Boston (1988) also reported annual exports by industry for 1981, 1985, and 1987 across a range of high, medium, and low tech industries. My analysis of their data suggests that from 1985 to 1987, exports of high tech industries such as computer, aerospace, and telecommunications increased an average of 11.1 percent. Medium tech exports such as passenger cars and piston engines grew at a slower rate of 7.9 percent. Low tech exports such as coal, corn, and wheat *declined* 10 percent over the 1985–87 period.

Why does high tech seem to imply higher international activity? Anecdotal evidence from the business press suggests that many U.S. computer hardware and software companies are turning to international markets because growth is considerably higher than in this country. There are also numerous stories of biotechnology, semiconductor, and computer companies who are forming global strategic alliances to help match the financial strength of larger partners with the creativity of high tech start-ups, or to marry the products and technologies of one partner with the market presence, access to customers, and knowledge of distribution channels of another.

The scramble for international alliances is not without its problems. Kosnik (1988) has listed five potential stumbling blocks of global partnerships for computer systems suppliers:

1. Partners are organized differently for making marketing and design decisions, leading to *problems in coordination.*
2. A company with special competence may align itself with several firms that are bitter competitors, leading to *problems of cooperation and trust.*
3. The "allies" with the best combination of complementary skills to build or market high tech products in one country may be ill-equipped to help one another in other countries, leading to *problems in implementing alliances on a global basis.*
4. The rapid pace of technological change virtually guarantees that the best partner tomorrow may be different from the best partner today, leading to *problems in maintaining alliances over a strategic (long-term) time period.*
5. The tendency of each partner to want as many allies and as few enemies as possible will make it difficult to say "no" to any alliance, leading to *problems in establishing unique competitive advantage.*

Kosnik (1988) also suggested a framework to compare what each partner "brings to the party," which is summarized in Figure 7.4.

Any venture requires a mix of the following:

- *resources* (money, information, people, and time)
- *relationships* (with customers, channels, and influencers)
- *reputation* (breadth of a firm's visibility and depth of its credibility)
- *capabilities* (technological expertise, industry experience, functional competencies, creative talent, managerial knowhow, marketing skill, and knowledge of the countries in the target market segment)

Each potential partner may offer a different mix of the these ingredients in each of the countries where the marketing will occur, which makes selection of a global ally an extremely complex decision.

Hypergrowth: Marketing When Time and Talent Are Scarce Resources

The combination of new technology solving new problems provides the opportunity to create markets where none existed. As a result, high technology products and services often undergo a period of slow growth in the initial stage, followed by spurts of sudden, dramatic growth as the new idea

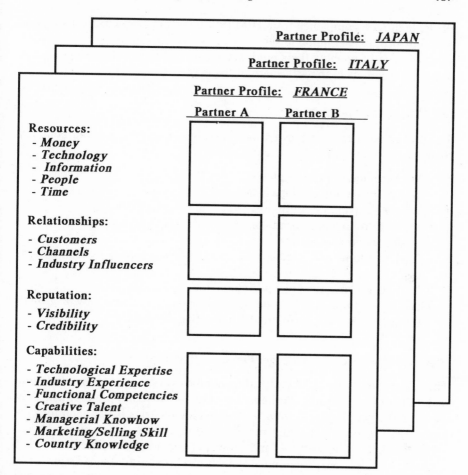

Figure 7.4 What Does Each Partner Bring to the Party? Does It Vary by Country?

catches on. During period of hypergrowth, time and talent are often more binding constraints than capital. The structures, systems, and procedures in the marketing organization are strained to the limit, thereby placing more pressure on the people to deal with problems in fire-fighting mode. This is an inherently more difficult task than following well-established rules and procedures.

There is another aspect of hypergrowth that increasing numbers of successful technology companies have had to address for the first time in the 1980s: managing and marketing when the growth slows. With all of its attendant problems, hypergrowth tends to attract excellent people, because the opportunities for advancement, financial rewards, and freedom from bureaucratic restrictions create an exciting work environment. The employees in hypergrowth settings frequently respond to problems with creativity and commitment that are rare in many other firms. However, it is extremely difficult to sustain that level of effort when opportunities dry up. In the late

1980s, high tech companies from IBM ($54 billion in sales) to Lotus Development Corp. ($396 million in sales) to a host of start-ups are grappling with thorny issues of pushing their products and motivating their marketing and sales professionals in the aftermath of hypergrowth.

PRACTICAL IMPLICATIONS

The preceding section suggested that high tech marketing is more complex than low tech marketing for seven reasons:

- Market uncertainty is higher
- Technological uncertainty is higher
- An ever-expanding set of new skills must be mastered
- Shorter product and technology life cycles imply that skills and wisdom quickly become obsolete
- Interfunctional and interfirm alliances are needed to pioneer new technology and enter unfamiliar markets
- High tech firms must manage global marketing efforts
- High tech implies a volatile pattern hypergrowth and slower growth that makes it difficult to build a marketing organization.

High Tech Marketing's Challenge: Perennial Renaissance

The seven sources of complexity affect almost every aspect of the marketing task in high tech settings. Perhaps the most fundamental requirement they place on the people and systems in high tech industries is the need for *perennial renaissance,* a constant renewal and rebirth of skills and structures as the markets, technologies, and problems change at breakneck speed. I have chosen the words "perennial renaissance" carefully because each has practical implications for getting the marketing job done. The dictionary definition of perennial is "consistent, enduring, constant." Renaissance is defined as "a period of vigorous artistic and intellectual activity; rebirth, revival." The combination of the two terms suggests that high tech marketing not only requires a tremendous amount of innovation to deal with the uncertainty and complexity; it also requires an ongoing level of intense effort for as long as the firm is in business, because the complexity and uncertainty are unlikely to diminish, despite the best efforts of the marketer.

Marketing Strategy: Focused, Flexible, Future Perfect

The need for perennial renaissance suggests several implications for both high tech marketing strategy and execution that are summarized in Figure 7.5. Marketing strategy decisions include (1) which market segments will be served, (2) how the firm will differentiate its products and services, and (3) how it will position itself as a company relative to its competitors in the minds of its customers. Figure 7.5 suggests that marketing in high tech settings must simultaneously be *focused, flexible, and future perfect.*

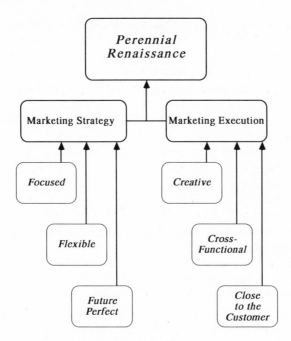

Figure 7.5 Keys to Successful High Tech Marketing

Focus in Commitments to Customers and Market Segments
The simultaneous requirement for focus and flexibility may appear at first to be a paradox, but both are required for different dimensions of high tech marketing strategy. Focus is imperative in selecting which customers and market segments the firm will serve over time. Given the high level of uncertainty in the buying and selling of high tech products, commitment to a specific, manageable number of customers and target industry segments is necessary to facilitate the successful adoption of the new technology, encourage the stimulation of new product ideas, and adapt and test new products throughout the design process to ensure they will be effective solutions to evolving customer needs.

Flexibility in Choice of Problems and Technological Solutions
If focus is required in the commitment to customers, flexibility is the watchword in selecting which of the customers' needs the marketer will address and which technologies will become part of the solution. These choices determine how the firm differentiates its products and positions itself relative to competitors. A marketing firm cannot focus doggedly on a particular set of customer needs if the customer cannot articulate them or if they are rapidly changing. Similarly, a firm cannot hope to "stick to the knitting" when today's knitting (technology) may be obsolete tomorrow.

For the marketer wondering how to translate the concept of flexibility into a tangible form, several alternatives are currently used. One approach is to design in *versatility*—the product's ability to be used for multiple purposes. One example of a product designed and marketed based on versatility is an integrated, multifunctional office productivity software tool, Microsoft Works. In 1987, product managers for Microsoft Corporation's application software products segmented the potential market based on whether or not people knew what they wanted in the way of "office productivity tools" to support number crunching, text processing, graphics, and file management. Microsoft positioned Works as the flexible solution for customers (called "breadth users") who were not sure what they needed. Other products, such as Microsoft Word (word processor) and Excel (spreadsheet) were designed and marketed as the best alternative for more experienced "depth users" who were very clear about the functions they wanted from their spreadsheet or word processor, and were less worried about flexibility across functions than they were about the capabilities of the product to support their most critical function(s).

A second way to provide flexibility is to offer *adaptability*, usually by providing support services to customize or modify the product to meet evolving needs. Many instrument manufacturers and some vendors of large, relatively costly computer software packages use this tactic. For example, American Management Systems (AMS) positions itself as a provider of information technology solutions to complex organizational problems. The firm targets only very large organizations with complicated application functions that defy a standard, "off-the-shelf" solution. It has software products that provide the foundation to meet many of the customers' needs at a fraction of the cost of a custom-built system. However, AMS also has a cadre of consultants who understand the details of the client's business functions and can design modifications to customize the solution at each site, thereby dominating standard packages.

A third approach is to design the product to offer *compatibility* with a wide variety of other products. Some computer software companies write their programs in languages that make them easily transportable across many different brands and models of computer hardware. AT&T's promotion of the Unix operating system, and IBM's commitment to its Systems Application Architecture are two other examples of vendors trying to broaden the compatibility of computer software products.

Finally, product flexibility can be enhanced through *modularity*—designing a set of products that can be bought one at a time, to meet a customer's particular need and budget at a given moment but that can be used together as part of an integrated system if and when the customer acquires more of the "building blocks." Modularity is used by a number of marketers of computer hardware, software, scientific instruments, and factory automation systems.

Future Perfect: A New Concept of Time and Strategy

The third implication for high tech marketing strategy is that is must be *future perfect*. Davis (1987) uses the term as the title of his book about linking strategy, science, technology, and organization. He suggests that implementing a strateg, in a radically new context requires an organization's leaders to "lead from a place in time that assumes you are already there, and that is determined even though it has not happened yet" (p. 25). He cites (p. 26) an earlier definition of this new sense of time from Weick's *The Social Psychology of Organizing* (1969): "The actor projects this [future strategy] as if it were already over and done with and lying in the past. . . . The fact that it is thus pictured as if it were simultaneously past and future can be taken care of by saying that it is thought of in the future perfect tense" (p. 26).

For those who may think suggesting that high tech marketing strategy be future perfect sounds farfetched, consider a few examples of future perfect strategizing in action from successful high tech marketing firms.

American Management Systems has successfully implemented numerous complex information systems over the period from 1970 to the present. At the beginning of each new custom-built system, they work closely with clients to develop the strategic concept of how the system, once completed, will add value to the organization. Consultant and client work together to create a "system concept" that describes in present tense, active voice, *as though it already existed,* the tangible details of how people and technology interact in new ways to create information, respond to requests for changes, and perform new functions in the various parts of the organization that the system will support. AMS's future perfect visualization of the strategy for a high tech product is distinctive. Although AMS's leading competitors engage in systems planning activities, most speak of the system in the *future* tense. The founders of AMS have used "future perfect" projective techniques to articulate their own marketing strategy over five-year time horizons—a lifetime in the software and systems consulting business.

Apple Computer's corporate university, Apple University, has recently begun implementing a series of learning programs for its managers called Living Programs℗, which also adopt a future perfect approach. At one of these programs, the Apple Management Seminar, groups of more than 100 managers spend four days together living life at Apple five years in the future. They are formed into self-managing teams of twenty to twenty-five people called learning circles, and are given the task of creating a product using a combination of cutting-edge computer technologies that will help solve a problem Apple will face in the future or communicate what Apple is like in the future to new Apple employees. Apple senior management, including CEO John Sculley, visit the seminar and conduct sessions that begin with something like: "This is (a date five years in the future). Let's talk about what Apple is doing, how it overcame some of the problems of five years ago, and where it is headed in the *next* five years." The learning and the concrete products/solutions that the Apple managers have developed and implemented in the course of these future perfect programs are nothing less than astonishing, compared with what I have seen many other competent and dedicated high tech marketers accomplish after the expenditure of much more time and effort both in management seminars and on the job.

In summary, marketing strategy must be focused, flexible, and future perfect in high tech settings, where the high rate of uncertainty and the rapid rate of change render strategy based on the lessons of the past obsolete before they can be implemented.

Marketing Execution: Creative, Cross-Functional, and Close to the Customer

Building Both Creativity and Discipline

Sculley (1987) points out a paradox in technology companies that provides the first implication for high tech marketing execution. He suggests that such firms need an environment that encourages creativity, to elicit the technological innovation essential to success in high tech domains. However, they also need a healthy dose of discipline, to avoid the problems of instability and lack of focus that are often present in high tech situations. Sculley evokes the image of a manager as an "impresario, to orchestrate a workshop of wizards" (p. 183) to characterize the skills needed for effective implementation high tech firms.

In my own work, when asked to summarize the task of high tech marketing execution, I have called it "managing creativity under the gun." It requires an appreciation for the fact that creativity and discipline are not polar opposites that must be traded off against one another. The most creative and talented people and organizations also have a healthy sense of self-discipline that allows the drive for technological innovation and the commitment to product quality to coexist with the need to meet some, but not all, deadlines and profit targets. Over the longer term, if careers in high tech marketing are to last a lifetime rather than the short span allotted to most rock stars, sports heroes, and research physicists, a certain amount of discipline is needed to ensure that the people involved in the process replenish their intellectual, emotional, physical, and spiritual resources so that they can be creative year after year.

Cross-Functional Collaboration and Communication

The second implication for high tech marketing execution is the requirement for cross-functional collaboration. Product design, manufacturing, sales, and marketing professionals need to improve their cross-functional communication and their understanding of customer needs if they are to design, make, and market products that provide value to the marketplace. There are several methodologies that show great promise in the area of enhancing cross-functional activities and communication. Hauser and Clausing (1988) have described a procedure known as quality function deployment (QFD) that originated at Mitsubishi in 1972 and was being piloted at high tech companies such as Digital Equipment Corporation, AT&T, and ITT in the late 1980s. Through a series of graphical forms, customer desires for intangible product qualities are linked to specific, tangible physical attributes of the product. For example, customers' desires for sportiness in a car may be linked to the presence of bucket seats or the shape of the automobile body. Then the physical product attributes are linked to design choices of technologies, components, or engineering specifications for the product. QFD is being used in a variety of ways to improve cross-functional communication and enhance product design.

Takeuchi and Nonaka (1986) and Hayes, Wheelwright, and Clark (1988) have provided concrete examples of how well-managed companies have organized the new product development to enhance cross-functional communication and reduce the time required to move from a big idea to the launch of a new product. One of the common themes of both approaches is that they recommend a great deal of interaction of marketing, sales, field service, R & D, and manufacturing throughout the process. This contrasts with traditional approaches to new product development, in which one function dominates the new product development process for one phase and then passes the baton to another function at a later phase. For example, under the old approach, marketing often originates a project, and then hands it off to R & D, who later returns it to marketing, who then passes it to manufacturing, and eventually to sales and field service. Under the new approach, manufacturing, sales, and service are involved from the early stages of the project.

In addition to new methodologies for product design and project management, many high tech firms are using management development and training experiences to foster cooperation and communication across the borders traditionally erected between functions, business units, and countries. AMS, Apple, Data General, and IBM are but a few of the high tech companies who use management seminars to promote boundary spanning. AMS and IBM use organizational and team-level simulations to give participants hands-on experience in developing group solutions to problems often encountered on high tech project teams. Data General routinely invites sales, field service, and R & D professionals to join its marketers as full participants during a series of marketing leadership development programs. As part of the Data General programs, cross-functional teams apply new marketing tools to "live" marketing problems that are currently being faced by the organization. As mentioned earlier, Apple's cross-functional teams develop concrete solutions to *future* marketing problems.

Although much is being done, there are still major opportunities to enhance the effectiveness of cross-functional marketing activities in high tech organizations. In addition to making marketing work better as a function, such activities can also begin to address the final issue in high tech marketing execution, the requirement for people in all functions throughout a high tech organization to become more sensitive and responsive to customers.

Close to the Customer: Technological Innovation Is Not Enough

Virtually every high tech company I have encountered in the last decade has gradually come to the realization that technological innovation is not enough to guarantee long-term success. The challenge in the 1990s is in learning how to sustain the commitment to technological advancement, while simultaneously becoming more market driven, or "getting closer to the customer."

However, getting close to the customer is more easily said than done.

Learning about them through market research is difficult and potentially misleading when technologies are changing rapidly and customers do not know what they want (McKenna, 1985). This calls for greater care in using existing techniques, and the development of new market research methodologies that are appropriate to conditions of high technological and market uncertainty (Workman, 1988). Urban and von Hippel (1988) provide an example of this new class of marketing methods by eliciting preferences from lead users, who understand their needs and potential application of new technology sooner than others.

Getting closer to customers also requires that high tech sales and marketing professionals focus less on the technology and more on the clients' business problems. One approach that has been widely adopted by computer hardware manufacturers is a training simulation in which the sales people and sales managers live in a customer organization for a week, and deal with the problems of a major technology purchase from the buyer's perspective. Various sales people play the roles of a customer's division general manager and his vice presidents of finance, marketing, sales, manufacturing, and management information systems. By "walking in the customer's shoes," sales professionals gain insights not easily acquired by simply talking about, or even listening to, their clients.

Some high tech marketers also use *technology* to get closer to customers. For example, Digital Equipment Corp., Sun Microsystems, Apple Computer, and Microsoft use electronic mail to allow customers to interact with people in sales, technical support, marketing, and in some cases even R & D and manufacturing, to ask questions or resolve problems that arise with new technology. American Management Systems and Index Systems, two information technology service firms, put select clients on their voice messaging networks so that they can interact with consultants and with other clients to discuss technical and other issues. It is really not surprising that some high tech companies use information technology to provide better service and get closer to customers. What *is* surprising is that many high tech suppliers do not put all of their own people on voice mail or electronic mail systems because the costs are allegedly too high and refuse to allow customers on the systems for fear of security leaks about new product plans.

The mechanisms for getting closer to customers appear deceptively straightforward. However, one difficulty many high tech firms have in becoming more customer focused is that the patience and long-term perspective required to nurture relationships with customers are antithetical to the mindset required to manage the intense pace and unpredictable change that characterize high tech products and technologies.

Conclusion

It is ironic that the recommendations for coping with complexity in high tech marketing seem very simple and low tech. Focused, flexible, future perfect marketing strategy; creative, cross-functional, and close-to-the-customer marketing execution—at first glance, these prescriptions may appear superficial. However, if one remembers that high technology is simply new technology in the service of evolving needs, and that the problems of coping with complexity and uncertainty in the face of innovation are timeless, the recommendations ring true. Besides, there is a world of difference between understanding the need for perennial renaissance and being able to sustain it over the decades that mark the life cycles of high tech companies and marketing careers. It is the difference between reading a biography of Michelangelo and setting out to paint your own Sistine Chapel.

8

Managing a High-Reliability Organization: A Case for Interdependence

KARLENE H. ROBERTS AND
GINA GARGANO

Among high technology organizations there is a set of organizations labeled "high risk" (Perrow, 1984). They are high risk in the sense that errors in them may lead not only to employee death or to the need to rebuild parts of the organization, but to catastrophic consequences of such magnitude that they are unacceptable to the organization or a larger public. For example, the result of the accident at Union Carbide's chemical plant at Bhopal in 1984 is unacceptable to the Indian government.

These organizations are high risk because, in order to provide goods or services deemed important to a society (e.g., power, defense), they engage in sophisticated complex technologies that have to be managed to avoid unanticipated interactions among parts of the organization. It was just such unanticipated interactions among organizational parts that resulted in the nearly catastrophic Three Mile Island nuclear power plant accident (Perrow, 1984).

Within this set of organizations there is a subset in which reliability rather than productivity is the bottom line. These are organizations with an avowed goal of safe operations and in which behaviors are engaged in to ensure those safe operations (Roberts, in press). The focus in these organizations is on extremely highly reliable operations. Such organizations are not to be confused with those in which steps to ensure safe operations should be, but are not, taken (e.g., the Union Carbide plant at Bhopal). It is entirely possible for a "high-reliability" organization to change its operations so that it becomes potentially unreliable.

This research was supported by Office of Naval Research contract N-00014-86-k-0312 and National Science Foundation grant 87-08046. The research is part of a multidisciplinary study of high-reliability organizations. The ideas in this chapter were drawn from the research team; professors Todd La Porte and Gene Rochlin; PhD students Jennifer Halpern and Paula Consolini, University of California; and Suzanne Stout, Stanford University. The authors would like to thank Comdr. Pat Madison and Capt. Denny Gladman for their help.

Most organizations attempt to avoid mistakes, and often go to great lengths to do so. Errors in judgment may lead to lost profits or opportunities, but organizations often learn from their mistakes and subsequently improve their performance. High-risk organizations do not have the luxury to learn by trial and error. The consequences of error in these organizations are often so great that when a major error occurs the organization effectively ceases to function or there is sufficient public outrage that it is significantly altered or put out of operation.

Aircraft carriers closely fit this description of high technology, high-risk organizations that are extremely reliable. Carrier operations are enormously complex, and the safety history of the U.S. Navy's nuclear aircraft carriers (of which there are now six) is extraordinarily good. No nuclear carrier has ever been destroyed, and the last major deck fire attributable to ship's operations on any of the U.S. aircraft carriers (of which there are fifteen) was in 1969 (aboard USS Enterprise). Each nuclear carrier is a floating city with an airport on its roof, 6000 men aboard, two to eight nuclear reactors, nine aircraft squadrons (with about ninety aircraft) and every imaginable service (food, barber, medical and dental, clergy, training, etc).

The sheer density of technologies and magnitude of activities that go on aboard carriers illustrate their high-risk potential. The modern carrier's principal offensive strike power are the A-6 Intruder (all weather attack) and A-7 Corsair (light attack) jet aircraft. The primary defense force for the carrier and its surface escort ships (of which there are about ten) are the F-14 Tomcat jet fighters and the propeller driven E-2 Hawkeye early airborne warning aircraft. Equipped with an array of electronic detection systems, the S-3 Viking propeller-driven aircraft and the SH-3H Sea King helicopter search for, locate, and relay information on submarines contacts. Finally, the EA-6 Prowler jet aircraft uses sensitive receivers and high-powered jammers to deny the enemy use of much of his radar and radio equipment. All of these systems operate simultaneously by a team whose job is to maintain a defensive barrier of several hundred miles around the carrier battle group and ensure that no unknown contacts cross this barrier without positive identification.

During battle exercises or duty in a hostile area the ships man their NATO Sea Sparrow missile system and the Phalanx close-in weapons system, a sophisticated version of the rotating-barrel Gatling gun. These ships are the most powerful self-contained combat platforms in the world.

The nuclear power plants allow the carriers to travel for extended periods at speeds in excess of 30 knots without the need to replenish propulsion fuel. Once on station, these ships can remain longer and fly more missions than oil-fired carriers because of their ability to carry aviation fuel in tanks that would otherwise be devoted to ship's fuel in the conventional carrier. Each ship has fuel for approximately fifteen years.

When the ships are at sea, all of these systems are maintained and operated simultaneously along with the 3360 compartments and spaces aboard, the more than 2000 telephones, and the over 1 billion tubes, transistors, and diodes. While these various kinds of technologies operate so the ship can carry out its missions, 18,150 meals are consumed and over 400,000 gallons of water are distilled daily (more than enough for 2000 homes), and electronic equipment output equals the output of about fifty broadcast stations operating simultaneously.

In addition to the complexities of running small cities, carriers at sea continually launch and recover aircraft at frequencies of 45 to 60 seconds and at speeds of up to 140 knots. Carriers basically operate today in eighteen-month cycles, beginning with an extensive maintenance after return from deployment, and ending with a six-month overseas deployment. (For an extensive discussion of characteristics of carriers, see Roberts, in press.)

For several years a group of researchers at the University of California has examined the design and operational characteristics of several high-reliability organizations, including nuclear aircraft carriers. During the course of their investigation they uncovered a unit aboard the carriers whose sole duty is to manage interdependence across other units. One purpose of this paper is to describe the nature of the interdependence that exists on carriers. First, however, it is necessary to define interdependence and to offer some suggestions for a theory of interdependence. Since the relationship of interdependence, complexity, and system stability are so closely intertwined in the literature, these will also be discussed.

INTERDEPENDENCE

Societal problems are increasingly framed in interorganizational terms. Interdependence is a fact of life for organizations in social systems (Blau, 1976; Bingham & Vertz, 1983), in networks of community organizations (Galaskiewicz & Krohn, 1984; Sheets, 1985), among governmental agencies (Weed, 1986), in corporations (Mizruchi & Bunting, 1981; Pfeffer, 1972), and within technical systems (Perrow, 1984). Consequently, there is growing interest in understanding intra- and interorganizational relations (Aiken & Hage, 1968; Benson, 1975; Pfeffer & Salancik, 1978) and networks of organizations (Burt, 1980; Galaskiewicz, 1979; Lincoln, 1982).

Systems with highly interdependent components pose problems of coordination and integration, in part because of new levels of system complexity. This complexity often results in the kinds of situations discussed by Eisenhardt and Bourgeois (chapter 5). In addition, failure in one part of the system can bring down the whole system or substantial parts of it because of unanticipated interactions (Perrow, 1984) and the nature of tight coupling (Thompson, 1967).

The technologies of high-risk organizations are dense; that is, they are packed one on top of another in overlapping and thick networks of components. Technological density may be a cause or an effect of tight coupling in these organizations. Tight coupling and dense webs of technology create environments in which complex interactions occur. These interactions may be baffling in the sense that their sequences are unfamiliar, unplanned, unexpected, and often either invisible or not immediately comprehensible. According to Perrow (1984, p. 75), in complex interactions "There are branching paths, feedback loops, jump[s] from one linear sequence to another because of proximity and certain other features. . . . The connections are not only adjacent, serial ones, but can multiply as other parts or units or subsystems are reached." According to Cook (1977, p. 63), "Not only is the environment becoming more complex and turbulent but the web of organizations within communities is becoming increasingly complex, interrelated and extensive." As the number of both high-risk and high-reliability organizations increases, the potential for these organizations (or units in them) to become interdependent with each other increases rapidly. Galbraith (chapter 3) suggests that high technology leads to networks of tightly connected organizations. Mohrman, Mohrman, and Worley (chapter 11) point out that the high levels of interdependence both within and between functions in high technology settings create a need for teamwork, cooperation, and codependence.

One definition of interdependence stresses the fact that "interdependent entities form a system whose members or parts cannot be identified except by the process of their interactive functioning" (Rorty, 1987, p. 3). For example, nuclear power plants and nuclear waste management organizations are interdependent; neither could exist without the other.

Researchers recognize the need for theories to aid in understanding of increasingly complex social systems. The organizational literature, however, has thus far failed to address problems that may be unique to or at least magnified in high-risk organizations.

COMPONENTS OF A THEORY OF INTERDEPENDENCE

Given the broad, far-ranging, and varied conceptualizations of interdependence that exist, it is not surprising that the organizational literature is characterized by few and imprecise attempts to measure it. Here we attempt to provide a testable conceptualization based on our understanding of previous literature.

Interdependence describes a relationship between two or more units that are mutually affecting and affected (Radcliff group, 1987). Their parts cannot be easily distinguished because of mutual interaction (Keller, 1987). Individual unit actions and goals are formulated in reference to other parties in the relationship and interlock to serve common ends, often because one party controls resources required to reach another party's goal (Pfeffer & Salancik, 1978). The relationship is enduring in such a way that there is not only exchange of resources to support mutual and individual goals but also an expectation of exchange (Cook, 1977; Emerson, 1970; Levine & White, 1961). In this sense, exchanges in an interdependent relationship are predictable (Rorty, 1987) and necessary for survival. Interdependence is a continuous variable; a system can have highly interdependent or minimally interdependent components.

The dimensions emerging from the literature that can be used to assess relationships are as follows:

1. Static or dynamic
2. Consensual or de facto
3. Providing checks on the actions/outcomes of the other party or having no such "veto" power
4. Symmetrical or asymmetrical
5. Pooled, sequential, standard reciprocal, asymmetrical reciprocal, and flexible reciprocal
6. Containing exchanges of goods and services, flows of information (communication), or exchanges of norms

These terms require clarification. Static versus dynamic relationships have commonsense meaning. If relationships are dynamic they change, if static they remain the same over time. If relationships are consensual, they are based on bargaining and negotiation; if de facto one party determines the relationship. If checks are in place, one party checks the other party, or both parties to the relationship have this right.

Pooled interdependence occurs when each party to a relationship contributes to the whole, but the parties may not interact in any other way. Sequential interdependence is serial in the sense that the job cannot be completed unless A provides a resource for B, that B, in turn, provides one for C, and so forth. Reciprocal interdependence occurs when the outputs from *each* party to a relationship become the inputs to the other parties (Thompson, 1967).

Interdependence is asymmetrical when both sides rely on each other but one relies on the other more (Kmetz, 1984). Flexible reciprocal interdependence exists when each party not only depends on the other but coordination is by mutual adjustment in which each unit depends on the other to act in a time-dependent manner (Eccles, 1986). Interdependencies based on various exchanges are self-explanatory.

To fully understand interdependence we must take into account that organizations are not "flat" but rather "thick." Systems are too often measured as one-dimensional arrays rather than n-dimensional forms. Fombrun (1986) claims that social collectivities contain three interactive but partially autonomous levels: the infrastructure, sociostructure, and superstructure. Within any one structural level, a number of interdependent relationships exist between two or more parties. Organizations become especially complicated and complex when interdependencies develop across levels.

In this distinction, we find one of the major differences between most organizations and high technology, high-risk organizations (Roberts & Rousseau, 1989). The structural levels are more tightly coupled and interact more extensively and unpredictably in high-risk organizations. Failure at one level is not isolated but spreads quickly in vexing ways to other levels and components in those levels. These organizations, like all complex organizations, are composed of layers of levels, one on top of another, with interaction across levels. This is the epitome of what Perrow calls interactive complexity and nonlinear interactions. This means interactions in which the processes occurring in two systems that should be independent and in parallel interact.

The ultimate goal of most organizations is to maintain a stable system, one that endures and avoids failure. Aldrich and Whetton (1981) believe that the ultimate predictor of network stability is the probability of a link failing, given that another has failed (disregarding external factors). Multiple links and built-in redundancy are purported to increase overall network stability (Landau, 1969). If A and B have three links among them, failure in one link does not significantly alter A's and B's ability to function together. This suggests that organizational subsystems overlap in function, with closely coupled backup links, to avoid a system breakdown. It is assumed that the links are independent of one another.

The "conventional wisdom" in ecology through the 1970s was that increased complexity by means of greater "connectedness" provides greater stability (Begon, Harper, & Townsend, 1986). Complexity is defined in this context as more interactions, a greater number of species (or units), and a greater length of interaction. May (1974, p. 75), however, offers the opposite prediction. He finds that mathematical models indicate complexity tends to beget instability rather than stability: "The greater the size and connectedness of a web, the larger the number of characteristic modes of oscillation it possesses: since in general each mode is as likely to be unstable as stable, the addition of more and more simply increases the chance for the total web to be unstable."

For May the units are not independent of one another. Failure in one link is likely to bring the entire system down, regardless of the amount of redundancy built into the system. The scenario is more likely to occur in an unstable environment. "A predictable or stable environment may permit a relatively complex and delicately balanced ecosystem to exist; an unpredictable or unstable environment is more likely to demand a simpler robust ecosystem" (p. 215).

PARADOXES

A number of tensions exist between what the organizational literature predicts about interdependence and related issues in high-risk organizations. That is, the literature offers propositions that, if pushed to their extremes in high-reliability organizations, are internally inconsistent. Scott[1] makes a number of propositions based on the literature:

1. Hierarchical structures should increase the reliability of performance.
2. In highly interdependent systems, tight coordination and close grouping enhances reliability.

3. Redundancy increases reliability in loosely coupled systems.
4. The better the match or congruence between complexity of work performed and complexity of performance (ability to exercise discretion), the higher the performance reliability.
5. The more uncertainty the organization faces, the more flexible the system must be to ensure high reliability (one way to manifest flexibility is through decentralization).
6. Resources are needed to coordinate and control for high reliability.

Based on our discussion, it is clear that interdependence leads to problems of coordination and control that are often resolved through extreme hierarchy, as seen in propositions 1 and 2. On the other hand, environmental uncertainty begs for decentralization (proposition 5). Hierarchy and decentralization do not coexist well (paradox 1).

Redundancy increases reliability (proposition 3) in loosely coupled systems. Highly interdependent systems such as those we discuss here are tightly coupled. As we discussed earlier, introducing greater redundancy into highly complex systems may actually destabilize them, resulting in low-reliability organizations (paradox 2).

Tightly coupled systems are also less adaptive to changing environments than are loosely coupled systems. High-risk organizations must confront environmental uncertainty but are tightly coupled (paradox 3). We might predict system failure under these circumstances (thus the term high risk). Increasing interdependence leads to system instability in organizations that absolutely require error-free operations.

From proposition 4 it is clear that simple systems require simple skills and complex systems require complex skills. Perrow (1984) points out that nuclear power plant operators have narrowly defined skills and often do nothing more than read meters and open and close valves in an uneventful day. The nature of the problems that may develop are complex, interactive, and unpredictable in high-risk systems. Can operators cope with these occurrences (paradox 4)?

Proposition 6 is intuitive: There are no free lunches, as starkly revealed in Shrivastava's (1987) analysis of the disaster in the Union Carbide plant at Bhopal. Coordination requires resources to ensure reliable performance. One characteristic of high-risk organizations is their lack of slack resources; these systems often operate at or near capacity (paradox 5).

How do high-risk organizations survive? This discussion points out how high-risk organizations deviate from theoretical predictions about reliable performance in organizations. But many high-risk organizations somehow mitigate these dilemmas, forming the subset of high-reliability organizations. One way they may do this is through explicitly acknowledging and managing the interdependence among their parts. To illustrate this point, we now return to the carriers.

AN ILLUSTRATIVE EXAMPLE

Interdependence

That a carrier is not just one system but rather a host of complex systems is clear from our previous description of carriers. Here we focus on one segment of these systems, the interdependence of ship's company and the air wing effected by the Carrier Air Wing Command (CAG, a unit that includes about fifteen people). This unit's sole purpose is to integrate the ship and air wing (the nine squadrons of aircraft). When a ship is in readiness training (about nine months) the Air Wing (composed of about 3000 men) flies on and off to qualify aviators for carrier landings and to accomplish other training. During these times the wing must effect quick connects and disconnects from the ship's company (another 3000 men) without doing harm to any of the complicated technologies involved (from aircraft to steam catapults, nuclear reactors, etc.). When the squadrons are not aboard the ships, they are engaged in training from land-based air fields. During the six-month ship deployment, the squadrons are aboard continuously. Squadrons are highly dependent on the abilities and cooperation of ship personnel, and ships are dependent on the squadron's ability to adapt to and work well with the ship. Neither the squadrons nor the ships can do their jobs without the other.

We have attempted to provide an overall description of interdependence between the ship and the air wing by assessing whether the dimensions (previously discussed as possible components of a theory of interdependence) exist. CAG staff and squadron representatives from the air wings aboard USS *Enterprise* and USS *Carl Vinson* completed questionnaires assessing their perceptions of the nature and extent of interdependence of the ship and air wing. Because CAG staffs are small, the data from them are used merely to illustrate and support our independent observations of the operations of the carrier and air wing. Data from ninety-two respondents from the squadrons aboard the two ships were aggregated to provide a picture of interdependence. The data were broken out by job function to assess whether one's job specialty influenced one's perception of various aspects of interdependence. Thus, we present here data from our own observations over a two-year period, combined with descriptive data from CAG and squadron personnel.

Our observations suggest the ships and their air wings are interdependent; that is, their functions are defined in relationship to each other. As an example, even at their home bases the squadrons train to go to sea; they are not entirely disconnected from the ships. And one of the goals of an aircraft carrier is to project power abroad, which is impossible without its aircraft. As one squadron commanding officer said, "we are CAGs reason for existence. They have no function without the squadrons." The parties are deliberately mutually affected and affecting. The deliberate nature of this is the activity of the CAG staff, which is analogous to the center of an hour glass, mediating the direction in which the sands flow. It is clear that the air wing and ship share desired outcomes and that neither controls entirely the conditions necessary for achieving these outcomes. The ship cannot realize its goals without the planes, nor can the planes without the ship.

The air wing and ship can be partitioned into parts as is done when the squadrons return to their home bases. These may set the limits to interdependence in this organization. Because of the nature of social organizations, one probably would find in them few instances of interdependence that are not deliberate. Nondeliberate interdependence may characterize ecological systems more than it does organizations. The fact that the air wing and ship can be and are partitioned makes the organizations interesting as a case study of interdependence, because one can look at what the partitioning does to dimensions of interdependence.

Observational data also provide a picture of interdependence along the six specific dimensions that might serve as a basis for theoretical development. Carriers are characterized by *dynamic* interdependence. It simply is not possible for ship personnel to drive the ship to specified locations, maintain the aircraft, provide ordnance, and engage in the thousands of other services it engages in for the squadrons without dynamic interaction between ship and squadron personnel. Squadron and CAG personnel report that when they are at sea they interact with their counterparts on the ship more than hourly or every few hours. The higher one's rank, the more frequent the interaction. One respondent reported, "during flight ops [operations] it's hourly, during non flight ops daily to every few hours, if we're developing a plan for future ops." A squadron member reported, "CAG staff serves as an interface between our squadron and the flag [admiral's] staff. As such, they may require short fuzed inputs or long range plans covering squadron planning on even day to day administrative matters." When the ship is in home port, interaction drops to weekly or monthly.

The interaction is obviously *consensual* in that it is not possible for the parties to reach their shared goals (getting aircraft off the ship to some destination, and then back onto the ship) without bargaining and joint consensus. The situation is characterized by too much uncertainty and too many possible courses of action not to behave in this way.

The mere existence of the CAG staff imposes a mechanism for *checks and balances*. Each member of CAG staff has counterparts in ship's company and the squadrons (e.g., there is an operations officer on CAG staff, one on each ship, and one in each squadron). Many activities conducted on carriers can be vetoed by anyone, regardless of rank, who believes the activity is placing the ship in harm's way. Ship and squadron maintenance workers are frequently intertwined, particularly because some squadron maintenance personnel are assigned temporary duty to ship's company when the ships are deployed. Checks and balances are worked into the system in many ways. A CAG weapons officer stated, "my primary responsibility is weapons safety/expertise. Afloat I work on the flight deck and provide direct liaison between the ship's weapons department and strike operations, and the air wing. We can look over the whole thing."

Interdependence can be *symmetrical* or *asymmetrical* independent of whether it is pooled, sequential, or reciprocal. In this case neither unit has the ultimate power to define the ends and directions of the systems. That power is left to flag command and sometimes even to the commander-in-chief. However, within the purview of day-to-day shipboard activities there is a good deal of symbiosis. CAG staff members reported that, in their interactions with ship's departments, they each ask for about equal resources from the other. They more frequently desire resources from squadrons than squadrons do for them. Among squadron personnel, higher job levels reported equal exchange of resources between squadrons and their ships, while lower ranks saw the relationships as more one-sided (squadrons demanded more from the ships than the ships did from the squadrons). In terms of their relationship with CAG, squadron personnel generally perceived the exchange of resources as equal. "CAG allows us to do our job" and it is an "organizational point for all squadrons to make a unified whole." A squadron maintenance officer said, "We assist as necessary for working out aircraft maintenance problems throughout the air wing." The commanding officer of the CAG stated, "We cut across different unit lines and coordinate 'functional' efforts for the squadrons. For example, CAG Operations Officer puts out a plan to all squadron ops officers ensuring they are all aware of the Battle Group's aviation ops. We also coordinate the diverse efforts of nine squadrons into a supportive whole in maintenance and safety. Finally, we relate with the ships counterpart people."

From the ships' perspectives, every maintenance, safety, and other activity is designed to support the movement of aviators safely on and off the ship. Thus, the matter of asymmetrical interdependence is one of perception. As an example, a member of the CAG staff said, "The squadrons don't do much for us individually. Collectively they are the air wing and comprise our primary mission [resource], air superiority." The same person added that CAG staff's job is "to liaise up and down the chain of command for the squadrons and to assist them in any way possible. We provide support, coordinate operational plans/schedules, material assistance, etcetera." In reality this may be analogous to a marriage in which each partner feels he or she gives 60 percent.

As in any complex organization, there is much *pooled, sequential,* and *reciprocal* interdependence on the ships. Since, by definition, if reciprocal interdependence exists, so do pooled and sequential interdependence, we looked for evidence of reciprocal interdependence. One indicator was descriptions from squadron officers about what CAG staff does for them. They reported that CAG staff's job is to coordinate and direct and to act in the chain of command between the squadrons and the ship. "The staff sets out requirements from higher authority, buffering the squadrons from direct intervention from the flag. . . . They consolidate the overall planning." Respondents from each of the squadron's job functions (from operations to ordnance to safety) reported that CAG staff provides liaison between them and the ship. In each case the squadron officer has contact with his counterpart both on CAG staff and in ship's company. Reciprocal interdependence exists with CAG serving as the fulcrum.

Is this reciprocal interdependence flexible (focusing on interdependence in which time is essential)? Since the entire operation of aircraft carriers is designed to be extremely time-dependent, it is pointless to ask organizational members whether it is. However, the frequency of communication with one another and the importance of interaction are indications of mechanisms in place to aid the time-dependent nature of activities. The fact that the pattern of interaction changes from home port to sea operations is an indicator of flexible reciprocal interdependence. A CAG staff operations officer reported, "We operate as a translator from mission requests or tasking. We manage training for the air wing in a macro sense with a goal of deploying in a combat-ready status."

On a five-point scale from very important to not at all important, all CAG staff respondents replied that their interaction with both ship's company and the squadrons is very important to the successful completion of their jobs. Squadron respondents reported that interaction with the ship is generally very important to the completion of their jobs (with some variation by job title). They believe that interaction is somewhat important in the ships' abilities to do their jobs. Squadrons found their interaction with CAG to be somewhat important for their ability to do their jobs and slightly more important for CAG's ability to do their job.

In summary, using both observations and questionnaire responses from key squadron and CAG staff personnel, we identified a number of dimensions of interdependence. While we demonstrated the existence of these elements, our metric is not a precise barometer of "how much" interdependence exists. We can say, "quite a lot," but that is all. We believe interdependence, particularly of the flexible reciprocal sort, is a characteristic of high-risk, high-reliability organizations and that, if high-risk organizations are not extremely well coordinated and managed, they will fail. This observation is based on Shrivastava's (1987) account of the accident at the Union Carbide Plant at Bhopal in which he alludes to the fact that various workers did not know what others had or had not done. If the organization had managed its interdependence with a coordination unit, perhaps failure would have been avoided.

Resolving Paradoxes Created by Interdependence

Not only do we find large amounts of interdependence aboard the carriers, particularly across the air wing and ship's company, we also find that in their efforts to maintain high degrees of reliability the carriers, as larger systems, defeat the paradoxes previously discussed.

Paradox 1 focuses on simultaneous hierarchy and decentralization. The military system of ranks and reporting by rank operates on carriers just as it does in all other parts of the military. Higher-level ranks can override decision making by lower-level ranks. In addition, however, the organization operates optimally when decisions are pushed to the lowest level commensurate with skill (Roberts, Halpern, & Stout, 1988).

An example of this is "fouling the deck" (preventing aircraft from landing). The decision is important because the ship may have aircraft in the queue or on final approach that are low on fuel. The lowest-level deck hand can call the deck foul if he sees something on the deck that might cause a problem for the returning aircraft. Small objects (such as tools and other paraphernalia) frequently get loose on decks and can be sucked into jet engines destroying them. While decision makers are careful not to call the deck foul if, in fact, it is clear, in this case the wrong decision is not punished. Interdependence across the system is strengthened through this kind of resolution of paradox 1.

The tension between tight and loose coupling among interdependent units requires resolution (paradox 2). Asymmetrical reciprocal interdependence leads to very tight coupling. Alternatively, flexible reciprocal interdependence requires loose coupling. Once the air wing is aboard the ship steps are taken to hook together the air wing and ship's company, particularly in the aircraft maintenance function. Large segments of squadron personnel are given over to the ship and fitted into the ship's operations. Air wing maintenance personnel and ship's company maintenance personnel become almost indistinguishable (tightly coupled). Just as quickly, these two groups disconnect and go their separate ways. When ships are in port air wing maintenance are miles from port while ship maintenance men remain with the ship. These two groups go from tightly coupled to not coupled at all, moving from extreme interdependence to complete independence from one another.

How does a tightly coupled organization deal with environmental uncertainty (paradox 3)? It is possible that carriers and other high-risk organizations are most subject to accident by failing to resolve paradox 3. A common response to demands made on high-risk organizations to increase service is to introduce more technology. A common response to budgetary concerns is to reduce manpower. What results is an even more tightly coupled system with more dependencies and fewer human monitors. Slack is squeezed out of the organization. Carriers do not readily embrace new technologies, and high-level decision makers continually do what they can to buffer against manpower cuts. Should an overzealous Congress win, however, the Navy might find itself in the condition just described.

Paradox 4 results when people are trained narrowly but face a complex set of interactive, unpredictable contingencies. Carrier design solves this problem by having narrowly trained people supervised by specialists trained more broadly and with long histories of experience. These men are, in turn, supervised by generalist officers. On top of this system of training and experience is layered enormous redundancy across jobs for the very purposes of identifying errors before they propagate.

Paradox 5 was alluded to in our discussion of paradox 3. High-reliability organizations are very expensive to operate, and pressures abound to reduce cost. At top "readiness" carriers operate at or near capacity. The challenge is to engage the level of peak activity that will not destroy the organization's ability to act continuously. Carriers engage in nine months of work-ups before they are ready for six-month overseas deployments in their readiness phases.

MANAGEMENT PRESCRIPTIONS

Managers in high technology, high-risk organizations might want to think about whether their organizations should operate with high reliability as a goal. If the consequences of error in the organization are severe, then it is prudent to take steps toward ensuring high-reliability operations. Observations, perhaps supplemented with questionnaire data, can be used to assess the degree to which interdependence exists in the organization. It is probably apparent from our previous discussion that increased interdependence can result in destabilization.

What we have not done that managers may want to do is develop a fairly precise metric for measuring interdependence in an organization or one of its units. Since there are yet no available instruments to do this, managers may wish to do informal assessments based on the categories discussed here. Not only can this categorical scheme be used to determine existing interdependence, it can be used as a basis for building in coordination where it is desired and for reducing interdependence when it is desirable to do so.

Where it is possible and desirable managers may want to decrease interdependence among subunits, making it easier to decouple systems when problems begin to develop. If they cannot do this and tight coupling and interdependence pose problems, they may want to build in specific decoupling mechanisms to use when necessary. Sometimes these strategies are mechanical (for example, physically unhooking units of an organization) and sometimes managerial (for example, when groups decide not to interact but each develop independent solutions to a problem).

It may be possible to lessen the potential destabilization problems introduced by increased interdependence through developing units, such as CAG, to manage interdependence. This unit is used to increase stabilization. CAG serves as an intermediary, controlling the flow and content of information. Both the ship's departments and the squadron rely on CAG for information and direction. Squadrons and ships departments refine their common goals through CAG. CAG is a coordinating device and coordination is expensive for organizations. It may be less expensive, however, than organizational annihilation or extreme damage to the organization and its surrounding public.

We believe that not only is the number of organizations designed for high reliability on the increase but other organizations not generally thought to be high reliability are developing characteristics that should make considering high reliability an objective. As more and more chemical plants in addition to sophisticated technologies handle products and processes that can lead to catastrophic consequences, they become candidates for management strategies to increase reliability. As power production moves from total reliance on hydro, fossil fuel, and geothermal sources to nuclear sources of power in which the production process itself creates the potential for both personnel loss and extreme environmental damage and community loss of life, reliability-enhancing strategies should be considered.

NOTE

1. W. Richard Scott; personal communication with K. H. Roberts, T. L. La Porte, and G. I. Rochlin, November 1987.

9

Implementing New Production Technologies: Exercises in Corporate Learning

DOROTHY LEONARD-BARTON

Some people never understood that the *way* you introduce something really matters.

a plant manager

Of all the things you spend money on, building a new organization is the most important, because whether you know it or not, that's really what you're doing when you introduce a new system.

implementation team member

Corporations described as high technology companies earn that title not only by competing through new product technology but also by embedding new technology in their operations. Therefore, managers in many firms today need to build the in-depth technological capability that will allow them to produce goods and services competitively.

In building that capability, they must make several critical decisions, foremost of which is the extent to which the technology is bought or otherwise obtained in an off-the-shelf form, ready to be used, versus developed within the corporation. Second, and closely related, is the decision as to how much organizational change implied by the new production technology can be tolerated, or perhaps deliberately stimulated. That is, to what extent should the new technology fit the skills, equipment, procedures, and job-performance criteria of the corporate site where it is to be used? (On this question, see Leonard-Barton, 1988a.) The closer the initial fit is, the less

The author is grateful for access to field sites provided by two anonymous corporations whose cultures permit learning, for the very competent research help of Linda Moffat and Cynthia Costello, and for funding by the Division of Research, Harvard Business School.

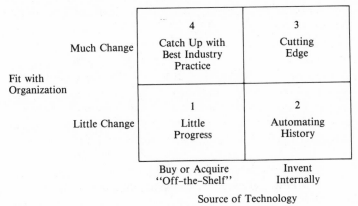

Figure 9.1   Four New Technology Implementation Situations

the manager has to be concerned with changing the organization or altering the technology.

These two dimensions, technology source and fit with the user organization, considered together describe four quite different new technology implementation situations that a manager can face (Figure 9.1). In the situation represented by quadrant 1 of Figure 9.1, the technology acquired is already very fully developed and almost perfectly fits the user environment into which it is introduced. This situation, though rare, occurs when an organization obtains technology that somewhat enhances the efficiency of current operations, with little or no alteration in current procedures—for example, an improved software package for payroll. Quadrant 2 describes a technology internally developed to fit into a user organization without disrupting or altering current practice at all. Although this situation is desirable in some circumstances, an invented technology that in every way fits the user organization provides little occasion for change, and change is needed for an organization to progress. At worst the corporation risks the possibility that the technology is automating history; that is, by the time the technology is ready to use, it fits the organization as it was at the project's inception rather than under current conditions. The third quadrant describes the case in which the technology is wholly invented but initially does not at all fit one or more important aspects of the user environment. Such large misalignments between the technology and the user organization necessitate significant change in the technology or in the organization or, in most successful implementations, adaptations in both (see Leonard-Barton, 1988a for an exploration of this case).

This chapter focuses on the situation described by quadrant 4. In this very challenging management situation, the technology, purchased or otherwise acquired in a fully developed form, does not match the current user organization. Frequently the reason for acquiring such a technology is to catch up with the best industry practice. Since the technology itself is unlikely to be amenable to alteration (it is off the shelf), implementing it will require making vast, often wrenching, changes in the adopting organization. In fact, the motive for acquiring the technology may be at least in part to force the organization to conform to the embedded standard procedures.

The managerial challenge in this situation is to figure out how to minimize the financial and human costs of making the necessary organizational alterations and still maximize the speed of the implementation so that the corporation can begin to realize productivity benefits. The following pages address that dual challenge and suggest managerial strategies for meeting it.

The strategies are illustrated with reference to an in-depth comparative study of two large new software programs introduced into the manufacturing operations of two companies in the same industry. One program, a manufacturing resource planning (MRPII) system, was purchased from a vendor, and the other, a purchasing control system, was internally developed. Despite their different origins, the two were at similarly advanced stages in their development when studied. That is, both were developed to a high degree of transferability with most "bugs" worked out, and both documentation and training were available. Each system was implemented in multiple sites within the corporation, and three such plant sites were studied in each corporation. Thus, it is possible to compare implementation management both between the two firms and among the six sites.[1]

The six cases are viewed from two perspectives: that of the whole corporation and that of the plant or technology user site. From the first perspective the key issue is how to manage corporate learning across implementation sites. Pioneering sites must be carefully selected. Then their organizational adaptations and their additions to the technology must be communicated so that later sites do not waste resources in recreating existing knowledge. As the between-corporation comparisons will demonstrate in the first part of this chapter, one of the companies was somewhat more successful than the other in transferring learning from early to later implementation sites (in the particular cases studied), and this transfer proved to be very valuable.

From the plant perspective the major managerial tasks are to anticipate the degree of technical and organizational change implied by the new production technology, and then to manage that change appropriately so as to keep implementation time and costs—human as well as financial—to a minimum. Within-corporation comparisons presented in the second part of the chapter will show that the six implementation projects differed in total financial and nonfinancial costs—including expenditure of plant resources, duration of disruption, and toll on plant morale—and that these differences are largely attributable to management practices. After a description of each technology, each of these two perspectives will be presented in turn. Since the study was focused on, and most of the data were collected, at the plant level, relatively more emphasis is placed on the plant perspective.

DESCRIPTION OF CASES STUDIED

The two large high technology corporations that were studied manufacture a wide variety of electronic components and systems. In both companies, manufacturing plants have historically had a lot of freedom in choice of production technologies, including software. However, recent pressures in the United States for manufacturing excellence, induced in part by Japanese competition (see Hayes and Wheelwright, 1984), have resulted in a push for more tightly integrated information and control systems across plants in both companies, and hence for standardization. Each of the software packages studied has been disseminated as a corporate standard, in large part because each package embodied operating principles that headquarters wanted to promulgate but that differed from current manufacturing practices. In short, management intended these technologies to stimulate organizational change. Although, as noted later, the two pieces of software differ in size and complexity and consequently in the *magnitude* of organizational disruption they occasion, they are similar in function and purpose.

PURCHASE

Corporation P's corporate materials management group developed PURCHASE in order to better control the materials that represent about 50 percent of its total manufacturing costs. The software replaces largely manual procurement systems in the plants, thus giving more efficient local materials control. It also provides standard data to corporate headquarters for critical shared-resources information on parts specifications, contract commitments, and both vendor and internal supplier performance.

Two system-design features affected implementation. First, PURCHASE was deliberately developed in modules, each of which was released to the field as it was ready. This divisibility was a desirable implementation characteristic in that plants could absorb the necessary changes in bite-sized pieces. (See Leonard-Barton, 1988b, for a discussion of divisibility and other generic implementation characteristics.) Second, most of the software code was provided by the corporate office in "object-code" form, meaning that plant-level software programmers did not have access to the building blocks of the technology and could not alter the basic program. The first few plants into which the program was released did adapt the technology to their conditions somewhat by influencing the design of the user interface. Moreover, a few small portions of the software were provided to all sites in source code, allowing some limited local construction of linkages to existing plant-specific software control and reporting systems. However, PURCHASE creators deliberately controlled the amount of local customization possible and thus ensured that the plant organization would adjust to their software rather than vice-versa.

The module of PURCHASE that affects the buyers' jobs more than all the others and that was consequently of greatest interest in this research, is PRO-PLAN, a procurement planning aid first released in early 1985. Once the buyer has entered desired planning parameters (e.g., levels of safety stock; lead time for vendors), PROPLAN works with manufacturing schedules and forecast information taken from the plant MRP (Materials Resource Planning) program to generate new orders for materials. This electronic linkage automates some buyer functions. However, manufacturing schedule changes, which cause PROPLAN to suggest exceptions to the original plan once every two weeks, still necessitate much buyer judgment in deciding whether or not to alter already placed purchase orders.

By late 1987, PROPLAN was in use in twenty-nine plants. Of the three PURCHASE sites studied, site A was the earliest corporate user of PROPLAN, and seventh of the twenty-nine in the corporation. Site A managers deliberately chose to have their site "be a guinea pig" so as to have the opportunity to influence user interface decisions still being made by the developers. These managers worried that "the way we operated would have to dramatically change if we did not get involved in the development of [PROPLAN]." Thus, although the basic PROPLAN was already developed before site A had the opportunity to influence the design, site A did induce some reinvention of the software, that is, some alterations. In contrast, sites B (18th implementation) and C (29th implementation) adopted PROPLAN as an off-the-shelf solution, neither requiring nor allowing any user-driven changes to the program itself.

MANFACT

MANFACT, a manufacturing resource planning program (MRPII), combines information about purchasing, receiving, billing, inventory, and production scheduling and routing into one large integrated software program used to drive an entire manufacturing operation. While PURCHASE affects receiving and finance departments in addition to purchasing operations, MANFACT links to every facet of manufacturing in the plant. Implementing MANFACT is thus a larger organizational undertaking than bringing PURCHASE on line, but the potential benefits to the manufacturing plant are commensurately larger.

In 1976, when MANFACT was first released, it was used by a single Corporation M site, in Europe. Another European site (X in this study) adopted the system in 1982, but there were still no U.S. users in the corporation. Then, in 1984, Corporation M put together a manufacturing task force that selected MANFACT over other MRPII systems as the company standard. In 1986, site Y became the first in the United States to adopt MANFACT as part of their drive toward manufacturing excellence. More than one year later, site Z followed suit as the twentieth implementation site. The research reported here focused attention on MANFACT use by the purchasing department (hence on the purchasing module) at each site, in order to maintain as much comparability to PURCHASE as possible.

THE CORPORATE PERSPECTIVE: TECHNOLOGY IMPLEMENTATION LEARNING CURVES

Viewed from the corporate rather than the plant-specific level, managing the introduction of new production technologies into multiple operational sites is a matter of managing organizational learning and knowledge. One way to conceive of the accumulation of knowledge through repeated experience is as a learning curve (Anzai and Simon, 1979). New technology implementation in each plant could be described in terms of one or more individual learning curves in that the implementation team members, as well as the factory-floor users, accumulated knowledge about the new technology. However, of greater interest from the corporate viewpoint are two overall organizational learning curves, each of which describes the aggregate corporate experience across a number of implementations: (1) a technical learning curve describing the cumulative knowledge about the technical aspects of implementing a particular technology (including additions that aid in aligning the technology with existing equipment or systems) and (2) an organizational learning curve describing the cumulative knowledge about the management of organizational issues (changes in user skills, procedures, performance criteria) raised by a particular technology.

The basic concept of a learning curve is that the accumulation of mental or physical experience with a task or phenomenon is accompanied over time by improvement along some performance dimension. For purposes of comparison between the two learning curves at a conceptual level, we can assume that an important performance dimension common to the two curves is the reduction of uncertainty. Uncertainty has been defined as "the difference between the amount of information required to perform the task and the amount of information already possessed by the organization" (Galbraith, 1977, p. 37). The more information that is transferred from previous implementations to each succeeding one, the smoother (more regular) and steeper will be the curve describing the reduction in uncertainty.

Of the two corporations studied, Corporation M was slightly more successful than Corporation P (in the limited instances studied) in managing the cross-site transfer of knowledge that enables later sites to benefit from both the technical and organizational learning of earlier implementation sites. A close examination of the six cases illustrates the kinds of learning that can be transmitted and the benefits to be derived from that transmission.

Technical Learning Curve

Figure 9.2 portrays schematically one key observation derived from the case data: that technical learning is transmitted more efficiently than organizational learning. One reason for this is that once new technical knowledge is acquired, it can usually be embodied in a readily transferable form. The smoothness and slope of the corporate technical learning curve depend on two factors: (1) how well learning about the particular technology is trans-

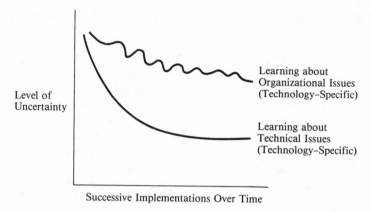

Level of
Uncertainty

Learning about
Organizational Issues
(Technology–Specific)

Learning about
Technical Issues
(Technology–Specific)

Successive Implementations Over Time

Figure 9.2 Schematic Representation of Implementation Learning Curves Within Corporations

mitted from site to site and (2) how representative of later sites the first ones that influence developers' design decisions are.

In the cases studied, the software-embodied learning that was transferred from early sites lowered costs and sped up implementation for later adopters in three ways. Early sites (1) debugged the software, that is, identified technical problems with the program that later sites therefore did not need to address; (2) persuaded the developers to add small enhancements to the user interface; and (3) created needed interfaces to other software programs. Each of these factors is considered in turn.

Managers at pioneering sites inevitably spend time and technical resources identifying and working with developers on "bugs." For this reason, the site C PURCHASE managers explicitly decided not to be the first implementers, but to "let someone else work out the bugs first." The site A PURCHASE information systems people, who were the "someone else," felt that the implementation there was difficult, even though their nontechnical colleagues rated it as very smooth.

However, pioneers derive some compensating benefits from working with developers, the major one of which is the opportunity to persuade the developers to add small locally desired enhancements that will become part of the standard package. For instance, users at PURCHASE site A convinced the corporate developers to add some coding spaces in the data base format so that both product designers and buyers would have information about parts status and could avoid obsolete ones. Also, some of the program screens were redesigned for easier use. Such refinements contribute to the technical learning curve in that later users do not need to make as many adjustments. "We feel very good that we influenced that [PURCHASE] developers positively," commented a site A manager.

The third way that transfer of software-embodied knowledge lowered costs and implementation time for later adopters in the cases studied was that these later sites were able to borrow existing interfaces created by ear-

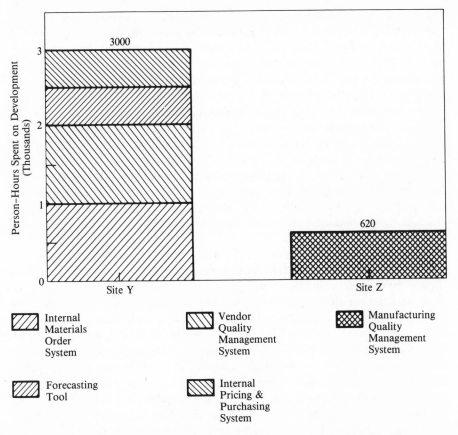

Figure 9.3   MANFACT Technology Interfaces (Comparison of Site Y & Site Z)

lier users. Figure 9.3 contrasts the more than 3000 person-hours spent at
MANFACT site Y on interfaces that were later borrowed and used by site Z
with the mere 620 person-hours invested at MANFACT site Z in building
one interface. Moreover, site Z developed that one interface module because the site had enough slack resources to do so, not because it was
essential.

Corporation P, in the cases studied, was less successful in transferring
local enhancements. Some software interfaces, inquiry tools, and report
functions developed at site B and at other Corporation P plants were discovered by PURCHASE site C only by accident and after they had begun work on
similar pieces of software themselves locally. The reverse was also true. Site
B did not know about later enhancements developed at site C. The failure
to transmit technical learning between the sites in Corporation P was attributed by participants in the PURCHASE project to a long-standing tradition of
independence among corporate plants. However, compared with the MAN-
FACT sites Y and Z described earlier, the Corporation P plants were more
geographically distant from each other. The PURCHASE program office tried

to overcome this lack of technical networking among Corporation P sites by publishing periodic notes and updates on the software. This formal mechanism, however, focused more on technical information originating at the corporate center, and hence on new releases and plans for future releases, than on announcing locally developed enhancements and hence on aiding site-to-site transfer of software-embodied knowledge.

As noted, the shape of the corporate technical learning curve also depends on the representativeness of the early sites. Those sites help developers to catch potentially dangerous interactions between the technology and the real-world situation that may not have been anticipated or simulated in the laboratory environment from which the technology is newly emerged. However, problems can remain undetected at this stage if the early sites are not typical user environments. This unrepresentativeness may force costly redesign later, making the learning curve lumpy with renewed surges of uncertainty.

That kind of delayed discovery of a design flaw occurred with PURCHASE. Six months after site B had fully implemented the fifth module of PURCHASE, the receiving dock at the plant was mysteriously and disastrously inundated with huge deliveries of purchased parts that were all scheduled to arrive on the same day. Although the individual buyers had not all entered the same delivery dates for their long lead-time purchases, PURCHASE was designed to batch orders within certain delivery windows. The problem could not be easily solved, for even when order dates for the long-lead-time parts were carefully randomized and reentered, the software program overrode the manual manipulations as if they were unintentional errors. Six months later, the peak occurred again, to the surprise of the plant technical staff, who did not know that their "fix" had been countermanded by the internal logic of the software. These "spikes'" in parts delivery occasioned heavy expenditures on overtime and extra help in the site B receiving department, plus hours of effort by purchasing and information systems staff attempting to solve the problem without access to the basic source code of the software program. At site C, six months after the system's implementation, the same phenomenon wreaked even greater havoc on the receiving docks, for almost 80 percent of parts ordered for site C fell within the long-lead-time category.

Why did the problem surface so late in the sequence of implementations? A partial explanation lies in the fact that at site A, where buyers had worked with the PURCHASE developers to design this particular module, only about 10 percent of their parts fall into the long-lead-time category that causes the problem. The danger was therefore invisible to developers because site A was not representative of later users. Had the problem been identified and solved at site A, and the solution embodied in the software, site C would not have experienced the same spike. Thus, this instance illustrates the sensitivity of the technical learning curve to the representativeness of the early user sites.

Organizational Learning Curve

The organizational learning curve is more erratic than the technical, that is, it evidences surges of renewed uncertainty each time the technology is implemented in new sites. These surges occur for a number of reasons. Each site has some unique situational characteristics, such as parts mix and locally developed procedures, that require tailored adjustments in the technology and the organization. Also, there is frequently inadequate continuity in job positions within the sites for someone to accumulate the organizational knowledge in one place. Moreover, much of the organizational learning is housed in people's heads rather than embodied in some more readily transferable form (software, written procedures, etc.), and it is not always possible to transfer the people in whose heads the knowledge resides. Finally, in many organizations, neither culture nor existing information channels support the transfer of organizational learning. In short, such transfer is not a specific part of anyone's job as the transfer of technical knowledge often is. For all these reasons, it is more difficult to identify and convey useful implementation knowledge about organizational impacts than about technical ones. However, such organizational learning *can* be transferred.

Among the sites studied, MANFACT site Z transferred more organizational (as well as technical) learning into their site than any of the other five sites. Site Z implementers not only visited other sites, but had implementation team members visit from the site Y plant to review plans, make suggestions, help conduct a peer "readiness audit," and point out before the system was turned on any likely pitfalls that had not yet been recognized. Site Y implementers spent two days during the audit explaining where their own prior implementation had gone astray and making suggestions about how to avoid the costly errors they had incurred. They might themselves have avoided some of these errors had they sought advice from their European predecessor, site X. However, at the time that site X brought MANFACT up, there was no program office guiding the overall corporate implementation; site Y was therefore unaware that they were not the first to implement MANFACT.

In contrast, even though the implementation team at PURCHASE site C knew they had been preceded by many sites and although they spent time visiting several other user sites before undertaking their own installation, they were taken totally by surprise when their parts delivery hit the same spike experienced thirteen months previously by site B. In fact, when the site C team contacted the PURCHASE program office to ask what to do about the spike, they were told it was unprecedented. Site C believed their experience was unique until the research reported here accidentally connected the two sites. Part of the reason for this lack of communication was apparently that parallel but separate channels existed between the corporate program office and implementation sites for communicating about technical versus organizational implementation issues. Both sites identified the problem to PURCHASE technical support staff as a technical problem—a delivery "surge" at site B and a "back order" problem at site C. The corporate program office did not equate the two problems for some time partly because they did not hear about the similar organizational impacts that were an integral part of the problem. Therefore, the program office did not serve as a conduit for either warning or aiding the afflicted sites.

The evidence from these cases suggests that unless organizational learning is systematically captured in a readily transferable form, the organizational learning curve can be rather shallow and extremely uneven. In the two corporations studied, the main function of the program office was to serve as the primary technology source in a vertical diffusion network, that is, a network in which the technology diffuses from the authoritative, standard-setting center down to plants as dispersed peripheral nodes. The potential of these offices to serve in a liaison role, linking dispersed nodes together in a horizontal diffusion network, was much less explicitly recognized. Yet some of the most useful implementation knowledge was the information that flowed accidentally from plant to plant through job transfers and peer contacts and enabled the corporation as a whole to move down the two learning curves.

HIGH- VERSUS LOW-COST IMPLEMENTATIONS

Individual production technologies are not usually highly visible at the corporate level unless they are disasters or spectacular successes. Changes at a plant level (both beneficial and destructive) are invisible from a distance because their specific effects are absorbed into general, overall measures of plant performance. Even at the plant level, it is often difficult to associate unique costs and benefits with the introduction of a particular technology. Therefore it is hard to judge the success of a given implementation effort. Yet the comparisons undertaken here of implementation projects involving the same technology at different sites revealed real and significant differences in both the time it took to realize productivity gains and the total implementation costs. A technology laboriously introduced with enormous disruption at one plant could be implemented at another site relatively quickly and smoothly.

It should be noted that, in one sense, the implementations at all six sites were successful. The new technology is in use at all six. Therefore, the differences among the sites lie in how long it took to get the software into routine use, how much disruption the plants experienced, how many resources were devoted to the effort, and how traumatized were people in the user organization (the plant) by the whole experience.

Tables 9.1 and 9.2 indicate that in Corporation P, the implementation at site B was relatively costly compared to those in the other two PURCHASE sites. Site B was in a state of disruption longer than the others, both in absolute terms (twelve months) and as a proportion (67 percent) of the total eighteen-month implementation period. This disruption delayed realization of productivity gains (Table 9.1: column III) and cost considerably more in

Table 9.1 Outcome Measures at Sites Studied

	I Rank Order of Implementation Sequence	II Disruption Period (months)[a]	III Time to Productivity Gains (months)[b]	IV Total Person-Days of Effort[c]	V Subjective Rating of Implementation User Management[d]
PURCHASE					
Site A	7	0	14	67	9
Site B	18	12	18	126	7
Site C	29	7	10	89	8
MANFACT					
Site X	2	9	13	NA[e]	Rough
Site Y	4 (1 in U.S.)	20	21	5915	Rough
Site Z	20	2	4	2576	Smooth

[a]Measured from cutover to time when purchasing department regained preimplementation level of efficiency.

[b]Measured from cutover to time when purchasing department realized gains in productivity.

[c]Number includes time spent by implementation team and purchasing department in planning and training for implementation. It does not include time spent by the Information Systems Department on programming. For PURCHASE sites the number is normalized as effort per buyer to allow comparison between sites of different sizes. The effort is measured in total person-days for MANFACT sites, since these two sites are about the same size.

[d]PURCHASE sites were asked to rank implementation on a scale from 1 to 10, where 10 means as smooth as possible. MANFACT sites were asked to rank implementation from rough to smooth.

[e]Completely comparable figures could not be obtained for site X. However, because many contract workers and consultants were hired, the figure is known to be larger than that for site Y.

Table 9.2 Proportion of Implementation Effort Devoted to Planning

	I Total Months in Implementation Period[a]	II Months in Planning (Precutover)[b]	III Person-Days Precutover (%)[c]	IV Person-Days Postcutover (%)[c]	
				Months 1–6	Months 7–12
PURCHASE					
Site A	19 (33)[a]	6	14[d]	21[d]	24[d]
Site B	18	6	19	48	33
Site C	21	13	32	65	4
MANFACT					
Site X	32	23	—	—	—
Site Y	28	8	64	36	—
Site Z	14	12	69	31	—

[a]Measured from the time the implementation team was established until the purchasing department regained preimplementation level of efficiency. The number for site A is not exactly comparable to those for sites B and C, because site A managers felt they never experienced any loss in efficiency. Their implementation was so slowly paced that learning time was absorbed into daily routine. Moreover, they believed they achieved "well over 50%" of the productivity gains they would ever realize from PURCHASE by fourteen months after cutover (nineteen months total implementation effort) because of careful selection of buyers and parts to put on the system. They did not put up their last buyer until thirty-three months after starting the implementation, as part of their strategy.

[b]Measured from the time the implementation team was established until cutover to the new system; that is, until the software was first installed in production mode.

[c]Measured as a percentage of total days spent on implementation.

[d]At site A. 45 percent of person-days of effort were spent twelve to thirty months after cutover; see the text for discussion.

terms of person-days (per buyer) of effort devoted to training and learning (Table 9.1: column IV). Moreover, the purchasing department regarded the implementation as somewhat rougher than did their counterparts at sites A and C (Table 9.1: column V).

Similarly, MANFACT sites X and Y were considered rough implementations compared with site Z and were in a state of disruption for much longer (Table 9.1: column II). Moreover, site Y expended more than twice as many person-days on planning, training, and learning as did site Z, although the two plants are roughly the same size (Table 9.1: column IV). Not only was the period of disruption in sites X and Y dramatically longer than that at site Z (Table 9.1: column II), but there were financially measurable costs associated with the disruption. At site X (although available cost figures are not exactly comparable to those in the other sites) we know that over a nine-month period, approximately $2 million was spent for temporary help, consultants' fees, and the costs associated with a large inventory build-up, including the rental of extra storage space. At site Y, costs to the purchasing department alone were estimated at about $230,000, including overtime worked by full-time employees and contract workers who were hired during the first twelve months following the installation of MANFACT.

These numbers do not tell the whole story, either. Managers at site X felt the whole plant was so demoralized by the traumatic experience of having horrendous order backlogs and total confusion for several months that even after order was restored, it "took a year for plant management to rebuild confidence in their judgment" among plant workers and also at the level of corporate area management. A new plant manager who took over site Y soon after the installation recalled that people in the plant seemed crushed by the rough MANFACT implementation experience and were "walking around with their shoulders hunched over as if they'd been beaten into the ground with a croquet mallet." At both sites, people at several organizational levels left the site, and a few fled the company because of implementation "burnout." Such costs are difficult to quantify, but some senior managers counted them as the highest expenses involved in the rough implementations.

The first explanation that comes to mind for such disparities in implementation costs among sites is that early implementations always take longer and inevitably cost more than later ones. Although it is true that pioneering can be very expensive, appropriate management can reduce financial and social costs. Site A was an early user of PURCHASE, but implementation was relatively painless compared with those of the other two PURCHASE sites. Although only a few months later in time, site B was many implementations later in terms of corporate experience. Yet it was the least successful of the three PURCHASE implementations studied. Therefore, pioneering is a contributing factor, but it cannot be the *total* explanation for high-cost implementation. Differences in the relatively low- and high-cost sites must instead be attributed, at least in part, to plant-level management of the new technology products.

Another appealing hypothesis is that more up-front planning among the lower-cost sites paved the way for smoother implementations. Table 9.2 shows that this simple explanation is again incomplete. Implementation at MANFACT site Y was much rougher than that at Z, and site Z did spend more time on preimplementation planning than site Y. However, the two sites spent roughly the same *proportion* of the total person-hours devoted to implementation on precutover planning (column III), and the absolute number of total person-hours expended was greater at the less successful site. Also PURCHASE site B spent *more* hours on precutover planning than the relatively less costly site A had (column III).

The likely explanation for the observed differences in implementation outcomes lies less in the number of person-hours of effort than in the nature and timing of the resources expended. That is, the *type* of planning is probably more important than *magnitude* of planning. The second part of this chapter is devoted to an examination of the way planning and other aspects of plant-level learning were managed differently among the sites.

THE PLANT PERSPECTIVE

Figure 9.4 suggests that the implementation effort in the plants required two kinds of knowledge about both the technology and the organization: (1) know-*how*—a detailed, hands-on familiarity with how both the technical and organizational systems work day-to-day; and (2) know-*why*—a more abstract comprehension of how the technical and organizational systems interact with their environments, and hence why the new technology is designed and operated in a given fashion. Using this model as a diagnostic tool, one can observe that relatively rougher implementations differed from more successful ones in two major ways. First, in the costly sites, relatively little effort was expended to create local expertise in all four quadrants of the knowledge grid. Second (and partly as a result of the first reason), resources were inadequately matched to the kind, magnitude, and timing of demands placed on the plant organizations. These two issues are examined in detail in the following pages.

Creating Local Expertise

The most successful sites (PURCHASE A and C; MANFACT Z) all deliberately invested in the creation of local user-experts, whose job it became to anticipate, model, and teach the new behavior necessitated by the software, especially during the critical period of the cutover from the old to the new system. For instance in PURCHASE site C, one buyer's regular parts load was cut 75 percent so that he could become an expert in the system and head up the implementation project. He spent three months simulating the system and then, with one other senior buyer, brought up all his parts on the system three months before the other fourteen buyers. "We told the other buyers that we were working out all the bugs before we turned it over to them," he explained. Similarly at site A, one buyer became the expert by putting all

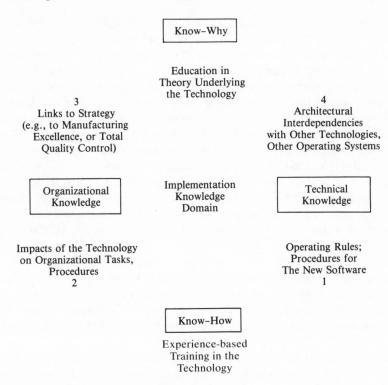

Figure 9.4   Implementation Knowledge Grid

his own parts on the system; then he trained all the other buyers, one by one, based on his own experience. At MANFACT site Z, the implementation team became local experts through extensive simulation with real data, since they could not use the actual system without involving the entire plant.

These user-experts served as scouts in foreign territory. They already knew their own organization's tasks and procedures intimately. Therefore, when they became knowledgeable about exactly how the software worked, they had personally experienced both quadrants 1 and 2 of the implementation grid. Their hands-on trial of the system was a form of organizational prototyping (Leonard-Barton, 1987)—that is, experimentation for the purpose of learning how the system would interact with its environment. By virtue of their contact with the software developers and their designation by management as the resident experts, they also became acquainted with the business and systems logic behind the software (quadrants 3 and 4 of the implementation grid).

They did not need to become the foremost available experts in all four quadrants. However, the organizational prototyping allowed them to identify those issues in each quadrant in the implementation knowledge grid that would be problematic at their particular site. They were well qualified to decide what kinds of information should be passed along to their fellow users and to anticipate where extra effort and resources would be needed to support the change. They not only selected those pieces of information that would be most important to convey to other users, but in the more successful sites, they rewrote the corporate documentation, breaking it down into bite-sized pieces and customizing it for the other buyers. The early scouting effort also helped the user-experts identify the quadrants for which knowledge already existed in a highly transferable form (e.g., software or training modules), and hence where experience could be gained vicariously. Thus, these user-experts helped diagnose the implementation situation, direct the learning effort, and model the needed changes in routine.

In contrast, at the more costly sites (MANFACT X and Y; PURCHASE B), very few resources were devoted to creating user-experts in advance of cutover. At sites X and Y, no user actually had detailed working knowledge of the system before the cutover (i.e., the day on which the new software was turned on for the first time and, in some cases, on which all current systems supporting the same functions became unavailable). At site B, a senior buyer was asked to learn the system one month ahead of cutover, but he managed to devote only 10 percent of his time to that effort. Site B users were also exposed to a demonstration program, but they did not actually load parts into the system; hence their operating know-how (quadrant 1) was very limited.

Consequently, none of these less successful sites developed the various kinds of site-specific knowledge needed for implementation. Implementation was viewed primarily as a technical issue. The technical support personnel were expert in the software (quadrant 1), but not in purchasing (quadrant 2). Nor were technical personnel from either the Corporation P program office or Corporation M's vendor ASC familiar with the in-house software systems to which the new technology was being linked at each site. Hence there was inadequate understanding of the technical system as a whole (quadrant 4). Finally, because the implementation teams in these sites generally viewed the technical realm, not the organizational, as their province, they were not prepared to deal with the changes in buying behavior required by the new system. Consequently, the implementation teams at the more costly sites spent months of fruitless effort in detailed planning for a system that they did not really understand in practice. At site Y, for example, the massive twenty-seven-person implementation team met daily for seven months before the cutover. They filled large notebooks with detailed plans of action. Yet no one took the time to actually use the available simulation that was later used to such good effect in site Z. When the day came to turn on the MANFACT system at site Y, the notebooks turned out to be largely irrelevant. "We did a lot of planning we could never use." No one had anticipated most of the real problems that experimentation with real data in the simulation might have revealed.

Not only were many organizational changes unanticipated, but there was no one to model, or even guide, the organizational transition. No one had been designated as organizational change agents. At MANFACT site Y, the manufacturing floor supervisors who had customarily made purchasing, scheduling, and inventory decisions were suddenly totally shorn of expertise. "We took all that [expertise] away from them, literally overnight. Everyone was reduced to the same baseline." They were afraid to make any decisions, for the new system might countermand them. Consequently, there was no one to shape the human systems and procedures into the necessary configuration. Knowledge about the interaction of the software with procedures (quadrant 2 of the knowledge grid) was almost totally missing at this site.

Furthermore, at site Y, the top half of the knowledge quadrant was inadequately addressed. Recognizing a need to educate everyone in the plant about the new push for manufacturing excellence that was also motivating the corporate decision to adopt MANFACT as a standard, plant management hired a well-known consultant in MRPII philosophy to conduct 558 hours of classes for the entire plant almost two years before cutover and before the final selection of the specific MRPII software package was made. The flaws in this seemingly sensible effort were apparent only with hindsight. First, the education was abstract, divorced from the new software system and its discipline both in content and in time (two years before cutover). Therefore, although plant management assumed that the educational foundation for MANFACT implementation had been laid, in fact few people could make a meaningful connection between the abstract course and the software. Second, the knowledge was never applied after the consultant left and was therefore lost by the time of the actual cutover. There was no one to select communicable parts of the manufacturing strategy and then link those high-level organizational issues to the needed changes in daily routine.

Site Y was also taken by surprise by the degree to which MANFACT was unable to link to other, existing computer systems on which their operations depended. Because the implementing team lacked systemic understanding of the whole technical architecture into which MANFACT was being introduced (quadrant 4), they did not foresee much of the technical disruption. As noted previously (Figure 9.3), site Y spent many person-hours creating necessary interfaces. Many noncritical but efficient functions available under the previous local system were unavailable on MANFACT—a fact that was an unpleasant surprise to many users. For example, the purchasing department had developed a homegrown "automatic buy card," which allowed them to access all vendor information needed on one screen, and to store purchase order histories in one data base. Because MANFACT did not have this functionality, it was less convenient to use than the old system. Only many months after the cutover date was software written to replace the lost functionality.

PURCHASE was an internal corporate invention. Its creators had had much less time to "work the bugs out" in production sites previously than had MANFACT vendor ASC. PURCHASE site A anticipated the costs of working with an immature system, but site B, which implemented PURCHASE only a few months later, was just as unprepared to devote resources to linking the software to local systems as site Y had been with MANFACT (quadrant 4). Because PURCHASE is so much smaller than MANFACT, fewer interfaces were needed with local operational controls, and more of the plant activities could proceed even if the new system did not fit as anticipated. Nevertheless, managers and users alike considered the implementation of PURCHASE at site B to be rougher than their colleagues at the other two PURCHASE sites studied, in part because their expectations about the transferability of the system had been unrealistically high. As one manager observed, "I don't think we understood how complex PURCHASE was. . . . We didn't expect [it] to be complex, so hard to tune and to understand what it was doing." Because no user-experts had been created ahead of the cutover point, the first three buyers who were asked to put all their parts on the system found use difficult (quadrants 1 and 2) and made little progress in implementation the first few months. Moreover, the information systems support staff were very unhappy about the number of perceived bugs in the code and the frequency of updates necessitating changes in code.

Figure 9.5 presents graphically the differences among the three PURCHASE sites in levels and timing of resources expended on the PROPLAN module for planning, training, and learning by the implementation team and buyers (excluding the time for information systems technical support, because exactly comparable data on that could not be obtained across sites). As the figure indicates, the learning and training costs at site B peaked later, higher, and longer than those at site C, where the large effort devoted to learning dropped off quickly after cutover. Site C brought up over twice as many buyers in six months (from first buyer's use to use by the entire department) as site B did in ten months. As noted previously, site A deliberately chose a low-cost but carefully targeted incremental implementation strategy, and the graph indicates the small, periodic surge in learning as the one designated user-expect brought up each fellow buyer on the system, one by one.

Matching Resources to Demand

Besides the presence or absence of user-experts, there was one other very apparent and probably related distinction between the relatively rough and smooth implementations—the appropriate allocation of resources. In the three sites where implementation was quite smooth (A, C, and Z) managers consciously matched their organizational resources to the anticipated demand that uncertainty placed on the organization, in part because their user-experts knew what resources would be needed. In the three more costly sites (B, X, and Y) managers either naively or consciously decided to implement quickly and with limited resources, and were then surprised at the cost of doing so. The ratio of resources to demand was inadequate. As Galbraith (1977), among others, has pointed out, one way to address uncertainty is to provide slack in the system. Partly because they lacked the scouts to sound an early warning about the extent of uncertainty left to be addressed, the less successful sites suffered from resource scarcity at critical times; they had no slack to cope with contingencies.

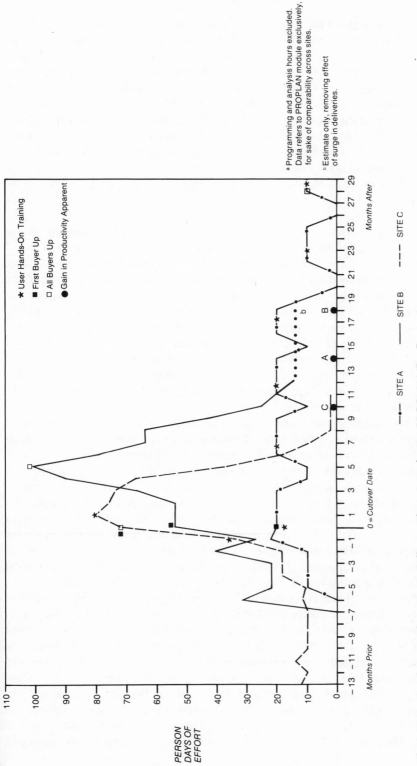

Figure 9.5 Purchase Implementation Effort[a]—Plants Introducing PROPLAN (Per Buyer, Team Meetings, Training, and Planning)

This mismatch between resources and demand on the system was exacerbated in all three cases by the deliberate management decision to "bite the bullet" and get on with the implementation. Managers were understandably impatient because they mistook their staff's seemingly endless planning for knowledge creation. They had no idea how inadequately the implementation knowledge grid was covered in this planning. In the absence of information, they assumed that business would proceed as usual, that is, that the advent of the technology would impose no extraordinary demands on the organization and therefore few extra resources would be needed. With hindsight, this assumption seems wildly naive, even to those who had made it. "As the guy who *caused* all the pain," one plant manager noted ruefully, "I feel we should have been able to [implement the new system] without so much pain."

At site X, the implementation of MANFACT was characterized as the "flying wedge technique," meaning the technology was driven into the heart of the organization with the expectation that the organization would adapt around the innovation with only minor discomfort. Similarly, at site Y the manager who had publicly committed to having his organization achieve manufacturing excellence within twelve months and who considered the implementation of MANFACT critical to attaining that goal was determined to see that the switchover would be immediate and complete with no chance of returning to the old systems. One of the staff members recalled this perceived philosophy as the "pocketless shirt strategy." "If you want to stop a heavy smoker and he keeps his cigarettes in his shirt pocket—then you make him wear shirts without pockets."

This "damn the torpedoes, full steam ahead" attitude was not supported by extra resources at the time of cutover at either site X or Y. In fact, as Figure 9.6 shows, hours of effort devoted to implementation support at Y dropped the day the system was introduced. As of that day, the responsibilities of the implementation team were assumed to end. The team members were immediately assigned new and entirely unrelated full-time duties. Resources were similarly constrained at site X, where the business was growing at an exponential rate, and many people were new hires. Furthermore, implementation here was scheduled for the final, and hence the busiest, quarter of the fiscal year. The organization was already stretched to conduct regular business and could not devote extra resources to implementation.

Perhaps it is not coincidental that at both sites X and Y the amount of physical computer power needed to run the new software was also vastly underestimated. Just as the organization needed extra resources to cope with the inevitable confusion, duplication of effort and extra communication burdens, so initially the computing demands were extremely high. The machine power was adequate once the system was up and running and everyone was inputting data correctly. However, in the first few days, when people were making errors, the machine slowly bogged down (especially at site X) until it could no longer physically keep up with the necessary flow of data. The output lagged behind the input by hours, leading to a vicious cycle

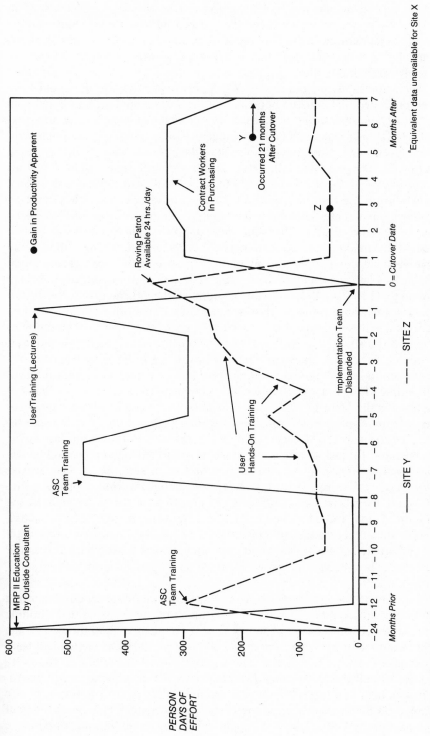

Figure 9.6 MANFACT Implementation Effort[a] (Team Meetings, Training, and Planning)

[a]Equivalent data unavailable for Site X

of ever-increasing inaccuracy. Unable to trust the output, people in the plant at site X reverted to their former manual procedures, further undermining the implementation effort. This recidivism was damaging to the plant and, ironically, was also the only factor that kept a small trickle of orders proceeding through the plant.

With hindsight, people at site X felt this capacity shortage could have been predicted had someone considered the exponential growth in demand on the system that would be caused when it was linked to all the other operating systems; that is, had anyone understood quadrant 4 in the implementation knowledge grid. They ran a pilot of the system, but on only one small part of the business, and failed to consider scale-up issues, that is, the difference between the level of activity for that small business segment and for the whole system. For instance, one manager observed, when they saw that loading a bill of materials took seven or eight minutes, they should have been able to extrapolate from that and understand that once the whole system was interconnected, the computer would be far too slow. Then they could have been selective about how much they tried to do at once. "There might still have been a period of inefficiency—but not everything would have ground to a halt [as it did]." At site Y, although the information systems staff foresaw a machine capacity shortage several months prior to cutover, they were unable to secure the needed resources until three months after cutover.

MANFACT site Z was better able to match the anticipated demand with resource allocations, since they had the advantage of learning from site Y's problems. In fact, they had more physical and personnel resources on hand at the time of the cutover than proved necessary (see Figure 9.6). "We kept waiting for the plant to blow up," explained one member of the implementation team, "and it never did." As Figure 9.6 shows, the "roving patrol" assigned to staggered shifts covering the entire twenty-four-hour day during cutover and following weeks was able to return to regular job schedules within just one month—a full month sooner than anticipated. One reason fewer resources were needed than were allocated is the *kind* of planning that was done by the implementation team. Drawing on their own experience with the system and what they had learned from site Y, they had anticipated in great detail the changes in individual jobs caused by MANFACT (quadrant 2 in the knowledge grid). They had also documented those changes and the new procedures in detailed manuals placed on every user's work desk (quadrants 1 and 2).

Moreover, the implementing team reduced some of the required learning load, and consequent strain on the organization, by focusing user training on operating issues. They did not try to pass on the top half of the knowledge grid to the rest of the plant immediately, although that knowledge had been crucial for them in their own planning effort. "We decided to deal first with [MANFACT] and then with MRPII [training] later." Consequently, user confusion was held to a minimum and the strain on the organization was considerably less than it had been in the early MANFACT sites. This postponement was not totally without cost. "People didn't have a good understanding of manufacturing, so they couldn't think in terms of it," commented one implementation team member in explaining why MANFACT and its required discipline were hard for many to understand. However, it was a cost deliberately incurred and relatively small compared with the price paid in other sites of failing to pass along operational-level know-how. After the initial learning during the cutover period was absorbed (quadrants 1 and 2), the team proceeded with the more abstract "know-why" training of users (quadrants 3 and 4).

With hindsight, it is clear that even pioneering sites X and Y could have addressed the resources-to-demand ratio from both sides of the equation. That is, they could have reduced the uncertainty and hence lessened demand placed on the organization by investing in hands-on experience ahead of cutover. They could also have allocated more resources, thus providing enough flexibility to handle unanticipated contingencies as well as the expected confusion. Looking back, one who had been a plant manager at the time of implementation commented that, given it to do over, he "would put more effort up front and at the cutover"; he would "be in force with trainers during the cutover."

Site A illustrates the advantages of creating local knowledge about the technology implementation process, and then using that knowledge to calibrate the ratio of resources to anticipated demands on the organization because of uncertainty. Although they committed themselves to early implementation because they wanted to influence PURCHASE development, site A managers had few excess resources to devote to implementation. They therefore reduced the demand side of the resources–demand equation. First, they targeted for implementation the one PURCHASE module they needed, and delayed introducing later modules until the first was well absorbed. Then, as previously noted, one buyer became an expert on PURCHASE and developed close ties with the program office. Based on this knowledge, this user-expert and the purchasing manager were able to identify those few parts categories responsible for 80 percent of the purchase order activity and constituting the most critical workload for the department and the plant. The buyers responsible for those parts were brought on to the system, one by one, by the user-expert, who "let people go at their own pace." The technology infiltrated the organization so slowly that the purchasing department experienced no productivity losses and the technology introduction was almost unnoticed by other departments at the site.

As Figure 9.6 and Table 9.2 indicate, this very low resource investment approach to implementation resulted in a thirty-three-month-long implementation period. However, because of the careful selection of the buyers (and hence types of parts) to be included first, the system started yielding some benefits after only two buyers were using it. Moreover, well over 50 percent of the anticipated productivity gains were achieved within the first fourteen months (nineteen months after the start of the project), with just half the buyers using the system. Therefore, there was no particular need to hasten the rest of the implementation process. Obviously this very low-key implementation approach would not be feasible in all cases, but the general strategy of first understanding the scope of the implementation task and then reducing it to manageable proportions, commensurate with available resources, may be widely applicable.

CONCLUSION

The major conclusion drawn from the study described herein is that the implementation of a new production technology intended for use in multiple sites is an exercise in corporate learning. That learning consists of two types: (1) vicarious learning, from the experiences of others, and (2) experimental learning, from one's own experimentation with the innovation. Both types of learning should occur at the corporate as well as at the plant level (Figure 9.7), and the challenge to managers is how to accelerate that learning process at both levels.

The Corporate Perspective

Site Selection
The first few sites into which a new production technology is introduced assume a large share of the corporate learning burden and potentially much of the responsibility for teaching other sites. Not surprisingly, then, these pioneering sites are often selected because they have a special need for the new technology, or because the technology developers have some strong interpersonal ties into the intended user organization.

However, if the new technology is to be dispersed to multiple sites, the most important criterion for selection of the pilot sites is representativeness rather than receptivity. If the first site is atypical of later ones in some important way, less technical and organizational learning can be transferred from this early user to later ones, and potentially costly problems with the new technology may not surface soon enough to be efficiently solved.

Horizontal Diffusion
Peers who have already implemented a new technology have what communication researchers have called "safety credibility" (Rogers, 1982) because people seeking their advice believe they know what it is really like to undertake this innovation. Therefore, people at the pioneering sites are well positioned to disseminate vicarious learning to their colleagues, whether their own endeavors went smoothly or not. As the case stories demonstrate, however, the transfer across sites of valuable learning about both enhancements to the technology and implementation pitfalls is neither inevitable nor naturally efficient.

The transfer of knowledge horizontally (i.e., from plant to plant) rather than vertically, from corporate office to plant is, by definition, a decentralized activity. Yet it requires corporate support. First of all, the sites imple-

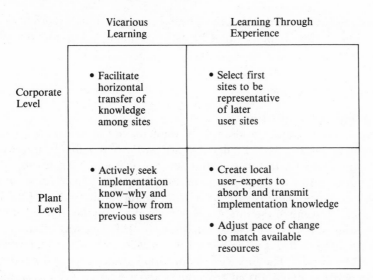

	Vicarious Learning	Learning Through Experience
Corporate Level	• Facilitate horizontal transfer of knowledge among sites	• Select first sites to be representative of later user sites
Plant Level	• Actively seek implementation know–why and know–how from previous users	• Create local user–experts to absorb and transmit implementation knowledge • Adjust pace of change to match available resources

Figure 9.7   Managerial Strategies for Successful Implementation Under Conditions of High Organizational Change

menting the new technology need to be able to identify each other. For large programs of technological change, the technology program office serves an important role not only in disseminating technical information directly, but also in linking sites together in a fertile horizontal network. However, program offices do not always place much importance on that role, perhaps because the rewards for serving as a central fount of corporate wisdom about a technology are much more visible than are those for facilitating learning among sites. It is not clear how to measure or reward such facilitating activities.

Moreover, many new technologies are too minor to warrant a dedicated program office. Thus, each site runs the risk of starting the implementation process anew, and in isolation, without the benefit of previous corporate technical and organizational learning. In such cases, the internal or external vendor serves as the carrier of knowledge. However, once again, the importance of site-to-site transfer of learning (especially organizational learning) is apt to be underestimated.

Assuming that the network exists and is active, the implementers at each site will still need some financial and possibly other support to visit each other and discuss the implementation as it proceeds. Because well-managed change is by definition not very dramatic, it is often undervalued and the amount of effort that went into making it a nonevent is often underestimated. One plant manager interviewed noted that the "corporate management may not fully understand what is involved in (such massive innovation)." A change that looks relatively small from the corporate perspective may in fact rate quite high on the Richter scale for that site, especially if the implementation proceeds without the benefit of building on previous experience. One of the points of this chapter is that investment in aiding horizontal transfer is likely to be cost-effective.

The Plant-Level Perspective

Learning from Previous Users

As the cases showed, the two kinds of implementation knowledge needed (know-how and know-why; Figure 9.4) are partly obtainable from previous users. Later users, for instance, could get tips on operating rules (quadrant 1), find out some of the organizational impacts to anticipate (quadrant 2), determine linkages made by previous users to corporate strategy (quadrant 3), and identify some of the interdependencies between the new system and other existing software packages (quadrant 4). This last was often easiest, because the knowledge was embodied in software code, that is, interfaces that could be copied. The linkages to corporate strategy were similarly embodied in easily imitated formal procedures and measures, such as standardized procedures for manufacturing to follow to reach Class A standing. Less formalized knowledge about potential organization impacts or software operating tricks had to be actively sought and assimilated on a person-to-person basis. This was a labor-intensive activity. At the more successful sites, the implementation supervisors were allowed the time and resources to actively scan and learn from their corporate environment. In the less successful sites, inadequate time and resources were allotted to this activity.

Organizational Prototyping by User Experts

The most successful sites studied here made a conscious investment in prototyping both the technical and the human systems, with real data and in real time. Representatives drawn from the ranks of the actual end-users, not computer specialists, were encouraged to become the experienced experts. This strategy was particularly wise for several reasons. First, these user-experts possessed a depth of experience with their own organization and job procedures that could not be easily assimilated by an outsider, whereas they could learn the software in a few days. At all three successful sites, one person or a small group therefore understood all four quadrants of the implementation knowledge grid (see Figure 9.4) and selectively conveyed that knowledge when and where it was needed. They could foretell where the interaction of technology and organization would be particularly stressful. Having gone through the learning experience themselves, they knew what was difficult to understand and could translate generic instructions into organization-specific ones.

Second, these user-experts were permanent staff members rather than consultants passing through. That was somewhat of a disadvantage for them personally, for other users depended on them for extensive hand-holding. One such user-expert commented that his availability made other users lazy about figuring the system out for themselves. They continued to lean on him long after he felt they could have mastered the software. However, his frustration derived in part from the fact that his important peer consulting was not explicitly rewarded or even acknowledged, once the initial implementation was complete. Other user-experts whose consulting roles were more adequately acknowledged, were more content with their status as resident gurus.

Even well rewarded user-experts can be expected to eventually tire of the role, of course. In the most successful implementation studied here, even that eventuality had been foreseen. The original user-experts trained others to take their places; that is, the trainers trained trainers rather than users. This strategy ensures a hierarchy of expertise and a more equitable distribution of consulting duties over time.

Matching Resources to Demand
One of the important contributions of the user-experts in the more successful sites was the ability, born of their vicarious learning and hands-on experience with the innovation, to judge the amount of resources needed to effect the cutover from old to new system. In the less successful sites, both machine and human resources were underestimated and ill-timed, for the most part because the implementers lacked accurate forecasts of the potential organizational impacts. In at least one site, the underestimation was also born of the desperate conclusion that, since resources were limited, a crisis was inevitable and one might as well get it over with. However, as noted in the body of this chapter, that is not always the only implementation option possible. One very successful site, faced with limited resources, instead decided to cut back on the demands made of the organization by slowing the speed of implementation and targeting only certain high-importance tasks. In this case, a manager had paused long enough in his fire-fighting to figure out how his organization could derive the most benefit from the innovation fastest, with the least immediate investment.

The research described here highlights the fact that the implementation of new technologies is a process of learning. Participants even at low-cost, successful sites felt this point was ill-understood. "Management saw [the technology] as a cassette you just plug in," one observed. Some technologies are obviously closer to being a cassette than others are, but any technology being used purposely to alter the way an organization operates likely involves a great deal of stressful change. Managers who understand that they are managing organization change, not just technical change, are well positioned to direct the learning process.

1. Although both the technologies reported on here are software packages, most management issues relevant to the implementation of new technologies are the same, regardless of the type of technology (hardware, new methodologies, or software). Therefore, the observations made here are expected to apply to many technology implementation projects besides those involving software.

10

Managing High Tech Processes: The Challenge of CAD/CAM

PAUL S. ADLER

THE PROBLEM

A process technology revolution is underway in industry today: computer-aided design (CAD) and computer-aided manufacturing (CAM) technologies are being interconnected (CAD/CAM) and linked with management information systems (MIS), moving toward what is often called computer-integrated manufacturing (CIM) or what might be better termed the computer-integrated enterprise (CIE).

These technologies promise great benefits (Manufacturing Studies Board, 1984). But there are indications that U.S. industry is not effectively exploiting this technological potential.

Consider these results from a recent study of CAD/CAM in printed circuit boards and aircraft hydraulic tubing over the 1980–87 time frame (Adler, 1988).[1] For printed circuit boards (PCBs), the good news is in data like these: in one company, boards of comparable complexity were being designed in one third the time; in another, layout and drafting time was reduced by three quarters; several companies reported that automatic insertion programming that used to take seventy hours per board now took only five hours; and many companies experienced quality improvements like those highlighted by one organization where the average number of revisions per drawing was reduced from 0.51 to 0.33.

But there was an important gap between these impressive improvements in specific suboperations and the relative paucity of perceptible efficiency benefits for the PCB organization as a whole. Over the same time frame, the total fabrication costs for boards of identical degrees of complexity had increased, suggesting that the rate of productivity improvement for this important segment had been lower than the inflation rate. More important, of the firms surveyed only a small minority could claim any improvement in their overall design-to-market cycle time. It is true that CAD/CAM had enabled these organizations to produce boards of somewhat greater complexity (more layers, closer spacings, more numerous, and more complex components) with only minimal engineering or technician headcount increases. But the sampled organizations were under very real cost and time-to-market pressure—they were not companies for whom product complexity was the overriding competitive priority—and yet most of the sampled firms had experienced little improvement in these efficiency dimensions.

Evidence of a similar gap was found in the application of CAD/CAM to the design and manufacture of hydraulic tubes in the aircraft industry. The companies studied experienced considerable reductions in the labor hours per tube in "mock-up" (engineering prototype), fabrication and assembly; the "first-time-fit" ratio between the third mock-up aircraft and the first production aircraft increased considerably, in one company from between 10 and 20 percent to 55 percent. But, despite these accomplishments, as yet none of these major aircraft manufacturers could boast any reduction in new aircraft development time, and tubing engineering change requests still took five months to accomplish unless they were expedited. Certainly the companies were happy to see that CAD/CAM had enabled them to design more complex aircraft with almost no engineering headcount increases; but the overall cost and time efficiency of their operations—a key strategic variable in this industry—was as yet little changed.

The study also found that even on a purely technological level, CAD/CAM efforts were cause for disappointment. One of the most promising elements of CAD/CAM is the possibility of linking design and manufacturing data bases, so that the factory can be driven from the design data. In both PCBs and hydraulic tubing this has been technically feasible for nearly a decade now. But one third of the larger and more progressive electronics businesses that were contacted for the survey declined to participate because, despite the fact the PCBs were a major component of their products, they had not yet established any direct linkage between their CAD and CAM systems. Most of these companies had developed stand-alone capabilities in CAD and CAM, but they had not yet ventured into integration. And while the other PCB organizations and all the aircraft companies had some downloading capability, none had developed a good set of producibility guidelines for their designers to ensure that the downloaded designs could be manufactured, nor had they developed any two-way communication link that would allow manufacturing to pass design revision suggestions directly into the design data base.

This evidence of US industry's difficulty in deriving competitive advantage from CAD/CAM comes from a sample of two industries. Some other industries, such as VLSI semiconductors and complex metal contouring, have been much more aggressive in their use of CAD/CAM. But these more aggressive industries are characterized by their use of CAD/CAM to achieve greater product complexity. Where it is a matter of using CAD/CAM to enhance manufacturing or design efficiency, evidence is accumulating that the United States is lagging its international competitors. In a recent article, Lester Thurow (1987) marshals evidence from a broad array of industries showing a serious gap between proven possibilities and current practice in process technologies. A recent survey by Arthur Young documents the same gap: surveying several hundred visitors to a factory automation trade show in November 1987, they found that middle managers and engineers disagreed strongly with the common assumption among senior executives that advanced process technology was being applied widely. The extent to which technology is being applied to manufacturing is "vastly lower than that generally assumed" (*Aviation Week and Space Technology*, April 11, 1988).

This chapter presents a framework for identifying the impediments to more effective use of new process technology and offers some guidelines for surmounting those impediments. I highlight five levels of organizational learning needed for effective process automation: skills, procedures, organizational structure, strategy, and culture. I use examples drawn from the previously mentioned survey of CAD/CAM in PCBs and aircraft tubing to illustrate a set of lessons that are surprising similar across different technical and industry contexts.

CAD/CAM TECHNOLOGY

Before we identify these lessons, it is important to understand the nature of the opportunities created by the new process technologies. This section uses the tubing and PCB examples to identify the different types of benefits offered by CAD/CAM, the opportunities for integration, and the underlying dynamics of technological development.

Potential Benefits of CAD/CAM

In the case of hydraulic tubing, the old manual system began with a point-to-point engineering specification: the task of defining a precise route for the tube and its brackets was left to the mock-up (engineering prototype) department, since tubes compete for space with structural elements and other subsystems (electrical, fuel, etc.). Using the old systems, it was virtually impossible for design engineers to develop more precise specifications because of these multiple interdependencies. Mock-up department workers ("plumbers") would fit flexible wire into the full-scale model aircraft and thereby establish the more detailed tubing specifications. Mock-up would generate sample tubes and tube bend cards describing this configuration. The cards were sent back to the design engineers, who would use them to generate production release drawings. The sample tubes and the bend data cards would go to the tooling department to generate tooling. When production orders were released, the fabrication shop would use the sample tubes, the data cards, and the tooling to bend the tubes needed by the assembly function. (This description is very simplified; Rutledge [1986] identifies no fewer than sixty-eight discrete tasks involved in this sequence.) Requests for design changes by the assembly group would go to mock-up, which would then initiate a new iteration.

CAD/CAM makes possible a new, more efficient process in aircraft tubing activities. If all the other structural elements and subsystems are visible to them on their CAD workstation, design engineers can now fully specify the tubing and perform sophisticated engineering analysis before prototypes are created. This specification can be accessed electronically by a much-reduced mock-up staff, who should be necessary only for resolving some of the residual space conflicts. The design data base is then accessed directly by fabrication, in which the specifications are directly downloaded into a numerically controlled tube bender, which has been programmed to compensate for springback[2] and interferences. This avoids the tedious and error-prone process of manually reentering product specifications into the machine control programs. The NC benders are not only more accurate and faster, but eliminate entirely the need for expensive special tools and fragile sample tubes. CAD/CAM systems also offer extraordinary possibilities for simplifying the elaborate administrative and control system for cost estimation, lot release, shop orders, materials, and performance tracking.

In the PCB case, under the old manual system, a design engineer hand-sketched a schematic and indicated the components to be used. This schematic passed to a design and drafting technician (titled "PCB designer" or "drafter," depending on the organization) who would develop a proposal for component placement and wire routing. (In aircraft tubing, no such division of labor between engineering and design/drafting, has emerged.) After several review and revision cycles between engineering and design/drafting, manually created drawings and mylar masks (artwork) for printing would be transmitted to the fabrication and assembly (component insertion) departments. Each department would in turn refer to these documents to (manually) generate the specific drawings and documentation that it required.

CAD/CAM makes possible important improvements in the PCB process. Design automation now allows for functional simulation even before routing is established. The schematic is then directly accessible by design/drafting, which has at its disposal interactive CAD programs for optimizing placement and routing, and for automating the physical drafting task. Timing tests can be conducted before any prototype manufacture needs to be undertaken. The manufacturing functions can code into the design software producibility guidelines or rules, facilitating the assessment by designers of manufacturing cost and quality. Instead of receiving drawings and mylar,[3] the fabrication department can access the design data base directly, using it to automatically generate more accurate photoplotted artwork, board profiling and drilling programs, and connectivity test programs. The assembly department can draw on the design data base to semiautomatically generate automatic component insertion programs, functional tests, process plans and other manufacturing documentation. Various ancillary manufacturing tasks such as materials handling can be automated. And in both departments the administrative control systems can be greatly simplified.

To summarize, in both tubing and PCBs, the potential benefits of CAD/

CAM are potentially large and multifarious, permitting both the elimination of many performance impediments and the enhancement of many performance contributors.

Levels of Integration

The preceding discussion showed the power of CAD/CAM integration as distinct from stand-alone CAD and CAM. It is useful to distinguish the following five levels or degrees of integration:[4]

1. *Downloading* of data for machine control programs from the design data base (i.e., without the need to reenter product specifications): This first level of integration is the simple existence of a direct electronic connection between a design data base and electronically controlled manufacturing equipment.
2. The presence in the CAD system of *producibility design rules:* This second level of integration represents the integration of critical manufacturing knowledge into design software, ensuring that downloaded designs are in fact producible through control of such variables as line and space width on PCBs.
3. The possibility of *uploading* revisions to designs from manufacturing: These revisions will typically need design engineering's approval, and thus necessitate extremely disciplined control systems; but ensuring that the CAD/CAM linkage is a two-way connection is a third, more advanced level of integration.
4. *Automated process planning* broadens the span (or bandwidth) of the integration link, to encompass not only discrete manufacturing processes but also the sequencing of these processes that is required to effectively and efficiently generate the final product.
5. Finally, an *automatic error recovery* capability of the CAD/CAM system—not yet feasible—would ensure that in the presence of contingencies in manufacturing such as tool breakage or machine failure, machine control programs and process plans can be altered automatically in real time. This level of integration would ensure the robustness of the previous levels.

The fifth level of integration may need more advanced sensors and artificial intelligence capabilities than are currently available. The first four levels of integration, on the other hand, are well within the spectrum of current technological feasibility. My survey revealed, however, that few organizations had pursued all the downloading possibilities; very few had even begun uploading; and only a small proportion had begun automated process planning, and these efforts were proceeding without any direct tie-in to the design data base.

The Acceleration of Automation

One of the most important features of the overall process of technological development is the way each new technological step appears to open up successively bigger and more numerous technological possibilities. Historically speaking, the developmental sequence in CAD/CAM is as follows:

- The development of drafting systems led to the emergence of engineering design workstations.
- The development of computer-controlled manufacturing systems made possible their interconnection and their linkage to production scheduling and control systems.
- These developments made possible, in turn, the lowest level of CAD/CAM linkage—the downloading of data from design to manufacturing.
- This fuels the development—as yet limited—of the higher levels of integration that would allow two-way communication between design and manufacturing and the automation of process planning using design data.

Behind the obvious fact that simpler innovations precede more sophisticated ones lies the proposition that technological change is cumulative: the higher the level of automation, the greater the opportunity for further automation. Prima facie support for this hypothesis lies in the approximately regular long-run productivity growth rate experienced in most industrialized economies.

The implications of this accelerating technology trend for management are potentially enormous. If over the long run the *rate* of technological change is constant, the *absolute* amount of change requiring active management in any given time frame is increasing. In slower-moving technological contexts, occasional discrete changes to equipment and operating systems may suffice for an organization to remain competitive. As technological change accelerates, however, organizations will need to develop the ability to aggressively pursue constant change. The next section identifies five key elements of such an ability.

THE MANAGERIAL CHALLENGES OF CAD/CAM

What conditions are required to realize competitive advantage from the potential offered by CAD/CAM technologies? What are the hurdles to the aggressive use of these advanced process technologies? Before we turn to these questions, we need, first, to identify an appropriate measure of CAD/CAM's contribution to competitive advantage.

A particularly useful yardstick for assessing CAD/CAM's contribution is improvement in new product development (NPD) effectiveness. In today's competitive context, companies can no longer content themselves with purely internal measures of process technology effectiveness such as process yield or labor hours. For high-tech companies with rapid product turn-over, NPD effectiveness is the key external measure of success.

For products within a given broad class of performance characteristics, NPD effectiveness can be measured on at least three dimensions: total cost, concept-to-market time, and quality conformance. Within broad classes of product performance characteristics, and contrary to popular prejudice, performance on any one of these dimensions does not necessarily trade off against performance in the other dimensions. Such trade-offs may appear inevitable in a static, all-other-things-being-equal analysis, just as cost and quality seem to trade off against each other in a static analysis of manufacturing operations. But in a dynamic analysis, sustainable improvements in any one dimension typically depend on and induce improvements in other. That is the rationale for the "quality is free" doctrine now well established in manufacturing (Crosby, 1980). It applies in new product development too.[5]

Turning now to the factors that can improve NPD effectiveness, many observers have focused either on the impact of process technology itself or on the approaches that an individual project manager can employ. By contrast, my starting point embeds these factors in a web of more enduring organizational features that shape both the technology development efforts and the project manager's margin of maneuver:[6]

- A first determinant of the benefits realized from new technologies is the *skill base* of the organization: do the personnel have the skills required to effectively select, develop, operate, and maintain the systems?
- Whether or not skills are effectively deployed depends on prevailing *procedures* (or, more broadly, organizational systems), in particular the procedures for coordinating design and manufacturing activities.
- Whether these procedures, which prescribe certain roles, are maintained in the spirit or are respected only in the letter, and therefore degenerate over time, depends on their congruence with the incentives created by the organizational *structure:* what specialized functions have been established? To whom do they report?
- These structures in turn evolve to reflect the priorities embodied in the organization's *strategy:* What are the competitive priorities of the firm? How are these formulated? How are they translated into resource allocation and organizational design?
- And behind these priorities, we often find *culture*—the values and assumptions that bind the organization and give it continuity over time.

These five factors can be thought of as five levels of organizational learning. Two factors argue for thinking of them as levels. First, with increases in the magnitude of the technological change that the organization seeks to effect, organizational adaptation needs to move progressively up this hierarchy (Pava, 1983). Simple technological changes typically require modest changes in skills and procedures. More radical technological changes, on the

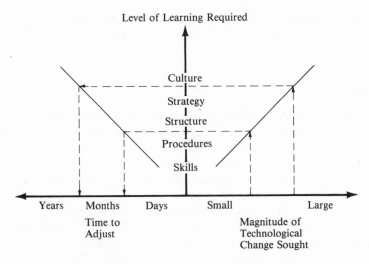

Figure 10.1 Organizational Learning

other hand, typically call for organizational changes not only in skills and procedures, but also in structure and strategy; and revolutionary technological changes usually call for changes in all five levels, including culture.

The second reason for thinking of these factors as a hierarchy is that the lower levels of organizational learning are typically amenable to faster change than the higher levels. The higher levels are more "viscous:" a department's skill level can be adapted through training and recruitment in a matter of weeks or months, whereas changes in organizational culture typically take years to accomplish.

This framework, summarized in the Figure 10.1, is not a theory—it does not tell managers what needs to be done. But it can serve as a heuristic device, pointing managers in the direction of useful questions about their process technology strategy. The following five sections discuss each of the five levels of learning in turn.

SKILLS

A growing body of research results contradicts the hopes of some managers that automation would shift the intelligence requirements from humans to machines and would thus reduce personnel skill requirements and the associated training and wage costs. CAD/CAM typically requires new and broader skills for personnel in manufacturing, design, and CAD/CAM system development, at engineer, technician, and operator levels.

This section first describes the general trend toward increases in skill requirements within specific occupational categories, then the changes in composition of the work force that typically reduce the share of less-skilled categories. The overall result is typically a shift toward greater training needs—and probably higher wage and salary rates—virtually across the board. CAD/CAM's personnel requirements can be summed up as "fewer but better."

Job Content

Turning first to job content shifts, my research supports others' in finding that CAD/CAM creates upgrading pressure in all the major occupational groups:

Design engineering: CAD/CAM drives engineering skills upwards through its impact on both engineering technology and engineering tasks. The new design tools are themselves complex and constantly evolving, requiring new skills and constant skill upgrading among engineers. The introduction of CAD/CAE and the integration of CAD/CAM considerably broadens the task of the design engineer. With CAD/CAE, the designer can access other parts of the design being worked on by other designers, and a much higher level of design optimization is possible and becomes expected. With CAD/CAM integration, plant equipment is driven directly from the design data, so design-for-manufacturability becomes much more important; as a result, a higher level of manufacturing knowledge is expected of the designer. A shift toward a higher skill profile is inevitable (see also Majchrzak et al., 1987; Wingert, Rader, & Riehm, 1981).

Design and drafting technicians: Design automation can reduce design/drafting headcount requirements (for a given output level), since some human tasks are eliminated; many managers extrapolate from this to thinking that automation like PCB autorouting will reduce technician skill requirements. However, the limitations of these systems and the emergence of other higher-level design/drafting tasks usually make deskilling impractical. Design technicians in CAD/CAM environments need higher levels of abstract problem-solving capability and computer expertise, and CAD/CAM integration requires of them a greater understanding of the manufacturing constraints summarized in producibility design rules. These increases typically outweigh the reduced requirements in manual drawing skills. As a result, most drafting managers are shifting their recruiting criteria upward, demanding at least an associate degree. (See also Salzman, 1985; Senker and Arnold, 1984; Allen, 1984; Majchrzak et al., 1987; Tucker and Clark, 1984; Marchisio and Guiducci, 1983; Jerahov, 1984).

Manufacturing workers: Manufacturing automation seems to be increasing manufacturing workers' skill requirements in almost all categories. The key factor behind the general trend toward higher skills is the greater speed of automated processes. As one manager of a PCB assembly plant put it, when component insertion speeds progress from 5000 to 12,000 units/hour, and when some of the newer machines operate at 120,000 units/hours, "the consequences of not thinking have gone way up." CAD/CAM also encourages upgrading of maintenance skill requirements: traditional mechanical, hydraulic, and electrical skills need to be supplemented by electronics expertise. Furthermore, as the span of automation—the integration within a single system of previously separate operations—increases, the need for multicraft maintenance people and broader responsibility for operators appears to be increasing (see also Manufacturing Studies Board, 1986).

Manufacturing engineering: This is perhaps the function in which skill upgrading is most dramatic. The proportion of degreed people tends to grow considerably with CAD/CAM: in one PCB shop I have surveyed, the proportion grew from 40 percent in 1980 to 68 percent in 1986; in another, the proportion grew from less than 15 percent in 1976 to 100 percent in 1986. The main impetus is the need for manufacturing engineers who can understand and program the new CAM systems and manage the software and communications links to the CAD data base. Moreover, CAD/CAM integration means that manufacturing engineers need to develop a rigorous characterization of the manufacturing process and of its producibility constraints. For organizations accustomed to promoting their manufacturing engineers from the shop floor, the change is dramatic (see also Battelle, 1979).

CAD/CAM system development engineers: The development of manufacturing and design engineering systems has, until recent years, been the province of more experienced manufacturing workers and design engineers. Automated design tools were very limited; even manufacturing automation was typically limited in most industries; as a result, operating systems were based not so much on equipment as on the organizational technology of work breakdown, process planning, and scheduling. With the development of computer tools, new skills are needed in CAD and CAM systems development departments. Even firms that plan to buy rather than to develop their own software find that both systems maintenance requirements and the value of customizing their software drive them to establish and maintain significant staffs of highly skilled systems developers (see also Traversa, 1984).

Work Force Composition

The organization's overall skill and human resource challenge is not only a function of the changing content of the specific occupations, but also reflects the changing proportions between these occupations:

Within *design,* there is a trend toward a higher ratio of engineers to design/drafting personnel. In one typical PCB operation I have studied, this ratio evolved from 2:1 in 1980 to 3:1 in 1986. CAE/CAD does not substitute technicians for engineers.

In the *manufacturing* area, we find similar compositional upgrading forces at work: manufacturing, engineering, and maintenance—typically the higher-skilled categories—increase their share compared to "direct" labor. There are some cases, however, in which highly skilled categories appear to be swept aside by automation. In the tubing case, for example, the mock-up department will shrink. Although compositional upgrading seems to be the general trend, each case needs to be carefully examined.

The ratio of CAD/CAM *systems designers* to system users grows over time. Some managers hope that once the systems are installed, most of this staff will no longer be needed. This is unrealistic and undesirable. The example of one highly automated PCB facility is enlightening. When their CAD/CAM development efforts began in 1980, they needed some sixteen highly skilled systems development engineers. By 1987, they had been up and running and debugged for over three years, and they found they still needed all sixteen in order to maintain the new systems and to pursue the continually expanding range of new automation opportunities.

Implications

Naturally some contingency factors, apart from technology, can influence skill trends—factors such as product complexity, production volume, and make/buy policy. Although these factors modify the relative strength of various upgrading pressures, they do not reverse the upgrading trend on a sustained basis. The reason is not hard to see. An increase in the automation level applied to a given task might, in a particular instance, reduce skill requirements, but automation typically leads to (a) further automation and (b) changes in product characteristics. Both these dynamic effects have strong skill upgrading effects—employees must be able to support and adapt to this dynamic change—and these effects typically far outweigh any static deskilling effect.

Just as important as the changes in skill levels, however, are the changes in the nature of the skill requirements. The general thrust of CAD/CAM is to shift the knowledge-base in both design and manufacturing toward the science end of the art–science spectrum. Tacit, firm-specific skills developed through the accumulation of experience lose in relative importance to formalized, conceptual, classroom-based, explicit, generic skills. Higher initial education levels and more formal training are required.

This trend in the *relative* importance of explicit versus tacit skills seems to coexist with the simultaneous increase in the *absolute* level of tacit skill requirements. As the knowledge base becomes more explicit, more potential "hooks" appear that can tie it into firm-specific opportunities to build tacit knowledge. To take an example from PCB manufacturing: autoinsertion machines require less manual dexterity than manual component insertion; on the other hand, they require not only greater formal generic training in machine operations, but also a more firm-specific knowledge of the broader variety of components being inserted at a given workstation.

This dual shift to (a) a higher level of both generic and tacit, firm-specific skill requirements and (b) a higher ratio of generic to tacit skills has serious implications for recruiting, training, and personnel retention policies. The increase in firm-specific skills makes turnover more costly, at the same time the even greater increase in generic skill requirements makes internal promotion increasingly insufficient as a source of high-level technical expertise.

A further factor adds to the tension. The accelerating automation curve, as well as CAD/CAM's effect of reducing the cost penalty associated with increased product variety, both imply that the rate of change of the requisite knowledge base is increasing. Whatever the firm's training versus hiring policy, the people in place will thus need a more proactive learning orientation toward both explicit and tacit skills.

Some organizations are taking the bull by the horns (a) by developing a pay-for-knowledge system (see Lawler, 1981) to replace their traditional job classification approach and (b) by making a more sustained commitment to development of their work force.

PROCEDURES

If the skill-base of the organization is the underlying condition for effective CAD/CAM implementation, the more immediately visible factor explaining the degree of overall NPD improvement, and the fact most directly responsible for the poor CAD/CAM performance of many U.S. firms, is the state of design/manufacturing coordination procedures. The proximate cause of the poor business pay-off to CAD/CAM efforts to date is the anarchy of interfunctional coordination procedures and the failure to revise these procedures when CAD/CAM is introduced:

- Drawings often sit idle, waiting to be worked on, just as long in electronic form as in paper form.
- Engineers rarely focus on using the new tools to reduce the frequency of revisions—they are much more inclined to focus on increasing product performance.
- Procedures for the coordination of design and manufacturing typically leave too much until too late in the cycle.

There are, of course, many other procedures that need attention when an organization moves into CAD/CAM, such as pay systems and investment evaluation rules. But this section concentrates on engineering procedures, since it is here that I have found both the greatest improvement opportunity and an important new area for research. Most discussion of procedures has taken as its unit of analysis the individual project. By contrast, I will attempt to characterize the procedural issues at a more aggregate level, using the organization as the unit of analysis and analyzing product and process design engineering as production processes (see also Clark and Fujimoto, 1987).

Just-in-Time Discipline for Engineering Activities

The typical part in the typical machining shop is being worked on only 2 percent of the time it spends there. The rest of the time is spent in transport or waiting (95 percent) and in set-up or other necessary nonmachining time (3 percent) (Hutchinson, 1984). What are the corresponding figures for an engineering drawing? Few organizations can answer this elementary question.

Certainly we can find cases in which rapid new product introduction is the overriding concern, and all efforts are devoted to minimizing the wait, transport and set-up times experienced by designs-in-process (to use an analogy to manufacturing work-in-process). But the machine shop, too, has its rush jobs. And at the other extreme, engineering changes in both civilian and military aircraft companies take an average of five months in calendar time unless they are expedited. The estimated average actual processing time of these ECs is about forty-eight hours, including redesign, retooling, revising plans, and reviews. The ratio of processing time (forty-eight hours) to calendar time (5 months × 20 days/months × 8 hours/day) is 6 percent—not much batter than the machining shop.

The same effects have the same cause: a management focus on maximizing utilization rather than on minimizing product throughput time. Engineers are thus kept busy working on many projects at once; their in-basket is constantly overflowing. But in engineering as in the job shop, dramatic reductions in the processing time of specific steps do not translate into improved NPD time if there are long wait times between steps. In most cases, however, firms implementing CAD/CAM merely automate the existing procedures and leave the old sequence of suboperations and the old wait times untouched. If they want to capture the benefits of CAD/CAM, it is imperative that firms reconfigure engineering procedures to improve engineering operations efficiency.

Total Quality Control Discipline in Engineering

In the domain of quality policies, just as in inventory control, engineering seems to lag behind modern manufacturing procedures. Although design engineers are often enthusiastic about the way CAD/CAM allows them to design more complex products, another of CAD/CAM's major potential benefits is improved quality conformance (minimizing errors). But very few organizations develop the procedures needed to tap this potential.

One PCB operation I have studied did track postmanufacturing-release engineering changes, and found that some 50 percent of the board designs released to manufacturing violated at least one design rule. Without aggressive quality improvement procedures, CAD/CAM will not translate into NPD improvement. But very few organizations hold project managers accountable for things like the number of engineering changes within the first three months of release to manufacturing.

Pre-manufacturing-release quality is also an important improvement opportunity. All engineering organizations have some procedure for controlling the quality of individual designs. But this is what modern manufacturing calls "inspecting design in" rather than "building it in;" to build quality in requires procedures for managing the quality of the design process, not only the quality of the products. Most design organizations have quite standard test and review milestones; a total quality control approach in design can track the yield at these checkpoints to catch systematic design process quality problems. (See Schrader, 1986; Murray, 1987; Melan, 1987.)

Design/Manufacturing Coordination Procedures

It is tempting to see CAD/CAM integration as the electronic solution to the problems frequently encountered when designs are "thrown over the wall" to manufacturing: in this vision, producibility rules guarantee manufacturability, and electronic communication allows the perfect throw. This vision is unrealistic.

A useful way of thinking about the design/manufacturing coordination problem is to distinguish coordination before, during, and after the design project. In each case, we can make a further distinction based on the interfunctional communication pattern: this pattern can be in the form of a one-way information flow, a "stilted" two-way information flow (or batch information transfer), or a collaborative and interactive two-way flow. (This latter distinction builds on the research of Clark and Fujimoto, 1987.)

Many writers wax eloquent on the virtues of joint design teams—collaborative two-way communication during the project. Clearly, earlier communication between the functions and a less-stilted dialogue can go a long way to improving NPD; but my research suggests that the joint design team formula needs to be buttressed by pre- and postproject coordination mechanisms. Activities prior to the project, such as the development by design engineers of their knowledge of manufacturing constraints, the elaboration of producibility design rules, and joint strategic planning by design and manufacturing managers, can economize on and focus design team meeting time. Aggressive management of issues after design release, such as the engineering change process, the maintenance of a judicious degree of manufacturing flexibility, and postproject appraisals, can leverage the prerelease efforts and ensure learning across projects.

Even coordination during the design project should not be restricted to joint design teamwork. More formalized design reviews can help the organization economize on meeting time and can bring a fresh perspective from outsiders. Moreover, although manufacturing engineering's contribution to product specifications is often valuable, it is clearly preferable to have the manufacturing staff focus as much as possible on the issues that require their special expertise; part of project coordination should therefore take the form of early release of design data to manufacturing, rather than joint teamwork.

In general, the better the earlier interaction modes and the more reliable the one-way information flows are, the more effective the later interaction modes and two-way information flows will be. But all these modes of coordination are important: they are complementary, not substitutes. CAD/CAM can be a powerful support tool for these coordination modes. But it only facilitates coordination; it does not itself accomplish it.

Implications

A powerful determinant of the ability to transform CAD/CAM's micro sub-operation benefits into macro NPD time-to-market, cost, and quality competitive advantages is the tautness and appropriateness of the procedures that regulate the design and manufacturing operations and the interface between them.

Regarding tautness, the potential gains associated with CAD/CAM automation encourage greater discipline in the organization. But many of the organizations I have studied have discovered, if only in retrospect, that much of the performance improvement associated with CAD/CAM was well within reach for organizations that took on such discipline even without CAD/CAM. CAD/CAM, however, makes the waste more apparent.

Regarding appropriateness, the key is the fit between the procedures and the coordination needs created by the underlying organizational structure. Structure is the subject of the following section.

STRUCTURE: DIFFERENTIATION AND INTEGRATION

The basic framework for understanding the organizational structure challenges of CAD/CAM is the dialectic of differentiation and integration (Lawrence and Lorsch, 1969). Greater environmental uncertainty, and in particular, more rapid technological change, encourages organizations to develop specialized, differentiated subunits, and these subunits in turn need new structural coordination mechanisms to ensure the consistency of their efforts.

Both developing and implementing CAD/CAM introduce new uncertainties, new differentiation needs and thus new coordination needs. In this section, I focus on CAD/CAM development to illustrate some of the structural challenges of the new process technologies.

Differentiation

CAD/CAM systems development calls for new forms of organizational differentiation. As indicated earlier, new systems development skills are required to develop and maintain CAD and CAM systems. When the change experienced in process technologies was slower, manufacturing and design engineering could absorb the task of managing such change. As the pace of change accelerates, the skill base of process technology development becomes progressively more distinct from the skills typically required of design and manufacturing engineers. New systems development groups are needed.

Interestingly, such an organizational redesign seems to come more naturally to manufacturing than to design. Most firms have advanced manufacturing technology groups that develop CAM capabilities, however, in many firms, the so-called CAD organization is simply the computer-equipped drafting group; there is often no specific CAD systems development organization. This relative weakness in the organizational differentiation of CAD development as opposed to CAM development exists partly because a buy-only policy is more feasible in CAD than in CAM. A more fundamental reason is that the design organization is quite unaccustomed to process automation, so has typically never had a design process engineering group parallel to manufacturing process engineering from which a system development organization could grow.

Nevertheless, as organizations push more aggressively into CAD, they often find that total reliance on vendors is insufficient, and they begin forming their own specialized in-house CAD systems development groups. Depending on their make/buy policy, these groups are smaller or larger and spend varying proportions of their time developing, selecting, installing, customizing, and maintaining the CAD/CAE systems.

Coordination Through Integrating Structures

The technological opportunities for CAD/CAM integration and the competitive pressures to capitalize on these opportunities create the need for some new mechanisms for coordinating CAD and CAM development efforts. We have already discussed some of the skill and procedural requirements of coordination. But it is organizational structure that creates the incentives for people to coordinate.

The pressures to improve coordination are destined to grow more important over time. As CAD/CAM ties the various functional departments closer together, costs and benefits are increasingly cross-functional. To take just one example: some mechanism is necessary for deciding who is going to fund the development of a parts data base when it is to be used by design but its primary payoff is in manufacturing efficiency. The CAD/CAM integration efforts of one electronics company I have studied have been stymied by the failure, three years in a row, to find such a budget mechanism.

I have found a variety of integrating mechanisms being deployed more or less successfully. These can be arrayed in a hierarchy from looser to tighter coordination:[7]

1. The loosest integration mechanisms are in the form of direct contacts and liaison roles. Many organizations have *CAD/CAM committees* in which representatives from design and manufacturing meet regularly to exchange information about current and future projects. Committees without budgets are powerless, however, in the face of "not-invented-here" syndromes.

2. Cross-functional CAD/CAM committees can play a more effective role when they take the form of *task forces,* with high-level management direction-setting, and with funds to allocate—in other words, where there is both authority and accountability.

3. An even more powerful integrating mechanism can be the requirement that all systems be able to communicate with, and all design specifi-

cations fit the format of, a *product definition data base* jointly specified by design and manufacturing: as long as this requirement is met, CAD and CAM developers can be left free to use or develop any system they see fit.

4. Some organizations nominate a *CAD/CAM manager,* to whom the separate CAD and CAM development groups report. This encourages a greater degree of strategic coordination, since the CAD/CAM manager is typically responsible for formulating an overarching strategy encompassing the two subgroups.

5. A small number of organizations have put into place a *central CAD/CAM organization.* The systems developers in CAD and in CAM have similar skill sets, so pooling them is less difficult than in the case of design and manufacturing engineers. But they still have very different clients and task environments; thus, even when such central groups are established, they do not replace so much as support distinct CAD and CAM development efforts located in design and manufacturing (see also Schaffitzel and Kersten, 1985).

Implications

As the value of CAD/CAM integration becomes more obvious. organizations will redesign themselves to ensure higher degrees of organizational coordination. To elaborate a strategic vision of CAD/CAM development over a five- or ten-year horizon and ensure its consistent implementation call for more than occasional committee meetings.

While the new technologies encourage new organizational structures, the existing structures can mask the need for this adaptation. One impediment to effective CAD/CAM development often lies in product-oriented (rather than functional or process-oriented) structures. Product, project, or program managers typically have little incentive to contribute to the longer-term task of CAD/CAM systems development, especially if it comes out of their project budget. Even if some funding mechanism is created, the product-oriented structure typically disperses key experts and thus often blocks the formation of a critical mass of systems development expertise. On the other hand, the functional, process-oriented structure common in manufacturing can also impede CAD/CAM development: the interfunctional coordination required for the integration of CAD and CAM is more easily ignored in the functional than in the product structure.

The implication is clear: strategic commitment to pursuing CAD/CAM opportunities will encourage many businesses to redesign their organizational structure. In some of these businesses, organization along product line will remain valid for design, while organization along process lines will remain valid for manufacturing. Matrix forms will therefore become more common, especially in firms with greater strategic commitment to CAD/CAM.

STRATEGY

In this section I first examine CAD/CAM development strategies, then the CAD/CAM strategy process, and finally the implications of these strategy issues for organizational structure.

CAD/CAM Development Strategies

CAD/CAM, by virtue of the accelerating technology curve it embodies, forces organizations to push their planning horizons further out. In the past, manufacturing technology was planned one or at most two years out, and design technologies were typically managed on a purely incremental basis. CAD/CAM choices, by contrast, can commit the organization's infrastructure for five years or more. Unfortunately, few organizations have even a rough sketch of a comprehensive strategy for tackling the longer-term issues.

Among the more popular CAD/CAM strategies, I have found three different approaches:

• The first could be called *energetic anarchy:* One aircraft company encouraged its subunits to plunge ahead, independently of each other if need be, into whatever automation efforts passed a rather generous set of investment criteria. They ended up with twenty-three different and incompatible computer-based systems. This strategy can nevertheless be considered successful, since they found that the accumulated automation experience and skill base outweighed the inconvenience and cost of having to reprogram or replace some systems when they decided to integrate them.

• A second strategy is a variant of the first, which could be called *minimal government:* Subunits are encouraged to automate in any way that seems appropriate, with the proviso that all systems be able to communicate with a central product definition data base. As in the energetic anarchy strategy, the rapid progress made in both CAD and CAM builds a competence-base and ensures that integration proposals are generally well-received, since there is already something worth integrating, and since the subunits' appetites for the potential gains of automation have been whetted.

• A third and more difficult strategy is that of *integrated planning*. One PCB operation I have studied has developed a detailed matrix of all the products to be introduced over the next five years and a year-by-year characterization of the process technologies to be used for each. Such an integrated approach has the major benefit of giving all the subunits a common reference point in their technology planning.

None of these models, however, captures the enormous long-term potential of CAD/CAM. The product-by-product approach of the integrated planning strategy, despite its detail (or perhaps because of it) does not offer an overarching vision of where design and manufacturing capabilities as a whole are going: planning has swamped strategy, leaving little room for creative initiative. Lacking even a planning framework, energetic anarchy and minimal government strategies create no process for coming to grips with new technologies (such as surface-mount for PCBs), which require true joint problem solving across the design and manufacturing functions.

Unfortunately, most organizations think of their CAD/CAM strategy as a detailed "architecture" document and a timetable for sequencing the projects necessary to realize that architecture (following a model like that proposed by Hales, 1984). Few organizations have identified the range of policies that would be required to effectively manage this sequence of projects and implement the new systems. A CAD/CAM strategy should specify all the relevant policies: skill formation, organizational interfaces, CAD/CAM make/buy policies, CAD/CAM systems capacity expansion policies, line versus staff roles in systems development and maintenance, centralization versus decentralization of CAD/CAM development capabilities, and so forth.

The chief impediment to developing a truly strategic vision of the development of CAD/CAM capabilities are (1) the lack of familiarity with the technology at senior management levels and (2) the lack of strategic management capability at the middle-management levels. Developing a CAD/CAM strategy seems to call for a new distribution of competencies within management and a new strategy process.

The Strategy Process

The previous subsection's vision of CAD/CAM strategy is premised on a simple proposition: as the rate of technological change accelerates, the strategy process must be decentralized, because general management cannot deal with the growing information-processing burden associated with the proliferation of technology options. This vision of strategic planning pushed down from general to functional management may appear utopian. It resembles the vision of "interactive planning" proposed by Ackoff (1970) nearly twenty years ago. But two factors argue for its growing realism. First, strategic analysis has become a more familiar process at the general management level. The preconditions for its downward diffusion within the organization are therefore probably in place. Second, the relative competitive effectiveness of such "participatory" strategy processes compared with that of the traditional top-down processes will encourage their diffusion.

The new strategy approach requires and encourages a reduction in the status and power differentials within the management team: (1) A more participatory process requires a reduction in the power differential that often separates functional from general managers. (2) When competition and CAD/CAM opportunities require greater consistency of functional strategies, it becomes more difficult to justify the traditional hierarchy separating the functions: finance and marketing have often dictated the overall strategic direction, while design engineering spelled out the desired new product characteristics and manufacturing was left to "implement" the strategy that the other functions had articulated. In companies hoping to capitalize on CAD/CAM, all the functions will need to enter the strategy formulation process as equals.

Implications

In the previous section on structure, I outlined some of the new forms of differentiation and integration necessitated by CAD/CAM. It is important, however, to note that strategy has important implications for organizational structure. Strategy can both influence the need for differentiation and facilitate integration:

Strategic aggressiveness in pursuing CAD/CAM opportunities pushes the organization out along the environmental uncertainty/technological opportunity axis, forcing it to confront greater differentiation requirements. An extreme case is one of the PCB fabrication operations I studied, in which they had discovered that the vendors of PCB drilling machines were not designing their equipment for maximum manufacturing efficiency. As a result, this PCB fabrication business decided to design its own 200-bit tool changer—a great improvement over the 20-bit capacity of standard equipment. This aggressiveness led naturally to a qualitatively new level of differentiation, as they developed a new subsidiary to build and sell this equipment.

Strategic focus, by contrast, can mitigate some of the effects of this increase in environmental uncertainty and technological opportunity: if a more careful and accurate analysis of the environment allows the organization to be more selective in focusing its attention, the differentiation requirements can be reduced for a given level of objective environmental uncertainty. Rutledge's (1986) analysis of aircraft tubing, for example, establishes an approximate relationship between cost and differentiation business strategy priorities, on the one hand, and emphasis on various subareas within tubing CAD/CAM on the other hand: both cost and differentiation strategies give great weight to the production data system (a prime opportunity area), but differentiation strategies tend to focus more on the design/manufacturing data interface, and cost strategies tend to focus more on integrating CAM applications.

Through the development and harmonization of *function-level long-term strategies,* the uncertainty surrounding other subunits' future actions and needs can be reduced, and therefore the requirements for organizational structural mechanisms of integration can also be reduced (see Wheelwright and Hayes, 1985, on functional strategy). In practical terms, if (1) the manufacturing function articulates a long-term vision of the development of its CAM capabilities, and if (2) the design function articulates a long-term vision for CAD capabilities, and if (3) these functional technology strategies are iteratively revised until they are consistent with each other and with the overall business strategy, then this strategic coordination reduces CAD and

CAM developers' need for day-to-day coordination and ensures that their efforts are nevertheless consistent.

This section's discussion of strategy has highlighted the need for new status and influence relationships. The following section on culture addresses these in more depth.

CULTURE

In many ways, the most difficult challenges of CAD/CAM are at the cultural level, the least tangible level of organizational learning. Three key relationships pose cultural challenges in CAD/CAM:

- *Between workers and manager:* When workers are asked to play a more active problem-identification and problem-solving role, as was the case in my analysis of CAD/CAM's skill requirements, commonly encountered authoritarian values become obsolete (Adler, 1986).
- *Between design and manufacturing:* Overcoming the great status gap becomes an imperative if firms hope to capitalize on the integration opportunities that hold so much competitive advantage potential.
- *Between lower and higher levels of managers:* The previous section discussed the need to shift from a more autocratic, top-down strategy process to a more participative process.

In this section, I take the second of these relationships to illustrate CAD/CAM's cultural challenge. This challenge can be analyzed at several levels of visibility: artifacts, values, and basic assumptions (Schein, 1984).

Cultural Artifacts

The clearest expression of the design/manufacturing divide is in the fact that in most PCB businesses, not only are design and manufacturing engineers not at the same average pay levels, but they are not even on the same pay curves. And such anomalies have strange ways of surreptitiously reappearing: when some companies move to common curves, they retain a lower maximum for manufacturing; in others, manufacturing engineers are not included in profit-sharing plans. In other industries, such as the aircraft industry, pay curves are similar across functions, but a multiplicity of other artifacts communicate the same message of inequality: amount and quality of office space, time to participate in professional activities, and so on.

Values

The hierarchy expressed in these artifacts reflects and reinforces an underlying hierarchy in values. The status hierarchy in PCB engineering typically follows the descending order of (1) circuit design, (2) board design, (3) mechanical design, (4) assembly engineering, and (5) fabrication engineering. In aircraft companies, a similar hierarchy of status and organizational influence distinguishes design engineering, various support engineering functions, and the various types of manufacturing engineers.

The inequality expressed in these artifacts and values would not be a major source of concern were it not for the fact that automation has shifted upward the skill and recruitment profiles of manufacturing engineering relative to design engineering. Whereas in the past many businesses did not need degreed manufacturing engineers with a solid theoretical knowledge base, the effective design and implementation of CAD/CAM has meant that recruitment criteria are becoming increasingly similar. The hierarchy separating design and manufacturing engineers is no longer a reflection of real differences in skill level or contribution and therefore becomes increasingly dysfunctional. Since all forms of coordination, especially the two-way forms, presuppose a willingness to cooperate, these obsolete values are increasingly debilitating.

Basic Assumptions

Value orientations typically reflect and reinforce an underlying set of implicit and usually unconscious assumptions. One important cluster of such assumptions may be the individualistic conception both of the nature of useful knowledge and of how such knowledge grows over time.

Many engineers, and especially design engineers, have an individualistic conception of knowledge: the organization's ability to design products is often seen as the arithmetic sum of the component individuals' capabilities minus the organizational impediments. Similarly, the development of new knowledge is often seen as the sum of each component individual's personal learning.

Many engineers see the organizational element as merely a potential impediment whose impact has to be minimized. It is rarely seen as an enabling factor, and almost never as a critical element of the organization's knowledge base. For most engineers, the ability to get something done through other people—one of the critical skills of the manufacturing engineer, but also an important skill in most design environments—is much less valued than individual creativity. Echoing these assumptions, specialized depth of knowledge is typically valued over the breadth required to effectively coordinate with complementary specialities. And the idea of tighter procedures in engineering is resisted not only because it seems to undermine the traditional autonomy of the professional, but because such individual autonomy is assumed to be the precondition of creativity.

With these assumptions, the image of collaboration with which most engineers would spontaneously identify is that of baseball or football, games with very clearly defined, specialized roles and based on primarily individual contributions; they rarely see themselves as part of a basketball team engaged in spontaneous reciprocal adaptation (Keidel, 1985).

Typically, this cluster of assumptions is also buttressed by the assumption that the most efficient principle of organization is competition rather than cooperation: let the best ideas, as products of the smartest individuals, win.

This emphasis on individual contributions and individual creativity undergirds the hierarchical values that elevate design over manufacturing rather than promote teamwork between different but equal contributors.

Associated with this individualistic assumption is a distinctive understanding of the nature of engineering knowledge and its growth. Although many engineers see continual education as an important means for avoiding technological obsolescence, few of them see themselves engaged in a collective enterprise of continual organizational learning. New projects are more or less interesting because they offer greater or lesser opportunity to apply available knowledge, not because as a team they are generating new insights. As engineers rather than research scientists, they see themselves applying existing knowledge, not creating new knowledge of any great significance. This reflects the assumption dominant in most engineering schools that science is more valuable than practical know-how.

The drawback of such a set of underlying assumptions should be obvious, especially compared with the culture fostered by many Japanese companies, in which even the most minor process improvements are celebrated as the key to progress and competitiveness (Imai, 1986). Many U.S. organizations are severely handicapped by a culture that embraces neither the challenge of collective learning, as opposed to purely individual learning or to the application of existing knowledge, nor the idea that this learning is about both technologies and organizational forms.

Implications

It is this cluster of assumptions that explains perhaps why so few companies pursue aggressive policies of colocating engineers from different functions— a proven powerful catalyst for improved communication. The efficacy of this organizational technology presupposes a more collective learning process. Similarly, few organizations seriously pursue a policy of designing managerial career paths in multiple functions. As a result, very few design engineering managers have ever worked in manufacturing for longer than a couple of months. Some manufacturing engineers and some manufacturing engineering managers have worked in design, but their move into manufacturing is usually seen as a one-way quasi-demotion.

These cultural problems, notwithstanding the relative invisibility of the underlying assumptions, are not beyond the reach of management. It is remarkable how quickly values can adapt when a few manufacturing managers are promoted into top management positions. More fundamentally, problems in the design/manufacturing relationship often stem from and are exacerbated by the absence of a clear common external objective. In the absence of such an external objective, design and manufacturing goals turned inward—toward rivalry with each other. When senior management, aided perhaps by real external challenges, can refocus the subunits on a common external rival, the hostile subunit relations can be turned into one of cooperative complementarity.

The difference in the performance of externally focused, internally cooperative organizations and the performance of organizations that have turned inward and become absorbed by rivalry and by hierarchical mechanisms for controlling it will grow over time. A culture of hierarchy was perhaps inevitable in more stable contexts; the increasingly dynamic character of CAD/CAM technology makes that culture obsolete. As CAD/CAM technologies accelerate, hierarchical approaches will be progressively less effective than a collaborative learning approach in all three critical organizational relationships mentioned in the introduction to this section.

CAD/CAM AND COMPETITIVE ADVANTAGE

The key problems framing the objective of this chapter were (1) the slowness of many firms in pursuing the technological potential for CAD/CAM integration and (2) the scarcity of major efficiency benefits from CAD/CAM for the organization as a whole.

The previous five sections have outlined the problems at five levels of organizational learning that seem to account for these facts: the need for broader skills, for more disciplined engineering procedures, for new structural forms of differentiation and integration, for a new strategy content and process, and for a new cultural context.

Can we, in conclusion, characterize a viable approach to seriously tackling these five levels of learning? One organization's history captures some key lessons. They have reduced their PCB design-to-market time from forty-five weeks to eighteen weeks. What did it take? In fact, CAD/CAM equipment itself played a very small role in this improvement. The factors highlighted by the former general manager were these:

- Forethought and discipline in the design stage—taking a little more time to define all the parameters before the schematic goes into layout— avoided several design iterations and cut design time (to manufacturing release) from sixteen to four weeks.
- The reduction in the number of design cycles cut the average number of prototypes from 3 to 1.5; this allowed the organization to eliminate the model shop and allowed manufacturing to run these remaining prototypes as initial production tryouts, which in turn allowed manufacturing earlier access to the product design, permitting an earlier start on tooling, on procurement, and on progress down the learning curve.
- Assuring that files sent to the fabrication shop contained all the necessary information and that the design did not violate any design rules meant that 100 percent as opposed to 50 percent of files received by fabrication were producible the first time.
- Improving the procurement cycle allowed them to cut two weeks out of the assembly process.

The key managerial challenges in this organization's improvement process were as follows:

- Empowering the downstream, typically lower-status, subunit to return inadequately prepared material, rather than use it and suffer quality failures as a result.
- Overcoming the "ego" pressures and managing the time pressures on the design engineers, to encourage them to "do it right the first time."
- Focusing the entire organization on new product development time as the key competitive variable and on total quality control through the design-to-market cycle as the key means of improvement.

Several of the aircraft companies I have studied are on the verge of similar cascade of improvements. After painstakingly building their product data bases—structural, hydraulic, electrical, insulation, controls, and so forth—they can now proceed to tie them together and engage the corresponding organizational learning challenges. One company estimated that this would eventually allow them to generate sufficiently detailed high-quality designs that they can eliminate three iterations of mock-up; this means saving some $300 million spread over the first 200 planes of a new aircraft series and gaining some twelve to sixteen months in new aircraft development time.

The lesson appears to be this: payoffs in enhanced competitive position are indeed possible with CAD/CAM, but they do not come in direct proportion to CAD/CAM development (Haas, 1987). The payoff curve to CAD/CAM, like that of other technologies, has an S-form, with most benefits appearing only after a certain threshold has been broken. Indeed, these benefits often appear only after some disruption effect has been absorbed.

The pathway to this breakpoint is well known: first simplify, then automate, finally integrate. My analysis suggests a few qualifiers to this prescription:

1. Simplify current processes, building understanding and mastery of its contingencies and streamlining it as far as possible: this discipline should be carried through into engineering activities that are often exempted in the name of professional autonomy.
2. Build islands of automation, developing the requisite skills and knowledge base: compatibility may not be as important as the automation experience acquired.
3. Integrate these islands: the details of a system architecture may be less important than interfunctional agreement on the direction of development and on comprehensive, consistent sets of policies that would constitute long-term functional technology strategies.

And I would add a fourth step:

4. Reconfigure the organization and its procedures to capitalize on this integration.

If CAD/CAM is on the early, and thus relatively flat, part of the S-curve, the managerial challenge is to get onto the steeper part sooner rather than later. The overarching strategic issue is thus not so much *learning,* since progress is certainly being made, but *learning to learn* faster and more effectively. This exigency is only reinforced by the fact that the currently identifiable CAD/CAM S-curve will certainly be followed by other manufacturing and engineering process technology S-curves that will have even higher levels of productivity potential. Longer-term competitiveness depends on the organization's ability to shorten the flat parts at both the bottom end and the top end of the S-curve.

The key conclusion of this chapter is therefore that capturing the potential competitive advantage payoff of CAD/CAM, and of the accelerating stream of design and manufacturing process technologies of which it is a part, requires substantial revisions to traditional policy focii. When automation came in small, discrete, occasional steps, it could be absorbed by marginal adjustments at the "lower" levels of the hierarchy of organizational learning—skills were updated and procedures were fine-tuned. But when automation no longer comes as discrete projects, but instead as an ongoing program, continually reaching further out into the expanding universe of technological opportunities, then learning must be pursued much more proactively at all five levels.

The challenge is considerable, since these higher levels of organizational learning do not respond as rapidly as lower levels. Changes in culture and in the type of strategy (as distinct from changes to specific objectives) typically take much longer to accomplish than changes in skills or procedures—as expressed in the earlier figure.

This analysis suggests that CAD/CAM calls for a subtle change in the whole fabric of the organization, away from a conception of the organization as a production system and toward a new conception of the organization as a system with a dual objective of production and learning. As a result, not only do the higher levels of learning assume greater importance, but the content of policies at each level needs to change. The technological dynamism that will increasingly characterize competitive conditions calls for distinctively "dynamic" policies at each of the five levels of learning:

1. More dynamic learning policies in the skills domain add a focus on problem-identification and problem-solving know-why to the static policy's focus on operational know-how; "training" becomes "development."

2. In a more static environment, it may have made sense to buffer departments from each other using procedures as bureaucratic walls; each department could thereby better focus on its own distinct mission. But in a more dynamic context, missions change more frequently and response-time becomes a critical competitive factor. Procedures, therefore, need to be seen as ways both to more tightly couple subunits and to better consolidate ongoing organizational

learning. Procedures make learning more explicit and thus more easily reproducible and improvable.

3. In a static approach, structure easily degenerates into fiefdoms, and such autarchy has the virtue of allowing each function to build its own expertise. But in a dynamic approach, structures must be as flat as possible and flexible in their configuration of specialized, differentiated, and coordinated subunits.

4. In the static model, strategy is primarily elaborated by general management; functional management's role is primarily that of implementing this strategy; and the strategy is focused on attaining one-time step-function improvements in market and financial outcomes. In the dynamic model, on the other hand, strategy is collaboratively elaborated by both functional and general management, and it defines both expected results and a capabilities growth path.

5. In the static model, culture is based on hierarchical authority; in the dynamic model collaboration replaces rivalry and culture is marked by encouragement to experiment and the right to fail.

CAD/CAM's challenge goes to the core of our conception of the firm.

NOTES

1. This research was supported by McKinsey & Co. Their financial, logistic and conceptual assistance is gratefully acknowledged. Managers and engineers at the companies surveyed graciously provided not only data but also their valuable insights. They must unfortunately remain anonymous. Duane Helleloid and Elaine Rothman provided extensive research assistance. This draft has also benefitted from comments by Kim Clark, Dave Grossman, Robert Hayes, John Nast, Steven Wheelwright, and participants at two McKinsey/Academic working sessions.

2. Springback is the tendency of the tube to spring back a little from a bending operation, so that a tube bent 90 degrees may be found to retain a bend only of 85 degrees. The amount of springback depends on the type of tubing and the angle bent.

3. Mylar has a number of limitations. Mylar artwork is hand-generated and therefore error-prone. It is not stable in changing atmosphere conditions. It cannot be used for up to twelve hours, until it fixes. Finally, only one original is generated, and vendors can find themselves working on a fifth- or even tenth-generation copy with the corresponding loss of definition.

4. This hierarchy was developed with the assistance of Mark Cutkosky, Mechanical Engineering, Stanford University.

5. Strong evidence for this can be found in Clark, Chew, and Fujimoto's (1987) comparison of automobile development projects: they found a strong positive correlation between total engineering hours and total calendar time in the development of comparably complex vehicles.

6. This framework was inspired by Pava (1983), to whose four-element model I have added a fifth, strategy level. It was only after my initial formulation that it became obvious that it can also be related to the so-called Seven S framework (Pascale and Athos, 1981; for an application to CIM issues, see Krakauer, 1984; for an application to information systems, see Crescenzi, 1987). Relative to the Seven S

framework, I have assimilated style into strategy and culture—since by style Pascale and Athos refer to the elements of leadership that reflect and reinforce strategy—and I have assimilated staff into culture and skills—since here Pascale and Athos focus on the socialization of new personnel and their skill mix. Following Pava, I have also characterized these domains as levels in a hierarchy, which Pascale and Athos do not.

7. This hierarchy was guided by that proposed by Galbraith (1977): direct contact, liaison roles, task forces, teams, integrating roles, managerial linking roles, matrix organization.

11

High Technology Performance Management

ALLAN M. MOHRMAN, JR., SUSAN ALBERS MOHRMAN,
AND CHRISTOPHER G. WORLEY

Performance requirements in high technology firms have become increasingly stringent. A few of the factors that require high performance on the dimensions of quality, cost, schedule, and service are global competition, shorter new product development cycles, shorter product life cycles, and the high cost of, but unquestionable need for, the organization to keep up with the rapid development of product, process, and administrative technology. Organizations must innovate, adapt to change, be efficient, and be responsive. To fail in any of these dimensions results in vulnerability.

Most high technology firms identify their cadre of highly trained and educated employees as their most important resource. These employees are expensive to attract, require ongoing maintenance of up-to-date skills and knowledge, and through experience develop local knowledge and networks of contacts useful to task accomplishment. Effective management of the performance of employees is key to the success of the firm. It can potentially constitute a competitive advantage as firms that manage their people well are better using this important resource, and will find it easier to attract and retain the level of talent required in a difficult technical and competitive environment.

The nature of high technology firms poses special challenges that make performance management difficult. The requirements of high technology work and of high technology employees both work against classical bureaucratic notions of control and require performance management practices that acknowledge uncertainty, rapid change, innovation, and professional standards and expertise. To some extent, the organizational requirements of the rapid-paced, highly interdependent technology and the professional standards and norms of professional and technical employees can work against each other.

This chapter reports the findings from the studies of performance management in twelve operating divisions of three large, mature high technology organizations. All have extensive research and development components, and scientists, engineers, and technicians are the major employee groups. Managers tend to come from the technical ranks. Organization A operates primarily in the defense sector. It produces sophisticated avionics systems. Organization B operates in both the commercial and the defense sector, producing state-of-the-art systems in the aerospace industry. Organization C is an oil and chemical company that uses rapidly developing, state-of-the-art technology in all phases of its enterprise, from exploration to production. Each of these organizations has extensive information systems groups as staff support which develop advanced administrative, design, and process systems.

In each of these corporations we conducted one-hour interviews with more than fifty employees who represented a diagonal cross section of the salaried workforce, and administered surveys to at least 10 percent of the salaried work force, randomly selected. The studies were sequential; information derived from earlier studies was used to frame new questions and to help in deciding what needed to be replicated. More detailed results from each of the studies exist elsewhere (Mohrman, Mohrman, & Worley, 1987, 1988; Mohrman and Mohrman, 1988). This chapter draws on both the qualitative and quantitative results, and integrates what we have learned so far. It then develops a framework for performance management in high technology settings, presents some prescriptions, and addresses important unresolved questions.

HIGH TECHNOLOGY

Since the kind of performance required depends partly on the technology being used, performance management techniques have to fit with the technology of the organization. In this vein high technology settings have certain characteristics that set constraints and requirements about how performance is managed. We must understand high technology before we can understand its performance management implications.

Technology is "any tool or technique, any physical equipment or method of doing or making, by which human capability is extended" (Schon, 1967). At the core of technology is the knowledge on which it is based (Tornatzky et al., 1983). Technology consists of this knowledge base, its technical content, and the tools, artifacts, and practices that embody this knowledge (Tornatzky et al., 1983; Pelz and Munson, 1980).

Although there are many definitions of "high" technology, most of them deal with correlate aspects such as the high number of technical professionals, heavy use of research and development, and the rate of change in the product offerings of the industry, rather than with characteristics of technology itself. If the essence of technology is knowledge, then high technology refers to knowledge with certain characteristics. We posit that high technology is at the high end of a number of interrelated dimensions of knowledge: it is complex rather than simple, new as opposed to established, at the boundaries of development and incomplete rather than complete, rap-

Table 11.1   High Technology and Its Implications

Dimensions of Technical Knowledge			
"High"		"Low"	Implications for People
Complex	vs.	Simple	Hard to learn
New	vs.	Established	Not generally understood
On edge of development	vs.	Complete	Requiring invention
Rapidly progressing	vs.	Static or slowly developing	Requiring quick response to keep up
Systemic	vs.	Isolated	Interdependence among people, individual knowledge bases incomplete for tasks, individual contribution has systemic effects
Contingent	vs.	Linear	Unpredictable development, uncertainty

idly progressing not static or slowly developing, systemic not isolated, and contingent rather than linear (see Table 11.1). Its position on each of these knowledge dimensions has implications for people.

High technology knowledge is complex. The source of this complexity lies in many of the other dimensions of knowledge; its result is that it takes a long time to acquire the knowledge, and mastery requires a fairly high level of ability and, frequently, advanced degrees. Even those who perform the lower-level tasks in high technology organizations find that training time is considerably higher than in other organizations (Von Glinow and Mohrman, in press). It is this attribute of high technology that prompts many to equate it with a high incidence of professionals (Von Glinow, 1988).

High technology is new. It is based on the most recent developments in scientific knowledge. As a result there has not been much time for the technology to achieve general understanding. There is a tendency for only a few "gurus" to have mastered it, and they are extremely valuable and scarce resources. At times whole product lines, companies, and industries have been built around individuals.

High technology knowledge is right on the edge of ongoing development; consequently, it is incomplete. There are still gaps to fill to use the technology and the knowledge behind it to their fullest extent. Therefore, people who use the technology need to constantly learn from their experiences, invent, and innovate. This means not only that high technology ventures tend to have large research and development components, but also that all employees to some extent will confront situations that demand innovative responses because the technology is not well understood.

Accelerating development is an ironically constant aspect of high technology, and the development feeds on itself. Rapid progress leaves more knowledge gaps. Profitable and competitive use of technologies depends on filling the gaps as quickly as possible, creating a base for further progress. People and organizations must respond quickly to these ongoing developments.

The knowledge behind high technology is systemic. It cannot be isolated into neat packages and disciplines; previously separate knowledge bases, for example, join forces to form the knowledge base of new technologies. This is happening in aerospace, where the new composite materials are literally revolutionizing aerospace engineering. Increasingly, high technology products and production processes are systems. They serve to link people and technological elements into mutually interdependent parts. The individual effects of a person's behavior are lost as they interact with the behaviors of others and aggregate to contribute to the performance of the system as a whole. These systems are in turn embedded in other systems. Interdependent systems are exemplified and exacerbated by networks of information technologies that permeate our modern organizations. As a result, in high technology settings, people are highly interdependent with one another, and the contributions of individual efforts to the effectiveness of the system as a whole are not always known.

Finally, high technology knowledge is contingent on which aspects of the technology have most recently been developed and which gaps in the developing knowledge domain people choose to fill next. The result is uncertainty. The development of technology content cannot be completely predicted, so the overriding need is to be able to respond to developments as they occur and to strategically choose points where subsequent development should be aimed. Much of the high technology of the defense industry, for instance, is fueled by strategic developments and counter developments between the Eastern and Western blocks. Sophisticated radar capabilities on one side are countered by the development of jamming technology on the other, which leads to further radar development by the first, and so on. These developments happen quickly, during the life of a development project, and can result in frequent changes in design. These design changes are not isolated but typically have ramifications for design of the entire system. On the domestic front the jockeying for position among computer manufacturers creates a similar dynamic. This uncertain, unpredictable nature of the direction of the high technology exacerbates the implications of the other dimensions.

We have spelled out these aspects of high technology in some detail because of their significant implications for the way performance is managed in high technology firms. Our interviews confirmed that the technologies in all three firms had these characteristics. More than 80 percent of survey respondents indicated that they were highly interdependent with the work of others. More than half reported that they frequently had to change their own work in response to changing requirements, information, and priorities from others. Almost 60 percent of the respondents could not immediately know the results of their work. Almost 60 percent reported that their job required them to use technical and scientific knowledge and keep it up to date. All of these factors correlated with one another; that is, if one was true, it was likely that all the other factors were true also. Sixty-five to seventy percent said that they frequently had to innovate and try out new approaches just to get their jobs done. This factor correlated most highly and consistently with all the other high technology factors and therefore appears to be a basic underlying component of high technology settings.

One particularly interesting pattern was that each of these attributes, though high for all, was even higher for managers than it was for nonmanagers. In these firms, a lot of the uncertainty reduction was being performed by management. Any prescriptions we make for performance management in high technology settings apply as strongly to the management of managers as it does to the management of professionals.

HIGH TECHNOLOGY AND PERFORMANCE

Settings where there is a lag in performance feedback, where tasks are often changing and being changed, that require experimentation with untested ways of doing things, and where interdependencies require ongoing interaction with others to get the work done pose special challenges for performing effectively. Our findings corroborated this. They show plainly that these characteristics of high technology settings can easily work against performance. Survey respondents who reported that requirements and priorities keep being changed and that they do not readily know the results of their efforts reported lower effectiveness of all types of performance: individual, work-group, and project level, quality, schedule, and cost. Respondents who reported that they frequently have to try out new and innovative approaches to get the job done and that they work extensively with others with whom they are interdependent saw their own work and that of their work groups and projects as being of higher quality. Nevertheless, the need for both innovation and extensive interaction negatively affected schedule and budget. Innovating and coping with interdependence by person-to-person interaction are critical to the quality of the work that is done, but are time-consuming and costly.

In each of these organizations, the characteristics of the technology impose work requirements that appear to work against employees' sense of accomplishment and of being part of a high-performance group. This is an especially important performance management issue given the professional nature of the employees and the fact that professional pride of accomplishment is an important motivator for professionals.

HIGH TECHNOLOGY EMPLOYEES

High technology workers are "knowledge workers." Many are highly educated and trained in specialized fields of knowledge and belong to professional groups that have norms and standards and are defined not only by the content of their knowledge but by accepted practices and approaches to solving problems or conducting investigations (Von Glinow, 1988; Resnick-West and Von Glinow, this volume). They arrive in the firm already "socialized" with a strong internalized set of expectations and values. They have internalized standards, expect to be able to exert professional autonomy within the narrow bounds of their expertise, and experience collegial influence and control as more legitimate than hierarchical control.

From the organization's viewpoint, a performance management problem arises because of natural clashes between the orientations of professional scientists and engineers and the business needs of the firm (Resnick-West and Von Glinow, this volume). The knowledge workers' concern for creative freedom, furtherance of the technology, and their own position in a professional community can conflict with the business concern for targeted investment in strategic areas, planning and control, and cost and budget. Interest in elegant solutions and autonomy clash with the business needs for a planned way to manage complex projects with many interrelated parts in a cost-effective manner that enhances competitiveness, and in a timely manner that brings the product to market before that of the competition.

Closely related to the adherence to professional standards and norms of autonomy is the individualistic orientation of many technical employees, particularly engineers (Adler, this volume). Organizational accomplishments are believed to be the sum of individual accomplishments, and individual creativity is valued more than working with and through other people. This analytic, individualistic notion of work conflicts with the required behaviors to work out the complex interdependencies of high technology work.

Because of these potential clashes between the professional and individualistic orientation of many high technology workers and the business and technological demands, the challenge of performance management is significant. It is not sufficient to simply hire employees with the requisite professional background and set them loose to use their talents, although this is frequently done. In fact, our interviews suggested that such an approach was quite common in these organizations, where little attention was paid to clearly defining needed performance, or to providing feedback and development plans. It is not uncommon to find managers who believe it unnecessary to help employees define their roles; in fact, they look upon such a need as a sign of lack of capability in the employee. Many scientists and engineers, in particular, reported that they knew what they were supposed to do and how they were to go about it by virtue of experience, modeling of others, and using their training and education. As a result, they were frequently unsure of how their activities fit into a larger set of business priorities.

The next section provides a framework for understanding performance management that will then be used in examining what approaches were effective and ineffective in our high technology companies.

PERFORMANCE MANAGEMENT

Performance management encompasses the many things done in organizations to manage and shape the performance of employees. It attempts to align effort and performance with standards and types of performance needed for organizational success.

The value expectancy model (Campbell, Dunnette, Lawler, and Weick, 1970) provides a framework for understanding performance management. It posits that employees will be motivated to expend effort to accomplish performances that they believe will lead to the outcomes they value. Their effort will result in the targeted performances if the goals are realistic, and if they fully understand what is expected of them and have the necessary skills to do them. Ongoing motivation depends on the extent to which attaining the targeted performances indeed results in valued outcomes. Thus, performance management includes at least in part the processes and practices that clarify expectations, ensure that individuals have the adequate skills and information to accomplish them, and link valued outcomes to successful performance.

A large portion of performance management occurs through ongoing processes in the organization, such as organizational communication processes of various kinds, and daily interaction within work groups and between supervisors and employees. Formal systems are also put in place to help manage performance. These include job definition and goal-setting to define the needed performances, performance appraisal and various review and feedback systems, training and development to keep skills and abilities commensurate with needed performances, and reward and recognition systems to provide valued outcomes. Traditionally these practices have been looked at as independent systems; increasingly it is coming to be understood that they all fit together into a performance management system and must reinforce each other and support an overall approach to managing human performance (Mohrman, Resnick-West, and Lawler, 1989).

Complicating the picture is the fact that these formal systems, particularly in a mature firm, have been developed over a number of years and exist for a number of purposes in addition to performance management. For instance, attraction and retention of scarce and valued employees and avoidance of legal charges of inequitable treatment are other important purposes of job evaluation, performance appraisal, and various pay programs. Consequently, in many firms practices have evolved that are not strongly linked to performance.

Traditional performance management practices are based largely on the legacy of the concepts of bureaucratic organization and scientific management. Work is divided into tasks that were grouped into jobs. These jobs are described and evaluated, forming the basis for selection, appraisal, training, and compensation (Mahoney and Deckop, 1986). Supervision exists to control organizational performance and to integrate the contributions of various jobs.

Related to this tradition, three fundamental assumptions have been the underpinnings of most approaches to performance management. First, it is assumed that managers are the appropriate and best managers of performance. Second, jobs are assumed to be relatively constant and definable. Third, it is assumed that the managing of performance means managing the performance of individuals. Each of these assumptions is challenged in the high technology setting, as we found in the open-ended interviews that were conducted in our three organizations. Next, we discuss each of these assumptions in more detail.

Hierarchical performance management. The belief that managers are the appropriate managers of performance stems directly from our beliefs about the role of hierarchy and leads to the corollary that supervisors should manage subordinates' performance. The high interdependence among employees in high technology firms creates conditions in which this assumption must be questioned. The interdependencies are generally lateral in nature, between employees and internal customers or between employees and peers who are working on other components of the technological system. Managers frequently get involved in working out such interdependencies, especially within a traditional bureaucratic framework. However, interdependencies are also worked out between peers, as was illustrated by the comments of a software engineer, who echoed a sentiment we heard many times:

> My boss insists on resolving all of the issues we have with all other groups. We generally have to pick up the pieces anyway—after a lot of time has been wasted waiting for a decision. He doesn't have any idea how we really resolve things since he's always in meetings. We try not to involve him if we can possibly keep him ignorant of what's going on.

This raises an interesting performance management challenge: If interdependencies are being worked out directly between employees, many aspects of an employee's performance are likely to be invisible to the supervisor.

In addition, many technical employees perform work that is not easily measurable and for which the behaviors are not readily observable. Often the supervisor does not have the kind or currency of technical knowledge of employees. Consequently, it is difficult for the supervisor to adequately evaluate the work of subordinates. Alternatively, many supervisors had been promoted into management ranks but remain, in many senses, technical contributors themselves. They spend long hours in meetings addressing technical issues, and do not spend enough time with their employees to have a good sense of each person's contribution or to adequately manage performance.

There are other indications that making performance management practices the responsibility of supervisors is a failing strategy. On the surveys, fewer than half of employees reported receiving direction or goals from their supervisor. Scientists and engineers, in particular, frequently reported that they had little contact with their supervisors and that, indeed, the supervisor knew little of what they did unless complaints were received. When asked who determines what work they do, employees in organization C ranked themselves and their internal customers over their supervisors.

Performance appraisal systems were most often judged by the interviewees to be good systems on paper but not to work because supervisors did not put in the requisite effort and time, or in some cases did not have the necessary skills. A common complaint was that the supervisor, while expected to carry out appraisals, had little first-hand knowledge of appraisee performance.

Nevertheless, it should be pointed out that most people interviewed believed that performance management is the responsibility of the supervisor and that more time and energy should be put into the process. Subordinates wanted their supervisor to spend more time helping them make developmental plans for their careers, and in general wanted the supervisor to keep them informed of "where they stood." They relied on the supervisor as their contact with outcomes—pay, job assignments, and promotional opportunities.

Constant and definable jobs. Traditional performance management mechanisms are based on the assumption that jobs and the organizational situation are relatively constant and stable, allowing for formalization of practices such as job definitions, job evaluations, written goals and standards, and other relatively permanent mechanisms of performance management. The characteristics of high technology settings dilute the effectiveness of these static mechanisms that violate the systemic nature of the work. Constant change coupled with the need to innovate and high interdependence mean that specifications and goals are quickly eroded. Static job evaluation systems as the basis for compensation practices can work against the need for employees to continually update skills, perform new tasks, and be flexible in their contributions (Lawler, 1986). In rapidly changing conditions, job definitions and goals have to be frequently updated. Organization A, for example, was spending thousands of hours updating job descriptions that the managers said would be obsolete within two years.

In organization C, where appraisals and merit pay were based on a strong management by objectives (MBO) system, great dissatisfaction was expressed with the fact that the system was unable to keep up with the frequent need to change goals and objectives. To do so would have involved many interim checks and updates of goals. Many felt the goal-setting process was unrealistic for the nature of their jobs, which involved solving unforeseen problems of unknown magnitude and dealing with unknowable change orders that arose along the way. Employees in all three organizations reported spending time on tasks that were of lower priorities than emerging workflow needs because they were locked into objectives. More insidiously, they often reported working on low-priority issues because their managers' yearly objectives and bonuses were at stake.

A strong lament from managers was the lack of flexibility in all the performance management systems. Within the context of rapid changes in strategy, technical specifications, and project requirements, employees were continually being thrown into periods of seven-day work weeks and extremely long hours just to get the product to market on time. Managers were especially unhappy with reward systems that were "controlled by an inflexible set of rules," and "unable to address stellar performance or extraordinary effort in a timely way." Even special awards programs were often tied to levels of bureaucratic approval and obsolete provisions that required the special performance to be outside of the employee's job description. "What about my team that spent seven-day weeks through the Christmas holidays so that we could get a proposal in on time?" In some operations teams were not eligible, or award limits were so small that to reward a team would seriously dilute the impact.

Managing individuals. It is often assumed that managing the performance of people means managing the performance of individuals. For instance, appraisal systems are aimed at individuals, and rewards are most frequently based on the individual's job, performance, skills, and potential. Nevertheless, because of the systemic nature of the work and the high interdependence in high technology firms, managing performance means managing the whole, which includes the interdependencies as well as the parts. This means treating the team, or group, as a unit of analysis for performance management purposes.

A theme that we heard, particularly from managers who were trying to establish and manage teams, was that the reward system not only did not provide for team rewards, but actually worked against teamwork. The pay for performance systems in these companies were based on a fixed pool of money and thus rewarded some individuals at the expense of others. At its very core, this system is competitive and could easily divide people who were interdependent. This was poignantly pointed out by one scientist who said that peer input to appraisals would be disastrous because appraisals determine pay and he and his peers were compared with one another for pay determination. "We're all out to get each other; they've turned us into enemies."

Perhaps partly to offset this dysfunctional consequence of merit pay, supervisors in practice differentiated very little between employees in either the raise or the performance appraisal unless they were required to force a distribution. A message we heard from some supervisors was that "the work of the group requires a true team effort. The foundation for cooperation would be destroyed if I began differentiating between people to any great degree." Where organizations required a forced distribution, many employees and supervisors took issue with the implicit assumption that every team or work group must include a normal distribution of weak and strong performers. They believed that a strong team could easily be composed entirely of excellent performers, and vice-versa.

All three companies had formal practices of ranking all employees, for either pay or retention purposes. Many managers and employees were conceptually comfortable with this, but concerned about it operationally. True to the quantitative orientation of this population, the major concern was to develop better ways to measure and compare employees. Those who opposed the practice did it on the basis of the inability of managers to accurately make such fine distinctions between employees and the lack of viable standards for comparison. In organization A, which was the only company in which we asked about this practice on the survey, only 20 percent of managers felt the ranking process worked well, and half believed it resulted in serious equity problems.

Although all three organizations were trying out a variety of new approaches to establishing teamwork, none had formal practices of team goal-setting or performance planning. All had systems of program or project reviews that were held with unequal regularity and vigor in different projects. In most cases, these reviews were a formal upward reporting of progress against plan with little or no actual team goal-setting, planning of performance strategies, or providing of feedback to one another. Individual contributors and even first-line supervisors were often not included in the reviews.

Nonetheless, informal group-level practices had evolved. In each company respondents reported that group meetings to discuss group performance happened at least as often, and sometimes twice as often (averaging from 2.5 to 5.5 times a year), as individual performance discussions with supervisors. For example, an exploration group of the oil company reported regular morning meetings ("without supervisors") to determine who would do what.

Some individual contributors were unhappy with the relative lack of attention to building the team: "I have no idea how my work fits in with the bigger picture"; "We're missing out on an opportunity to learn from one another and to coordinate better"; "I don't even know what the guy in the cubicle next to mine is doing, even though we're working on the same program. Perhaps if we understood each other's tasks we could avoid reinventing the wheel"; "My boss doesn't like to bring our team together. She's afraid we might challenge her decisions about how the work is divided up"; "We've got about three different groups working on reliability issues for each project, but we never bring them together. There's a duplication of effort and endless arguments over which group is using the right approach."

Indeed, all three companies had various kinds of efforts to establish increased teamwork, including quality circles, quality action teams, interfunctional business development teams, and design-to-production teams. Managers who were champions of these efforts were the most adamant in their message that individually oriented performance management systems were major blocks to teamwork in the organization.

COMPARING THE EFFECTS OF PERFORMANCE MANAGEMENT PRACTICES

The questionnaire portions of the studies were designed to test the predictions about what constitutes effective performance management in high technology firms that emerged from the interviews and that sprang from the

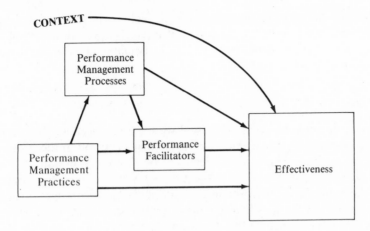

Figure 11.1 Model of Performance Management Effects

assumptions that we had about the nature of performance in high technology firms. The model in Figure 11.1 shows the various aspects of performance management that we measured and how we expected them to relate to one another and to effectiveness.

Performance management practices include reward and appraisal practices that are established to ensure that performance is reviewed and leads to valued outcomes. *Processes* are the interpersonal processes that manage performance on a day-to-day basis. *Performance facilitators* are conditions that exist in the job, the work group, or the person that enable people to know what is expected of them in their job and to do it.

According to the model, performance management practices can influence effectiveness directly, such as merit pay might do by motivating people. Practices can also encourage processes or facilitators. For instance, performance appraisal is often expected to encourage feedback or to result in the establishment of goals that may, in turn, promote effectiveness. Interpersonal processes such as supervisor structuring of work may directly contribute to effectiveness or operate by setting up facilitators such as performance standards, which then contribute to effectiveness.

Our general approach in analyzing the relationships among these variables has been to use multiple regressions. First, we regress each of the processes on the practices. This gives us a picture of how the practices contribute to the processes. Second, we regress each facilitator on both the practices and processes, giving a pattern of how each contributes to the establishment of the facilitators. Finally, we regress each of the measures of effectiveness on the practices, processes, and facilitators. This gives us the pattern of how each of the practices, processes, and facilitators has contributed to effectiveness directly. This approach to analyzing the data allows us to discover paths that begin with practices and end with effectiveness, and enables us to see both direct and indirect relationships. In this chapter, we report only the paths that were consistently found in the three organizations and discuss the variables in these paths as well as those that failed to lead directly or indirectly to the measures of effectiveness. More complete reporting of particular regression analyses is available elsewhere (Mohrman, Mohrman, & Worley, 1988).

Practices

The five practices that were measured were chosen because they were the major performance management activities that occurred in these organizations. Three were appraisal practices and two were rewards practices. *Supervisor–individual appraisal* is the frequency with which the supervisor gives the subordinate performance feedback. *Formal work group appraisal* refers to the degree to which the work group or project team is formally assessed by the organization. *Work group self-appraisal* is the extent to which work groups and project teams discuss the group's performance among themselves. *Pay for individual performance* measured the degree to which respondents perceived the pay for performance system to be working. Similarly, each company had instituted a special awards program for various kinds of one-shot awards to both individuals and groups. These programs were the only avenue available in these companies to reward teams with cash bonuses. *Special awards* reflects how well employees thought these programs were working.

Two of these practices, supervisor–individual appraisal and formal work group appraisal, do not consistently or significantly appear in the paths to any form of organizational effectiveness! These formal, hierarchical processes have very little performance impact in these companies.

Processes

Three supervisory and three work group processes measured the extent to which each (1) gave feedback to group members, (2) structured tasks and set goals, and (3) stressed and exhibited a high performance orientation (performance norms).

None of the supervisory processes is consistently and significantly related directly or indirectly to any of the organizational effectiveness outcomes that were measured, supporting the prediction that hierarchical processes are not highly effectual in high technology settings!

Facilitators

We measured five facilitators. *Skill level* measured the degree to which the employee felt adequately trained and sufficiently skilled for the job. *Clear job duties* refers to the degree to which employees report that they have clearly specified jobs and clearly prioritized job responsibilities. *Performance standards* refers to the extent to which employees have jobs for which goals and performance standards can be and are defined. *Understanding role in group* refers to how well employees know how their work fits into that of the work group. *Teamwork* is the active assistance that work group members give to one another.

Clear job duties and performance standards do not appear in any of the paths to organizational effectiveness. These relatively static (and common) approaches to performance management do not consistently contribute to performance outcomes in our high technology settings!

Effectiveness

By effectiveness we mean the degree to which the needs of various organizational stakeholders are met. We obtained survey measures of six aspects of performance: individual performance; work group effectiveness; project effectiveness; on schedule performance; on-cost performance, and human affective outcomes (satisfaction, pay equity, and trust). Next, we discuss the paths by which the performance is not presented because in each company less than 10 percent of the variance was explained by the performance management variables, and no clear paths emerged.

Individual performance. Employees rated their own performance on several dimensions and reported their perceptions of their supervisor's ratings of their performance on the same dimensions. Previous research had indicated that subordinates usually have an accurate sense of their supervisors' ratings (Lawler, Mohrman, & Resnick, 1984). Figure 11.2 illustrates the consistent paths through which the performance management variables were related to individual performance.

Performance is very strongly facilitated by the employee's skill level and by employee understanding of his or her role in the group. These facilitators strongly result from work group structuring and goal-setting and by work group feedback. Thus, both skill and understanding of how one's work fits into the larger context are the result of group processes to a significant extent.

Work group performance norms have a direct path to individual performance. Thus, individual performance is both directly and indirectly related to all three group-oriented processes. They in turn are strongly related to the practice of group self-assessment.

The two reward practices have an interesting relationship to individual performance. Pay-for-performance is surprisingly related to work group feedback, indicating that if people feel their pay depends on their performance they are more likely to give feedback to one another about what they need, evidently to aid their own performance. The relationship of pay for performance to work group feedback is minor compared to its main process effects, which are the bolstering of the three supervisory processes. These relationships do not appear in the figures, however, because the supervisor processes of feedback, structuring, and stressing productivity have no consistent link to the outcomes we measured.

Special awards has a direct and *negative* path to individual performance,

Practices   Processes   Facilitators   Effect

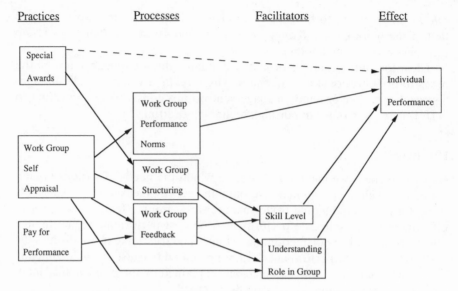

Figure 11.2   Paths Leading to Individual Performance

but a positive indirect path through work group structuring and goal-setting. Evidently, the fact that special awards were often used to reward groups has provided some support to encourage work groups to set goals.

Group Performance. Work group effectiveness and project effectiveness measure the quantity and quality of work group and project performance. The paths leading to these two effectiveness measures are the same, and are indicated in Figure 11.3. Group performance is strongly related, either directly or indirectly, to every group level practice, process, and facilitator except formal work group appraisal. In addition, group performance can be directly helped by the skill levels of its members, which are also affected by work group processes and by teamwork. Again, pay for performance and special awards operate only through the work group processes.

On Schedule. This aspect of group performance was singled out because of its central importance in the fast-paced world of high technology. On schedule is directly impacted (Figure 11.4) by the skill levels of employees, and by work group processes of structuring and goal-setting and stressing of high performance. Again, the practices of work group self-appraisal, special awards, and pay for performance operate through the work group processes.

Affect is the dimension of effectiveness that reflects the degree to which the individual's needs are being met by the organization. We measured satisfaction, pay equity, and trust. These affective reactions (Figure 11.5) are directly and positively impacted by teamwork and by pay for performance. This is interesting because it is the first time that pay for performance has had a direct link to any outcome. Individuals have a favorable reaction to this practice when they think it is working. The work group processes of stressing performance and structuring and setting goals are indirectly linked

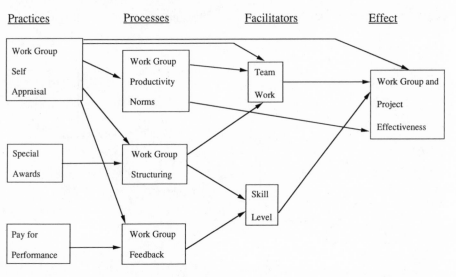

Figure 11.3 Performance Management Paths Leading to Work Group Performance

to affective outcomes through their relationship to teamwork. And of course, work group self-appraisal and special awards relate to these work group processes.

It is important to note that individuals respond favorably to teamwork and to pay for individual performance. Thus, the dual pressures on high technology are captured: the orientation of employees to individual creativity and autonomy, and the fact that they are engaged in a highly interdependent work.

Figure 11.4 Performance Management Paths Leading to Meeting Schedules

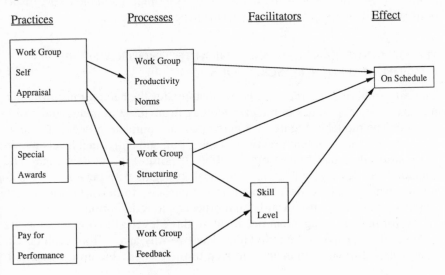

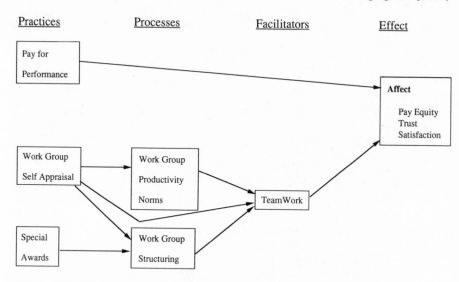

Figure 11.5   Performance Management Paths Leading to Affective Outcomes

In summary, these performance management paths to effectiveness illustrate the erosion of the three assumptions underlying traditional performance management practices. First, none of the effective practices relied on the supervisor or, to put it another way, none of the practices that rely on the supervisor were effective. Second, the centrality of the work group is abundantly clear. Even a traditionally individual practice like pay for performance, though it is important to the affective responses of employees, contributes to performance only by supporting the work group. Third, the reality of change has resulted in the erosion of such traditional mainstays of performance management as job specifications and performance standards. Neither of these consistently showed any impact on effectiveness. In short, it does indeed appear that the nature of work in high technology organizations demands new approaches to performance management.

PERFORMANCE MANAGEMENT IN HIGH TECHNOLOGY FIRMS: A MODEL AND SOME PRESCRIPTIONS

The pattern of findings reported here substantiates the need for performance management approaches in high technology firms to be dynamic and multi-faceted. The model in Figure 11.6 illustrates the complete process. It shows performance management practices at the group and individual levels within the context provided by the organization, its strategy, and its design. The sequence in Figure 11.6 is quite traditional. It begins with performance definition, which leads to development of the capacity to perform, the review of performance, and its rewards, and proceeds to redefinition.

Performance management occurs at all three levels: the organization, its teams and groups, and the individual. The two-way arrow from each organizational performance management step to the comparable group step indi-

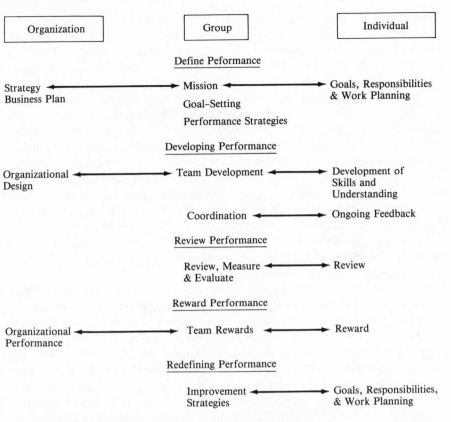

| Organization | Group | Individual |

Define Peformance

Strategy ◄──────────► Mission ◄──────────► Goals, Responsibilities
Business Plan   Goal-Setting   & Work Planning
                        Performance Strategies

Developing Performance

Organizational ◄──────────► Team Development ◄──────────► Development of
Design   Skills and
                                       Understanding

                         Coordination ◄──────────► Ongoing Feedback

Review Performance

                         Review, Measure ◄──────────► Review
                         & Evaluate

Reward Performance

Organizational ◄──────────► Team Rewards ◄──────────► Reward
Performance

Redefining Performance

                         Improvement ◄──────────► Goals, Responsibilities,
                         Strategies   & Work Planning

Figure 11.6 Team and Individual Performance Management

cates that group and individual performance management must consciously and openly be linked to organizational performance needs, and vice-versa. Processes and practices should be designed to raise the level of awareness of teams and individuals of how they fit into this overall picture, and to involve them as much as possible in organizational goals and effectiveness.

The two-way arrow between group and individual performance management steps indicates the ongoing reciprocal relationship between the performance cycles at these two levels of analysis. Individual performance can be defined and interpreted only within the context of what the team is trying to accomplish and the performance strategies it uses. Individual performances that are excellent according to static or external standards but do not add up to a team accomplishing its mission are not organizationally excellent performances.

Although this model may appear quite traditional, some prescriptions for how it must be done in high technology settings are quite different from traditional approaches:

   1. *The performance management cycle should be flexible and frequent.* Most organizations operate with a yearly operational planning cycle and quarterly updates. Their individual performance management cycle gener-

ally follows the yearly business cycle. In a high technology firm these sequences cannot easily be shoehorned into a yearly cycle. The competitive arena changes more frequently than that, technology advances steadily, at irregular rates and in unpredictable directions, and customer specifications and requirements are articulated and changed frequently.

Because of the rapid rate of these changes, the quarterly planning cycle drives many high technology firms. Group and individual performance management must occur many times a year as well. Furthermore, the cycle for these events will most likely not be regular or predictable. Ongoing monitoring of performance at all three levels should be able to trigger review of performance and redefinition of goals, performance strategies, and work plans at any time. Outstanding accomplishments that need reinforcement can occur at any time, which argues against relying on the yearly merit increase or bonus as the sole reward system. On the other hand, projects can have natural life spans longer than one year. The ultimate success of endeavors may not be known for quite some time. Performance management needs to reflect this reality also.

2. *Lateral and self-management are more important than hierarchical mechanisms.* Group self-management includes processes by which the group can set its own goals, determine its own strategies, ensure that individuals within it have the needed skills and are being effectively used and interdependencies are being worked out. Group self-management does not rule out that the supervisor has a legitimate role in the group, as was indicated by our survey data showing that team self-appraisal enhances both supervisory and work group feedback, goal-setting, structuring, and performance norms (Mohrman, Mohrman, & Worley, 1988). The message for the supervisor is that team mechanisms are a more effective route to influence than one-on-one relationships with subordinates.

Most professional employees expect individual self-management of technical task performance based on standards and accepted practices that were learned in school. It is essential, however, that processes be in place to link individual task performance directly to needed team objectives or goals. This requires that much attention be given to the team as a performing unit; to team development of its ongoing processes of goal-setting, reviewing, and improving itself; and to rewards and recognition of team accomplishments. It also requires team input into the management of individuals: their tasks and goals, determining how individuals fit together into the team, their skill improvement, and the review and reward of their performance.

3. *An important role of supervision is to link performing units to the greater organizational performance requirements and to create a climate for effective self-management.* It is essential that teams and individuals have full cognizance of organizational goals and performance, and of how they fit into this larger picture. Very clear performance values (Shuster, 1984) are required to align personal and team effort with organizational performance needs. Creating an overall climate that stresses performance and is information-rich is a key managerial task in the high technology firm.

Supervisors must create conditions for effective team and individual self-management by serving as communication links to the rest of the organization, ensuring that the teams have the resources they need, and building the team's capacity for self-management.

Supervisors are also the link between the individual and the organization in such issues as career and placement. Our interview data suggest that it would be a serious mistake to overlook the importance that individuals attach to learning "where they stand," and to their supervisor's responsibility to attend to their development and career issues. They also suggest, however, that it is important to develop mechanisms for co-worker and customer input into the evaluation of individual performances that lead to individual reviews, rewards, and career actions.

4. *Team management occurs in a series of embedded and interlinked processes.* The preceding prescription makes it sound as if organizations are a sum of a number of self-contained groups or teams. In fact, teams are embedded within bigger teams, and interdependent with other teams. Performance management must take place at multiple levels and in many overlapping teams. Intergroup performance management between two interdependent teams may have to establish the mission of each, within which team self-management may then occur. Individuals may be part of the performance management processes of several teams, and may find their roles being determined by several groups of people. Consequently, part of the role individuals must play is to manage how they personally are used in multiple groups.

Traditionally, this complexity has been handled by managers, who specify who does what and how teams relate to one another. In high technology organizations, ongoing lateral processes are very common, because the rate of change and amount of uncertainty makes hierarchical decision making too slow a response mechanism. Since it is impossible to prestructure all the needed interfaces and coordination functions, temporary task groupings will continually spring up. Team self-appraisal and improvement mechanisms must become part of the culture and be adapted to many forms of self-standing, overlapping, permanent, and temporary teams.

CONCLUSION: SOME UNRESOLVED ISSUES

Based on an analysis of high technology work and studies of performance management in three high technology firms, we have called for significant reframing of traditional performance management theory and practice. New approaches involve managing interdependencies as well as individual performances; consequently performance management practices must meet the performance requirements of both teams and individuals. They must be flexible enough to adjust continually to changing requirements. Furthermore, they must bridge the gap between the performance orientation of professional high technology scientists and engineers that stresses autonomy, creativity, and furtherance of knowledge and that of business managers who must ensure financial and market viability and live by plans and controls. Some interesting questions that are raised deserve much more investigation.

First, although these results indicate the current supervisory role has little relationship to effective performance, they do not describe a new role. Organizations have some hard decisions to make in this regard. Working through teams is certainly as time-consuming and perhaps more difficult than working with individual subordinates. Furthermore, results clearly indicate that subordinates expect individual attention to their career and development needs, indicating that a team supervisory role does not alleviate the need for individual attention as well. Currently, technical, administrative, and coordinative roles prevent many managers from doing a good job at either the team or the individual level of performance management.

Second, the notion of the team as the performing unit conflicts with cultural, professional, and hierarchical tendencies to value individual creativity and initiative and to want to find an individual to hold accountable. Our data suggest that individual affective responses depend on both teamwork and acknowledgment of personal contribution and career needs. What is less clear is whether performance management practices, rewards and appraisals in particular, can be designed at both team and individual levels that do not subtly undermine one another. Much more work is needed to define compatible approaches at these two levels.

Third, there is the question of to what extent performance management practices and processes can be or should be formalized in high technology settings. In our studies, formal group appraisal, for example, had no relationship to effectiveness, although self-appraisal by teams was a key driver of the performance processes that led to effectiveness. The challenge will be to encourage dynamic lateral processes but not to formalize them to the extent that they are no longer responsive to the changing context and rapid innovation that must occur.

In sum, high technology drives its own special brand of performance management. As high tech firms grow and mature, they must evolve practices and processes that fit with their own nature.

12

Beyond the Clash: Managing High Technology Professionals

SUSAN RESNICK-WEST AND
MARY ANN VON GLINOW

On January 28, 1986, millions watched as the spaceship Challenger blew up only seconds after takeoff. Some say the incident was avoidable. Hours before the tragedy, Thiokol project engineers pleaded with authorities to delay the launch. They feared the inevitable, that the cold temperatures would cause the O-rings and joints to malfunction. Much to the nation's regret, the engineers were overruled by their management.

The President's Commission investigating the causes of the incident concluded that "The Thiokol Management reversed its position and recommended the launch of 51-L, at the urging of Marshall (an intermediary vendor) and contrary to the views of its engineers in order to accommodate a major customer" (Presidential Commission, 1986, p. 82).

Individuals who work in high tech environments were not at all surprised by this incident. To some degree it happens every day. In the final analysis decisions are routinely made by managers concerned with profit and loss statements, not engineers concerned with product integrity. The trade-off between the firm's need for financial profitability and product quality is at the core of most high tech firms today (Kleingartner and Anderson, 1987). In most cases the primary emphasis on financial soundness, fortunately, does not result in lost lives. The tension between these two systems—one motivated by profit and the other by expertise—makes the management of high tech firms a crucial balancing act. This chapter examines those critical tensions and offers recommendations for the management of the high tech firm.

WHO ARE THESE HIGH TECH WORKERS?

High tech professional workers are, first and foremost, knowledge workers—highly educated, autonomy-seeking, and career-oriented (Drucker, 1988; Von Glinow, 1988). They engage in knowledge exchange as the currency of trade and pursue intellectual and technical challenges. Typically they strive for technical breakthroughs. Their allegiances are suspect, but generally they join a firm because of the challenge of the work, and the management practices (Raelin, 1985; Bailyn, 1985). They expect to be rewarded accordingly. They also demand autonomy, abide by a set of ethics, expect to live up to professional standards set by collegial, or occupational groups, and tend to have more sunk cost in their skills, abilities, and education than they do in the employment contract with their organization. They prefer to identify with other high tech and professional workers who are engaged in similarly important, challenging tasks. In short, high tech professionals are a new breed of worker with strong ties to their technical specialty through their profession.

The difference between high tech professionals and their organizational counterparts is significant. For many years sociologists and organizational scientists have studied the differences between professional and nonprofessional employees (Hughes, 1967). It is generally concluded that the two groups—professional workers and organizational workers—tend to be significantly different from one another. Their motivations for working are different, their values tend to be different, and their work-related behaviors reflect these differences. Over the years and through considerable empirical study, it is now fairly well established that professional and nonprofessional workers have vastly different "worldviews" about work (Von Glinow, 1988; Bailyn, 1985; and Benveniste, 1987). When we discuss high tech professionals, we refer to the professionalized segment of the work force engaged in high technology industries, such as electronics computing equipment, chemicals, drugs, semiconductors and related services, electronic components, aircraft and parts, communications robotics, and computer-based instruction (Belous, 1987). In general, a high technology industry is one which has a higher proportion of engineers and scientists than other industries, has a higher percentage of expenditures on R & D, has technology-oriented goods and services, and has a proportion of technology-oriented workers equal to 150 percent of the rate for all U.S. industries (Von Glinow, 1988). Thus, we refer to high tech workers as professionals such as engineers and scientists engaged in knowledge exchange. Typically, they work within high tech industries; however, many industries other than those just mentioned may employ high tech workers.

Recently, we investigated some of these differences in a large Fortune 100 electronics firm. Among the factors probed was pride in work and organizational satisfaction. The data from a sample of managers and engineers revealed that technical and professional employees were more likely to take pride in the quality of the technology than were their management counterparts, who focused on the health of the business. When both groups were asked for sources of satisfaction, professional and technical workers mentioned challenging work, autonomy, and variety in their work while their management counterparts were more likely to mention opportunities for promotion (Resnick, 1985). Although the sample for this particular study was relatively small, these results have been consistently supported in studies of high tech employees in contrast to organizational employees (Miller, 1986; Von Glinow, 1988; Raelin, 1985).

The nature and cycle of their work differ as well. High tech employees frequently work within the realm of ideas, engaged in the innovation process. This creativity or innovation process is *at best* difficult to define, measure, evaluate, or control (Von Glinow, 1988). Ideas are also difficult to schedule and when the time between conceptualization and product development is continually decreasing, this becomes particularly important for the highly competitive high tech firm. Scientists and technologists are never quite sure when the breakthrough will come, how long it will take to debug a program or, in the case of the Challenger disaster, develop O-rings that do not freeze. In development work, creation often takes on a life of its own, and breakthroughs rarely come at a controlled or predictable pace. Equally problematic here is knowing at what point in the innovation process to cease improving and refining the core ideas. One manager criticized the engineers' overattention to this idea-generating process by claiming "these kind of people don't know when to quit. They don't seem to know when good enough means good enough. This can destroy product scheduling." Thus, the organizational goals of prediction and control are difficult organizational criteria for the high tech employee to attend to while engaging in the innovation process. They are, however, the focal point for organizational employees.

The work of the manager involves considerable predictability and tends to be well controlled. Business planning cycles are reasonably predictable. They are conducted at the same time each year; dividends are distributed and taxes are paid at the same time every year as well. Innovations, however, seem to come at unpredictable and uncontrollable intervals, and applying pressure only delays them. In essence, we believe that not only are there fundamental differences between high tech workers and their organizational counterparts, but these differences transcend the culture of the firm as well.

THE BUREAUCRATIC AND PROFESSIONAL CULTURE CLASH

Siehl, Ledford, Silverman, and Foy (1988) liken culture to a magnet that holds a company together through shared patterns of meaning. But magnets with similar poles can repel one another. It is our contention that if improperly managed, the culture of the high tech employee strongly resists the organizational culture of predictability and control, which we have labeled the "bureaucratic culture." The culture of the high tech employee is the culture of innovation. This culture lacks organizational boundaries. Whereas the bureaucratic culture appears dominated by profit-maximizing constraints, the culture of high tech is inspired by the constant search for new ideas and applications quite apart from financial criteria. The time span is necessarily long and forward-looking. At the core of the high tech culture is autonomy. High tech employees generally prefer not to be strategically or operationally involved with their bureaucratic counterparts (Bailyn, 1985).

The bureaucratic culture is one dominated by control systems that emphasize company loyalty, short-term profitability, hierarchical authority, and control. It measures growth in terms of production output, volume, and size. In view of these polar cultures, it is not surprising that inherent tensions arise within the high tech firm.

A key dilemma in managing high technology and professional employees is to skillfully manage the interface between the creative and innovative roles played by high tech workers and the roles played by managers in attempting to control the output and energies of these human resources (Von Glinow, 1988).

The clash of these cultures is perhaps no different from the myriad of other culture clashes that take place in American firms. What is more alarming about this clash is that it takes place at the core of the high tech business. It cannot be unobtrusively cast aside to fester or be relegated to a staff function. This issue is fundamental to the business and affects day-to-day operations of the firm. Because this is integral to the firm's overall health, the following section examines the core clashes in greater detail.

THE EXPERT CLASH

Expertise, or prolonged specialized training in a technical specialty, is a requisite characteristic of high tech professionals. However, the expertise that characterizes these high tech workers leads to overspecialization, communication problems, and unnecessary turf battles (Raelin, 1985). In discussing product delivery delays one engineer offered a typical comment elucidating the expert clash. "There were far fewer communication problems and misunderstandings with the engineers from the Japanese part of the company than with the managers in headquarters."

The communication barriers become particularly frustrating for the technical employee when they are compounded by issues of power and decision authority. This was the case of the Thiokol Engineer describing his futile attempt to delay the Challenger:

> So we spoke out and tried to explain once again the effects of low temperature. Arnie actually got up from his position which was down the table and put a quarter pad down in front of the table, in front of the management folks, and tried to sketch out once again what his concern was with the joint, and when he realized he wasn't getting through he just stopped. (Presidential Commission, 1986, p. 92)

The education and training of technical professionals reinforces their position, but they ultimately do not have the power to make the decision. In some high tech firms, R & D managers perceive their future, salary, and power in the organization to be lower than that of their marketing manager counterparts. Marketing managers, particularly in industries such as consumer products in which marketing is perceived as a high-status function, seem keenly aware of these status differences (Gupta et al., 1986). On the other hand, some industries such as aerospace frequently limit hierarchical advancement into line management for those who lack the appropriate scientific and technical background. Status differences abound in such industries, with the high tech employees receiving the lion's share of the perks.

Of course, to some extent the expert clash may be somewhat industry-specific. Industries not employing a large number of both technical professional and organizational employees would likely suffer less from this clash than would industries such as electronics, aerospace, and defense, where a large number of both types is critical to the business.

Technical professionals have been known to exacerbate this clash by failing to discuss or communicate with their hierarchical superiors. To maintain their mystique and culture, or because their language tends to be filled with technical or scientific jargon unknown to most outside the specialty, they frequently establish barriers between their technical specialty and lay people. When the layperson happens to be their hierarchical superior, coordination can be a nightmare (Raelin, 1985).

THE AUTONOMY CLASH

Stemming from high tech professionals' belief in their expertise is their desire for autonomy or control over selecting projects on which they work (strategic autonomy), and how the work is to be performed (operational autonomy). To some extent, granting these employees control over the day-to-day operational autonomy of how the work is done is just good management practice. High tech employees, because of their expertise, are particularly sensitive to control in this arena.

From an organizational perspective greater tension arises over the former type of autonomy—the strategic autonomy, or what work is done (Bailyn, 1985).

This autonomy clash also reinforces the expert clash. Since technical professionals have a tremendous investment in their expertise, understanding a few areas very thoroughly, they tend to resist outsider interventions into those specialized areas of expertise.

Yet all business, including high tech, requires balancing the demands of many stakeholders against the pull of technological advancement. The best business decisions are not always the best technical decisions, yet ideally they reflect technical inputs.

Funding feuds frequently erupt around these balancing acts. Technologists, trying to convince management they are on the brink of discovery and worthy of funding, frequently underestimate the time required to turn technical innovation into usable customer-oriented product. Thus, another aspect of the autonomy clash, in addition to the quality of the decision, involves the amount of time it takes. Meeting customer requirements may directly conflict with engineering requirements.

Technological advancement frequently conflicts with the market for a given product. Rather than finding a niche and filling it, high tech professionals prefer to find cutting edges and advance them.

Keeping market and technological goals aligned is one of the more difficult problems in managing high tech firms and industries, such as banking, which routinely have a large high tech component. Gibson (1987), for example, relays the tale of a debacled Citibank automation project. The initial intent of the project was to automate every aspect of bank work. Instead of giving the bank a huge competitive edge, it produced big bills and internal anguish. According to one insider, "The problem was that the computer power available then was inappropriate to the task, but those working on it said, "Just give us another budget review." They went from overrun to overrun. Eventually the bank brought in another technical team that reengineered and scaled down the project" (Gibson, 1987, p. 23).

Like strategic autonomy over goals, timing, and the perception of time is a continual tension between technical professionals and managers. Technologists, motivated by innovation, often become furious when projects are canceled for reasons relating more to short-term profitability than to long-term technical success.

In highly competitive, shifting markets, strategic decisions often cancel well-run projects, as in the case of GM's Fiero automobile. The business demands shifting goals but threatens the professional's autonomy over what they do and how they do it (Raelin, 1985; Bailyn, 1985; Von Glinow, 1988).

THE STANDARDS CLASH

Most technical professionals believe only colleagues with similar specialties are capable of evaluating their work. Because the work is frequently exploratory and abstract, they reason, one must understand the process of the work in order to evaluate it. Results may or may not be a measure of performance. In many professions one can do flawless technical work and not obtain short-term profitability. When that happens, as it frequently does early in the research process when there are no tangible outcomes to assess, it poses a problem. Assessments by colleagues particularly early in a project are more likely to focus on *how* the work was done and how much it contributes to the growth of the field than on the project's financial performance. To technical professionals, how well the activity is done is frequently more important than its achieved results. Absent interim measures, results are the *sine qua non* for high tech managers who need a common denominator to evaluate across professional groups. Herein lies one of the greatest strains between managers and technical professionals: the use of bureaucratic versus professional standards (Raelin, 1985), which we refer to as the standards clash.

As we have mentioned, technical professionals working on the creation of new knowledge generally believe ownership of these ideas resides in the public domain. This is why they prefer collegial maintenance of standards. When standards are promulgated, maintained, and upheld by a professional group of experts, they are less apt to be arbitrarily altered to meet organizational results.

When overt conflict over standards occurs, or when technical professionals become frustrated with seemingly insoluble problems, they often share those conceptual frustrations with colleagues outside the business. The frustration often leads to problem solving, and the problem solving frequently leads to new discoveries. Because discovery occasionally occurs at a "watering hole" after work (Rogers & Larsen, 1984), another dilemma emerges: To whom does this new knowledge, created by a group effort independent of the employing organization, belong? If such a problem-solving group stumbles upon a new innovation, which firm is the rightful owner? Some high tech firms, including those that comprise the many R & D consortia around the country today such as MCC in Austin, Texas, believe that "discovery" is part of the public domain. Once those ideas shift to product development and new products begin to emerge, ownership shifts to the firm.

Professionals like to publish their findings in professional journals where they can receive recognition from their peers. Organizations, on the other hand, are reluctant to release information prematurely for proprietary reasons and fear of losing their competitive edge. Thus, the dissemination of professional knowledge tends to be a strong point of contention. Technical professionals believe their careers are best served by maintaining professional contacts, and thus they want to publish their research results to ensure that their name remains "top of the mind." A clash occurs when the firm wants to keep the information confidential, or is under time pressure to meet changing markets. Under those conditions, the firm prefers that the professional spend time strictly on business issues, not on enhancing their career marketability.

Role models and feedback are critical for a professional's growth. Because these employees are more likely to identify with their professions than their company, their role models are likely to be external to the employing firm. As a measurement of their development, professionals look to the standards set by their external role models and are likely to be motivated by feedback from those valued sources.

As we have noted, tension occurs when professional standards are in conflict with organizational goals. The management of this tension is a challenge for the professional as well as the firm.

Of course, not all high tech professionals are like this; there are those who are solely interested in achieving rank and status within their own organizations. These people, referred to as "locals" (Gouldner, 1957) are more likely to accept the standards established by the firm, and thus are less prone to the standards clash.

THE ETHICS CLASH

Ethics was at the core of the Challenger tragedy. Not only did Thiokol management reverse their decision to launch, but levels of management above Thiokol withheld information from key decision makers. As unfortunate as this case was, it is not an isolated incident. Ethics clashes like this appear routinely and range from the highly publicized aircraft brake scandal of B. F. Goodrich, the Chernobyl crisis, and Three Mile Island to more minor product delays or product malfunctions that disappear from the public attention rather quickly. Typically the technical professional sounds an alarm, which gets muffled by the middle so as not to upset the top.

The Thiokol management did not intentionally act unethically; most of us rarely do. Ethics frequently becomes the area of ambivalence in which unethical behaviors inadvertently are rewarded and reinforced through regular organizational practices. Because they see themselves as members of a larger community, professionals are more likely to make judgments based on the well-being of that professional community than on the well-being of the business.

Tension around ethical issues can take several forms. The professional's code of ethics may conflict sharply with an organization's seemingly deceptive product marketing. The firm's desire for secrecy around new products may conflict with the professional's commitment to disseminate information, or a firm's overt disregard for ethical considerations in the use of research may conflict with the professional code.

Professional ethics generally define the do's and don'ts of the profession. Since these ethics are written across organizational boundaries, professionals view themselves as having responsibilities beyond the boundaries of any one organization. Problems arise when the ethics of the profession clash with the interest of the firm (Benveniste, 1987).

Given our current technology, decisions made in the context of a single organization can have tremendous repercussions for the general public. Problems of pollution, and chemical and nuclear dumps typify this concern. Professionals' training alerts them to the danger of these acts before the layperson notices them. Frequently, business people trained to focus solely on their goals and their short-term results fail to observe the implications until it is too late. One manager in our sample noticed that "obstacles are those frightening things you see when you take your eyes off the goal." Though it is sometimes motivational, a company culture built on that philosophy can suffer from tunnel vision. When that gap in perspective becomes regularized, ethics clashes frequently will arise.

Sometimes the tension is covered up, as in the case of the Challenger. With almost machismolike fever, middle management "bet the store" that they could outrun the technologists' concerns. Other times, the tension is illustrated by the professional's open dissent and challenge to managerial authority. This tension, like the others, must be managed effectively if one is to effectively manage the high tech professional.

THE CLASH OVER COMMITMENT TO CALLING/LOVE OF WORK

At the core of many employee involvement movements in the United States today, is the notion of ownership. If workers feel they "own" the project, their motivation increases (Lawler, 1986). Without any effort on the part of management to build employee ownership, technical professionals already experience ownership. The very nature of the socialization process instills a sense of commitment, of love of work that very frequently has little to do with the rewards attached. Benveniste (1987) calls this quasi-religious fever commitment to one's calling.

Commitment to calling is the very thing that caused the Thiokol engineers to get down on the floor with a quad pad and repeatedly try to infiltrate the barriers to communication. It is a type of magic that, once engendered, is exceptionally powerful as a motivational tool. Professionals' training instills in them a sense of commitment to calling and love of work that cannot be duplicated by the organization. Nevertheless, the organization can influence the extent to which professionals may participate in projects in which their commitment will be evident. Although it is very difficult for the firm to create this commitment, it is somewhat easier to erode. The erosion begins when communication barriers are impenetrable, budgets are cut below a level that allows a competent job, and turnaround is too short for existing tasks. Much of the mismanagement of these professionals comes from the organizationally enforced erosion of their sense of commitment (Von Glinow, 1988).

THE EXTERNAL IDENTIFICATION CLASH

The knowledge base for scientific and technical professionals changes rapidly. Professional groups emerge to help professionals keep in touch with the advancements in new knowledge (Hall, 1985). In order to keep current in their technical specialty, professionals tend to seek out other professionals through professional alliances. These external referents serve as reinforcement and encourage professionals to push for their own standards within bureaucratic structures. The professional associations exert tremendous social and political influence through the dissemination of knowledge, updating members on current trends, affording contact with other professionals, accrediting and establishing standards of ethics, conduct, and behavior. Thus, the professional who identifies with the profession over the employing organization can receive considerable support from his or her peers. This sup-

Table 12.1 Culture Clashes Between Professionals and Organizations

Clash Categories	Bureaucracy		Professional
Expert clash	Hierarchical/organizational control	vs.	Expert evaluation and control
Standards clash	Rules of the company	vs.	Professional standards
Ethics clash	Organizational secrecy	vs.	Dissemination of information
Commitment clash	Organizational loyalty	vs.	Commitment to the field or profession
Autonomy clash	Organizational decision making	vs.	Professional demands for strategic and operational autonomy

port, professionals claim, is rarely offered by the firm, particularly if there are few specialists in the technical specialty.

In summary, Table 12.1 highlights some of these common clashes between the high tech professional and the firm.

ATTAINING CULTURAL COMPATIBILITY

Professionals, fueled by their expertise and demands for autonomy, chafe at overly rigid bureaucratic structures. Organizations, designed for prediction and control, typically tighten the supervision of professionals when that occurs. The task of leadership is to harmonize these two approaches, which is an extremely difficult task. For this to happen, both the professional and the bureaucratic culture must learn to tolerate and accommodate aspects of the other. The result of this fusion is a third type of culture, a new kind of organization in which professional integrity is maintained and organizational goals are valued.

Drucker (1988) likens this new organization type to a hospital or symphony. Like them, he hypothesizes, these new organizations will be "composed largely of specialists who direct the discipline of their own performance" (p. 45). Organizational goals will be based on this performance and reflect professional inputs far more significantly than today's organizations do.

Drucker (1988) refers to this as an information-based organization in which the management side of most high tech firms will be cut from one third to one half its current members. He notes that this structure bears little resemblance to our current organizational forms, noting that organizations of the future will have little choice but to become information-based. This is due partly to demographic factors that have shifted employment away from manual and clerical workers to knowledge workers who, as we have noted, resist the "command and control" model borrowed from the military over a century ago (Drucker, 1988).

We believe ultimately organizations that employ high tech professionals will evolve structurally and philosophically to this position. Currently, most high tech firms are undergoing transitions that reflect the demographic changes and cultural clashes that we have highlighted.

Organizational change is often neatly defined as a three-step process. One defines the future state, assesses the current state, and manages the transition (Beckhard, 1969). Drucker (1988) and others involved in high tech management have defined the future state. This chapter is intended as a first attempt at addressing transitional issues in a positive way. We believe managers can begin to systematically deal with the clashes we have highlighted by incorporating the following suggestions into their day-to-day interactions with high tech professionals. These suggestions have met with success across a wide array of high tech organizations employing numerous high tech professionals. We offer them here as harmonizing methods for easing culture clash.

SET A VISION

It is common for most firms to have a mission statement. What is less common is the fact that few high tech firms involve their technical staff in creating that mission or vision. Since these employees are central to the firm and comprise the organizational knowledge bank for generating ideas and products, these employees should not be merely an afterthought. Particularly when so many high tech firms today concentrate a tremendous amount of energy on attracting, compensating, and retaining these workers, their inputs should be sought before the mission or vision of the firm is generated. The firm should ideally include the high tech professional in creating the vision and putting it into operation. An effort should be made to include the professional's opinions. These workers generally come to the table with a demonstrated capacity for commitment to their technical specialty and a work ethic that is strong. Company leaders need to build on that commitment by considering them not as adjunct prima donnas, but as *critical* stakeholders. This is a difficult task, particularly since professional and organizational goals are frequently "at an angle" to one another, but one that successful firms, such as Apple, Hewlett Packard, and Intel manage to accomplish. Establishing a vision that all stakeholders share is a fundamental step in creating a loyal work force.

Implementing a vision sounds easy enough to accomplish, but in reality it is extremely difficult. Setting a vision is reasonably easy. Communicating the vision and causing others to believe it is more complex. It takes vigilance, attention to detail, and use of every possible aspect of the organization (Lawler, 1986). One company president went to great expense to develop a video message to share part of his vision and the state of the business with his 8000 employees. One year later he lamented, when at a staff meeting no one sitting around the table had seen or remembered the video. Alternatively, another CEO used the same format to communicate massive restructuring and culture change, and that video has become part of the folklore of the firm.

Although, communicating a vision that treats the high tech employee as a stakeholder is an important element for mobilizing change, the real key to managing the transition lies in concrete actions. We turn next to a discussion of those.

Show Them the Big Picture

Many of the tensions that arise between high tech professionals and their management stem from differences in their perspective and ability to understand the demands of the other's position. Concerted efforts to show both groups the big picture and the role they play in it are helpful. This suggests rotating high tech employees periodically through some of the other functional areas.

For example, an engineer in one high tech firm was sent to Europe to install, and work with the marketing department as they presented, a new product at a trade show. The engineer was amazed by both the intelligence and depth of the marketing people and the customers; on his return he suggested that more engineers be allowed to experience the same type of activity.

Bemis Company, involved in packaging, often has its engineers accompany salespeople to listen to customer needs. We not only advocate technical specialists spending time in a functional role, but we also advocate the reverse. The latter is done less frequently; however, the few cases of which we are aware reported favorable results. Thus, marketing, manufacturing, and staff personnel would also be well served by spending time in product development turf.

An important result of showing employees the big picture is that they usually begin to feel they play a part in it. But inspiring employees to feel part of the business does not do any good if they do not have the skills to gainfully participate. Many corporations, Xerox and General Electric among them, are training all employees in basic fiscal management. When everyone understands the financial impact of such things as too much inventory, for example, they are capable of making financially sound decisions, and as a result, more likely to participate in the business.

When the technical professional's interests go toward expanding their repertoire of skills, they should be encouraged to rotate through other functions or seek advanced training through either in-house educational programs or university-based programs. Job rotation affords an excellent opportunity to experience another function's job-related problems. When marketing employees are pulled from the ranks of the technical community in which they have rotated, many of the differences between the two have reportedly dissolved (Gupta et al., 1986).

This type of rotation has been shown to be extremely successful and is the hallmark of most Japanese sogo sosha, or large trading firms such as Mitsui and Mitsubishi, including their American subsidiaries. It does, however, require some willingness on the part of the technical employee as well as careful manpower planning to ensure distribution of skills and equitable rewards.

A natural way to both improve products and expand the horizon of both technical professionals and others is to use cross-functional teams to develop products. We now discuss those teams as well as other structural solutions to the problem of culture clash.

CREATE INTERDISCIPLINARY TEAMS

Developing a product is more like playing rugby than participating in a relay race. In today's competitive market, speed and flexibility are as important as high quality, low cost, and differentiation. The traditional sequential "relay race" approach to product development, exemplified by the National Aeronautics and Space Administration's Phased Program Planning (PPP) system, may conflict with the goals of maximum speed and flexibility. Instead, a holistic or "rugby" approach, in which a team tries to go the distance as a unit, passing the ball back and forth, may better serve today's competitive requirements (Takeuchi & Nonaka, 1986).

Many companies now use product development teams composed of members from engineering, manufacturing, sales, marketing, and service. When structured correctly, these interdisciplinary teams have been highly successful in reducing the time it takes to get a product to market. Referred to as quasi-structure by Schoonhoven and Jelinek in their chapter, these teams exist in concert with the traditional formal organizational structure, as well as the more "informal" networks of the organization. These intermediate-level structures have a considerable success record in high tech firms that must constantly innovate to remain competitive. Xerox, for example, has been able to halve both the number of people and the time it takes to develop a product (Hought, 1987). Sun Company, in its upstream activities always involve experts and technicians in interdisciplinary project teams.

Working together on a common goal is also one of the most effective means of reducing cultural tension (Sherif, 1951). Nevertheless, when the teams are not established and managed appropriately, cultural differences polarize the team rather than serve as a means of pulling the organization together. The cultural differences sited earlier in this chapter can cause problems in communication that are not ameliorated by simply putting a group of technical and marketing people together and instructing them to "be creative." These teams need to be given skills to work with each other. Cultural differences need to be made explicit so that problems stemming from them can be addressed and subsequently resolved. To some extent, quality circles (QC) serve the same purpose. Although QC has had a checkered history in firms where the culture has not supported the activities, firms that have blended competing cultures together successfully, such as H-P and Honeywell, claim their interdisciplinary QC teams work satisfactorily.

This type of interdisciplinary team tampers with the normal power structure of the organization. Team members need to have new skills in group decision processes. These teams, by their nature, also lead to flatter organizations, since the teams provide their own management. Flatter organizations in turn increase the probability that technical problems are heard by key decision makers. At NASA, at the time of the Challenger disaster, the organizational structure had become so complex that the people with technical expertise were isolated from important technical decisions. People who designed the product were no longer involved in decision making.

To address the problem of group decision making, both TRW and Xerox Corporation heavily involve their organizational development specialists in product development, so that the latter can transfer the skills necessary for team performance. The use of these teams has reduced the number of organizational levels at Xerox, thus reducing the middle level's muffling of technical messages.

One frustrated ex-technical professional-turned-entrepreneur suggested that development teams be allowed to pick their own team members. However, not all development teams have the big picture in mind when they select team members. The selection of team members and the development of employees capable of working in this arrangement become key functions for management in the high tech firm. To guarantee interdisciplinary team success, management must ensure that the environment is ripe for teamwork. This does not mean that management should squelch conflict. On the contrary, too little conflict has been cited as the primary reason for many organizational failures, including Penn Central. Some prior training in conflict resolution and problem solving may enhance team activities.

TOLERATE CONFRONTATION

One important key to managing corporations with high tech employees is to learn to tolerate confrontation. In the bureaucratic organization, confrontation is tantamount to insubordination. In technical professional cultures, confrontation and disagreement is frequently the way the sciences or professions advance themselves. As with the problem of working in interdisciplinary groups, management needs to support the statement that "disagreement is health" and encourage the teaching of confrontation skills. Since disagreements are inevitable, learning to confront without hostility is critical to achieving a creative synergistic work force.

Tolerance for diversity has been labeled a cognitive style—one in which some individuals may be more psychologically suited to greater levels of diversity than others. This, then, argues for some type of cognitive style or skill assessment to ensure that interdisciplinary teams are composed of individuals who are most likely to tolerate and grow from diversity.

SHARE THE WEALTH

Many high tech firms fail to share the wealth with all relevant stakeholders. The concept of wealth-sharing involves providing greater return to high tech workers from a profitable season. This might take the form of stock options, profit sharing, gain sharing, and other means of sharing wealth (Schuster, 1985). When profitability stems from direct contributions by interdisciplinary teams, all team members should benefit, not just senior management.

Generally, wealth-sharing plans include both a short- and a long-term incentive plan. The short-term plan emphasizes a period of twelve months or less, and the long-term plan typically is based on performance over a longer period of time. This is particularly relevant to the high tech professional, because many innovations take far longer than twelve months to reach fruition. Nevertheless, the product life cycle for new high tech products is being reduced daily. In fact, the average period for electronics and computers may be less than one year (Riggs, 1983).

Most high tech firms use stock options as the principal form of long-term incentive (Schuster, 1985) and use a pool of incentive dollars distributed on the basis of some measure of performance as short-term incentives (Von Glinow, 1988; Gomez-Mejia & Balkin, 1985).

We are not altogether comfortable with these methods, for reasons we discuss in the next section. What is relevant for managers involved in managing high tech workers is that compensation and wealth-sharing schemes should ideally be designed to communicate and reward performance that is consistent with the firm's performance objectives (Von Glinow, 1988). If the link between wealth-sharing and performance is missing, predictable woes occur for most high tech firms caught in the drive for increased productivity to bolster their competitive edge. A key question for managers is, just what is meant by the term "wealth"?

Reward Appropriately

When wealth-sharing is mentioned, we typically think of money and other financial components. However, review studies in a variety of high tech industries have consistently shown that traditional rewards, including money, promotions, status symbols, and the like, are consistently less important in controlling the performance of professional and high tech workers (Von Glinow, 1988). When we suggest that wealth-sharing is important, we mean that rewards should be appropriately distributed, that is, seen as important to those who receive them.

In general, financial rewards lack the leverage to give high tech workers incentive to perform (Von Glinow, 1988; Griggs & Manring, 1986; Miller, 1986). They tend to be weak motivators for professionals and still weaker as retention devices. Money is cited as less important than almost all other categories or rewards for high tech professionals. When we remember that

Table 12.2 Rewards Most Valued by High Technology and Professional Workers

Professional Rewards
  1. Opportunity to work with top-flight professionals
  2. Freedom to make the most of your own work decisions
  3. Intellectually stimulating work environment
  4. Not working on repeating yesterday, but working on tomorrow
  5. Having an impact on national legislation

Job Content Rewards
  1. A productive atmosphere
  2. Flexible work hours
  3. Long-term project stability
  4. Opportunities to address significant human needs
  5. Diversity of business that creates continuing new opportunities
  6. Patriotic projects
  7. Projects of an altruistic nature

Career Rewards
  1. Working for a leading-edge company
  2. Diverse opportunities for personal growth and advancement
  3. Opportunity to participate in the company's successes
  4. Career opportunities to stay ahead of the crowd
  5. The chance to get in on the ground floor of important projects
  6. Opportunities for self-expression
  7. Being able to play a role in the company's future

Social Status or Prestige Rewards
  1. Beautiful location
  2. Open-door management
  3. Extensive recreational facilities

Financial
  1. Twice yearly salary reviews
  2. Compensation for unused leave
  3. Cash bonuses

Source: Von Glinow, 1988.

professionals value the work they do because they are committed to their "calling," it is easier to see that they are motivated not by financial incentive but the nature of the work itself.

Table 12.2 illustrates the rewards that are most valued by high tech and professional workers. The key is that the most important rewards are the professional rewards and the nature of the work itself. There are, of course, some rewards that may be valued by different age categories. For example, people in their twenties seem to respond to job content rewards (or the nature of the work itself) and a few financial rewards; those in their thirties respond to professional rewards; professionals in their forties respond to professional, career, and job content rewards; people in their fifties want greater social, financial, and career rewards; and finally, people in their sixties seem to value financial and some social status rewards (Von Glinow, 1988).

In all, it seems exceedingly important to us that managers be aware of the different rewards and their appropriateness for different age categories. This awareness should be followed by systematizing those meaningful rewards into a reward system aimed at different types of individuals. In other words, some tailoring to the high tech professional is strongly advocated.

CONCLUSION

This chapter has identified key clashes that separate technical professionals from their organizational counterparts and suggested ways of ameliorating those clashes. Successfully managing the transition from today's high tech firm, riddled with culture clash, to tomorrow's high tech firm harmonized with diversity requires attention to multiple factors. The firm must be willing to set a vision, which includes all its stakeholders, and communicate that vision so all involved understand the firm's goals. To facilitate this vision, we recommend that managers encourage rotation of technical professionals with other functional areas of the high tech firm, so that each side comes to better understand the requirements of the other's position. This entails showing everybody the "big picture."

Similarly, we encourage the formation of interdisciplinary teams, composed of not only technical professionals, but marketing, manufacturing, and other personnel involved in getting the product from idea stage to market. Since this de facto means a certain element of conflict and confrontation, we suggest that such conflict not be "avoided at all costs," but rather be encouraged, with appropriate conflict-resolution and confrontation-handling skills as part of the training program of the interdisciplinary teams.

Finally, we recommend that the wealth be shared more with all members of the team, not strictly the key contributors. Key contributor programs have generally failed to give professionals incentive to perform since, by definition, a key contributor program singles out individuals, not teams. We believe that rewards may be more appropriately administered if attention is paid to which rewards are most salient for technical professionals. We cite new research that weighs the relative salience of a variety of rewards, across different age categories, for technical professionals.

Perhaps one of the most important recommendations for the successful management of high tech firms is to be aware of the perception held by the international community of the current management of U.S. high tech industry today.

Since the 1960s, the world opinion of the competence with which U.S. high tech firms are managed has declined dramatically (Sexton, 1988; Madique & Hayes, 1984). The United States has failed at keeping pace with many other countries, most notably Japan and many of the NICs, in terms of patents, invention rates, and important new innovations, and this has been attributed to poor management (Riggs, 1983). All of our recommendations become highly pertinent when world opinion of U.S. high tech management is so low.

We believe these recommendations are particularly salient for managers and leaders concerned with managing the transition from today's firm to tomorrow's. The transition will undoubtedly be a difficult one for most managers, and for firms based on the military model or that of old-line manufacturing firms. Given that such outdated emphases have predominated management thinking, it is time that high tech management in particular be alert and receptive to change. To some extent, a change of worldview may be necessary to attain competitive advantage.

We began this chapter with an excerpt from the President's Commission analyzing the causes of the Challenger disaster. Since the event, many organizational researchers and case writers (Maier, 1988; Marx, Stubbart, Traub, & Cavanaugh, 1987; Schwartz, 1987) have studied the events that led to the disaster. Some have hypothesized that the disaster was inevitable given NASA's post–moon landing environment. They believe post–Apollo NASA lacked vision and direction, was racked with an overpoliticized environment, funding deficits, and a culture so infiltrated with "can do" that they could not hear "we can't." The problems that led to the Challenger disaster were equally systemic.

NASA and its contractors are not unlike many firms that employ high tech professionals. Perhaps they are more mature than some and, precisely because of that, we believe the Challenger incident has a lesson to offer. In this chapter we have made systemic recommendations because we believe the problems stemming from the clash between technical professionals and their organizations are widespread and multifaceted.

The reason we advocate such massive change is that many of the previously mentioned clashes arise from the fact that most high tech professional workers are considered difficult to manage. Attributions such as prima donna and space-cadet abound. It is our contention that these high tech professional workers are not eccentricities the firm must endure to produce new product and process innovations. They are not adjuncts, nor peripherals, to be "put up with" in one manager's words. Rather, these people are essential to the production process. They are the raison d'etre for the high tech firm, and managing to accommodate them is central to the mission of the firm. Without a change of organizational philosophy that promotes toleration and respect for differences, we predict that firms of the 1990s will fail in their attempt to attract, motivate, and retain these valued workers. When that occurs, these firms will cease to remain competitive.

Thus, in conclusion we believe that managing the transition is necessary to achieving organizational growth. But for high tech firms to competitively enter the 1990s, committed managers and diverse high tech professionals must respect each other's diversity, and change outdated structures and practices to reflect the new high tech firms of our future.

13

The Role of Compensation in the Human Resource Management Strategies of High Technology Firms

LUIS R. GOMEZ-MEJIA AND
THERESA M. WELBOURNE

High technology firms have created some of the most desirable jobs in the economy, expanded the demand for highly skilled employees, and created millionaires and heroes overnight. For example, Apple's 1981 public offering resulted in 100 individuals becoming millionaires. Curiosity about how these high tech firms tick has prompted a flurry of research in recent years. This was vividly demonstrated in a recent academic conference on "Managing the High Technology Firm" (1988) sponsored by the University of Colorado–Boulder. While original plans called for 60 participants and 25 paper presentations, the total attendee count exceeded 350 and many more were turned away because of capacity constraints. Over 150 research papers were presented at this conference, spanning several management subfields, including human resource management systems. High technology has become the trademark of the late twentieth century, and our knowledge of why these companies are different is only beginning to blossom.

This chapter focuses on the compensation policies and practices developed by high technology firms in an effort to cope with the unique problems and issues facing the industry. The first section of this chapter attempts to go "behind the scene" and uncover the reasons why compensation plays such a prominent role in the human resource management strategies of these companies. The second section of the chapter details the types of rewards that have been employed by high technology organizations. These are divided into those that provide short-term incentives and those that encourage long-term goal attainment. In addition, they are further categorized by their ability to reward group or individual goal accomplishment. The third section examines contingency notions and empirical findings related to compensation practices in high technology firms. Finally, the last section poses some questions for future research.

Table 13.1   Features Distinguishing High Technology from Traditional Firms

Dimensions	High Technology	Traditional
Product	Cutting edge of technology	Well established
Industry	Electronics/computers/chemical	Mfg./services/misc.
Rate of innovation	High	Low
R & D expenditures	High	Low
R & D employees	High proportion	Low percentage
R&D employee attrition	High	———
Firm size	Smaller	Larger
Mortality rate	Higher	Lower
Rate of growth	Higher	Lower
Profits	Higher but variable	Lower but stable
Geographic concentration	High	Low
Organizational life cycle	Start-up/growth	Mature/decline
Product life cycle	Three years	Eight years

FACTORS SHAPING THE COMPENSATION STRATEGIES OF HIGH TECHNOLOGY FIRMS

Most empirical research on the human resource management practices of high technology firms has been conducted using comparative case studies and surveys of high tech versus traditional firms. For example, several recent studies by Balkin and Gomez-Mejia (1984; 1987) and Gomez-Mejia and Balkin (1988) used a 5 percent cutoff in the ratio of R & D expenditures to sales revenues to distinguish between high technology (5 percent or more) and traditional (less than 5 percent) firms. Based on this dichotomy, they found that several features distinguish these two types of companies (Table 13.1). Although definitions of high technology firms vary and there is no clear-cut measure, there seems to be a general consensus that R & D is of vital importance to these companies and that product life cycles are exceedingly short (Cascio, 1988). Competing products must be monitored constantly, and research projects, as well as business plans, may have to be altered overnight as a result of a new product release. Competition is very stiff, and new product introduction is a "race to the marketplace." To be successful in this industry requires a sophisticated R & D operation and a supporting set of human resource management strategies that foster innovation and are designed for a risky and turbulent environment.

Categorizing businesses into two mutually exclusive types such as high technology versus traditional may be useful for comparative purposes, but it is obviously an oversimplification of reality. In fact, the level of technological intensity across firms varies on a continuum from very low to very high. When we discuss compensation strategies of high technology firms in this chapter, we are referring to plans used by firms at the high end of the technology spectrum. This does not mean that firms with lower technological intensity do not use these types of reward programs but that these methods are used less frequently and might be less effective for them given the limitations, challenges, and needs they face.

To understand why compensation has played a dominant role in shaping the human resource policies of high technology firms, this section examines the complex factors that account for the flagship role of compensation in the human resource strategies of these companies (Table 13.2). The next section provides a more detailed description of the actual pay plans used by high technology firms.

DEMOGRAPHIC CHARACTERISTICS

Nature of Work and Employee Attributes

Jobs in high technology companies are in a constant state of flux. Business priorities can switch overnight with changes in the industry. Products become obsolete more quickly than in traditional firms. According to Gomez-Mejia and Balkin (1985) the product life cycle is between two and three years for high technology firms while in traditional companies the product life cycle is eight years. Employees who work for companies undergoing constant change find that their own jobs are continually being revised, and individuals who are successful in this environment must quickly adapt to changing conditions. For example, the authors found that former long-term government employees who attempted to work in secretarial, clerical, or administrative positions in start-up high technology firms were often not successful as rated by their supervisors, and these employees noted in exit interviews that they were extremely dissatisfied with their jobs. Their previous government positions were highly predictable, and the change to a situation in which their job description could be altered overnight was unduly stressful to them. Individuals who enjoy working for high technology companies thrive in the ambiguous working environment in which they operate; they are independent persons who take advantage of the loose job descriptions provided by their employers. Because tasks are fluid and jobs are difficult to define, formal job evaluation procedures are used infrequently in high technology firms.

High technology employees tend to be younger than their counterparts in more traditional organizations (Gomez-Mejia & Balkin, 1985). This trend is particularly prevalent in smaller high tech firms. These younger workers generally accept lower base salaries and benefits and work longer hours than employees in more established corporations. Older employees who usually have substantial financial burdens such as home mortgages or children in college are often uncomfortable in high-risk environments because financial security is an important need at this point in their lives. The risk accepted by employees in these firms is tempered by promises of rapid wealth if the business succeeds. Employees who work the long hours demanded share in both the risks and the rewards experienced by the firm.

Table 13.2 Factors Shaping Compensation Strategies in High Technology Firms

Demographic Characteristics	Compensation Strategies
Nature of Work and Employee Attributes • Fluid tasks • Short product life cycles • Younger employees	• Emphasis on risk sharing • Lower fixed compensation in pay • Shared ownership
Influence of Founder • Technical/scientific background • Antibureaucratic attitudes • Cynical about formal personnel programs • Play active role in human resource management	• Willingness to experiment with creative pay plans • Avoid use of mechanistic compensation approaches, e.g., job evaluation • Minimize use of policy/procedures as tools to control behavior • Shared ownership to foster employee commitment
Role of Scientists and Engineers • Crucial role in eventual success or failure of high tech firm • Loyal to discipline rather than organization • Own research agendas • Team projects • Willingness to move and/or start new firm	• Rewards to promote cooperation and group cohesiveness • Rewards to induce employee to internalize firm's goals and mission • Rewards to promote an entrepreneurial environment within firm • Rewards to tie individual to firm

Organizational Environmental Characteristics	Compensation Strategies
Cash Flow • Limited capital • Need to siphon scarce cash to R & D	• Keep fixed labor costs to a minimum • Flexibility in the reward structure • Risk-sharing by maximizing variable components in pay mix
Venture Capitalist Influence • High-risk investment • Unsecured position in firm	• Keep fixed labor costs to a minimum • Risk sharing by maximizing variable components in pay mix • Strong emphasis on pay for performance
Geographic Concentration • Low transition costs of charging employers • Competitive labor market	• Long-term incentives to tie employees to firm • Rewards that increase the opportunity costs of quitting • Front-end hiring bonuses
Pay Compression • Market forces bid-up entry level salaries • Narrowing of pay differentials by rank • Potential feelings of inequity and morale problems	• Incentives a high proportion of total compensation to shift focus from salary base • Long-term incentives and rewards that implicitly incorporate length of service as payment criterion

Extensive use of employee ownership programs such as offering generous stock options promote risk sharing, and induce employees to remain in the firm under extremely stressful and uncertain situations. Shared ownership plans promote a feeling that everyone is important for the organization's success, and the resulting internal commitment permits employees at all levels to continue to be productive under adverse conditions.

Influence of the Founder

Most original founders of high tech firms have technical backgrounds; they are often scientists and engineers who have left previous positions to become entrepreneurs (Gomez-Mejia & Balkin, 1985). Many of these individuals have been disillusioned by the expansive bureaucracy and miles of red tape that had to be sifted through in their previous positions. Much of this bureaucracy stemmed from administrative functions, including the human resources department. Although legislation has been responsible for the personnel department's increased status and power in many corporations, this same phenomenon has led to stacks of policies and procedures generated to guarantee compliance and avoid lawsuits.

For instance, a story often relayed to us by engineering managers and presidents of high tech firms is the dysfunctional consequences resulting from the employment policies enacted by their previous employers. The internal posting procedure generated months of delay for managers with an immediate need to add staff. The entire process of posting, recruiting, and sorting through resumés by personnel resulted in at least a two-month gap between the time an employee was needed and the time applicants could be interviewed for the position. Making an offer also entailed pigeon-holing the prospective employee into a predetermined pay hierarchy derived by job evaluation procedures such as the point factor system. These managers report that their inability to quickly hire a new employee and pay for unique skills not easily assessed by standard job evaluation methods resulted from the personnel department's unnecessary and rigid policies and procedures.

When these technical managers form their own companies, their negative impression of personnel procedures often leads them to curtail the amount of influence exercised by the department. They often do not trust the personnel function to develop systems that will provide equity and harmony essential to maintain the "happy family" atmosphere that is desired by entrepreneurs. Therefore, the founder takes an aggressive and leading role in guiding the human resource function, particularly the reward system. The entrepreneur's lack of reliance in the traditional personnel function and insistence on breaking tradition results in the minimization of mechanistic personnel policies, and the development of creative compensation strategies that tend to remain with the company as it matures. Employees' pay tends to be highly customized in these firms, and formal grade hierarchies with an associated standardized pay scale for each grade are less common.

As noted earlier, a common practice in start-up high technology firms is the entrepreneur's commitment to sharing ownership of the firm with all employees. Rather than writing policies and procedures intended to control behavior, chief executive officers have indicated to us in interviews their belief that if employees own a portion of the company and share in the risks and rewards, decisions and behaviors that are in the best interests of the organization will ensue. Employees working under these plans often take pay cuts in the short-term in the hope that the long-term will bring significant returns on their investment. There is a strong belief that the shared ownership will breed commitment to the organization and its purpose and help ensure that the entrepreneur's goal of "one big happy family" can come to fruition.

Pivotal Role of Scientists and Engineers

Scientists and engineers play a crucial role in the eventual success or failure of high technology firms. These employees tend to be more loyal to their discipline than to their organizations (Balkin, 1987). Research and development (R & D) employees have their own research agendas that are not necessarily consistent with those of the firm, or perhaps even those of other scientists on the team. These individuals want to be part of a company that they perceive has a product likely to succeed in the market and that will make a major contribution to the advancement of their scientific discipline. The organization needs a method for promoting teamwork and ensuring that the technical team works toward the firm's goals.

As will be discussed later, high technology firms have developed highly sophisticated, aggregate incentive systems, such as profit sharing and group-based cash award programs, that provide financial rewards to multiple contributors based on the achievement of common goals. According to the empirical findings of Gomez-Mejia and Balkin (1988), an aggregate incentive strategy is more appropriate than an individual-based reward strategy in an R & D environment for several reasons. First, an aggregate incentive strategy is more congruent with the cooperative structure of R & D work than individual based rewards. In a conceptualization derived from learning theory, Kelley and Thibaut (1969) defined a cooperative structure as one in which the individual's rewards are directly proportional to the quality of the work group. For Kelley and Thibaut, the reward distribution motivates group members to behave as a team or as individuals competing with each other. An aggregate-based reward strategy may be used to reinforce cooperation among members in R & D units while an individual-based strategy reinforces just the opposite. Second, given the team nature of R & D work, measurement difficulties with an aggregate incentive strategy are significantly less than those posed by individual rewards. Aggregate incentive plans are easier to implement because it is not necessary to identify individual contributors. They do not require unrealistic distinctions across employees. The financial reward may also be made more meaningful to the employee because it is less contaminated with other nonperformance factors such as seniority and cost of living adjustments. Third, aggregate incentive systems offer great flexibility in timing the reward close to actual task accomplishment or in making rewards contingent on specific targets or goals. Both timing and reward contingencies are important determinants of the reinforcement value of financial incentives (Nadler, Hackman, & Lawler, 1979; Opsahl & Dunnette, 1966). For instance, a group bonus for engineers can be timed right after a new product leaves R & D and goes into production in accordance with the planned time table.

Aggregate incentive systems may also be an effective management control tool for the R & D scientists who have personal and professional goals that might not match the organization's objectives. Group incentive programs may be set up to induce R & D workers to adopt the firm goals for themselves by making organizational rewards contingent on the achievement of those objectives.

As noted earlier, many high technology firms are founded by entrepreneurs who were dissatisfied with large bureaucratic organizations. They view aggregate incentives as a mechanism to create an entrepreneurial climate in R & D teams. The kinds of risks that an R & D group faces on the magnitude of the financial incentive can be made to resemble the risks that entrepreneurs face. In this manner, by creating an entrepreneurial environment, aggregate incentive systems would force scientists and engineers to share the risks of success or failure with the firm and its owners.

CHARACTERISTICS OF THE HIGH TECHNOLOGY ORGANIZATION AND ITS ENVIRONMENT

Cash Flow Problems

A constraint faced by many start-up high tech companies is limited cash flow into the firm. This phenomenon has forced these organizations to devise compensation systems that enable them to compete with more mature companies. Regardless of firm size, R & D expenditures are quite high; sometimes exceeding 25 percent of total operating costs. Management is forced to devise methods by which it can conserve cash in the early stages of product development.

Cash flow is also affected by the method in which the business is funded. Cash flow can be more or less of a constraining factor, depending on whether the firm is funded by, for example, a small group of owners' personal wealth, venture capital money, or a generous large organization that is supporting a new subsidiary. The employees working in a start-up subsidiary will tend to have more job security and more assurance that cash is available for payroll than individuals working under the other two alternative conditions mentioned.

To grapple with the constraint of limited cash flow into the business, incentive systems have been utilized that enable high tech firms (particularly throughout the start-up phase) to channel scarce resources into R & D while at the same time maintaining labor costs under control as these would fluctuate according to business conditions. Because group-based incentives are not a part of base salary, the organization has greater flexibility to be generous with the magnitude of the reward without having to fear inability to pay in future pay periods.

Gomez-Mejia and Balkin (1985) found that incentive-based programs were more effective at the growth stage of the product life cycle. This is consistent with the fact that firms at the growth stage face more difficulty with maintaining adequate cash flow than do those at the later stages when income is being derived from sales.

Influence of Venture Capitalists

High tech entrepreneurs offer both an idea that may have commercial value and the technical expertise for the research and development necessary to transform the idea into a product. The venture capitalist can provide start-up capital along with other resources such as critical management expertise and connections to other financial institutions or marketing distribution channels. In this exchange process, venture capitalists are willing to invest their funds and provide expertise on very risky investments anticipating a potential high rate of return.

The high tech entrepreneur accepts the financial assistance from the venture capitalist but in return gives up substantial equity in the firm and may also have obligations to accept advice from the venture capitalists. Venture capital is in short supply (Silver, 1985), giving venture capitalists significant leverage. They do not invest at one point in time, but rather in the stages. Workers have no guarantee that the investors will continue to pump money into their company, and the risks that they might be on the streets with a short notice are high.

Venture capitalists provide much of the financial support for high tech firms and, because of their unsecured equity position in the firm, are interested in maintaining fixed labor costs to a minimum (Gomez-Mejia, Balkin, & Welbourne, 1988). Since venture capitalists are able to influence management within the company, the desire to retain a ceiling on fixed costs is a prime goal of many high tech firms. As a result, many creative incentive systems are developed so that a significant portion of an employee's income (sometimes in excess of 50 percent) is *not* in the form of salary and benefits. This ensures that financial statements meet the goals of the venture capitalists and that the management team can better meet its annual plan and cash flow projections. At the same time, the employees' income and job security risks are counterbalanced by a high potential pay-off if the company succeeds.

Geographic Concentration and Staffing Problems

High technology firms are usually congregated in "high tech centers," such as Silicon Valley in California. The geographic concentration results in high turnover in the work force because jobs within similar organizations are easy to find with little cost to the employee (Gomez-Mejia & Balkin, 1985).

A single scientist or engineer can have significant impact on an organization's success. It is essential for a firm to induce these key employees to stay with the company during the critical stages of product development. The combination of weak organizational loyalties and easy access to new positions makes moving to another organization an easy decision for R & D employees. Not only are opportunities available for these employees to move to other companies, but with an attractive product idea they can obtain financing and start their own company, often in direct competition with their current employer.

Compensation schemes designed to "glue" employees to the firm are often used to cope with this problem. A wide array of long-term incentives has been developed with the objective of increasing the opportunity costs of moving. Once hired, the employee stands to gain substantial rewards if the company succeeds. Leaving the firm before some stipulated amount of time, or before the company "goes public," generally involves forfeiting the long-term gains.

The highly competitive nature of the business combined with the shortage of highly skilled research and development personnel results in recruitment being a prime concern for high technology companies. High technology firms gain a competitive advantage by being able to syphon scarce technical talent from other organizations. Front-end bonuses provided upon hire are used quite frequently to attract R & D employees from other firms.

Pay Compression

The intense competition for technical staff and increasing market rates result in bidding up entry-level salaries. Unless pay levels within the organization increase proportionately with new hire salaries, severe pay compression problems will ensue. Pay compression reduces the pay differentials between jobs at different levels, so that incumbents at the higher ranks may feel underpaid and unfairly treated. Those feelings of inequity will have a negative effect on employee morale and can further compound the attrition rates.

Pay compression problems are complex and difficult to avoid. Long-term incentives, particularly stock options that tend to be allocated in greater amounts and lower exercise prices for early employees, are used to shift the focus of attention away from base pay and inevitable inequity problems. These programs also tend to ameliorate the pay compression problem by implicitly incorporating length of service as a criterion for payment.

Table 13.3   Compensation Practices of High Technology and Traditional Firms

Compensation Practices	High Technology	Traditional
Salary as percentage of total pay	Lower	Higher
Short-term "plantwide" incentives		
• Profit sharing	Very common	Infrequent
• Gain sharing	Infrequent	More common
Short-term individual rewards		
• Merit pay	Universal	Universal
• Equity adjustments	Very common	Common
• Cash bonuses	Very common	Infrequent
• Nonfinancial rewards	Very common	Infrequent
Long-term incentives		
• Stock option plans	Very common	Infrequent
• Stock purchase plans	Very common	Infrequent
Other reward policies		
• Nontraditional benefits (e.g., flexible hours, recreational activities, education grants)	Very common	Infrequent
• Dual-career ladders	Very common	Infrequent

COMPENSATION PRACTICES OF HIGH TECHNOLOGY FIRMS

As noted earlier, high technology companies have developed innovative compensation strategies that are congruent with the nature of the work force, the organization, and its environment. This section describes, in some detail, the compensation practices and policies of these firms. Table 13.3 summarizes much of this discussion by outlining the compensation practices of high technology vis-à-vis traditional firms.

Short-Term Rewards

Available research indicates that most high tech firms take advantage of short-term incentives for all employees and that salary tends to be a smaller percentage of total pay relative to traditional companies (Schuster, 1984; Gomez-Mejia & Balkin, 1985) Short-term incentives refer to a program duration of twelve months or less. Most plans pay the employee a percentage of base salary based on some preestablished qualitative or quantitative criteria. Quantitative criteria may include revenues from the commercialization of a product, return on investment, return on assets, or net profit. Qualitative criteria may include meeting a deadline, saving the company money through suggestions, completing an important project, or achieving a preestablished goal.

Gomez-Mejia and Balkin (1985) cite three reasons for the importance of short-term incentives in high technology companies:

1. They are instrumental in maintaining an egalitarian culture and team approach in order to nurture technological innovation.
2. Short-term pay incentives such as a cash bonus are a powerful sig-

naling device that management can use to communicate corporate objectives.
3. Short-term incentives give management more flexibility in distributing compensation dollars to employees.

Appropriate feedback, which results from implementation of short-term incentives, helps ensure that members of the organization understand the important strategic goals that must be attained for corporate success. In this manner, the reward system provides a mechanism for management to communicate goals and priorities to employees. Grissom and Lombardo (1985) interviewed human resource directors of twenty high technology companies and found that one of their prime concerns, and an area which needs improvement, is corporate communication. These companies are rapidly changing and doing business in an unstable environment where facts are subject to constant reappraisal and alteration. It is essential that all of the employees be updated on events that affect their jobs, their priorities, and their goals. An incentive system that enhances understanding of strategic concerns can be helpful in attaining these communication goals.

Short-term incentives appear to be more popular among younger employees. As noted earlier, the majority of employees working in high technology companies are under thirty years of age (Gomez-Mejia & Balkin, 1985). Given these facts, short-term incentives provide a sensible way of matching the interests of employees with rewards provided by the employer.

Prompt payment of rewards also provides employees with the feeling that they are appreciated (Humphrey, 1987). The family atmosphere that so many entrepreneurs try to attain requires that individuals feel they are viewed as contributing members of the group. Short-term incentives offer one opportunity to ensure that employees feel they are "part of the family," thus providing further impetus to encourage loyalty and commitment to the firm. The various types of short-term aggregate incentives and individual rewards used by high technology firms are discussed next.

Short-Term Aggregate Incentives

Profit Sharing

Profit-sharing plans are not new, but the innovative use of these programs in high technology firms is that they have been extended to a broad cross-section of employees rather than restricted to top management. Profit-sharing plans are also more common in high technology companies than in traditional firms. For instance, Balkin and Gomez-Mejia (1984) found that 55 percent of high technology firms used profit sharing for research and development employees compared to only 33 percent in traditional firms. A more recent survey by Gomez-Mejia and Balkin (1988) found that 68 percent of scientists and engineers in high technology firms receive profit-sharing benefits in their compensation package.

Profit sharing rewards the individual employee for organizationwide performance. Although the link between an individual's performance level and the bonus is not always well understood by employees because net profit is affected by many factors outside the employee's range of influence (Welbourne & Gomez-Mejia, 1988), the advantage of profit sharing is that it allows an individual to understand the goals of the organization. It gives employees a broader view of their role in the company and provides a mechanism by which the organization reports corporate performance to the employees. Communication is enhanced by the formal policy developed in such a plan.

This feature can be particularly helpful with research and development personnel who tend to focus energy on their various research projects and scientific discipline (Balkin, 1987). Profit sharing forces them to look beyond the goals of their specific work group and consider the implications of their tasks on the total organization and "bottom line." Profit-sharing plans can provide a mechanism for enhancing cooperation between work units or departments. The scientist is motivated to consider the marketability of the product that is being generated in the lab.

Gain Sharing

Gain-sharing programs are increasingly popular in the United States (Welbourne & Gomez-Mejia, 1988). They provide a group of several hundred employees, within a division or a plant, with a bonus based on productivity improvements over a historical base that is determined by past performance. Most plans also provide a participative component that allows employees to filter suggestions to top management for consideration and implementation.

Although gain-sharing plans are being implemented in many industries, according to Kanter (1987), "in incentive-conscious high technology companies, gainsharing is rare" (p. 62). She cites a survey by Hay and Associates that reports only 6 percent of the high technology companies had gain-sharing plans.

One possible explanation for their disinterest in gain sharing is rooted in the mechanics of the system. Gain-sharing plans require that historical standards be developed based on stable, prior performance levels. High technology companies do not have consistent manufacturing performance from which to draw a historical base.

In addition, it has been recommended by proponents of gain-sharing plans that the bonus formulas remain constant for a number of years. In the changing environment in which a high technology firm does business, the bonus formula would need continual adjustments. These revisions would tend to erode the trust between management and employees that is necessary for plan success.

Although the components of gain-sharing plans (group-based bonus, participative management, and teamwork) are congruent with high technology goals, the mechanics of the system do not work well in the business environment in which these firms are immersed. Profit sharing and group-based cash bonuses accomplish many of the same functions that gain-sharing plans serve in traditional firms.

Short-Term, Individual Rewards

Merit Pay

High technology firms' use of merit pay is similar to that of traditional firms. Balkin and Gomez-Mejia (1985) found that the average merit increase for high technology companies was 8.0 percent compared to 8.3 percent in traditional firms. In a more recent survey, Gomez-Mejia and Balkin (1988) found that close to 100 percent of high technology firms use merit pay programs.

Unfortunately, merit pay suffers from some serious drawbacks. According to Lawler (1987), "despite the widespread adoption of merit pay, there is considerable evidence that in most organizations merit pay systems fail to create a perceived relationship between pay and performance" (p. 20). Lawler (1987) cites several problems with merit pay, including poor performance measures that are often based on subjective judgments of managers, poor communication systems which are shrouded in secrecy and require employees to trust management's interpretation of the merit pay increase, poor delivery systems that are complex and inadequate for their purposes, and management attitudes that has been found to consistently resist the performance appraisal process.

Merit pay, with its multitude of problems, continues to be widely used by industry. Lawler (1987) suggests that we do not abandon merit pay but, instead, use it when it is most appropriate. He notes that "overall, merit pay systems seem to fit best where work can be designed for individuals who work independently of others" (p. 24).

Gomez-Mejia and Balkin (1988) agree with Lawler's (1987) logic, arguing that merit pay is particularly inadequate for a research and development environment. The interdependent nature of the work requires teamwork and cooperation that they believe are not fostered through a merit pay system. In addition, they comment, the individual differences necessary to maintain a merit pay system are not easily apparent in the project work generated by the R & D personnel. They found no relationship between merit pay and a variety of pay effectiveness measures for R & D workers, such as pay satisfaction, attrition rate, and performance levels.

Equity Adjustments

Equity adjustments are permanent increases to base salary allocated to maintain equity with the external labor market. These adjustments are necessary when the salaries for specific jobs are raised as a result of an inadequate supply of qualified personnel. Equity adjustments are required for a company that does not want to lose its top performers to competitors. Although equity adjustments do not motivate an individual toward a specific job goal, they do induce an employee to remain with the firm. Lack of equity adjustments motivates the top performers to seek employment elsewhere.

Balkin and Gomez-Mejia (1984) found that 73 percent of high technology firms provided equity adjustments of approximately 12 percent for research and development personnel versus 54 percent of traditional firms that provided an average of an 8 percent equity adjustment. In other words, high technology firms provided equity adjustments more often, and when they did, the adjustments were higher than in traditional firms. This is not surprising considering the high attrition rate in high technology firms discussed earlier.

Cash Bonuses

Balkin and Gomez-Mejia (1984) found that 82 percent of high technology companies used bonus compensation for research and development personnel compared to 35 percent of traditional firms. Cash bonuses were based on both financial and nonfinancial criteria and awarded to all technical employees, regardless of job title or grade level. A cash bonus is awarded in addition to merit pay and equity adjustments. The purpose of the bonus is to reward special accomplishments. These incentives can be based on either group or individual performance. High technology companies appear to use both, with group bonuses being more common in research and development teams. Balkin (1987) reports that team based bonuses, designed in part to promote group cohesiveness, usually range between 15 and 20 percent of base salary for R & D employees.

Cash bonuses provide an organization with a flexible mechanism for rewarding employee performance without committing the organization's future dollars. The lump sum payment is made based on a specific accomplishment and is not a permanent addition to the base salary; thus, the money is not committed in upcoming years. This is an attractive feature for organizations that face an uncertain horizon, particularly for firms at the start-up phase dependent on the acquisition of additional venture capital funds for continued growth. The less fixed expenses an organization can show in its business plan, the more favorable the prospect will look to the venture capital community. Cash flow is an important variable in determining the company's ability to manage its growth.

Cash bonuses are often used for individuals who make significant contributions above the work of other team members. Although often an informal compensation policy, incentives for key contributors are used to reward outstanding performance of individuals (Balkin & Gomez-Mejia, 1985).

The availability of a cash bonus is often welcomed by managers who cannot reward employees within the current compensation system. Highly paid employees are often assigned a smaller range for their merit pay because they are already at the top of their pay range. This is a source of constant frustration for the manager who is trying to motivate these high performers. Cash bonuses allow the manager to reward the top performer without permanently raising the salary structure.

Miscellaneous Awards

Noncash awards, such as paid trips, dinners, and recognition plaques, can provide a company with flexibility to reward significant contributions immediately. This immediate feedback should make employees feel that they are appreciated and encourage loyalty to the firm.

An awards program, which can be either formal or informal, is often used by high technology firms for incremental or annual results (Schuster, 1984). Humphrey (1987) suggests that awards should be provided for clearly visible achievements and that the award should be given in public only after the project or task is completed. He suggests that incentives are provided for sustenance and comfort while awards are given for special recognition. This implies that incentives might be viewed as rewards for meeting agreed-upon standards, whereas awards are unexpected positive feedback for a job well done.

LONG-TERM, AGGREGATE INCENTIVES

Long-term financial incentives are defined as covering a period over one year—commonly, three to five years. Their goals should be congruent rather than competitive with those of short-term incentives. In many instances a manager is faced with a dilemma requiring him or her to forgo a short-term bonus to make the best long-term business decision. The limited tenure of most employees and lack of loyalty to the company may result in selecting alternatives that maximize the short-term bonus. For example, the best long-term business decision might be to build a new plant rather than lease a building. If the annual bonus is based on net profit and construction expenses will erode net profit for the year, management may opt to lease in order to secure the annual bonus payment. This is not the best long-term business decision but may be the choice made by executives in response to the incentive package.

To prevent this from happening, high technology firms offer incentives that encourage managers to consider the long-term benefits of their decisions as well as the short-term consequences. According to Lauenstein and Skinner (1980) "performance measures that reward executives for developing long-term resources are essential to provide incentives to spend more effort on activities that can be decisive with respect to longer-term results" (p. 10). The objective of long-term incentives is to link the goals of the management team to that of the shareholders (Schuster, 1984). This goal has led to the increasing popular use of stock purchase and stock option plans in high technology firms as long-term incentives (Lawler, 1987; Schuster, 1984). Balkin and Gomez-Mejia (1984) found that 73 percent of high technology companies implemented a stock purchase plan for scientists and engineers versus 25 percent in traditional firms.

Stock plans were initially implemented by many firms in response to the tax advantages that could be realized by the company and the employees covered by the plan (Kanter, 1986, 1987). Stock plans also allow the corporation to raise capital, improve cash flow by diverting the labor dollars until the time of stock sale, and retain key employees through restrictions on time of stock sale (Kanter, 1987; Gomez-Mejia & Balkin, 1988).

Perhaps the reason for the predominance of stock-based programs in high technology firms is that no better options exist for encouraging a long-term orientation. In a quickly changing environment how are long-term goals realistically set? If all the employees realize that long-term plans and objectives are unreasonable because of the severe fluctuations experienced by the industry, can these goals actually be expected to motivate long-term decision making? On the other hand, most employees understand that the stock price is related to corporate performance and that if they want to sell their stocks at some future time, their current decisions must be made with long-term performance in mind. It is the contention of these authors that stock options are the only realistic mechanism that high technology companies have at their disposal to motivate long-term orientations among their top management team and key personnel.

Stock option plans are generally implemented during the start-up phase of the company and can be issued to broad levels of employees, often all employees in the start-up team. At this time, there is no price for the stock in the market; employees are betting that their commitment to the firm will result in their stocks gaining considerable value at the time of public offering. The goal of stock option plans at this stage in the company's life cycle is to motivate the early contributors through partial ownership. The company cannot afford to pay high salaries and often asks employees to take pay cuts, in some cases working at half pay when cash flow is a critical problem. The only method for retaining these employees is to lure them into continued employment through the promise of substantial long-term rewards.

After the company goes public, stock purchase plans are implemented by most firms. Under these programs employees can purchase stocks at a discount of 15 to 20 percent of the market price (Gomez-Mejia & Balkin, 1985). At this point the price of the stock is known to the employee because it is being openly traded. They do not know what the price will be at the point when the stock can be sold. Stock purchase plans assist companies in retaining employees and in promoting long-term decisions for the same reasons that stock options plans motivate this behavior.

Stock purchase plans are less likely to have a significant behavioral impact than stock options for two reasons. First, a greater number of employees are covered under the stock purchase plan; thus, the novelty of a stock option plan is not present. The plan might be viewed as a benefit rather than an incentive. This is the case with many high technology firms that fail to provide retirement plans but, instead, allude to the stock purchase plan as a retirement savings. Second, the price of the stock constantly fluctuates, and many of the causes of this change in stock price are not within the control of the employees or even the firm. General economic conditions or actions by a competitor can cause the stock price to quickly rise or drop.

OTHER REWARDS

Benefits Package

Benefits provided by high technology companies appear to be comparable to those of traditional firms. Balkin and Gomez-Mejia (1984) found that both high technology and traditional companies provided benefits amounting to

35 percent of payroll. High technology companies might spend the benefit dollars on slightly different programs than traditional firms. Gomez-Mejia and Balkin (1985) suggest that in an effort to reduce some of the stress caused by employment with high technology companies, these firms have implemented programs such as flexible work hours, recreational activities, generous travel allowances, and employee assistance programs. They suggest that these programs are implemented in an effort to "pamper these employees" and help retain them.

Benefits packages in high technology firms also have extensive educational components for research and development personnel. A sampling of educational benefits offered by high technology firms are 100 percent tuition reimbursement, fees for publishing, reimbursement for attendance to seminars and trade shows, association fees, and journal subscriptions (Balkin, 1987). Continuing education is essential to the corporation and individual (Solomon & LaPorte, 1987). Half of a scientist's or engineer's knowledge is obsolete within three to five years (Cascio, 1988). The reward system allows research and development personnel to maintain and update their skills and abilities through continuing education programs.

Dual-Career Ladders

The compensation systems of high technology firms have contributed to an alteration of the traditional corporate hierarchy (Kanter, 1984; 1986). Although dual-career ladders are a myth in many firms because it is common knowledge that technical personnel can seldom achieve the same level of income and status as professional managers, high technology companies take them seriously (Milkovich, 1987; Gomez-Mejia & Balkin, 1985; Grissom & Lombardo, 1985; Madique & Hayes, 1984; Kanter, 1986; Martin, 1984). The dual-career ladder refers to an alternate career path that technical personnel can choose to pursue rather than the traditional route through management positions.

The typical corporate hierarchy promotes competent scientists and engineers who progress in their careers into management positions. According to Martin (1984), "This is a method whereby the firm may lose the services of a good researcher and gain the services of a poor manager—clearly an undesirable outcome" (p. 217). In this case, a competent scientist or engineer who has been rewarded for outstanding performance is put into a working situation where his or her performance often becomes less than satisfactory. The outcome is negative for both the corporation and the employee. Poor performance outcomes are demoralizing to employees who have been previously producing outstanding work, and poor managers affect the attitudes and work of subordinates. The result is less effective performance and unsatisfied employees.

High technology organizations have worked hard at implementing "true" dual-career ladders as a solution to this dilemma. They provide a means by which technical personnel can attain status, rewards, pay, and recognition normally granted to top executives (Madique & Hayes, 1984). Rather than moving into management positions, scientists and engineers can be promoted in a technical career track to a position comparable to the parallel management position. The result is that the company allows the employees who have expertise in research to make research their permanent career (Martin, 1984).

Kanter (1984) suggests that implementation of dual-career tracks allows the organization to treat the technical employee in a manner similar to that of university professors. She notes that scientists and engineers who choose this path often share in patent rights, are granted sabbaticals, are provided with awards for outstanding accomplishment, and take advantage of continuing education programs.

Grissom and Lombardo (1985) note that failures of dual-career ladders are a result of a poor implementation process and not the system itself. The key to success appears to be that the technical career path exactly parallels the traditional path. This ensures not only that employees who choose this path are accorded the recognition, status, and pay a management position grants but also that the individuals become involved with corporate decisions at a level at which a manager would be involved. Entrepreneurs who were active in the early stages of the company, when everyone participated in corporate decisions, will particularly need this feature (Madique & Hayes, 1984). Start-up companies call on the resources of all of their employees, regardless of professional discipline, to assist in developing and writing the business plan, presenting the information to acquire capital, hiring and firing employees, and an entire range of decisions from finance to marketing to product development. Involvement in corporate decisions enables those key employees who choose the technical career ladder to feel they are still contributing to the survival and growth of the company.

Job rotation is also used by high technology firms. Moving employees across disciplines allows the company to expand the knowledge base of its key personnel and weakens the links of the traditional hierarchy. Job rotation and matrix or project management allow people to work together in different roles and reduce reliance on hierarchical decision makers.

Job rotation can lead to what Kanter (1986) refers to as the generalist track. Rather than specializing in one discipline, a key employee is groomed by moving into various specialty areas for training and experience. The result is a competent high-level executive who understands the entire organization rather than a small component of it.

CONTINGENCY FACTORS AS DETERMINANTS OF OBSERVED COMPENSATION PRACTICES AND THEIR EFFECTIVENESS IN HIGH TECHNOLOGY FIRMS

From a contingency perspective, two important questions come to mind. First, is "high technology" the causal factor in the observed compensation practices of high technology organizations? It is quite possible that other variables that have little to do with high technology per se may explain these

Table 13.4 A Contingency Theory of Compensation Strategy:
Propositions and Findings

Propositions	Findings
1. Incentive pay as a proportion of the total compensation package is greater for firms at the growth stage of the product life cycle.	Strong support
2. An incentive-based reward strategy is more effective for firms at the growth stage of the product cycle.	Strong support
3. The proportion of fixed compensation costs in the total pay package increases as a function of organizational size.	Strong support
4. The effectiveness of an incentive-based strategy is inversely related to company size.	Moderate support
5. The compensation mix in high tech firms contains a higher proportion of incentive rewards and a lower proportion of fixed pay.	Strong support.
6. Considering all firms at the growth stage of the product life cycle, those that are high tech have a pay mix with a greater incentive component.	Strong support
7. Smaller high tech firms have a pay mix with a greater incentive component than similar non–high tech firms.	Strong support
8. An incentive-based compensation strategy is more effective in high tech firms than in non–high tech companies.	Strong support
9. For organizations at the growth stage in the product life cycle, an incentive-based reward strategy is most effective for high tech firms.	Moderate support
10. For smaller companies, an incentive-based strategy is most effective for those that are high tech.	Moderate support

ADAPTED FROM: Balkin, D.B. and Gomez-Mejia, L.R. (1987). Toward a Contingency Theory of Compensation Strategy. *Strategic Management Journal*, 8(1): 169–182. Published with permission.

practices. Some of these were alluded to earlier. For example, smaller firms and those at the growth stages in the life cycle may benefit from an incentive-based reward strategy to conserve cash regardless of their technological intensity. On the other hand, one could argue that technological intensity of a firm makes those practices more appropriate for the reasons outlined earlier (e.g., group nature of R & D work, entrepreneurial culture of those firms, beliefs of technical founders). It is also possible that exogenous variables to high technology such as company size and technological intensity of a firm may have a unique as well as an additive impact on the observed compensation practices. A second important question from a normative angle is whether the effectiveness of the observed compensation practices increases as expected for firms that use pay schemes that appear to be most appropriate given their technological intensity and standing on relevant variables such as firm size and life cycle stage.

In a recent study, Balkin and Gomez-Mejia (1987) tried to answer both of these questions by testing a series of propositions (Table 13.4) in a sample of thirty-three high tech and seventy-two non–high tech firms or business units in the Boston Route 128 area. Based on self-report data provided by managers responsible for compensation policies in these firms or business units, their findings suggest that technological intensity, in addition to firm size and life cycle stage, does make a difference in terms of observed pay practices and their effectiveness. Balkin and Gomez-Mejia (1987) concluded that "small firms at the growth stage of the life cycle, with a high proportion of R & D expenditures, tend to rely on incentive rewards, and this compensation strategy makes a greater contribution to effectiveness for firms sharing those characteristics" (p. 180). Because of the "soft" perceptual measures used in that study, those findings should be viewed as suggestive; much research remains to be done before more definite answers can be provided.

AN AGENDA FOR THE FUTURE

Much of our knowledge of high technology compensation is experiential or based on "armchair" conjectures. With the exception of the self-report perceptual data shown by Balkin and Gomez-Mejia (1987) and Gomez-Mejia and Balkin (1988), we know very little about the contributions of alternative reward strategies in high technology firms to the achievement of individual, organizational, and R & D goals. From a practitioner's perspective, it would be important to ascertain the relative cost–benefits of nontraditional versus traditional compensation approaches in the high technology industry. For example, is reliance on stock ownership more cost-effective for the firm than the use of fixed pay (i.e., salary and benefits)? What is the relative impact of various compensation schemes (e.g., individual and team bonuses, profit sharing, stock-based plans, gain sharing) on such variables as pay satisfaction, withdrawal behaviors, individual performance, team effectiveness, and profitability? The answers to these questions, though difficult to ascertain through rigorous scientific procedures, are essential for sound policy making. Some of the key issues that are badly in need of more study are outlined next.

The Role of Individual Differences

We know little about compensation strategy implementation at the unit level. Since R & D units are relatively independent within the high tech firm (Gomez-Mejia, McCann, & Page, 1985), they provide a significant research opportunity. On a prima facie basis, the effectiveness of strategy implementation in organizational units has been argued to be a function of (a) the characteristics of the individuals comprising the unit, including the general manager (Galbraith & Nathanson, 1978; Kerr, 1985; Gupta & Govindarajan, 1984); (b) the unit's internal organization (Lawrence & Lorsch, 1967; Miles & Snow, 1978); and (c) the nature of corporate control over the unit (Bower, 1974; Vancil, 1980). The relationship between the effectiveness of pay policy strategies and the last two dimensions noted here have been examined by

Gomez-Mejia and Balkin (1988). These findings were presented earlier in this chapter, when we discussed the cooperative structure of R & D and the role of rewards as an important managerial control mechanism for R & D units. Little is known about the first dimension; that is, the relationship between reward strategies, employee characteristics, and pay effectiveness for R & D units.

Indirect support for the expectation of a contingency relationship between reward strategies, employee characteristics, and pay effectiveness comes from the literature dealing with the behavioral consequences of a fit between personality and job. Although undertaken in diverse organizational contexts, several empirical studies (Griffin, 1980; Lorsch & Morse, 1974; O'Reilly, 1977) have discovered that congruence between personality and task characteristics is associated with improved work performance as well as greater job satisfaction. Conceptually, Fiedler (1965) argued for the need to match managerial characteristics with job requirements, while Lawler (1986) emphasizes the need for congruence between pay strategies and individual needs.

For example, two individual characteristics are likely to interact with reward strategies and moderate their effect: willingness to take risks and tolerance for ambiguity. Gupta and Govindarajan (1984) used those two characteristics to differentiate between effective and ineffective general managers in strategic business units following a "build" versus a "harvest" strategy. One would expect that those individual characteristics will also be relevant in the R & D context of high technology firms because employees receiving a significant portion of their pay on a variable basis face a more uncertain situation than do employees whose pay includes a lower variable component; and reward strategies associated with greater uncertainty require a greater willingness to take risks and a greater tolerance for ambiguity on the employee's part. As decision theory points out, with uncertainty goes risk and ambiguity (Luce & Raiffa, 1957). The greater the number of possible outcomes are, the greater the uncertainty and risk involved in the situation. Alternatively stated, for variable pay policies to be effective, the employee must be able to tolerate ambiguity and accept the associated risks. These are issues that require closer examination in future research.

Reward Systems in "Intrapreneurial" or Business Unit High Technology Organizations

Most of the research conducted to date has focused on the pay practices of start-up or entrepreneurial single-product high technology firms. In reality, the vast majority of high technology organizations are business units within larger diversified firms or conglomerates. Yet we know very little about the reward system of these business units or the extent to which the compensation strategies of entrepreneurial high tech firms compare with those of "intrapreneurial" high tech organizations. We suspect that part of the reason for this is that it is extremely difficult to get access to these business units, particularly if one is interested in comparative research requiring several organizations. Start-up or smaller firms, on the other hand, are normally less reluctant to collaborate with research projects. Whatever the reasons that may account for this, we need to be tentative in generalizing present survey findings to all high technology organizations.

TOO MUCH FOCUS ON RESEARCH AND DEVELOPMENT PERSONNEL

High technology firms are perceived by many as exciting, busy places to work that provide constant stimulus and a challenging work atmosphere. But not all jobs in high technology firms are glamorous (Anderson & Kleingart- ner, 1987; Belous, 1987). Wages for many semiskilled and unskilled workers are among the lowest in manufacturing industries, and many jobs are mo- notonous. The companies that do employ only highly skilled employees sub- contract much of their work out to other firms which are responsible for hiring assemblers to perform the laborious tasks needed to manufacture the product. Therefore, in some cases individuals observing high technology firms' operations never actually see the jobs that do not fit the stereotype described earlier.

In addition to the many unskilled and semiskilled workers who are em- ployed in high technology firms, the industry makes extensive use of part- time employees. These jobs help cushion them against cyclical events in the economy and industry.

Unskilled, semiskilled, temporary, part-time, and clerical workers are usually not offered the vast array of benefits and incentives allocated to the technical and management staffs of high technology firms. Madique and Hayes (1984) point out that "any policies that appear to elevate one of these functions (e.g., marketing, manufacturing, etc.) above the others—either in prestige or rewards—can poison the atmosphere for collaboration and co- operation" (p. 22). To gain a competitive advantage, high technology firms should be using every resource available to them, including the employee groups that have, to date, been ignored or underutilized.

Gerpott and Domsch (1985) make an intriguing argument regarding the elevation of "professionals" (technical and management personnel) over the manufacturing staff. They claim that the overemphasis in the United States on product development and lack of interest in production technology could be one reason that many U.S. companies have been unable to follow through on their innovative ideas with a marketable product. They claim that the whole concept of professionalism artificially elevates the research and de- velopment personnel to a status that is not necessarily deserved.

Gerpott and Domsch (1985) argue that "the concept of 'professionalism' and the resulting concentration on the management of 'true' professional technical experts in research and development may lead to practices which are detrimental to effective technological management through the whole company" (p. 209). Their argument has considerable merit; concentrating on one employee group, when the efforts of the entire organization are needed for corporate success, may be dysfunctional for the business.

It appears that in high technology companies the external labor market controls the internal actions of many firms, including their approach to research and development. In a fast-changing environment, integrating skills can be more important to success than concentrating on a few specialty areas. Gerpott and Domsch (1985) criticize the use of dual-career ladders as promoting a dichotomy within the organization rather than harmony. They claim that the system is doomed to failure because employees soon realize that transfer to the technical ladder moves them away from the true power and control within the business.

Some of the points made here about poor working conditions in the manufacturing environment and the preferential treatment, in terms of pay and benefits for R & D workers, may have future implications for labor relations in high technology organizations. Most human resource directors in high technology firms would argue that union activity is unlikely because of the vast array of benefits and incentives that are available to employees. However, Kassalow (1987) argues that "poorly paid assembly and related semi-skilled workers in many high technology companies would appear to be a likely target for unionization" (p. 173). In fact, high technology employees offer promise to union organizers who are actively looking for new sources of union membership.

Early and Wilson (1986) propose an interesting list of reasons why high technology workers might benefit from unionization. Low wages, inability to effectively deal with grievances, lack of career progression for unskilled employees, low representation of women and minorities, and lack of job security and inadequate layoff practices were mentioned as current problems that have not been adequately addressed by many high technology companies. In fact, union activity has recently been targeted against IBM (Howe, 1986), the giant that many people perceive would never be threatened by organized labor.

High Technology Organizations: A Synthesis

SUSAN ALBERS MOHRMAN AND
MARY ANN VON GLINOW

Throughout this volume, we have been exposed to controversial statements, provocative findings, and counterintuitive messages. Most of the authors readily admit that high technology demands a departure from traditional organizational and management thought and practice. Yet the messages of this book recognize the contributions of the past, revealed in wholly new perspectives—perspectives on high technology management that will shape future research and practice.

This chapter integrates the wealth of perspectives that have emerged and provides a synthesizing framework for conceptualizing the task of high technology management. We look first at the context of high technology firms, next at organizational design issues, and then at human resource issues. Finally, we tease out common themes that weave through the texture of the high technology world, presenting challenges and dilemmas at every conceivable level of analysis. In drawing this chapter and this book to an end, we extend our framework's conceptual parameters by asking some interesting questions that are as yet unanswerable. They demand our attention if the study of high technology management is to continue to provide a needed theoretical basis and provide practical guidance.

THE HIGH TECHNOLOGY CONTEXT

The environment for high technology organizations is extraordinarily complex, and presents an unending series of challenges to the firm. Figure 14.1 illustrates the context in which a firm is embedded. Each of the ovals represents not only one aspect of the organization's context, but also a perspective for analyzing and understanding the high technology firm. That is, the high tech firm can be viewed as a player in a global economy, an industry member, a firm in a local (community, regional, or national) society, or an

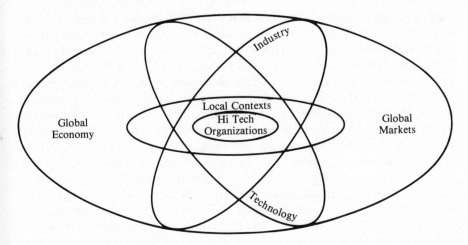

Figure 14.1   The High Technology Context

element in the constellation of institutions and organizations that advance the development and application of technology.

Obviously each perspective is intricate, and the organization cannot remove itself from any of these relevant environments. Traditional notions of competitive strategy (e.g., Porter, 1980) have analyzed the position of the firm within its industry. Relevant elements are competitors and markets, whether regional, national, or international. We depart from this "traditional" view of competitive strategies by noting that the high tech organization is in many cases simultaneously a member of the global marketplace and of the global economy—no longer operating as a domestic entity that is simply competing in foreign markets.

In this volume, Geraldo Ungson expands our thinking by comparing strategies across three different societies, at least raising the possibility that the most important competition may be between industries in different countries. Firms are strongly impacted by the laws, cultural values, technology policies, and economic practices in their countries. This may result in similarities in the competitive "recipes" for a given country that could consequently strengthen or weaken that country's firms in the global competitive arena. Taking a different approach, Jay Galbraith looks at the firm first and foremost as a member of a global economy and discusses forces pushing firms to become truly "global" in their operations as well as their marketing, sales, and distribution. Such an orientation, in its extreme, is blind to national boundaries. A country is important only for the barriers and facilitators that it presents, and for the particular requirements that are presented for doing business within its boundaries. Global financing and ownership and international management and careers are challenging the traditional ways of thinking about organizations and international competition.

The technological environment is perhaps the most interesting and complex of all, and certainly is the one that most distinguishes the high technology arena from lower technology settings. High technology organizations are fueled by the relentless march of technology—by the generation and communication of knowledge that can be used to solve a problem or accomplish a function. Each new breakthrough in basic scientific knowledge and in engineering and design capabilities can propel an entire industry to a new level of product or process. It can simultaneously create new opportunities for entry, bankrupt existing companies, and overnight render obsolete entire product lines and manufacturing and design processes. Technology progresses in diverse directions. No one firm has sufficient resources to keep up with all directions and aspects—from basic research to product development in multiple technical areas. Consequently firms must develop a technology strategy (Friar and Horwitch, 1986; Hamilton, 1986) that enables them to focus their investment dollars and develop alliances necessary to obtain the knowledge that they cannot generate on their own, or competencies they cannot afford to develop.

Technology strategy locates the firm among elements in an interorganizational network that advances the generation and application of technical knowledge. Rogers and Chen's chapter describes one manifestation of this network, the technopolii. These are clusters of organizations that create both the critical mass and the diversity of elements necessary for technology advance to occur and for commercialization to result. The research university or research institute is the growth stimulus, providing the energy for technological innovations that can then be converted into products and processes. Financial elements such as venture capitalists or banks are available to underwrite the costs of this conversion. The symbiotic nature of the relationship between the research organizations, financial organizations, and the entrepreneurial organizations that exist to commercialize the ideas is significant. Rogers and Chen have argued that there is a symbiosis among all elements of the technopolis that provide ideas, support, models, and even manpower for one another and that breed the entrepreneurs who spawn new organizations. One can argue that, whether located in a technopolis or not, a high technology firm must find a way to link into the loosely coupled interorganizational network that enables high technology to advance.

These different perspectives on the context of high technology organization interact with one another. Technopolii, for example, enable a country to support and advance the development of an industry, and thus can be viewed as a domestic phenomenon. However, the presence in most technopolii of elements representing several countries makes them global. As companies enter these global markets, they become subject to many different local contexts; alliances with overseas competitors both magnify and erode the national identity of the firm (Von Glinow and Teagarden, 1988), by making clear the cultural differences and demanding a resolution of conflicting interests. National technology policy and the social and economic context provided by each unique national setting have strong implications for firm technology strategy and for the relative success of a country's firms in the various arenas of high technology and consequently their success in the world economy.

High technology managers must cope with the complexity of this environment. Two factors magnify this complexity. First is the rapid pace at which it changes. Rapid technological development results in an ever-changing combination of elements at local, national, and global levels. Figure 14.1 is deceptive in capturing that changing complexity. It does not portray the rapid churn that occurs in each of the ovals—the change in the elements that compose the industry, the local environment, and the global economy. It does not depict the rapid technological development, the ongoing entry and exit of competitors, or the mergers and acquisitions that move competencies and resources from one competitor to another. The global economy assumes an ever-changing form as newly developing countries emerge as fierce competitors, countries make forays and gain strongholds in new national markets, and governments pass protectionist or trade-enabling laws. This turbulence is the constant state of the high technology context.

Second, new entities such as joint ventures, consortia, and technopolii emerge which pool and magnify influence on the unfolding of the future. New forms of social organization are being created to deal with the complexities of the high technology arena and the information age and with the enormity of the global economy. These forms are themselves presenting more strategic choices and more strategic uncertainty. They are not well understood and not easily managed.

Thus, one can understand a certain preoccupation with strategy. A successful firm must keep its eye on and find a path through many layers of ever-changing complexity. While keeping an eye on the environment, however, the organization must also tend to its internal functioning. Designing, building, and updating an organization that can function well in these turbulent seas is an equally difficult challenge, one that is discussed in more detail in the next section.

THE HIGH TECHNOLOGY ORGANIZATION

The nature of the high technology organization is a direct reflection of its environment and of the characteristics of the technology that it produces and uses. As described earlier, all aspects of the environment of high technology firms are changing rapidly. Complexity is increasing because of the increasing number of players in the arena and the proliferation of national laws, trade policies, and cultures that are relevant to the global economy. In addition, diverse kinds of entities have emerged or proliferated, such as technopolii, consortia, and various strategic alliances (Rogers and Valente, 1988). These new forms have blurred the lines between competition and cooperation, increased the potential influence of any one entity, tied the fates of various entities in the system more closely together, and increased the options and the difficulty of strategic decision making (Bourgeois and Eisenhardt, 1987). At the same time that complexity has increased, so has the interdependence among elements in the high technology arena.

The rapidly developing global high technology arena provides a moving context and a more complex one to which the organization must adapt. It also has compressed the time frame within which the organization has to accomplish its tasks. As more research institutions are formed and funded, technology progresses more rapidly and in more directions. The life of a product, and indeed of whole generations of technology, has shrunk, resulting in less time for an organization to commercialize and reap the return from those products. The impact is magnified for high technology firms that both use high technology as tools and produce high technology as their product. The life cycle of process technologies is similarly shrinking. Scientific and technical knowledge is becoming obsolete more quickly, placing a burden on organizations to more rapidly reeducate their employees (Kleingartner and Anderson, 1987). As more competitors enter the arena, each with special competencies, the time frame for each step in the sequence from research to the production and distribution of product has been shortened.

In addition to its rapid rate of development, certain characteristics of the technology itself have strong implications for the organization of high technology firms. All aspects of the technology sequence involve extremely complex technical problems (Riggs, 1983), as evidenced by both the depth and the breadth of knowledge required to solve them. This is true not only of the research and development process, but also in the product design phase, the design and operation of manufacturing and test processes, and the assessment of and application to customer needs.

The solution to these complex problems is, to a greater or lesser extent, a creative process: one that requires invention and innovation (Mohrman, Mohrman, & Worley, this volume). As such, uncertainty and consequently risk are involved. In adopting a strategy, high technology firms are gambling that they can solve these complex puzzles fast enough to secure a position in the market (Ottensmeyer & Snow, 1988). In many cases, the costs of staying in the game are extremely high (Galbraith, this volume).

The solution to technical puzzles frequently involves a number of distinct areas of expertise. The interdependence of individuals in research and development laboratories has long been acknowledged in the literature (Allen et al., 1969, 1980), and labs have been organized to acknowledge it. As time frames are being compressed, organizations are coming to more fully understand the crucial reciprocal interdependencies between functions that once were handled sequentially and buffered from one another: design, manufacturing, test, marketing, and field applications. Innovation involves the simultaneous coupling of all aspects of the organization—it is not a linear or sequential process (Galbraith, 1982; Van de Ven, 1986). Once treated as separate sequential technical puzzles, in today's environment the sequence of puzzles must be treated as an interconnected system, simultaneously solved, and with the solutions fitting together.

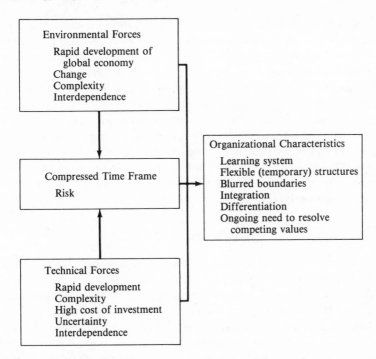

Figure 14.2   Organizational Imperatives in High Technology Firms

Figure 14.2 depicts the relationship of these aspects of high technology and its environment to their organizational implications. Each of these implications is discussed next.

High Technology Organizations as Learning Systems

The discussion of the environment implies not only a rapid rate of change, but also a directionality. The rapid pace of technological change and the emergence of a global economy not only create new and different situations to which the organization must adapt, but also imply development in a distinct direction. Development enhances the performance capacity of the developing unit. Consequently, to secure their position in the constellation of organizations that constitute the high technology arena, firms must in an ongoing way develop their performance capabilities; that is, they must learn to be more effective.

Clearly a major way in which they must develop is in their capacity to adjust to ongoing change. Eisenhardt and Bourgeois's discussion of strategic decision making (this volume), for example, depicts a decision-making process that is characterized by continual monitoring of key information, rapid input from various individuals who have differing perspectives, and decisive but not always consensual decision making from the top. This ability to make quick but informed decisions is coupled with a posture toward action that maintains multiple options as long as possible, collecting additional information to test the appropriateness of the decision. This sequence describes a learning process.

Learning has also been stressed in this volume by both Leonard-Barton and Adler in their discussions of the introduction and utilization of computer systems. Leonard-Barton deals with implementation learning, and makes the case that effective implementation requires organizational learning. Adler goes even further in suggesting that the ultimate bounty to be gained from CAD/CAM systems is their ability to enable organizational learning, but that to use it as such requires not only individual learning but also learning at the structural, strategic, and cultural levels.

The Use of Flexible and Temporary Designs

High technology organizations have to respond to rapid change in their environment with frequent changes in strategy and direction. Since design follows function and function is a consequence of strategy (Galbraith, 1977), this implies that these organizations must frequently change their design. For example, Schoonhoven and Jelinek found that successful high technology organizations are able to change their formal organizational structure rapidly and frequently. Kosnik reports a predilection for interfirm alliances that are flexible and temporary, and that can be changed as the strategic needs of the organization change. Gomez-Mejia and Wellbourne (this volume) and others (e.g., Shuster, 1984; Von Glinow, 1988) describe the importance of being able to change systems such as compensation and reward systems to fit the current needs of the firm. These all imply that a high technology firm must become competent at the process of self-design (Mohrman and Cummings, in press): redesigning themselves to adapt to a continually changing environment.

Permeable Boundaries

The complexity and rapid rate of change of the environment make boundary-spanning activities extremely important in high technology organizations (Miller, 1986). They need diverse, timely, and reliable ways to collect and process information from the environment. Several forces blur the boundaries of the organization and establish linkages with various aspects of the environment. Close coupling of the technical population of the organization with the greater technical environment stems from both the professional orientation of technical employees and the need of the firm to be well integrated into the technology advancement process. The clustering of high technology organizations in technopolii facilitates this process by creating close linkages between high technology firms and research-generating institutions such as universities (Rogers and Valente, 1988). It also creates a critical mass of technologists who interact informally and share information and problem-solving approaches (Rogers and Chen, this volume). The highly mobile career patterns in these areas further blur boundaries, as individuals carry with them information and skills that they gained from previous employers.

The high cost of the development of technical competencies and the need to share the risk cause organizations to band together in alliances that create overlapping interests and involve members of several organizations in collaborative efforts (Von Glinow and Teagarden, 1988). Becoming global competitors entails establishing operations in countries with diverse patterns of laws and cultural expectations, and adapting organizational practices to diverse work forces. This often requires sharing ownership and influence over decisions. Both of these factors open the organization to strong influence from other organizations.

High technology companies tend to work hard to establish close relationships with other organizations such as suppliers and customers, with whom they are highly interdependent. Locating field applications personnel in major customer facilities has been a long-standing practice in many high technology firms. Many companies are now also involving suppliers and customers in the new product development process (e.g., Heiko, 1988), a practice that further blurs boundaries.

Integration

The extreme interdependence of high technology work means that integration of effort is a key challenge in these organizations. Kosnik has argued that integration is also demanded by the uncertainty of product and market, and the need for ongoing reciprocal modification, interdisciplinary cooperation, and cross-training in multiple specialties. Adler contends that the greatest benefit of CAD/CAM lies in its ability to integrate manufacturing and design; the faster the development of the technology is, the greater the need for special integrating mechanisms to pull together the various CAD/CAM activities into a common framework and to provide an incentive for integrated effort. Roberts has illustrated the use of special integrating units in the extremely complex and interdependent world of a nuclear aircraft carrier. Schoonhoven and Jelinek's concept of quasi-formal structure (task forces, committees, interdisciplinary teams, etc.) plays a large role in integrating efforts across organizational lines.

The culture also can serve as a facilitator or barrier to integration. For example, Adler, Kosnick, and Resnick-West and Von Glinow point out that status differentials built into the fabric of the organization inhibit integration between individuals and groups who perceive themselves as unequal.

Human resources practices can, if properly designed, be used to encourage integrative behavior (Cascio, 1988). The chapters by Mohrman et al. and by Gomez-Mejia and Wellbourne discuss the role that performance management practices such as reward systems play in promoting or discouraging teamwork and integration. In addition, cross-functional career paths and cross-training are means of building integrative capability into individuals.

Differentiation

Although integration is a key concern in high technology organizations, differentiation is equally important (Lawrence & Lorsch, 1969). Rapid change in technology, uncertainty, and the proliferation of products and product lines contribute to the need to establish differentiated units.

An organization is likely to be involved simultaneously with multiple products and technology lines in different stages of the technical cycle. In dealing with emergent technologies, exploration, invention, and entrepreneurial behavior are key performance values. Firms tend to work more closely with one another to share the risk (Friar & Horwitch, 1986). As the technologies become better understood, commercialization and diffusion become key performance values. Cost reduction and niche marketing assume greater importance during the mature period. At these later stages, when firms are better able to focus their efforts, they tend to bring their operations inside in order to exploit the technology.

At these different stages, different performance values are relevant, different kinds of people are required, and different organizational designs are appropriate. This argues for differentiating units that are engaged in significantly different kinds of businesses. For example, large mature organizations often establish units that are free from their bureaucratic constraints, in order to elicit entrepreneurial behavior and invention (Schoonhoven, 1986; Schoonhoven and Eisenhardt, 1987; Von Glinow, 1988).

Ironically, the need to integrate can contribute to differentiation as well. Roberts and Gargano, in discussing nuclear aircraft carriers, and Adler in describing the implementation of CAD/CAM systems give examples of special (differentiated) units arising to provide systems integration for other parts of the organization. And considerable attention has been paid to reexamining the role dual ladders play in differentiating between technical and managerial functions (Raelin, 1987).

Ongoing Resolution of Competing Tensions

The rapid pace of environmental change and technological development presents an organization with ongoing choices as to how to apply its scarce resources. Preferences often fall along functional or discipline-based lines. For example, technologists prefer investment of scarce resources in activities that prepare the organization to be on the cutting edge with respect to developing technologies (investment activities); financial managers think about market position and cash flow (Mitchell, 1986). Kosnik describes a similar tension in the marketing area between the need to be creative and inventive and the need for ongoing business discipline. Resnick-West and Von Glinow, in this volume, graphically describe how that tension influences the daily interactions of managers and technologists. Strategic decisions need to be made in a manner that takes both perspectives into account (Mitchell, 1986).

Even within the technical ranks there are tensions between the orientations of those dealing with the front-end processes (development and design) and those dealing with the back end (manufacturing, test, and assembly). Adler's chapter emphasizes the need for multiple input into such decisions as a CAD/CAM strategy, so that the needs of all groups are met, all groups are moving in the same direction, and the organization can take full advantage of the technology.

The resolution of these tensions requires structural mechanisms and processes for resolving conflicts between groups with different interests and preferences. Quasi-structure (Schoonhoven and Jelinek) such as task teams and committees and various management groups such as the executive committee will need processes and schemata to help them surface information and make conscious trade-offs. Compressed time frames and potentially fundamental underlying value differences may combine to attenuate a consensus-building process. This combination of high input and nonconsensual decision making is the key to the decision-making processes described by Eisenhardt and Bourgeois.

Organizations that have the characteristics described here place extraordinary demands on their human resources. People are expected to learn, function within ongoing processes of renewal and reorganization, accomplish their highly specialized tasks, and be part of an ongoing integration of very different parts of an organization and a resolution of conflicting values and preferences. Once past the first entrepreneurial period of excitement and creation, organizations struggle to find human resource practices suitable for the long term. The next section deals with the people management issues and practices of the high technology world.

HIGH TECHNOLOGY HUMAN RESOURCES

A key factor differentiating high technology firms from firms not engaged in high technology outputs or processes is the concentration of high technology human resources. Some have referred to these scientists and engineers as "gold collar" workers (Kelley, 1985), others have referred to them as knowledge workers (Drucker, 1988), and still others refer to them, first and foremost, as professionals (Kleingartner and Anderson, 1987; Von Glinow, 1988). Extraordinary pressures befall these people, requiring innovative human resource practices designed to initially attract this talent, motivate it, and finally retain these valued employees. Since these professionals are the high tech organization's life blood and among its most important assets, innovative strategies and practices have been developed to cultivate them.

Excellent high technology human resources are in scarce supply, and are difficult to attract and retain. Technopolii represent fluid job markets, in which people can readily move from firm to firm, carrying with them ideas, experiences, and learning from previous employers (Rogers and Chen, this volume). There is an active grapevine, and employees feel they know if the grass is greener somewhere else. Thus, recruitment and retention strategies occupy a great deal of attention in high technology organizations.

High technology workers are also difficult to maintain. In some fields, for example, engineers become technically obsolete within three years of finishing their degrees (Miljus and Smith, 1987). Most organizations employ individuals in a wide variety of disciplines each of whom must develop as fields of expertise develop. Some fields diminish in importance as others emerge as preeminent. In electronics, for example, many firms are busy trying to transform "hardware people" into "software people." Ongoing development, retraining, and reskilling are continual imperatives in firms already burdened by the quick pace of strategic and organizational change and by the increasing tempo of the work.

Gold collar workers expect and demand careers, and yet the traditional organization and general social values offer hierarchical movement as the most desirable route. This is generally accomplished by having technical people move out of their technical specialty and into management. Dual-career ladders frequently do not go to levels equivalent to top management. Many fine technical employees jump ship to management jobs, often without training, aptitude, or interest in managing people. They often take the interesting technical tasks with them, further diluting the technical ladder and the amount of interesting work that goes to individual contributors. The answer to this problem has yet to be fully developed.

A key challenge, noted by Resnick-West and Von Glinow, echoed by Gomez-Mejia and Wellbourne and by Mohrman et al. in this volume, is that a firm's human resource systems must have reflexive capabilities built into them. These systems have the extremely complex task of matching the needs of the high technology organization with those of the high tech workers. Given the pace of change, to successfully manage high technology workers one must recognize that a certain amount of tension, dissent, and conflict is not only inevitable, but necessary (Von Glinow, 1988). If we keep in mind that most prescriptions of the past for managing professionals attempted to lessen the frictions and tensions, we begin to realize that the human resource practices of the high technology firm are at variance with most firm practices. For example, most organizational control systems are established to control the performances of people. Yet, in high tech organizations, considerable attention is devoted to buffering the high technology professionals from excessive controls. Not only are these workers given intellectual space (Von Glinow, 1988), but since the creative process is difficult to manage, they are frequently given "controlled freedom" to do what they want to do.

This human resource practice, analogous to the firm's quasi-formal structure, recognizes that what motivates these technical professionals to perform is somewhat different from traditional organizational incentives. A key here is challenging work, and meaningful work accomplished through team efforts or projects. Very few technical professionals work in isolation from one another, thus traditional methods of performance appraisal, evaluation, and rewards that focus on the individual as the unit of analysis and scrutiny will not work for these employees. Rather, team-related human resource practices are required in these high technology organizations.

Traditional theories of organizational control (Eisenhardt, 1985; Ouchi, 1979) suggest two underlying control strategies. Tasks that are easily programmed or measurable can be controlled through performance evaluation that focuses on behaviors or outcomes. The nature of high technology work is not highly programmable nor are the outcomes readily measurable. The second strategy is to minimize the diversity of preference among organizational members through policies such as selection, training, and socialization that lead to internalized goals and performance values. In high technology firms, the split in frame of reference between technical employees and business managers complicates the use of this second control strategy as well. It is far easier to get professional scientists and engineers to adhere to well-specified norms of their professional field than to the norms and values of the business world. Thus, it is critical that a culture be established that supports high performance in both the technical and business arenas.

Critical in addressing this issue is the matching of the firm's human resource practices with the organization's culture (Miller, 1986). If the culture of the firm supports strong performance values, then that must be communicated consistently by means of the human resource practices (Shuster, 1984). Similarly, in view of the constant changes occurring in the high technology organization's environment, technical professionals must be sensitized to the need or rationale for internal change. They must be linked to the business imperatives of the firm by the creation of open communication and meaningful technical input into business decisions. Even with this communication and input, tensions are bound to erupt. It will be the high technology firms that can learn from and manage these tensions through skillful human resource practices that will successfully navigate the sea of technological change. Figure 14.3 depicts the dynamic and kaleidoscopic nature of human asset utilization in high technology firms.

CIRCULAR THEMES

A number of words recur in almost any description or analysis of high technology organizations: complexity, invention, risk, change, uncertainty, learning, ambiguity, and renewal. One might image these organizations as playing a game on a playing field that is both moving and changing shape, in which the players keep changing, the content of the game becomes more complex through time, and the rules are made up as the game progresses. The winners are those that can learn, invent, survive, and ultimately recognize that within any circular relationship, beginnings and endings are difficult to pinpoint.

Effective high technology organizations are able to deal with many conflicting demands. We have already described a number of them in some detail:

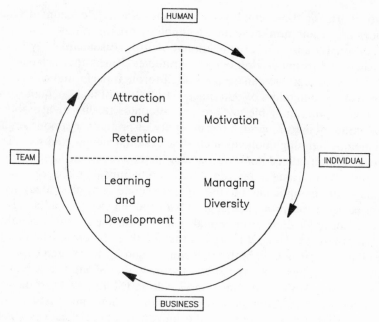

Figure 14.3   Dynamic Human Asset Utilization

1. The organization needs creativity and invention in the accomplishment of the technical task and the solution of organizational problems;
   it needs predictability, control, and planning to remain viable as a
   business.
2. In the rapidly changing environment, there is a tremendous amount of
   information that may be relevant to the organization's strategic decisions; however, decisions must be made very rapidly to avoid falling
   behind the swiftly moving environment.
3. The organization is simultaneously cooperating and competing with
   many other organizations in its environment.
4. A clear, well-understood structure and disciplined procedures facilitate efficient accomplishment of the complex high technology tasks;
   but they do not eliminate the need for informal and quasi-formal structure and communication to integrate the various parts and keep them
   working in the same direction. In addition, the structure must be
   changed frequently as the needs of the organization change.
5. Good decisions require input from various stakeholders who hold relevant perspectives and information; yet strong directive leadership is
   required because there is rarely sufficient time for consensual decision
   making to occur.

   In each of these areas a balance must be found. We do not think of balance as a trade-off, however; instead, an escalation of both kinds of activity
may be required for the high technology organization to survive and excel.

For example, increased differentiation brings with it requirements for increased integrating mechanisms (Lawrence & Lorsch, 1969). As the competitive environment becomes more intense, collaborative efforts are called for. Optimal use of CAD/CAM requires that formal procedures and communication and face-to-face and informal integration increase. Hierarchical decision making is most likely to be accepted by professional employees (probably all employees) if time has been spent getting their input and making them partners in the business.

High technology organizations exist in a high-velocity environment, perform extremely complex tasks in a compressed time frame, and demand high intensity from their employees. They use every possible uncertainty reduction mechanism (Galbraith, 1977). Traditional hierarchical mechanisms such as goal-setting, rules, vertical information systems, and hierarchical resolution of conflict are vital. In addition, the organization could not function without effective use of more organic approaches that involve lateral integration such as project teams, integrating roles, task teams, and lateral information exchange.

Almost everyone in the organization is affected. All functions must change rapidly to keep up with the changing environment; consequently, many people find themselves learning, innovating, and inventing to perform their jobs. Contact with the environment is not limited to a few specialized "boundary spanners," as we were traditionally taught to believe. On the contrary, all technical people span the boundary with the technical environment, and many functions relate directly to environmental entities such as customers, suppliers, competitors, and allies. The resolution of conflicting perspectives occurs at all levels in the organization.

Certainly traditional bureaucratic representations of an organization as a carefully designed machine in which each job has well-defined responsibilities and standards and a clear set of needed skills, and in which the hierarchy can control what goes on, does not fit the organization described here. A high technology organization is one in which hierarchy, structure, and differentiation of tasks into jobs is just the skeleton; the flesh and blood are the processes that occur.

Communication, coordination, complex problem-solving under conditions of uncertainty, the introduction of change, redesigning, addressing multistakeholder perspectives, resolving conflicting preferences, and monitoring the environment are the substance of high technology organizations. These processes must become *routine:* they must be built into the fabric of the organization. Structure and systems can support these processes by providing well-understood and agreed-upon procedures, clarifying authority and responsibility, and providing incentives. However, they can only begin to make a dent in the uncertainty reduction that must occur.

Cybernetic technology such as integrated CAD/CAM systems, E-mail, and other new communication technologies can greatly facilitate the flow of information and introduce discipline into task accomplishment and communication, and they can integrate the tasks of individuals and groups that are widely dispersed. Technology may provide the tools for organizations to handle the extreme information processing demands of the high technology environment. But the processes that are key to resolving the tensions and guilding the learning of the high technology firm depend on human behavior.

INTERESTING QUESTIONS

The chapters in this volume have just begun to scratch the surface of interesting issues in the management of high technology firms, and they raise as many questions as they answer. Nevertheless, the questions we raise now will most likely become the basis for testable propositions and future empirical research. Three of the more interesting of these questions are briefly discussed next.

Are high technology organizations qualitatively different from other organizations? Do they require new concepts and theories, or do they fall comfortably within the current ways of understanding organizations? It can be argued that high technology organizations are simply extreme examples of organic organizations (Burns and Stalker, 1961). Contingency theories of organization design (Lawrence & Lorsch, 1969; Lawrence, 1989) have posited that a different profile of design characteristics is necessary for organizations trying to accomplish regular, efficient performance from that for those requiring innovation and flexibility to introduce new products into a changing environment. Galbraith's information processing approach to organizational design (1977) also provides concepts that are very useful in understanding high technology organizations.

There does appear to be an aspect of high technology firms that is not adequately covered by traditional views of management and organization. The pace of technological advancement, which fuels continual change and development, provides an organizational challenge that is not easily dealt with using a static contingency model. These organizations must continually and quickly redesign themselves. They make decisions at a pace that prevents conventional strategic planning. They present an ever-changing set of tasks, responsibilities, and jobs. They require continual learning and renewal at both the organizational and individual levels. A model of the learning organization is required to truly understand high technology organizations.

A case can be made that most organizations are dealing with many of the same environmental requirements as high technology organizations. Most industries today are dealing in some ways with the unfolding of the global economy. They are confronting a different competitive environment, having to radically improve their efficiency and quality, and establishing closer ties with customers and suppliers. Most organizations are implementing cybernetic process technology that changes the nature of the work that is done and upgrades the skills required to do it. They are changing in ways that require individuals to learn new skills and knowledge bases, setting up continuous improvement processes, and redesigning to avoid some of the inefficiencies of their bureaucratic structure.

Considering this, it may be that high technology organizations are a laboratory for learning new organizational concepts that have broad application in this period of turbulence that accompanies the transition to the global economy and the emergence of the information society. The question still remains, do factors such as the pace of change, the risk, and the seeming unending potential for technological advance, and the need to be embedded in the larger technological environment create a context that requires a different kind of organization in the high technology world?

Is this period of extreme turbulence a temporary phenomenon or will it be the lasting context for high technology firms? If the generation of knowledge is the fuel that creates the growth and development in the high technology world, then it follows that a slowdown in such knowledge generation might result in stability in technology-based firms. As more products and technologies reach maturity, high technology firms may come to resemble more closely their lower technology counterparts. As the transition to the global economy proceeds, a new status quo may emerge that will enable firms to better plan around their competition and the marketplace.

Perhaps this is a question that will have to await the unfolding of history for its answer. For now, it appears that a new generation of technology continues to become available to replace each previous one, that new industries continue to be made possible by emergent technologies that can be harnessed for commercial application, and that more and more technopolii are emerging to continue to fuel the fire (Rogers & Valente, 1988). If this is so, then the world of high technology will continue to be one of risk, compressed time frames, and continual change (Schoonhoven & Eisenhardt, 1987).

Does cybernetic technology make possible organizational forms that are quite different from those we have studied in the past? Perhaps a new logic of organization is embodied in these technologies and their information processing capabilities. Adler's chapter began to shed light on this issue: in his words, the changes required to use the integrative capabilities of CAD/CAM optimally "go to the very core of our conception of the firm." Flat, flexible, collaborative, dynamic learning, and orientation toward capabilities are some of the organizational imperatives that emerge from the logic of the technology.

Information technology has made possible the integration of widely dispersed performers and units (c.f., telecommuting articles such as Metzger and Von Glinow, 1988; Olson, 1987). It enables information to be widely shared throughout the organization, theoretically providing the line worker with sufficient information to work without supervision and to make decisions from a perspective that goes well beyond the individual job. It enables organizations to intertwine their data bases, and to be able to enter into much closer collaborative and market relationships based on full disclosure and sharing of information (Miles & Snow, 1986). It provides the basis for simultaneously accomplishing the many pieces of the puzzle that, in the end, must fit together to create and deliver the technological product.

It is possible that even without the rapid pace of development of new technology, an organization designed to fully use cybernetic technology would look quite different from the traditional organization. This process technology may be a force that is pushing all organizations, high and low technology, toward a similar design.

Implications

The perspectives presented in this volume have implications for research and for practice. With respect to the former, we believe there are a considerable number of puzzles that remain unanswered by traditional management and organization theory. We strongly believe that the questions and the paradoxical statements raised throughout this volume warrant empirical investigation. Virtually no such large-scale empiricism has prevailed in the field of high technology management, in part because of the relative recency of some of the important phenomena (e.g., R & D consortia, strategic alliances, and the like). Nevertheless, the field is rich with anecdotal and case-based research, which enhances our knowledge of how particular firms innovate and get their products to commercial use. It is time to go beyond this type of methodology, for as any scientific inquiry proceeds, it alters its lens from qualitative to quantitative analyses. Further, just as the authors have attempted to do in this volume, large-scale empirical research efforts must be appropriately designed for different organizational forms. When we keep in mind that these organizational forms resemble the picture noted in Figure 14.1, we begin to appreciate the problems of inquiry associated with new forms, such as nuclear aircraft carriers, strategic alliances, and trend-setting entrepreneurial companies. Nevertheless, empirical research is the next step in the research chain that has as its primary goal the explanation, understanding, and prediction of high technology management.

Equally important to note are the important implications for practitioners in the field of high technology management. We believe that the findings of the authors in this volume have enormous and instantaneous application. Prescriptions range from establishing technology policy, to implementing CAD/CAM systems, to transitional management arising from culture clash. The prescriptions are varied, yet we reiterate our notion that much of what was initially learned by managers must be unlearned for management of high technology industries. Manage teams not individuals; change structure often; make every employee a boundary spanner; collaborate with competitors—these are prescriptions that fly in the face of traditional management practices. Managerial practices that have emerged from the study and practice of low technology organizations in stable environments cannot and should not be imported unquestioningly into high technology firms.

Although we do not believe that high technology organizations are the opposite of traditional organizations, we do believe that many have aspects that run counter to most of our organizational prescriptions, particularly those that have prevailed in large organizations. The key is in recognizing that high technology management is not just a variation of "good management practice"; it is often at an angle to what we used to know and demands new techniques and practices. The successful management of the high technology organization rests with this knowledge: elements of complexity, invention, risk, change, uncertainty, learning, ambiguity, and renewal are not only contextual but fundamental aspects to internal organizational functioning as well. The challenge is in simultaneously managing both the internal and the environmental, and the tensions between the two. It is not enough for managers to continue to make important trade-offs between internal and external elements. The future demands balancing both.

References

Chapter 2

Bell, D. (1973). *The Coming of Post-Industrial Society: A Venture in Social Forecasting.* New York: Basic Books,

Birch, D. L. (1978). *The Job Generation Process.* MIT Program on Neighborhood and Regional Change. Cambridge, Mass.

Birch, D. L., and S. J. MacCacken (1984). *The Role Played by High-Technology Firms in Job Creation.* MIT, Program on Neighborhood and Regional Change. Cambridge, Mass.,

Bloom, J. L., and Shinsuke Asano (1981). "Tsukuba Science City: Japan tries planned innovation." *Science,* 212, 1239–1247.

Chen, Xiangming (1988). "China's special economic zones (SEZs): Origins and initial consequences of a new development strategy." In G. Gereffi (ed.), *Origins and Consequences of National Development Strategies: Latin America and East Asia Compared.* Duke University Press, Durham, N.C.

Commonwealth: A Business Monthly, November 1987, Taipei, Taiwan.

Eveland, J. D. (1986). "Diffusion, technology transfer, and implementation: Thinking and talking about change," *Knowledge,* 8, 303–322.

Farley, J., and N. J. Glickman (1986). "R & D as an economic development strategy: The microelectronics and computer technology corporation comes to Austin, Texas." *Journal of the American Planning Association,* 52, 407–413.

Gibson, D. V., and E. M. Rogers (1988). "The MCC Comes to Texas." In F. Williams (ed.), *Measuring the Information Society: The Texas Studies.* Newbury Park, Calif.: Sage.

Miller, R., and M. Côté (1985). "Growing the Next Silicon Valley," *Harvard Business Review,* 4, 114–123.

Ouchi, W. G. (1984). *The M-Form Society: How American Teamwork Can Recapture the Competitive Edge* Reading, Mass.: Addison-Wesley.

Rogers, E. M. and J. K. Larsen (1984). *Silicon Valley Fever: Growth of High-Technology Culture.* New York: Basic Books.

Rogers, E. M. and T. W. Valente (1988). "Technology Transfer in High Technology." Paper presented at the second Annual IBEAR Research Conference on the Dialectics of Technology Transfer, Los Angeles.

Rogers, E. M. (1983). *Diffusion of Innovations.* New York: Free Press.

Rogers, E. M. (1986). *Communication Technology: The New Media Society.* New York: Free Press.

Rosenweig, R. M. (1982). *The Research Universities and Their Patrons.* Berkeley: University of California Press.

Segal, Quince, Wicksteed (1985). *The Cambridge Phenomenon: The Growth of a High-Technology Industry in a University Town.* Cambridge, England: Segal, Quince, Wicksteed Report.

Segal, Quince, Wicksteed (1987). *University-Industry Research Links and Local Economic Development: Food for Thought from Cambridge and Elsewhere.* Segal, Quince, Wicksteed Economic and Management Consultants. Report to the Manpower Services Commission, Cambridge, England.

Singhal, A. and E. M. Rogers (1989). *India's Information Revolution.* Newbury Park, Calif.: Sage.

Smilor, R. W., G. Kozmetsky, and D. V. Gibson, eds. (1988). *Technopolis: Technology and Economic Development in the Modern City State.* Boston: Ballinger.

Tatsuno, S. (1986), *Technopolis Strategy.* Englewood Cliffs, N.J.: Prentice-Hall.

Williams, F., R. E. Rice, and E. M. Rogers (1988). *Research Methods and the New Media.* New York: The Free Press.

Chapter 3

Abegglen, J. C. and George Stalk (1985). *Kaisha: The Japanese Corporation.* New York: Basic Books.

Galbraith, J. R. (in press) "From Recovery to Development." In Ralph Kilman, and Inez Martin and Associates (eds.). *Making Organizations More Competitive.* San Francisco: Jossey-Bass.

Hage, G. (1988). *Futures of Organization.* Lexington, Mass: Lexington Books, 1988, chap. 1.

Kotler, P., L. Fahey, S. Jatusripitiak (1985). *The New Competition.* Englewood Cliffs, N.J.: Prentice-Hall.

Miles, R., and C. Snow (1986). "The Network Organization," *California Management Review,* Spring.

Prahalad, C. K. and Y. Doz (1987). *The Multi-National Mission.* New York: The Free Press.

Chapter 4

Abegglen, J. C., G. Stalk, Jr. (1985). *Kaisa: The Japanese Corporation.* New York: Basic Books.

Bergsten, C. F., W. R. Cline (1987). *The United States-Japan Economic Problem.* Washington D.C.: The Institute for International Economics.

Borrus, M. (1988). *Competing for Control.* Cambridge, Mass.: Ballinger Publishing Company.

Borrus, M., J. Millstein, and J. Zysman (1983). *Responses to the Japanese Challenge in High Technology.* Berkeley Roundtable on the International Economy. Berkeley: University of California.

Botkin, J., D. Dimancescu, and R. Stata (1984). *Global Stakes: The Future of High Technology in America.* New York: Penguin Books.

Cohen, S., and J. Zysman (1987). *Manufacturing Matters.* New York: Basic Books.

Dekker, W. (1985). "Europe 1990: An Agenda for Action." *European Management Journal 3 (1):1–6.*

ESPRIT (European Strategic Programme in Informational Technology) Report. (1986). Issued by the European Economic Community. Brussels, Belgium.

Finan, W., and A. LaMond (1985). "Sustaining U.S. Competitiveness in Microelectronics: The Challenge to U.S. Policy." In Bruce R. Scott & George C. Lodge (eds.), *U.S. Competitiveness in the World Economy*. Boston: Harvard Business School Press, pp. 77–175.

Gerlach, M. (1988). "Business Alliance and the Strategy of the Japanese Firm." *California Management Review*, 30, 126–142.

Hamel, G., and C. K. Prahalad (1988). *When Competitors Collaborate*. Working Paper. London: The London Business School.

"Industrial Policy—Yes or No?" (1983, July 4). *Business Week*.

Johnson, C. (1985). "The Institutional Foundations of Industrial Policy," *California Management Review*, 27, 59–69.

Lincoln, E. J. (1988) *Japan: Facing Economic Maturity*. Washington D.C.: The Brookings Institute.

MacKintosh, I. (1986). *Sunrise Europe: The Dynamics of Information Technology*. Oxford, U.K.: Basil Blackwell Ltd.

Magaziner, I. C., and R. B. Reich (1983). *Minding America's Business*. New York: First Vintage Books Edition.

McClean, W., ed. (1986) *Status 1986: A Report on the Integrated Circuit Industry*, Integrated Circuit Engineering Corporation. Scottsdale, Az.: ICE SCOT.

McKenna, R., S. Cohen, and M. Borrus (1984). "International Competition in High Technology," *California Management Review*, 2, 15–32.

Ohmae, K. (1985). *Triad Power: The Coming Shape of Global Competition*. New York: The Free Press.

Okimoto, D. I., T. Sugano, and F. B. Weinstein (1984). *The Competitive Edge: The Semiconductor Industry in the U.S. and Japan*. Stanford, Calif.: Stanford University Press.

Ouchi, W. (1981). *Theory Z: How American Business Can Meet the Japanese Challenge*. Reading, Mass.: Addison-Wesley.

Palmer, S. (1983, December 21). *Panic in Silicon Valley: The Semiconductor Industry's Cry for Help* (Cato Institute Paper No. 30)–. Washington, D.C.: Cato Institute.

Pascale, R. T., and A. G. Athos (1981). *The Art of Japanese Management*. New York: Simon & Schuster.

Porter, M. (1980). *Competitive Strategy*. New York: The Free Press.

The Semiconductor Industry Association (1983). *The Effect of Government Targeting on Worldwide Semiconductor Competition: A Case History of Japanese Industrial Strategy and Its Costs for America*. Cupertino, Calif.: Semiconductor Industry Association.

International Newsweek, April 6, 1981.

Reich, R. B., and E. D. Mankin (1986). "Joint Ventures with Japan Give Away Our Future." *Harvard Business Review* (March–April 1986).

Reid, T. R. (1984). *The Chip*. New York: Schuster & Schuster.

Riggs, H. (1983). *Managing High-Technology Companies*. Belmont, Calif.: Wadsworth Publications.

Shanklin, W., R. Ryan (1984). *Marketing High Technology*. Boston: Lexington Books.

Ungson, G. R. (1988a). "Developing Flexible Infrastructures: Responding to the Japanese Challenge in High Technology." Working paper, Graduate School of Management, University of Oregon.

300   References

Ungson, G. R. (1988b). "International Competition Between Japanese, U.S. and European High Technology Firms: An Institutional Approach." In L. Meija and M. Lawless, *Managing the High Technology Firm Proceedings.* Graduate School of Management, University of Colorado at Boulder.

Ungson, G. R., A. W. Bird, and R. M. Steers (1988). "The Institutional Foundations of Competitive Strategies: Comparing Japanese and U.S. High Technology Firms." Working paper, Graduate School of Management, University of Oregon.

Ungson, G. R., and N. Van Dijk (1987). "Concurren in de postindustriele semeleving: de Verenigde Staten, Japan en Europa." *M & O,* Tijdschrift voor organisatie-kunde en sociaal beleid, 41c, jaardang, (semtember/October), 378–389.

United States Industrial Outlook, 1986, 1987. Washington, D.C.: U.S. Department of Commerce Publications.

Yamamura, M. (1986). Joint research and antitrust: Japanese vs. American strategies. In Hugh Patrick and Larry Meissner, *Japan's High Technology Industries.* Seattle: The University of Washington Press.

Chapter 5

Bell, G. (1984). The mini and micro industries. *IEEE Transactions on Computing,* October.

Bourgeois, L. J., and Eisenhardt, K. M. (1987). Strategic decision processes in Silicon Valley: The anatomy of a "living dead." *California Management Review,* 30, 143–159.

Bourgeois, L. J., and Eisenhardt, K. M. (1988). Strategic decision processes in high velocity environments: Four cases in the microcomputer industry. *Management Science,* 34, 816–835.

Bulkeley, W. M. (1987). Two computer firms with clashing styles fight for market niche. *Wall Street Journal,* July 6, 1.

Business Week (1982). The incredible explosion of startups. August 2, 53–54.

Business Week (1986). Computers: When will the slump end? April 21, 58–66.

Cameron, K. S., and Quinn, R. E. (1988). Organizational paradox and transformation. In R. E. Quinn and K. S. Cameron (eds.), *Paradox and Transformation: Toward a Theory of Change in Organization and Management.* Cambridge, Mass.: Ballinger.

Chandler, A. D. (1962). *Strategy and Structure.* Cambridge, Mass.: M.I.T. Press.

Dess, G. D., and Beard, D. W. (1984). Dimensions of organizational task environments. *Administrative Science Quarterly,* 29, 52–73.

Eisenhardt, K. M., and Bourgeois, L. J. (1988). The politics of strategic decision making in high velocity environments: Toward a mid-range theory. *Academy of Management Journal,* 31, 737–770.

Eisenhardt, K. M., (1988b). Making fast strategic decisions. *Academy of Management Journal,* forthcoming.

Hofer, C. W., and Schendel, D. (1978). *Strategy Formulation: Analytical Concepts.* St. Paul, Minn.: West Publishing.

Janis, I. L. (1982). Groupthink. Boston: Houghton Mifflin.

March, J. G., and Olsen, J. P. (1976). *Ambiguity and Choice in Organizations.* Bergen, Norway: Universitesforlaget.

Mintzberg, H. and Waters, J. A. (1982). Tracking strategy in an entrepreneurial firm. *Academy of Management Journal,* 25, 465–499.

Pfeffer, J., and Salancik, G. R. (1974). Organizational decision making as a political process: The case of a university budget. *Administrative Science Quarterly,* 19, 135–151.

Porter, M. E. (1980). *Competitive Strategy.* New York: The Free Press.

Quinn, J. B. (1980). *Strategic Change.* Homewood, Ill.: Dow–Jones Irwin.

Schweiger, D. M., Sandberg, W. R., and Ragan, J. W. (1986). Group approaches for improving strategic decision making: A comparative analysis of dialectical inquiry, devil's advocacy, and consensus. *Academy of Management Journal,* 29, 51–71.

Sharma, A., and Bourgeois, L. J. (1988). Note on the microcomputer industry: 1987. UVA-BP-288, Darden Case Series, Darden School, University of Virginia.

Sutton, R. I., Eisenhardt, K. M., and Jucker, J. V. (1986). Managing organizational decline: Lessons from Atari. *Organizational Dynamics.* Spring 17–29.

Van De Ven, A. H. (1983). Review of in search of excellence. Administrative Science Quarterly, 28, 621–624.

Vroom, V. H., and Yetton, P. (1973). *Leadership and Decision Making.* Pittsburgh: University of Pittsburgh Press.

Yin, R. K. (1984). *Case Study Research: Design and Methods.* Beverly Hills, Calif.: Sage Publications.

Chapter 6

Blau, P. M. (1955). *The Dynamics of Bureaucracy.* Chicago: University of Chicago Press.

Burns, T., and G. M. Stalker (1961). *The Management of Innovation,* London: Tavistock Publications.

Business Week (1984). Why Hewlett-Packard overhauled its management, July 30, 111–112.

Connor, P. E. (1980). *Organizations: Theory and Design.* SRA Associates, Chicago.

Donnelly, J. H. Jr., J. L. Gibson, and J. M. Ivancevich (1984). *Fundamentals of Management.* 5th ed. Plano, Tex.: Business Publications, Inc.

Gouldner, A. W. (1954). *Patterns of Industrial Bureaucracy.* New York: The Free Press.

Hatch, M. J. (1987). Physical barriers, task characteristics, and interaction activity in research and development firms. *Administrative Science Quarterly,* 32, 3, (September), 387–399.

Jelinek, M. (1979). *Institutionalizing Innovation.* New York: Praeger Publishers.

Jennings, D. F., and D. H. Sexton (1985). Managing innovation in established firms: Issues, problems, and the impact on economic growth and employment. *Proceedings,* 1985, Conference on Industrial Science and Technological Innovation. Sponsored by National Science Foundation. The Center for Research and Development, Publishers, State University of New York at Albany, New York.

Lawrence, P. R., and D. Dyer (1983). *Renewing American Industry: Organizing for Efficiency and Innovation.* New York: The Free Press.

Leavitt, H. J. (1973). *Managerial Psychology.* Chicago: University of Chicago Press.

Lundstedt, S. B., and E. W. Colglazier, Jr. (1982). *Managing Innovation.* New York: Pergamon Press.

Mintzberg, H. (1979). *The Structuring of Organizations.* Englewood Cliffs, NJ: Prentice-Hall.

Mintzberg, H, and A. McHugh (1985). Strategy formulation in an adhocracy. *Administrative Science Quarterly,* 30, 160–197.

Roethlisberger, F. J., and W. J. Dickson (1939). *Management and the Worker.* Cambridge, Mass.: Harvard University Press.

Saporito, B. (1984). Hewlett-Packard discovers marketing. *Fortune,* October 1, 50–56.

Schermerhorn, J. R. Jr. (1984). *Management for Productivity.* New York: John Wiley & Sons.

Schoonhoven, C. B. (1980). The management of innovation revisited: Volatile environments, structure, and effectiveness in high technology corporations. Paper presented at Pacific Sociological Association, San Francisco, Calif., April 20.

Schoonhoven, C. B. (1985). High technology firms: Where strategy really pays off. *Columbia Journal of World Business,* Winter, 49.

Schoonhoven, C. B., K. M. Eisenhardt (1985). Influence of organizational, entrepreneurial, and environmental factors on the growth and development of technology-based start up firms (pp. 12–14). A research proposal funded by U.S. Department of Commerce, Economic Development Administration.

Selznick, P. (1949). *TVA and the Grass Roots.* Berkeley: University of California Press.

Toffler, A. (1970). *Future Shock.* New York: Random House.

Tornatzky, L. G., J. D. Eveland, M. G. Boylan, W. A. Hetzner, E. C. Johnson, D. Roitman, and J. Schneider (1983). *The Process of Technological Innovation: Reviewing the Literature.* National Science Foundation, May.

Tushman, M. L., and W. L. Moore (1982). *Readings in the Management of Innovation.* Boston: Pitman Publishers.

Tushman, M. L., and P. Anderson (1986). Technological discontinuities and organizational environments." *Administrative Science Quarterly,* 31, 439–465.

Van De Ven, A. H. (1986). Central problems in the management of innovation. *Management Science,* May.

Van De Ven, A. H. (1988). Processes of innovation and organizational change. Technical report of the Strategic Management Research Center, University of Minnesota, February.

Webbink, D. W. (1977). *The Semiconductor Industry: A Survey of Structure, Conduct, and Performance.* An Economic Report to the Federal Trade Commission by the Bureau of Economics, January.

Weick, K. (1976). Educational organizations as loosely coupled systems. *Administrative Science Quarterly* 21, 1 (March), 1–19.

Weick, K. (1977). Organizational design: Organizations as self-designing systems. *Organizational Dynamics* (Autumn), 31–46.

Chapter 7

Ambrosino, G., J. Green, L. Kein, and M. Lyons (1988). "Entrepreneurial Needs Assessment: A Review of Massachusetts Smaller Businesses," A study co-sponsored by Arthur Young & Company and the U.S. Small Business Administration.

Alex Brown & Sons, Inc., Communications & Information Systems Group Company Update (1988). *Apple Computer, Inc.* Baltimore: Alex Brown & Sons, Inc.

Bank of Boston, Economics Department (1988). "Summary of Findings of Bank of Boston Survey on Exporting by Young High Tech Companies," Boston: Bank of Boston.

Bonoma, T. V. (1985). *The Marketing Edge: Making Strategies Work.* New York: The Free Press.

Burgelman, R. A., T. J. Kosnik, and M. Van den Poel (1987). "The Innovative Capabilities Audit Framework." In Burgelman and Maidique, *Strategic Management of Technology and Innovation,* Homewood, Ill.: Richard D. Irwin.

Capon, N., and R. Glazer (1987). "Marketing and Technology: A Strategic Coalignment," *Journal of Marketing,* 51 (July), 1–14.

Clark, K. B. and T. Fujimoto (1986). "Overlapping Problem Solving in Product Development," Harvard Business School Working Paper #87–048.

Davidow, W. H. (1986). *Marketing High Technology—An Insider's View.* New York: The Free Press.

Davis, S. M. (1987). *Future Perfect.* Reading, Mass.: Addison-Wesley.

Foster, R. (1986). *Innovation: The Attacker's Advantage.* New York: Summit Books.

Jacobson, G., and J. Hillkirk (1986). *Xerox: American Samurai.* New York: Macmillan Publishing Company.

Harrigan, K. R. (1985). *Strategies for Joint Ventures.* Lexington, Mass.: Lexington Books.

Hauser, J. R., and D. Clausing (1988). "The House of Quality," *Harvard Business Review,* 3 (May–June), 63–73.

Hayes, R. H., S. C. Wheelwright, and K. B. Clark (1988). *Dynamic Manufacturing: Creating the Learning Organization.* New York: The Free Press.

Kosnik, T. J. (1985). "Ambiguity of Preference and Brand Flexibility: How We Keep Our Options Open When We Don't Know What We Want." Unpublished doctoral dissertation, Palo Alto, Calif.: Stanford University.

Kosnik, T. J. (1986). "Flexibility Seeking and Delay: The Effects of Ambiguity of Preference and Experience on Selecting a Short List," Unpublished working paper, Harvard Business School.

Kosnik, T. J. (1988). "Five Stumbling Blocks to Global Strategic Alliances," *Systems Integration Age* (October).

Kosnik, T. J., and R. T. Moriarty (1988). "High-Tech vs. Low-Tech Marketing: What's the Difference?" AMA Research Workshop, Research at the Marketing/ Entrepreneurship Interface proceedings.

Levitt, T. (1975). "Marketing Myopia," *Harvard Business Review* (September– October), 26.

Lorsch, J. W., and P. R. Lawrence (1965). "Organizing for Product Innovation," *Harvard Business Review,* 43 (January–February), 109.

McKenna, R. (1985). *The Regis Touch: Million-Dollar Advice from America's Top Marketing Consultant,* Reading, Mass.: Addison-Wesley.

March, James G. (1978), "Bounded Rationality, Ambiguity, and the Engineering of Choice," *Bell Journal of Economics (March),* 587–688

Moriarty, R. T., and T. J. Kosnik (1987). "High-Tech vs. Low-Tech Marketing: Where's The Beef?" Harvard Business School case series, #9-588-012.

Sculley, J. (1987). *Odyssey: Pepsi to Apple.* New York: Harper & Row.

Shanklin, W. L., and J. K. Ryans, Jr. (1984). *Marketing High Technology.* Lexington, Mass.: D.C. Heath & Company.

Shanklin, W. L., and J. K. Ryans, Jr. (1985), "Organizing for High-Tech Marketing," *Harvard Business Review,* 62 (November–December), 164.

Spekman, R. E., and L. W. Stern (1979). "Environmental Uncertainty and Buying Group Structure: An Empirical Investigation," *Journal of Marketing,* 43 (spring), 54–64.

Systems Integration Age (1988). "SIA Alliance Report," (February), 6–19.

Takeuchi, H., and I. Nonaka (1986). "The New New Product Development Game," *Harvard Business Review*, 64 (January–February), 137–146.

Urban, G. L., and E. A. von Hippel (1988). "Lead User Analysis of New Industrial Product Concepts," *Management Science*, 34 (May).

von Hippel, E. A. (1978). "Users as Innovators," *Technology Review*, (January), 31–39.

Weick, K. (1969). *The Social Psychology of Organizing*. Reading, Mass.: Addison-Wesley.

Workman, J. P., Jr. (1988). "Linking Technology with Market Opportunities: An Ethnography of New Product Development in the Micro-Electronics Sector." Unpublished working paper, Massachusetts Institute of Technology, Cambridge.

Chapter 8

Aiken, M., and J. Hage (1968). Organizational interdependence and intraorganizational structure. *American Sociological Review*, 33, 912–919.

Aldrich, H., and Whetton, D. A. (1981). Organization-sets, action-sets and networks: Making the most of simplicity. In P. C. Nystrom and W. H. Starbuck (eds.), *Handbook of Organization Design* vol 1. New York: Oxford University Press, pp. 385–408.

Benson, J. (1975). The interorganizational network as a political economy. *Administrative Science Quarterly*, 20, 229–249.

Bingham, R. D., and L. L. Vertz (1983). The social structure of an academic discipline: Networks and social prestige in political science. *Social Science Quarterly*, 64, 275–287.

Blau, P. M. (1976). Social exchange in collectivities. In W. M. Evan (ed.), *Interorganizational Relations*. Pittsburgh: University of Pennsylvania Press.

Burt, R. (1980). Cooptive corporate actor networks: A reconsideration of interlocking directorates involving American manufacturing. *Administrative Science Quarterly*, 25, 557–582.

Cook, K. (1977). Exchange and power in networks of interorganizational relations. *Sociological Quarterly*, 18, 62–82.

Begon, M., Harper, J. L., and Townsend, C. R. (1986). *Ecology: Individuals, populations, and Communities*. Sunderland, Mass.: Sinauer Associates, Inc.

Eccles, J. (1986). Interdependence in a highly complex organization. A report submitted in partial fulfillment for the requirements for the degree of Master of Business Administration, Graduate School of Business Administration, University of California, Berkeley.

Eisenhardt, K. M., and L. J. Bourgeois (1989). Top management teams in high velocity environments. In M. A. Von Glinow and S. Mohrman (eds.), *Managing Complexity in High Technology Industries: Systems and People*. New York: Oxford University Press.

Emerson, R. M. (1979). Social exchange theory. *Annual Review of Sociology*, 2, 335–362.

Fombrun, C. J. (1986). Structural dynamics within and between organizations. *Administrative Science Quarterly*, 31, 403–421.

Galaskiewicz, J. (1979). *Exchange Networks and Community Politics*. Beverly Hills, Calif.: Sage.

Galaskiewicz, J., and K. R. Krohn (1984). Positions, roles, and dependencies in a community interorganizational system. *Sociological Quarterly*, 25, 527–550.

Galbraith, J. (1989). Technology and global strategies and structures. In M. A. Von Glinow and S. Mohrman (eds.), *Managing Complexity in High Technology Industries: Systems and People*. New York: Oxford University Press.

Keller, E. F. (1987). Demarcating public from private values in evolutionary discourses. The project on interdependence at Radcliffe College, Working paper series, No. 3.

Kmetz, J. L. (1984). An information-processing study of a complex work flow in aircraft electronic repair. *Administrative Science Quarterly*, 29, 255–280.

Landau, M. (1969). Redundancy, rationality, and the problem of duplication and overlap. *Public Administration Review*, 29, 346–358.

Levine, S., and P. E. White (1961). Exchange as a conceptual framework for the study of intraorganizational relationships. *Administrative Science Quarterly*, 5, 538–601.

Lincoln, J. R. (1982). Intra (and inter) organizational networks. In S. Bacharach (ed.), *Research in the Sociology of Organizations*. Greenwich, Conn.: JAI Press, pp. 1–38.

May, R. M. (1974). *Stability and Complexity in Model Ecosystems*. Princeton, N.J.: Princeton University Press.

Mizruchi, M., and D. Bunting (1981). Influence in corporate networks: An examination of four measures. *Administrative Science Quarterly*, 26, 475–489.

Mohrman, A. M., S. A. Mohrman, and C. Worley (1989). Performance management in high technology settings. In M. A. Von Glinow and S. Mohrman (eds.), *Managing Complexity in High Technology Industries: Systems and People*. New York: Oxford University Press.

Perrow, C. (1984). *Normal Accidents*. New York: Basic Books.

Pfeffer, J. (1972). Merger as a response to organizational interdependence. *Administrative Science Quarterly*, 17, 382–394.

Pfeffer, J., and Salancik, G. (1978). *The External Control of Organizations*. New York: Harper & Row.

Radcliffe College (1987). *Project on Interdependence*. Cambridge, Mass.: Radcliffe College.

Roberts, K. H. (in press). Some characteristics of high reliability organizations. *Organizational Sciences*.

Roberts, K. H., Halpern, J., and Stout, S. (1988). Decision making in high reliability organizations: Four tensions. Working paper, Univ. of California, Berkeley.

Roberts, K. H., and Rousseau, D. M. (1989). Research in nearly failure free, high reliability organizations: Having the bubble. *IEEE Transactions on Engineering Management*, 36, 132–139.

Rorty, A. (1987). Interdependence and the concept persons. Working paper series No. 1, Radcliffe College.

Sheets, R. G. (1985). The political economy of interorganizational relations in central cities: CETA and economic development. Ph.D. diss., Dept. of Sociology, Univ. of Illinois.

Shrivastava, P. (1987). *Bhopal: Anatomy of a Crisis*. Cambridge, Mass.: Ballinger.

Thompson, J. D. (1967). *Organization in Action*. New York: McGraw-Hill.

Weed, F. (1986). Interorganizational relations in welfare agencies as rituals of cooptation. *Social Science Journal*, 4, 431–438.

Williamson, O. E. (1975). *Market and Hierarchies: Analysis and Anti-Trust Implications*. New York: Free Press.

Chapter 9

Anzai, Y., and H. A. Simon (1979). "The Theory of Learning by Doing," *Psychological Review* 86, 124–140.

Eveland, J. D. et al. (1977). *The Innovation Process in Publication Organizations: Some Elements of a Preliminary Model.* Ann Arbor: Department of Journalism, University of Michigan.

Galbraith, J. (1977). *Organization Design*, Reading Mass.: Addison-Wesley.

Hayes, R. H., and S. C. Wheelwright (1984). *Competing Through Manufacturing.* New York: John Wiley & Sons.

Leonard-Barton, D. (1987). "The case for integrative innovation: An expert system at digital," *Sloan Management Review*, 29 (1), 7–19.

Leonard-Barton, D. (1988a). "Implementation characteristics in organizational innovations," *Communication Research.*, 15, 5 (October).

Leonard-Barton, D. (1988b). "Implementation as mutual adaptation of technology of technology and organization," *Research Policy*, 17, 5 (October), 1–17.

Mintzberg, H., D. Raisinghani, and A. Theoret (1976). "The structure of 'unstructured' decision processes," *Administrative Science Quarterly*, 21, 246–275.

Pelz, D., and F. Munson (1982). "Originality level and the innovating process in organizations," *Human Systems Management* 3, 173–187.

Rogers, E. M. (1982). *Diffusion of Innovations.* New York: The Free Press.

Chapter 10

Ackoff, R. L. (1970). *A Concept of Corporate Planning.* New York: John Wiley & Sons.

Adler, P. S. (1986). New technologies, new skills. *California Management Review* (fall), 9–28.

Adler, P. S. (1988). "The managerial challenges of integrating CAD/CAM." IEEM, Stanford University, July.

Allen, C. W. (1984). "A case history of introducing CAD into a large aerospace company." In P. Arthur (ed.), *CAD/CAM in Education and Training.* London: Kogan Page.

Battelle (1979). *Final Report on the Manufacturing Engineer-Past, Present, and Future*, Society of Manufacturing Engineers.

Clark, K. B., and T. Fujimoto (1987). Overlapping problem-solving in product development. Harvard Business School, Working Paper no. 87–048.

Clark, K. B., B. W. Chew, and T. Fujimoto (1987). "Product development in the world auto industry: Strategy, organization and performance." *Brookings Paper on Economic Activity*, 3, 729–771.

Crescenzi, A. (1987). "Implementing strategic information systems." *Indications: A Publication of Index Group, Inc.* 4, 3.

Crosby, P. B. (1980). *Quality Is Free.* New York: Mentor.

Foster, R. (1986). *Innovation: The Attacker's Advantage*, New York: Summit.

Galbraith, J. R. (1977). *Organizational Design*. Reading, Mass.: Addison-Wesley.

Haas, E. (1987). Breakthrough manufacturing. *Harvard Business Review*, 2, 75–81.

Hales, H. L. (1984). "How small firms can approach, benefit from computer-integrated manufacturing systems." *Industrial Engineering* (June), 43–51.

Hutchinson, R. (1984). "Flexibility is the key to economic feasibility of automated small batch manufacturing." *Industrial Engineering* (June).

Imai, M. (1986). *Kaizen*. New York: Random House.

Jerahov, G. E. (1984). "Training requirements for an interactive CAD/CAM system." *Autofact 6*.

Keidel, R. (1985). *Game Plans*. New York: Dutton.

Krakauer, J. (1984). Implementing automation systems: Implications for manufacturing managers. *Autofact 6*.

Lawler, E. E. III (1981). *Pay and Organization Development*. Reading, Mass.: Addison-Wesley.

Lawrence, P. R., and J. W. Lorsch (1969). *Organization and Environment*. Homewood, Ill.: Irwin.

Majchrzak, A., T. Chang, W. Barfield, R. Eberts, and G. Salvendy (1987). *Human Aspects of Computer-Aided Design*. Philadelphia: Taylor and Fracis.

Manufacturing Studies Board. (1984). *Computer Integration of Engineering Design and Production: A National Opportunity*. Washington, D.C.: National Academy Press.

Manufacturing Studies Board (1986). *Human Resources Practices for Implementing Advanced Manufacturing Technology*, Washington, D.C.: National Academy Press.

Marchisio, O., and G. Guiducci (1983). "Effect of the introduction of the CAD system upon organizational systems and professional roles." In U. Briefs, D. Ciborra, and L. Schneider (eds.), *Systems Design for, with, and by the Users*. Amsterdam: North Holland.

Marks, P. (1985). *Sink or CIM?* Campbell, Calif.: Automation Technology Products.

Melan, E. H. (1987). Quality improvement in an engineering laboratory. *Quality Progress* (June), 18–25.

Murray, T. J. (1987). "Meeting the new quality challenge." *Research Management* (November–December), 25–30.

Pascale, R. T., and A. G. Athos (1981). *The Art of Japanese Management*. New York: Simon & Schuster.

Pava, C. (1983). *Managing New Office Technology*. New York: The Free Press.

Rutledge, A. L. (1986). "An exploration of the adoption, design, and implementation of computer integrated manufacturing (CIM) in the aircraft industry." Ph.D. dissertation, Georgia State University, College of Business Administration.

Salzman, H. (1985). The new Merlins or Taylor's automations? The impact of computer technology on skills and workplace organization. Department of Sociology, Brandeis University and Center for Applied Social Science, Boston University, Boston.

Schaffitzel, W., and U. Kersten (1985). "Introducing CAD systems: Problems and role of user-developer communication in their solution." *Behavior and Information Technology*, 4 (1), 41–61.

Schein, E. H. (1984). "Coming to an awareness of organizational culture." *Sloan Management Review* (winter), 3–16.

Schrader, L. J. (1986). "An engineering organization's cost of quality program." *Quality Progress* (January), 29–34.

Senker, P., and E. Arnold (1984). "Implications of CAD/CAM for training in the engineering industry." In P. Arthur (ed.), *CAD/CAM in Education and Training*. London: Kogan Page.

Thurow, L. (1987). "A weakness in process technology." *Science* (December), 1659–1663.

Traversa, L. L. (1984). "High-touch requirements for high-tech CAD/CAM." *Autofact 6*.

Tucker, W. W., and R. L. Clark (1984). From drafter to CAD operator: A case study in adaptation to the automated workplace. SME Technical paper, MM 84-629.

Wheelwright, S. C., and R. H. Hayes (1985). "Competing through manufacturing." *Harvard Business Review* (January–February).

Wingert, B., M. Rader and U. Riehm (1981). "Changes in working skill in the fields of design caused by use of computers." In J. Mermet (ed.), *CAD in Medium Sized and Small Industries*. Amsterdam: North Holland.

Chapter 11

Campbell, J. P., M. D. Dunnette, E. E. Lawler, III, and K. E. Weick, Jr. (1970). *Managerial Behavior, Performance and Effectiveness*. New York: McGraw-Hill.

Lawler, E. E. III (1986). *High Involvement Management*. San Francisco: Jossey-Bass.

Lawler, E. E. III, A. M. Mohrman, Jr., and S. M. Resnick (1984). "Performance appraisal revisited," *Organizational Dynamics* (September), 20–35.

Mahoney, T. A., and J. R. Deckop (1986). "Evolution of concept and practice in personnel administration/human resources management (PA/HRM)." In J. G. Hunt and J. D. Blair (eds.), *1986 Yearly Review of Management of the Journal of Management*. 12, 223–241.

Mohrman, A. M. Jr., and S. A. Mohrman (1988). Technical report on performance management in an oil company. The Center for Effective Organizations, University of Southern California.

Mohrman, A. M. Jr., S. A. Mohrman, and C. G. Worley (1987). Technical report on performance management in an aerospace corporation. The Center for Effective Organizations, University of Southern California.

Mohrman, S. A., A. M. Mohrman, Jr., and C. G. Worley (1988). "Performance management in the highly interdependent world of high technology." In L. R. Gomez-Mejia and M. W. Lawless (eds.), *Proceedings: Managing the High Technology Firm*. University of Colorado Boulder, 43–49.

Mohrman, A. M., S. M. Resnick-West, and E. E. Lawler, III. (1989). *Designing Performance Appraisal Systems: Aligning Appraisals and Organizational Realities*. San Francisco: Jossey-Bass.

Pelz, D. C., and D. Munson (1980). *The Innovating Process: A Conceptual Framework*. Ann Arbor, Mich.: Working Paper, Center for Research on Utilization of Scientific Knowledge, University of Michigan.

Schon, D. A. (1967). *Technology and Change*. New York: Delacorte Press.

Shuster, J. (1984). *Management Compensation in High Technology Companies*. Lexington, Mass.: Lexington Books.

Tornatzky, L. G., J. D. Eveland, M. G. Boylan, W. A. Hetzner, E. C. Johnson, D. Roitman, and J. Schneider (1983). *The Process of Technological Innovation: Reviewing the Literature*. Washington, D.C.: National Science Foundation.

Von Glinow, M. A. (1988). *Managing High Technology and Professional Employees*. New York: Ballinger.

Von Glinow, M. A., and S. A. Mohrman (in press). "Attachment and Withdrawal Patterns of High Technology Workers." *Journal of High Technology Management and Research*, vol 2.

Chapter 12

Bailyn, L. (1985) "Autonomy in the Industrial R&D Lab." *Human Resource Management,* 24 (2) 129–146.

Beckhard, R. (1969). *Organizational Development: Strategies and Models,* Reading, Mass.: Addison-Wesley.

Belous, R. (1987) "High technology labor markets: Projections and policy implications." In A. Kleingartner and C. Anderson (eds.), *Human Resource Management in High Technology Firms.* Lexington, Mass.: Lexington Books, pp. 24–25.

Benveniste, G. (1987). *Professionalizing the Organization.* San Francisco: Jossey-Bass.

Drucker, P. F. (1988). "The coming of the new organization." *Harvard Business Review* (January–February), 45–53.

Gibson, R. (1987). "Managing the techies: Closing the lab coat-pinstripe gap." *Wall Street Journal, Special Report,* (June 12), 23.

Gibson, R. (1987). "Managing the techies." *Wall Street Journal, Special Report* (June 12).

Gomez-Mejia, L., and Balkin, D. (1985). "Managing a high tech venture." *Organizational Dynamics* (February).

Gouldner, A. W. (1957). "Cosmopolitans and Locals—Toward an Analysis of Latent Social Roles I" *Administrative Science Quarterly* 2, December, 281–306.

Griggs, W. H., and S. Manring. (1986). "Increasing the effectiveness of technical professionals." *Management Review,* May.

Gupta, A. R., and D. Wilemon (1986). "R&D and marketing managers in high-tech companies: Are they different?" *IEEE Transactions on Engineering Management,* EM33, 1, February.

Hall, R. (1985) "Professional Management Relations: Imagery vs. Action." *Human Resource Management Journal* (Summer, 24, 2, 227–236.

Hought, T. M. (1987). "Working better and faster with fewer people," *Wall Street Journal,* 15 May.

Hughes, E. (1967). "Professions." In Lynn (ed.), *The Professions in America.* Boston: Beacon Press.

Kleingartner, A., and Anderson, C. (1987). *Human Resource Management in High Technology Firms.* Lexington, Mass.: Lexington Books.

Lawler, E. E. (1986). *High-Involvement Management.* San Francisco: Jossey-Bass.

Lawler, E. E. (1971). *Pay and Organizational Effectiveness: A Psychological View.* New York: McGraw Hill.

Madique, M. A., and R. H. Hayes. (1984). "The art of high technology management," *Sloan Management Review,* winter.

Maier, M. (1988). *The Final Hours of Flight 51-L: Using the Space Shuttle Tragedy to Teach About Ethics and Organizational (Mis)Communication.* A bibliography of references compiled for 2nd Annual Regional Organizational Behavior Teaching Conference. Philadelphia, March 12.

Marx, R., C. Stubbart, V. Traub, and M. Cavanaugh (1986). "The NASA space shuttle disaster: A case study," *Journal of Management Case Studies,* 3, 300–318.

Miller, D. B. (1986) *Managing Professionals in Research and Development.* San Francisco: Jossey-Bass.

President's Commission Report on the Challenger (1986). *Report to the President by the Presidential Commission on the Space Shuttle Challenger Accident.* Washington, D.C.

Raelin, J. (1985). "The basis for the professional's resistance to managerial control," *Human Resource Management*, 24, 147–176.

Raelin, J, C. K. Sholl, and D. Leonard (1985). "Why professionals turn sour and what to do." *Personnel* (October) 62 (10), 28–41.

Resnick, S. M. (1985). *Pride in Xerox: A Study of Employee Attitudes and Morale*, Technical Report. El Segundo, Xerox Corporation.

Riggs, H. E. (1983). *Managing High-Technology Companies*. Belmont, California: Lifetime Learning Publications.

Rogers, E., and J. K. Larsen (1984). *Silicon Valley Fever: Growth of High Technology Culture*. New York: Basic Books.

Rogers, E. M., and T. W. Valente (1988). "Technology transfer in high technology industries." Paper presented at the Second Annual IBEAR Research Conference, University of Southern California, April 1988.

Schuster, J. (1985). "Compensation plan design." *Compensation Plans*, May.

Schwartz, H. (1987). "On the psychodymanics of organizational disaster: The case of the space shuttle Challenger." *The Columbia Journal of World Business* (spring) XXII, 1.

Sexton, D. L. (1988). "Propensity for change: A prerequisite for growth in high technology firms." Paper presented at the Managing the High Technology Firm, Boulder, Colorado, January 1988.

Sherif, M. (1951). "Experimental study of intergroup relations." In J. Rohrer and M. Sherif (eds.), *Social Psychology at the Crossroads*. New York: Harper & Row, pp. 388–426.

Siehl, C., G. Ledford, R. Silverman, and P. Foy (1988). "Managing cultural differences in mergers and acquisitions: The role of the human resource function." *Mergers and Acquisitions* (March–April), 22 (5)

Takeuchi, H., and I. Nonaka (1986). "The new product development game." *Harvard Business Review* (January–February), 64, 1, 137–147.

Von Glinow, M. A. (1988). *The New Professionals: Managing Today's High Tech Employees*. Cambridge, Mass.: Ballinger Publishing Company.

Chapter 13

Anderson, C. S., and A. Kleingartner (1987). "Human resources management in high technology firms and the impact of professionalism." In Kleingartner, A., and Anderson, C. S. (eds.), *Human resources management in high technology firms*. Lexington, Mass.: D.C. Heath, pp. 3–21.

Balkin, D. B. (1987). "Compensation strategies for research and development staff." In *Topics in total compensation* (Winter) 2 (2), 207–215.

Balkin, D. B., and L. R. Gomez-Mejia (1987). "Toward a contingency theory of compensation strategy." *Strategic Management Journal*, 8 (1), 169–182.

Balkin, D. B., and L. R. Gomez-Mejia (1985). "Compensation practices in high technology industries." *Personnel Administrator* (June), 111–118, 122–124.

Balkin, D. B., and L. R. Gomez-Mejia (1984). "Determinants of R & D compensation strategies in the high tech industry." *Personnel Psychology*, 37, 635–650.

Belous, R. S. (1987). "High technology labor markets: projections and implications." In Kleingartner, A., and Anderson, C. S. *Human resource management in high technology firms* Lexington, Mass.: D.C. Heath, pp. 25–45.

Bower, J. L. (1974). *Managing the resource allocation process*. Boston, Mass.: Harvard University Press.

Bright, D. S. (1985). *Gearing up for the fast lane*. New York: Random House.

Cascio, W. F. (1988). "Strategic human resource management in high technology industry." *Proceedings Managing the High technology Firm Conference*, Boulder, Colo.: High Technology Management Center, University of Colorado, pp. 9–16.

Early, S., and R. Wilson (1986). "Do unions have a future in high technology?" *Technology Review*, (October), 57–65, 79.

Fiedler, F. E. (1965). "Engineer the job to fit the manager." *Harvard Business Review*, 43:115–122.

Galbraith, J. R., and D. A. Nathanson (1978). *Strategy implementation: The role of structure and process*. St. Paul, Minn.: West Publishing Co.

Gerpott, T. J., and M. Domsch (1985). "The concept of professionalism and the management of salaried technical professionals: a cross national perspective. *Human Resource Management*, 24(2), 207–226.

Gomez-Mejia, L. R., and D. B. Balkin (1988). "The perceived effectiveness of individual and aggregate compensation strategies in an R & D setting." *Industrial Relations*.

Gomez-Mejia, L. R., D. B. Balkin, and T. Welbourne (1988). "The influence of venture capitalists on human resource management practices in the high technology industry." *Proceedings Managing the High technology Firm Conference*, Boulder, Colo.: High Technology Management Center, University of Colorado, (pp. 23–28).

Gomez-Mejia, L. R., and D. B. Balkin (1985). "Managing a high-tech venture." *Personnel* (December), 31–36.

Gomez-Mejia, L. R., J. E. McCann, and R. C. Page (1985). "The Structure of Managerial Behaviors." *Industrial Relations* 24, 147–154.

Griffin, R. W. (1980). "Relationship among individual, task design, and leader behavior variables." *Academy of Management Journal*. 23, 665–683.

Grissom, G. R., and K. J. Lombardo (1985). "The role of the high-tech human resources professional." *Personnel* (June), 15–17.

Gupta, A. K., and V. Govindarajan (1984). "Business unit strategy, managerial characteristics, and business unit effectiveness at strategy implementation." *Academy of Management Journal*, 27, 25–41.

Howe, C. L. (1986). "Big labor and big blue." *Datamation* (January), 30–32.

Humphrey, W. S. (1987). *Managing for innovation*, Englewood Cliffs, N.J.: Prentice-Hall.

Kanter, R. M. (1987). "The attack on pay." *Harvard Business Review* (March–April), 60–67.

Kanter, R. M. (1986). "Pay and hierarchy." *Management Review* (June), 11–12.

Kanter, R. M. (1984). "Variations in management career structure in high technology firms: the impact of organizational characteristics on internal labor market patterns." In Osterman, P. (ed.), *Internal labor markets*, Cambridge, Mass.: The MIT Press.

Kassalow, E. M. (1987). "The unions' stake in high tech development." In Kleingartner, A., and C. S. Anderson (eds.). *Human resource management in high technology firms*. Lexington, MA: D.C. Heath, pp. 157–182.

Kelley, H., and J. Thibaut (1969). "Group problem solving." In Lindzey, G., and Aronson, G. (eds.), *The handbook of social psychology*. Reading, Mass.: Addison-Wesley.

Kerr, J. L. (1985). "Diversification strategies and managerial rewards; An empirical study." *Academy of Management Journal*, 28 (1), 115–179.

Lauenstein, M. C., and W. Skinner (1980). Formulating a strategy of superior resources." *The Journal of Business Strategy*, 1(1), 4–10.

Lawler, E. E. III. (1987). "Pay for performance: a strategic analysis." Unpublished manuscript. University of Southern California.

Lawler, E. E. III. (1986). "The new pay." In Rynes, S. L., and Milkovich, G. T. (eds.), *Current issues in human resources management: Commentary and readings*. Plano, Tex.: BPI, pp. 404–412.

Lawrence, P. R., and J. W. Lorsch (1967). *Organization and environment*. Boston, Mass.: Harvard University Press.

Lorsch, J. W., and J. J. Morse (1974). *Organizations and their members: A contingency approach*. New York: Harper & Row.

Luce, D., and H. Raiffa (1957). *Games and decisions*. New York: John Wiley & Sons.

Madique, M. A., and R. H. Hayes (1984). "The art of high-technology management." *Sloan Management Review* (Winter), 17–31.

Martin, M. J. C. (1984). *Managing technological innovation and entrepreneurship*. Reston, Va.: Reston Publishing Company.

McCann, J., Hinkin, T., and L. R. Gomez-Mejia (1988). "A comparative study of managerial mobility patterns in high technology and traditional industries." Unpublished technical report, University of Colorado.

Miles, R. E., and C. C. Snow (1978). *Organizational strategy, structure, and process*. New York: McGraw-Hill.

Miljus, R. C., and R. L. Smith (1987). "Key human resource issues for management in high tech firms." In Kleingartner, A., and C. S. Anderson (eds.), *Human resource management in high technology firms* Lexington, Mass.: D.C. Heath, pp. 115–131.

Milkovich, G. T. (1987). "Compensation systems in high technology companies." In Kleingartner, A., and C. S. Anderson (eds.), *Human resource management in high technology firms*. Lexington, Mass.: D.C. Heath, pp. 103–114.

Nadler, D. A., J. R. Hackman and E. E. Lawler III. (1979). *Managing organization behavior*. Boston: Little, Brown.

Opsahl, R. L., and M. D. Dunnette (1966). "The role of financial compensation in industrial motivation." *Psychological Bulletin*, 66, 94–118.

O'Reilly, C. A. (1977). "Personality–job fit: Implications for individual attitudes and performance." *Organizational Behavior and Human Performance*, 18, 36–46.

Schuster, J. (1984). *Management compensation in high technology companies*. Lexington, Mass.: D.C. Heath.

Silver, D. A. (1985). *Venture Capital*. New York: John Wiley & Sons

Solomon, L. C., and M. A. LaPorte (1987). "The educational implications of the high technology revolution." In Kleingartner, A., and Anderson, C. S. (eds.), *Human resource management in high technology firms*. Lexington, Mass.: D.C. Heath, pp. 47–66.

Vancil, R. F. (1980). *Decentralization: Managerial ambiguity by design*. New York: Financial Executives Research Foundation.

Welbourne, T. M., and L. R. Gomez-Mejia (1988). "Gainsharing revisited." *Compensation and Benefits Review*. (July–August) 20 (4), 19–29.

Chapter 14

Adler, P. S. (1989). Managing high-tech processes: The challenge of CAD/CAM." This volume.

Allen, T. J., and S. I. Cohen (1969). "Information flow in research and development laboratories." *Administrative Science Quarterly, 14, 12–19.*

Allen, T. J., D. M. S. Lee, and M. Tushman (1980). "R&D performance as a function of internal communication, project management, and the nature of work." *IEEE Transactions on Engineering Management,* 27, 2–12.

Balakrishnan, S., and M. P. Koza (1988). "The emergence of supranationals in global industry." *The Proceedings of Managing the High Technology Firm,* A conference at the University of Colorado, 391–395.

Birnbaum, P. H. (1988). Coping with environmental and market forces impacting high technology industry in the 1990s. *The Proceedings of Managing the High Technology Firm.* A conference at the University of Colorado, 293–299.

Bourgeois, L. J., and K. M. Eisenhardt (1987). "Strategic decision processes in Silicon Valley: The anatomy of the living dead." *California Management Review,* 30 (1), 143–159.

Burns, T., and G. M. Stalker (1961). *The Management of Innovation.* London: Tavistock Publications.

Casio, W. (1988). "Innovative human resource practices for the high tech firm." *The Proceedings of Managing the High Technology Firm.* A conference at the University of Colorado, 9–15.

Davidson, W. (1988). "A technology-based theory of management." *The Proceedings of Managing the High Technology Firm.* A conference at the University of Colorado, 71–77.

Drucker, P. (1988). "The coming of the new organization." *Harvard Business Review* (January–February), 45–53.

Eisenhardt, K. M. (1985). "Control: Organizational and economic approaches." *Management Science,* 31, 12–149.

Eisenhardt, K. M. (1989). "Charting strategic decisions in the microcomputer industry; profile of an industry star." This volume.

Friar, J., and M. Horwitch (1986). "The emergence of technology strategy: A new dimension of strategic management." In *Technology in Society,* Vol. 7, New York: Pergamon Press, pp. 143–178.

Galbraith, J. (1977). *Organization Design.* Reading, Mass.: Addison-Wesley,

Galbraith, J. (1982). "Designing the innovating organization." *Organizational Dynamics* (winter), 3–24.

Galbraith, J. (1989). "Technology and Global Strategies and Organizations." This volume.

Hamilton, W. F. (1986). Corporate strategies for managing emerging technologies." In *Technology in Society,* Vol. 7. New York: Pergamon Press, pp. 197–212.

Heiko, L. (1988). "The role of manufacturability in managing new product development." *The Proceedings of Managing the High Technology Firm.* A conference at the University of Colorado, 149–153.

Jelinek, M., and C. B. Schoonhoven (1988). "Lessons for the future in high technology management: The strategy of innovation where it counts." *The Proceedings of Managing the High Technology Firm.* A conference at the University of Colorado, 318–323.

Kelley, R. E. (1985). *The Gold Collar Worker: Harnessing the Brainpower of the New Workforce*. Reading, Mass.: Addison-Wesley.

Kleingartner, A., and C. S. Anderson (1987). *Human Resource Management in High Technology Firms*. Lexington, Mass.: Lexington Books.

Kosnik, T. J. (1989). "Perennial Renaissance: The marketing challenge in high-tech settings." This volume.

Lawrence, P. (1989). "A reassessment of why organizations change." In A. Mohrman, S. Mohrman, G. Ledford, T. Cummings, and E. Lawler (eds.), *Large Scale Organizational Change*. San Francisco: Jossey-Bass.

Lawrence, P., and J. Lorsch (1969). *Organization and Environment*. Boston: Division of Research, Harvard Business School.

Leonard-Barton, D. (1989). "Implementing new production technologies: Exercises in corporate learning." This volume.

Metzger, R., and M. A. Von Glinow (1988). "Off-site workers at home and abroad." *California Management Review*, 30, 3, 101–111.

Miles, R. and C. C. Snow (1986). "New concepts for new forms." *California Management Review* (spring).

Miljus, R. C., and R. L. Smith (1987). "Key Human Resource Issues for Management in High Tech Firms." In Kleingartner, A., and Anderson, C. S. (eds.), *Human Resource Management in High Technology Firms*. Lexington, Mass.: Lexington Books.

Miller, D. B. (1986). *Managing Professionals in Research and Development*. San Francisco: Jossey-Bass.

Mitchell, G. R. (1986). "New approaches for the strategic management of technology." In *Technology in Society*, Vol. 7, New York: Pergamon Press.

Mohrman, A. M., Jr., S. A. Mohrman, and C. G. Worley (1989). "High Technology Performance Management." This volume.

Mohrman, S. A., and T. G. Cummings (in press). *Self Designing Organizations: Learning How to Create High Performance*. Reading, Mass.: Addison-Wesley.

Olson, M. H. (1987). "An investigation of the impacts of remote work environments and supporting technology." Working paper, Graduate School of Business Administration, New York University.

Ottensmeyer, E. J., and C. C. Snow (1988). "Managing strategies and technologies." In *The Proceedings of Managing the High Technology Firm*. Boulder: University of Colorado.

Ouchi, W. (1979). "A conceptual framework for the design of organization control mechanisms." *Management Science*, 25, 833–848.

Pavitt, K. (1984). "Sectoral patterns of technical change: Toward a taxonomy and a theory." *Research Policy*, 13, 343–373.

Pennings, J. M., and F. Harianto (1988). "Innovation in an interorganizational context." *The Proceedings of Managing the High Technology Firm*. A conference at the University of Colorado, 228–234.

Porter, M. (1980). *Competitive Strategy: Techniques for Analyzing Industries and Competitors*. New York: The Free Press.

Raelin, J. (1987). "Two track plans for one track careers." *Personnel Journal*, 66, 1 (January), 96–101.

Resnick-west, S., and Von Glinow, M. A. (1989). "Beyond the Clash: Managing High Tech Professionals. This volume.

Riggs, H. E. (1983). *Managing High-Technology Companies*. Belmont, Calif.: Lifetime Learning Publications.

Roberts, K. H., and Gargano, G. (1989). "Managing a high reliability organization: A case for interdependence." This volume.

Rogers, E., and Chen, A. (1989). "Technology Transfer and the Technopolis." This volume.

Rogers, E. M., and Valente, T. (1988). Technology transfer in high technology industries. Paper presented at the Second Annual International Business Education and Research Program (IBEAR) Research Conference, University of Southern California, April 7–9.

Scherer, F. M. (1982). "Interindustry technology flows in the U.S.," *Research Policy,* 11, 227–245.

Schoonhoven, C. B. (1986). "Organizational adaptation caused by technological change: issues and analysis." A paper presented at the Western Academy of Management, Los Angeles, California. March 20-23.

Schoonhoven, C. B., and K. Eisenhardt (1987). "Surviving the liability of newness: A model for successful entrepreneurship in technology-based ventures." Paper presented at the Academy of Management, New Orleans, August 10–12.

Schoonhoven, C. B., and M. Jelinek (1989). "Dynamic tension in innovative, high technology firms: Managing rapid technological change through organizational structure." This volume.

Shuster (1984). *Management Compensation in High Technology Companies.* Lexington, Mass.: Lexington Books.

Ungson, G. R. (1988). International competition between Japanese, U.S. and Europe high technology firms: An institutional approach. *The Proceedings of Managing the High Technology Firm.* A conference at the University of Colorado, 477–481.

Ungson, G. R. (1988). "A research agenda on the management of high technology firms." *The Proceedings of Managing the High Technology Firm.* A conference at the University of Colorado, 490–491.

Ungson, G. R. (1989). "International competition in high technology: The case of the United States, Japan and Europe." This volume.

Van De Ven, A. H. (1986). "Central problems in the management of innovation." *Management Science,* 32, 590–607.

Von Glinow, M. A. (1988). *The New Professionals: Managing Today's High Tech Employees.* Cambridge, Mass.: Ballinger Publishing Company.

Von Glinow, M. A., and M. B. Teagarden (1988). "The impact of contextually-embedded influences on cooperative strategic alliances: The case of Sino–U.S. joint ventures." Working paper, University of Southern California.

Weick, K. (1977). "Organizational design: Organizations as self-designing systems." *Organizational Dynamics* (autumn), 31–46.

Index

N.B.: Page numbers in italics refer to figures; page numbers followed by an italic *t*, refer to tables

Adaptability, 140
Adhocracies, organic, 99–100
Affect, 230–231
Agency of Industrial Science and
  Technology (AIST), 26
Agglomeration, 34–35
Aggregate incentives
  long-term, 269–270
  short-term, 265–266
Aircraft carriers, 147, 148
  interdependence in, 153–158
Alberding, Dick, 102
American Management Systems, custom-
  built systems of, 141
American Research Development
  Corporation (ARDC), founding of,
  19
Annual bonus, 269
Antitrust legislation, 72–73
Apollo, 80
Apple Computer
  corporate university of, 141
  cross-functional teams in, 143
  defense of Macintosh interface of, 52
  as Fortune 500 company, 76–77
  introduction of Macintosh by, 79
  marketing of, 119–120
  public offering of, 255
Apple University, 141
Appraisal practices, 227–228
Asia
  quality of life in technopolii of, 33–34
  technology transfer in, 29
Assumptions, basic, 209–210
AT&T, QFD in, 142
Austin, Texas, technopolis, 15
  history of, 22–24
  MCC and, 17
Automated process planning, 192
Automatic error recovery, 192

Automation, 212
  acceleration of, 193
Autonomy
  day-to-day, 241
  strategic, 241–242
Awards program, 269

Balkin, D. B., 256–260, 262–275
Beijing technopolis, 16
Bemis Company, 248
Benefits packages, 270–271
Benetton, as network organization, 53–54
Better mousetrap marketing, 121
Big picture, 248–249, 253
Biotechnology, from Route 128
  technopolis, 22
Boleky, Edward, 95–96
Boston University, Route 128 and, 22
Boundary-spanning activities, 132–133,
  284–285
  methodologies of, 143
Brand recognition, 51
British Petroleum, subsidiaries of, 51
Bureaucracy vs. professional culture, 239–
  240
Bureaucratic organization concepts, 222
Burns, Tom, 93–95, 98
Business environment
  deregulation in, 40
  government role in, 39–40
  new competitors in, 39
  oversupply problem in, 38
  takeovers in, 40
  technology in, 37–38
Buyers, wait and see approach of, 130. *See
  also* Customers
Buying process, 126

CAD/CAM
  acceleration of automation with, 193

317